CCNA

ICND2

Study Guide

Third Edition

DISCARD

CCNA®

ICND2

Study Guide

Third Edition

Todd Lammle

Senior Acquisitions Editor: Kenyon Brown
Development Editor: Kim Wimpsett
Technical Editor: Todd Montgomery
Production Editor: Christine O'Connor
Copy Editor: Judy Flynn
Editorial Manager: Mary Beth Wakefield
Production Manager: Kathleen Wisor
Executive Editor: Jim Minatel
Book Designers: Judy Fung and Bill Gibson
Proofreader: Josh Chase, Word One New York
Indexer: Johnna vanhoose Dinse
Project Coordinator, Cover: Brent Savage
Cover Designer: Wiley
Cover Image: Getty Images Inc./Jeremy Woodhouse

Copyright © 2016 by John Wiley & Sons, Inc., Indianapolis, Indiana

Published simultaneously in Canada

ISBN: 978-1-119-29098-8

ISBN: 978-1-119-29100-8 (ebk.)

ISBN: 978-1-119-29099-5 (ebk.)

Manufactured in the United States of America

For general information on our other products and services or to obtain technical support, please contact our Customer Care Department within the U.S. at (877) 762-2974, outside the U.S. at (317) 572-3993 or fax (317) 572-4002.

Wiley publishes in a variety of print and electronic formats and by print-on-demand. Some material included with standard print versions of this book may not be included in e-books or in print-on-demand. If this book refers to media such as a CD or DVD that is not included in the version you purchased, you may download this material at http://booksupport.wiley.com. For more information about Wiley products, visit www.wiley.com.

Library of Congress Control Number: 2016949702

10 9 8 7 6 5 4 3 2 1

Acknowledgments

There are many people who work to put a book together, and as an author, I dedicated an enormous amount of time to write this book, but it would have never been published without the dedicated, hard work of many other people.

Kenyon Brown, my acquisitions editor, is instrumental to my success in the world of Cisco certification. Ken, I look forward to our continued progress together in both the print and video markets! My technical editor, Todd Montgomery, was absolutely amazing to work with and he was always there to check my work and make suggestions. Thank you! Also, I've worked with Kim Wimpsett, the development editor, for years now and she coordinated all the pages you hold in your hands as they flew from thoughts in my head to the production process.

Christine O'Connor, my production editor, and Judy Flynn, my copyeditor, were my rock and foundation for formatting and intense editing of every page in this book. This amazing team gives me the confidence to help keep me moving during the difficult and very long days, week after week. How Christine stays so organized with all my changes as well as making sure every figure is in the right place in the book is still a mystery to me! You're amazing, Christine! Thank you! Judy understands my writing style so well now, after doing at least a dozen books with me, that she even sometimes finds a technical error that may have slipped through as I was going through the material. Thank you, Judy, for doing such a great job! I truly thank you both.

About the Author

Todd Lammle is the authority on Cisco certification and internetworking and is Cisco certified in most Cisco certification categories. He is a world-renowned author, speaker, trainer, and consultant. Todd has three decades of experience working with LANs, WANs, and large enterprise licensed and unlicensed wireless networks, and lately he's been implementing large Cisco Firepower networks. His years of real-world experience are evident in his writing; he is not just an author but an experienced networking engineer with very practical experience working on the largest networks in the world, at such companies as Xerox, Hughes Aircraft, Texaco, AAA, Cisco, and Toshiba, among many others. Todd has published over 60 books, including the very popular *CCNA: Cisco Certified Network Associate Study Guide*, *CCNA Wireless Study Guide*, *CCNA Data Center Study Guide*, and *SSFIPS (Firepower)*, all from Sybex. He runs an international consulting and training company based in Colorado, Texas, and San Francisco.

You can reach Todd through his forum and blog at www.lammle.com/ccna.

Contents at a Glance

Contents

Chapter   8   Evolution of Intelligent Networks   365

Introduction

Welcome to the exciting world of Cisco certification! If you've picked up this book because you want to improve yourself and your life with a better, more satisfying and secure job, you've done the right thing. Whether you're striving to enter the thriving, dynamic IT sector or seeking to enhance your skill set and advance your position within it, being Cisco certified can seriously stack the odds in your favor to help you attain your goals!

Cisco certifications are powerful instruments of success that also markedly improve your grasp of all things internetworking. As you progress through this book, you'll gain a complete understanding of networking that reaches far beyond Cisco devices. By the end of your studies, you'll comprehensively know how disparate network topologies and technologies work together to form the fully operational networks that are vital to today's very way of life in the developed world. The knowledge and expertise you'll gain here are essential for and relevant to every networking job, which is why Cisco certifications are in such high demand—even at companies with few Cisco devices!

Although it's now common knowledge that Cisco rules routing and switching, the fact that it also rocks the security, collaboration, data center, wireless, and service provider world is also well recognized. And Cisco certifications reach way beyond the popular but less extensive certifications like those offered by CompTIA and Microsoft to equip you with indispensable insight into today's vastly complex networking realm. Essentially, by deciding to become Cisco certified, you're proudly announcing that you want to become an unrivaled networking expert—a goal that this book will get you well on your way to achieving. Congratulations in advance on the beginning of your brilliant future!

> For up-to-the-minute updates covering additions or modifications to the Cisco certification exams, as well as additional study tools, review questions, videos, and bonus material, be sure to visit the Todd Lammle website at www.lammle.com/ccna.

Cisco's Network Certifications

It used to be that to secure the holy grail of Cisco certifications—the CCIE—you passed only one written test before being faced with a grueling, formidable hands-on lab. This intensely daunting, all-or-nothing approach made it nearly impossible to succeed and predictably didn't work out too well for most people. Cisco responded to this issue by creating a series of new certifications, which not only made it easier to eventually win the highly coveted CCIE prize, it gave employers a way to accurately rate and measure the skill levels of prospective and current employees. This exciting paradigm shift in Cisco's certification path truly opened doors that few were allowed through before!

Beginning in 1998, obtaining the Cisco Certified Network Associate (CCNA) certification was the first milestone in the Cisco certification climb, as well as the unofficial prerequisite to each of the more advanced levels. But that changed when Cisco announced the Cisco Certified Entry Network Technician (CCENT) certification. And then in May 2016, Cisco once again proclaimed that all-new tests will be required beginning in October of the same year; now the Cisco certification process looks like Figure I.1.

FIGURE I.1   The Cisco certification path

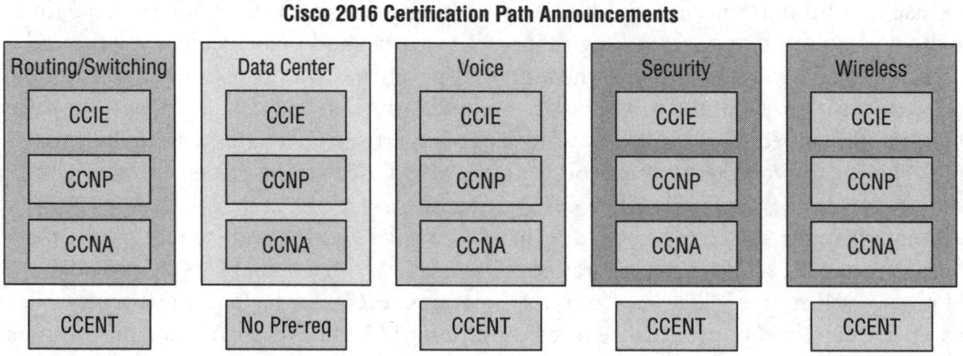

Cisco 2016 Certification Path Announcements

Routing/Switching	Data Center	Voice	Security	Wireless
CCIE	CCIE	CCIE	CCIE	CCIE
CCNP	CCNP	CCNP	CCNP	CCNP
CCNA	CCNA	CCNA	CCNA	CCNA
CCENT	No Pre-req	CCENT	CCENT	CCENT

> **NOTE** I have included only the most popular tracks in Figure I.1. In addition to the ones in this image, there are also tracks for Design and Service Provider.

The Cisco Routing and Switching (R/S) path is by far the most popular and could very well remain so, but soon you'll see the Data Center path become more and more of a focus as companies migrate to data center technologies. The Security and Collaboration tracks also actually provide a good job opportunity, and an even newer one that is becoming more popular is the Industrial CCNA. Still, understanding the foundation of R/S before attempting any other certification track is something I highly recommend.

Even so, and as the figure shows, you only need your CCENT certification to get underway for most of the tracks. Also, note that there are a few other certification tracks you can go down that are not shown in the figure, although they're not as popular as the ones shown.

Cisco Certified Entry Network Technician (CCENT)

Don't be fooled by the oh-so-misleading name of this first certification because it absolutely isn't entry level! Okay—maybe entry level for Cisco's certification path, but definitely not for someone without experience trying to break into the highly lucrative yet challenging IT job market! For the uninitiated, the CompTIA A+ and Network+ certifications aren't official prerequisites, but know that Cisco does expect you to have that type and level of experience before embarking on your Cisco certification journey.

All of this gets us to 2016, when the climb to Cisco supremacy just got much harder again. The innocuous-sounding siren's call of the CCENT can lure you to some serious trouble if you're not prepared, because it's actually much harder than the old CCNA ever was. This will rapidly become apparent once you start studying, but be encouraged! The fact that the certification process is getting harder really works better for you in the long run, because that which is harder to obtain only becomes that much more valuable when you finally do, right? Yes, indeed!

Another important factor to keep in mind is that the CCENT 100-101 exam, which is the exam this book was written for, costs $150 per attempt and it's anything but easy to pass! The good news is that this book will guide you step-by-step in building a strong foundation in routing and switching technologies. You really need to build on a strong technical foundation and stay away from exam cram type books, suspicious online material, and the like. They can help somewhat, but understand that you'll pass the Cisco certification exams only if you have a strong foundation and that you'll get that solid foundation only by reading as much as you can, performing the written labs and answering the review questions in this book, and practicing lots and lots of hands-on labs. Additional practice exam questions, videos, and labs are offered on my website, and what seems like a million other sites offer additional material that can help you study.

However, there is one way to skip the CCENT exam and still meet the prerequisite before moving on to any other certification track, and that path is through the CCNA R/S composite exam. First, I'll discuss the Interconnecting Cisco Network Devices 2 (ICND2) exam, and then I'll tell you about the composite CCNA exam, which will provide you, when you're successful, with both the CCENT and the CCNA R/S certification.

Cisco Certified Network Associate Routing and Switching (CCNA R/S)

Once you have achieved your CCENT certification, you can take the ICND2 (200-105) exam in order to achieve your CCNA R/S certification. This is now the most popular certification Cisco has by far because it's the most sought-after certification by all employers.

As with the CCENT, this exam is also $150 per attempt—although thinking you can just skim a book and pass any of these exams would probably be a really expensive mistake! The CCENT/CCNA exams are extremely hard and cover a lot of material, so you have to really know your stuff. Taking a Cisco class or spending months with hands-on experience is definitely a requirement to succeed when faced with this monster!

And once you have your CCNA, you don't have to stop there—you can choose to continue and achieve an even higher certification, called the Cisco Certified Network Professional (CCNP). There are various ones, as shown in Figure I.1. The CCNP R/S is still the most popular, with Voice certifications coming in at a close second. And I've got to tell you that the Data Center certification will be catching up fast. Also good to know is that anyone with a CCNP R/S has all the skills and knowledge needed to attempt the notoriously dreaded but coveted CCIE R/S lab. But just becoming a CCNA R/S can land you that job you've dreamed about, and that's what this book is all about: helping you to get and keep a great job!

Still, why take two exams to get your CCNA if you don't have to? Cisco still has the composite exam called CCNA 200-125 that, if passed, will land you with your CCENT and your CCNA R/S via only one test priced at only $250. Some people like the one-test approach, and some people like the two-test approach; this ICND2 book will help you with the two-test method.

Why Become a CCENT and CCNA R/S?

Cisco, like Microsoft and other vendors that provide certification, has created the certification process to give administrators a set of skills and to equip prospective employers with a way to measure those skills or match certain criteria. And as you probably know, becoming a CCNA R/S is certainly the initial, key step on a successful journey toward a new, highly rewarding, and sustainable networking career.

The CCNA program was created to provide a solid introduction not only to the Cisco Internetwork Operating System (IOS) and Cisco hardware but also to internetworking in general, making it helpful to you in areas that are not exclusively Cisco's. And regarding today's certification process, it's not unrealistic that network managers—even those without Cisco equipment—require Cisco certifications for their job applicants.

Rest assured that if you make it through the CCNA and are still interested in Cisco and internetworking, you're headed down a path to certain success!

What Skills Do You Need to Become a CCENT?

This ICND1 exam tests a candidate for the knowledge and skills required to successfully install, operate, and troubleshoot a small branch office network.

The exam includes questions on the operation of IP data networks, LAN switching technologies, IPv6, IP routing technologies, IP services network device security, and basic troubleshooting.

What Skills Do You Need to Become a CCNA R/S After You Have Passed ICND1?

The Interconnecting Cisco Networking Devices Part 2 (200-105 ICND2) exam is a 90-minute, 45–55 question assessment that is associated with the CCNA Routing and Switching certification. This exam tests a candidate's knowledge and skills related to LAN switching technologies, IPv4 and IPv6 routing technologies, WAN technologies, infrastructure services, and infrastructure maintenance.

Another test you can take instead of taking both of the ICND1 and ICND2 is the composite CCNA v3.0 exam, number 200-125.

How Do You Become a CCNA R/S with Just One Test?

The way to become a CCNA R/S is to pass one little test (CCNA composite exam 200-125) without having to take the CCENT and ICND2 exams. Then—poof!—you're a CCNA R/S. Oh, but don't you wish it were that easy? True, it's just one test, but it's a whopper, and to pass it you must possess enough knowledge to understand what the test writers are saying and you need to know everything I mentioned in the sections above! Hey, it's hard, but it can be done!

What does it cover? The 200-125 CCNA exam is the composite exam associated with the CCNA Routing and Switching certification. Candidates can prepare for this exam by taking the Todd Lammle authorized Cisco boot camps. This composite exam tests a candidate for the knowledge and skills required to install, operate, and troubleshoot a small to medium-size enterprise branch network. The topics include all of the areas covered under the 100-105 ICND1 and 200-105 ICND2 exams.

You can take the one composite test (200-125), but it is good to remember that Cisco offers the two-step process to become a CCNA as I discussed earlier in this introduction. It may be easier for you than taking that one ginormous exam, but don't think the two-test method is easy. It takes work! However, it can be done; you just need to stick with your studies. The two-test method involves passing the following:

- Exam 100-105: Interconnecting Cisco Networking Devices Part 1 (ICND1)
- Exam 200-105: Interconnecting Cisco Networking Devices Part 2 (ICND2)

I can't stress this point enough: It's critical that you have some hands-on experience with Cisco routers. If you can get a hold of some basic routers and switches, you're set, but if you can't, I've worked hard to provide hundreds of configuration examples throughout this book to help network administrators, or people who want to become network administrators, learn the skills they need to pass the CCENT and CCNA R/S exams.

 For Cisco certification hands-on training with CCSI Todd Lammle, please see www.lammle.com/ccna. Each student will get hands-on experience by configuring at least three routers and two switches—no sharing of equipment!

What Does This Book Cover?

This book covers everything you need to know to pass the ICND2 200-105 exam. But as I've said, taking plenty of time to study and practice with routers or a router simulator is the real key to success.

You will learn the following information in this book:

Chapter 1: Enhanced Switched Technologies This chapter will start off with STP protocols and dive into the fundamentals, covering modes as well as various flavors of STP. VLANs, trunks, and troubleshooting are covered as well. EtherChannel technologies, configuration, and verification are also covered. There are hands-on labs, a written lab, and plenty of review questions to help you. Do not even think of skipping the fundamental written and hands-on labs in this chapter!

Chapter 2: Network Device Management and Security   This chapter describes how to mitigate threats at the access layer using various security techniques. AAA with RADIUIS and TACACS+, SNMP, and HSRP are also covered in this chapter. Don't skip the written lab and review questions at the end of the chapter.

Chapter 3: Enhanced EIGRP   This is a full chapter on nothing but EIGRP and EIGRPv6. There are lots of examples, including configurations, verification, and troubleshooting labs, with both IP and with IPv6. Great hands-on labs are included, as well as a written lab and review questions.

Chapter 4: Open Shortest Path First (OSPF)   This chapter dives into more complex dynamic routing by covering OSPF routing. The written lab, hands-on labs, and review questions will help you master this vital routing protocol.

Chapter 5: Multi-Area OSPF   Before reading this chapter, be sure you have the previous chapter down pat with a strong OSPF foundation. This chapter will take off where that CCENT OSPF chapter left off and add multi-area networks along with advanced configurations and then finish with OSPFv3. Hands-on labs, a written lab, and challenging review questions await you at the end of the chapter.

Chapter 6: Troubleshooting IP, IPV6, and VLANs   I want to say this is the most important chapter in the book, but that's hard to do. You can decide that yourself when you take the exam! Be sure to go through all the troubleshooting steps for IP, IPv6 and VLANs. The hands-on labs for this chapter will be included in the free bonus material and be dynamic labs that I'll write and change as needed. Don't skip the written lab and review questions.

Chapter 7: Wide Area Networks   This is the longest chapter in the book. It covers multiple protocols in depth, especially HDLC, PPP, MLP, and PPPoE, along with a new section on BGP. Good troubleshooting examples are provided in the PPP PPPoE and BGP configuration sections, and these cannot be skipped! Hands-on labs meant to focus squarely on the objectives are included at the end of the chapter, as well as a written lab and challenging review questions.

Chapter 8: Evolution of Intelligent Networks   I saved the hardest chapter for last. What makes this chapter challenging is that there is no configuration section so you really need to dive deep into the cloud, APIC-EM, and QoS sections with an open and ready mind. I stuck as close to the objectives as possible in order to help you ace the exam. The written lab and review questions are spot on for the objectives.

Appendix A: Answers to Written Labs   This appendix contains the answers to the book's written labs.

Appendix B: Answers to Chapter Review Questions   This appendix provides the answers to the end-of-chapter review questions.

Be sure to check www.lammle.com/ccna to find out how to download bonus material I created specifically for this book.

Interactive Online Learning Environment and Test Bank

I have worked hard to provide some really great tools to help you with your certification process. All of the following tools, most of them available via www.wiley.com/go/ sybextestprep, should be loaded on your workstation when you're studying for the test. As a fantastic bonus, I was able to add to the download link a preview section from my CCNA video series! Please understand that these are not the full versions, but they're still a great value for you, included free with this book.

Sample Tests   All of the questions in this book are provided, including the Assessment Test at the end of this Introduction and the chapter tests that include the review questions at the end of each chapter. In addition, there is a practice exams with 50 questions. Use these questions to test your knowledge of the study guide material. The online test bank runs on multiple devices.

Electronic Flashcards   The online text bank includes 100 flashcards specifically written to hit you hard, so don't get discouraged if you don't ace your way through them at first! They're there to ensure that you're really ready for the exam. And no worries—armed with the review questions, practice exams, and flashcards, you'll be more than prepared when exam day comes!

Glossary   A complete glossary of CCENT, CCNA, and Cisco routing terms is available at www.wiley.com/go/sybextestprep.

Todd Lammle Bonus Material and Labs   Be sure to check www.lammle.com/ccna for directions on how to download all the latest bonus material created specifically to help you study for your ICND2 and CCNA Routing and Switching exams.

Full and demo versions of the CCNA and other Todd Lammle videos can be found at www.lammle.com/ccna.

How to Use This Book

If you want a solid foundation for the serious effort of preparing for the Interconnecting Cisco Network Devices 2 (ICND2) 200-105 exam, then look no further. I've spent hundreds of hours putting together this book with the sole intention of helping you to pass the ICND2 exam as well as really learn how to correctly configure Cisco routers and switches!

This book is loaded with valuable information, and you will get the most out of your study time if you understand why the book is organized the way it is.

So to maximize your benefit from this book, I recommend the following study method:

1. Take the assessment test that's provided at the end of this introduction. (The answers are at the end of the test.) It's okay if you don't know any of the answers; that's why you bought this book! Carefully read over the explanations for any question you get wrong and note the chapters in which the material relevant to them is covered. This information should help you plan your study strategy.

2. Study each chapter carefully, making sure you fully understand the information and the test objectives listed at the beginning of each one. Pay extra-close attention to any chapter that includes material covered in questions you missed.

3. Complete the written labs at the end of each chapter. (Answers to these appear in Appendix A.) Do *not* skip these written exercises because they directly relate to the ICND2 exam and what you must glean from the chapters in which they appear. Do not just skim these labs! Make sure you completely understand the reason for each correct answer.

4. Complete all hands-on labs in each chapter, referring to the text of the chapter so that you understand the reason for each step you take. Try to get your hands on some real equipment, but if you don't have Cisco equipment available, try the LammleSim IOS version, which you can use for the hands-on labs found only in this book. These labs will equip you with everything you need for all your Cisco certification goals.

5. Answer all of the review questions related to each chapter. (The answers appear in Appendix B.) Note the questions that confuse you, and study the topics they cover again, until the concepts are crystal clear. And again—do not just skim these questions! Make sure you fully comprehend the reason for each correct answer. Remember that these will not be the exact questions you will find on the exam, but they're written to help you understand the chapter material and ultimately pass the exam!

6. Try your hand at the practice questions that are exclusive to this book. The questions can be found only at www.wiley.com/go/sybextestprep. And be sure to check out www.lammle.com/ccna for the most up-to-date Cisco exam prep questions, videos, Todd Lammle boot camps, and more.

7. Test yourself using all the flashcards, which are also found on the download link. These are brand-new and updated flashcards to help you prepare for the ICND2 exam and a wonderful study tool!

To learn every bit of the material covered in this book, you'll have to apply yourself regularly, and with discipline. Try to set aside the same time period every day to study, and select a comfortable and quiet place to do so. I'm confident that if you work hard, you'll be surprised at how quickly you learn this material!

If you follow these steps and really study—*doing hands-on labs every single day* in addition to using the review questions, the practice exams, the Todd Lammle video sections, and the electronic flashcards as well as all the written labs—it would actually be hard to fail the ICND2 exam. But understand that studying for the ICND2 exam is a lot like getting in shape—if you do not go to the gym every day, it's not going to happen!

Where Do You Take the Exams?

You may take the ICND2 or any Cisco exam at any of the Pearson VUE authorized testing centers. For information, check www.vue.com or call 877-404-EXAM (3926).

To register for a Cisco exam, follow these steps:

1. Determine the number of the exam you want to take. (The ICND2 exam number is 200-105.)

2. Register with the nearest Pearson VUE testing center. At this point, you will be asked to pay in advance for the exam. At the time of this writing, the exam is $150 and must be taken within one year of payment. You can schedule exams up to six weeks in advance or as late as the day you want to take it—but if you fail a Cisco exam, you must wait five days before you will be allowed to retake it. If something comes up and you need to cancel or reschedule your exam appointment, contact Pearson VUE at least 24 hours in advance.

3. When you schedule the exam, you'll get instructions regarding all appointment and cancellation procedures, the ID requirements, and information about the testing-center location.

Tips for Taking Your ICND2 Exam

The ICND2 exam contains about 50 questions and must be completed in 90 minutes or less. This information can change per exam. You must get a score of about 85 percent to pass this exam, but again, each exam can be different.

Many questions on the exam have answer choices that at first glance look identical—especially the syntax questions! So remember to read through the choices carefully because close just doesn't cut it. If you get commands in the wrong order or forget one measly character, you'll get the question wrong. So, to practice, do the hands-on exercises at the end of this book's chapters over and over again until they feel natural to you.

Also, never forget that the right answer is the Cisco answer. In many cases, more than one appropriate answer is presented, but the *correct* answer is the one that Cisco recommends. On the exam, you will always be told to pick one, two, or three options, never "choose all that apply." The ICND2 exam may include the following test formats:

- Multiple-choice single answer
- Multiple-choice multiple answer
- Drag-and-drop
- Router simulations

Cisco proctored exams will not show the steps to follow in completing a router interface configuration, but they do allow partial command responses. For example, show run or sho running or sh running-config would be acceptable.

Here are some general tips for exam success:

- Arrive early at the exam center so you can relax and review your study materials.

- Read the questions *carefully*. Don't jump to conclusions. Make sure you're clear about *exactly* what each question asks. "Read twice, answer once," is what I always tell my students.

- When answering multiple-choice questions that you're not sure about, use the process of elimination to get rid of the obviously incorrect answers first. Doing this greatly improves your odds if you need to make an educated guess.

- You can no longer move forward and backward through the Cisco exams, so double-check your answer before clicking Next since you can't change your mind.

After you complete an exam, you'll get immediate, online notification of your pass or fail status, a printed examination score report that indicates your pass or fail status, and your exam results by section. (The test administrator will give you the printed score report.) Test scores are automatically forwarded to Cisco within five working days after you take the test, so you don't need to send your score to them. If you pass the exam, you'll receive confirmation from Cisco, typically within two to four weeks, sometimes a bit longer.

ICND2 Exam Objectives

Exam objectives are subject to change at any time without prior notice and at Cisco's sole discretion. Please visit Cisco's certification website (www.cisco.com/web/learning) for the latest information on the ICND2 exam.

TABLE I.1   26% 1.0 LAN Switching Technologies

Objective	Chapter
1.1 Configure, verify, and troubleshoot VLANs (normal/extended range) spanning multiple switches	1
1.1.a Access ports (data and voice)	1
1.1.b Default VLAN	1
1.2 Configure, verify, and troubleshoot interswitch connectivity	1
1.2.a Add and remove VLANs on a trunk	1
1.2.b DTP and VTP (v1&v2)	1
1.3 Configure, verify, and troubleshoot STP protocols	1

Objective	Chapter
1.3.a STP mode (PVST+ and RPVST+)	1
1.3.b STP root bridge selection	1
1.4 Configure, verify, and troubleshoot STP-related optional features	1
1.4.a PortFast	1
1.4.b BPDU guard	1
1.5 Configure, verify, and troubleshoot (Layer 2/Layer 3) EtherChannel	1
1.5.a Static	1
1.5.b PAGP	1
1.5.c LACP	1
1.6 Describe the benefits of switch stacking and chassis aggregation	8
1.7 Describe common access layer threat mitigation techniques	1, 2, 6
1.7.a 802.1x	2
1.7.b DHCP snooping	2
1.7.c Nondefault native VLAN	1, 6

TABLE I.2   29% 2.0 Routing Technologies

2.1 Configure, verify, and troubleshoot Inter-VLAN routing 1	1
2.1.a Router on a stick 1	1
2.1.b SVI 1	1
2.2 Compare and contrast distance vector and link-state routing protocols	3, 4, 5
2.3 Compare and contrast interior and exterior routing protocols	3, 4, 5
2.4 Configure, verify, and troubleshoot single area and multiarea OSPFv2 for IPv4 (excluding authentication, filtering, manual summarization, redistribution, stub, virtual-link, and LSAs)	4, 5

2.5 Configure, verify, and troubleshoot single area and multiarea OSPFv3 for IPv6   4, 5
(excluding authentication, filtering, manual summarization, redistribution, stub,
virtual-link, and LSAs)

2.6 Configure, verify, and troubleshoot EIGRP for IPv4 (excluding authentication,   3
filtering, manual summarization, redistribution, stub)

2.7 Configure, verify, and troubleshoot EIGRP for IPv6 (excluding authentication,   3
filtering, manual summarization, redistribution, stub)

TABLE I.3   16% 3.0 WAN Technologies

Objective	Chapter
3.1 Configure and verify PPP and MLPPP on WAN interfaces using local authentication	7
3.2 Configure, verify, and troubleshoot PPPoE client-side interfaces using local authentication	7
3.3 Configure, verify, and troubleshoot GRE tunnel connectivity	7
3.4 Describe WAN topology options	7
3.4.a Point-to-point	7
3.4.b Hub and spoke	7
3.4.c Full mesh	7
3.4.d Single vs dual-homed	7
3.5 Describe WAN access connectivity options	7
3.5.a MPLS	7
3.5.b MetroEthernet	7
3.5.c Broadband PPPoE	7
3.5.d Internet VPN (DMVPN, site-to-site VPN, client VPN)	7
3.6 Configure and verify single-homed branch connectivity using eBGP IPv4 (limited to peering and route advertisement using Network command only)	7

TABLE I.4   14% 4.0 Infrastructure Services

Objective	Chapter
4.1 Configure, verify, and troubleshoot basic HSRP	2
4.1.a Priority	2
4.1.b Preemption	2
4.1.c Version	2
4.2 Describe the effects of cloud resources on enterprise network architecture	8
4.2.a Traffic path to internal and external cloud services	8
4.2.b Virtual services	8
4.2.c Basic virtual network infrastructure	8
4.3 Describe basic QoS concepts	8
4.3.a Marking	8
4.3.b Device trust	8
4.3.c Prioritization	8
4.3.c. (i) Voice 4.3.c. (ii) Video 4.3.c. (iii) Data	8
4.3.d Shaping	8
4.3.e Policing	8
4.3.f Congestion management	8
4.4 Configure, verify, and troubleshoot IPv4 and IPv6 access list for traffic filtering	6
4.4.a Standard	6
4.4.b Extended	6
4.4.c Named	6
4.5 Verify ACLs using the APIC-EM Path Trace ACL analysis tool	8

TABLE I.5   15% 5.0 Infrastructure Maintenance

Objective	Chapter
5.1 Configure and verify device-monitoring protocols	2
5.1.a SNMPv2	2
5.1.b SNMPv3	2
5.2 Troubleshoot network connectivity issues using ICMP echo-based IP SLA	6
5.3 Use local SPAN to troubleshoot and resolve problems	6
5.4 Describe device management using AAA with TACACS+ and RADIUS	2
5.5 Describe network programmability in enterprise network architecture	8
5.5.a Function of a controller	8
5.5.b Separation of control plane and data plane	8
5.5.c Northbound and southbound APIs	8
5.6 Troubleshoot basic Layer 3 end-to-end connectivity issues	6

Assessment Test

1. What is the `sys-id-ext` field in a BPDU used for?

   A. This is a 4-bit field inserted into an Ethernet frame to define trunking information between switches.

   B. This is a 12-bit field inserted into an Ethernet frame to define VLANs in an STP instance.

   C. This is a 4-bit field inserted into a non-Ethernet frame to define EtherChannel options.

   D. This is a 12-bit field inserted into an Ethernet frame to define STP root bridges.

2. You have four RSTP PVST+ links between switches and want to aggregate the bandwidth. What solution will you use?

   A. EtherChannel

   B. PortFast

   C. BPDU Channel

   D. VLANs

   E. EtherBundle

3. What configuration parameters must be configured the same between switches for LACP to form a channel? (Choose three.)

   A. Virtual MAC address

   B. Port speeds

   C. Duplex

   D. PortFast enabled

   E. VLAN information

4. Between which two planes are SDN southbound interfaces used?

   A. Control

   B. Data

   C. Routing

   D. Application

5. Which option is a layer 2 QoS marking?

   A. EXP

   B. QoS group

   C. DSCP

   D. CoS

6. Which QoS mechanism will drop traffic if a session uses more than the allotted bandwidth?

    A. Congestion management

    B. Shaping

    C. Policing

    D. Marking

7. Which three layers are part of the SDN architecture? (Choose three.)

    A. Network

    B. Data Link

    C. Control

    D. Data

    E. Transport

    F. Application

8. Which of the following is NOT true about APIC-EM ACL analysis?

    A. Fast comparison of ACLs between devices to visualize difference and identify misconfigurations

    B. Inspection, interrogation, and analysis of network access control policies

    C. Ability to provide layer 4 to layer 7 deep-packet inspection

    D. Ability to trace application-specific paths between end devices to quickly identify ACLs and other problem areas.

9. When you're stacking switches, which is true? (Choose two.)

    A. The stack is managed as multiple objects and has a single management IP address.

    B. The stack is managed as a single object and has a single management IP address.

    C. The master switch is chosen when you configure the first switch's master algorithm to on.

    D. The master switch is elected from one of the stack member switches.

10. You need to connect to a remote IPv6 server in your virtual server farm. You can connect to the IPv4 servers, but not the critical IPv6 server you desperately need. Based on the output, what could your problem be?

```
C:\>ipconfig
   Connection-specific DNS Suffix  . : localdomain
   IPv6 Address. . . . . . . . . . . : 2001:db8:3c4d:3:ac3b:2ef:1823:8938
   Temporary IPv6 Address. . . . . . : 2001:db8:3c4d:3:2f33:44dd:211:1c3d
   Link-local IPv6 Address . . . . . : fe80::ac3b:2ef:1823:8938%11
   IPv4 Address. . . . . . . . . . . : 10.1.1.10
   Subnet Mask . . . . . . . . . . . : 255.255.255.0
   Default Gateway . . . . . . . . . : 10.1.1.1
```

    A. The global address is in the wrong subnet.

    B. The IPv6 default gateway has not been configured or received from the router.

C. The link-local address has not been resolved so the host cannot communicate to the router.

D. There are two IPv6 global addresses configured. One must be removed from the configuration.

11. What command is used to view the IPv6-to-MAC-address resolution table on a Cisco router?

A. show ip arp

B. show ipv6 arp

C. show ip neighbors

D. show ipv6 neighbors

E. show arp

12. An IPv6 ARP entry is listed with a status of REACH. What can you conclude about the IPv6-to-MAC-address mapping?

A. The interface has communicated with the neighbor address and the mapping is current.

B. The interface has not communicated within the neighbor reachable time frame.

C. The ARP entry has timed out.

D. IPv6 can reach the neighbor address but the addresses has not yet been resolved.

13. Serial0/1 goes down. How will EIGRP send packets to the 10.1.1.0 network?

```
Corp#show ip eigrp topology
[output cut]
P 10.1.1.0/24, 2 successors, FD is 2681842
          via 10.1.2.2 (2681842/2169856), Serial0/0
          via 10.1.3.1 (2973467/2579243), Serial0/2
          via 10.1.3.3 (2681842/2169856), Serial0/1
```

A. EIGRP will put the 10.1.1.0 network into active mode.

B. EIGRP will drop all packets destined for 10.1.1.0.

C. EIGRP will just keep sending packets out s0/0.

D. EIGRP will use s0/2 as the successor and keep routing to 10.1.1.0.

14. What command produced the following output?

```
via FE80:3:201:C9FF:FED0:3301 (29110112/33316), Serial0/0/0
via FE80::209:7CFF:FE51:B401 (4470112/42216), Serial0/0/1
via FE80::209:7CFF:FE51:B401 (2170112/2816), Serial0/0/2
```

A. show ip protocols

B. show ipv6 protocols

C. show ip eigrp neighbors

D. show ipv6 eigrp neighbors

E. show ip eigrp topology

F. show ipv6 eigrp topology

15. You need to troubleshoot an adjacency between two EIGRP configured routers. What should you look for? (Choose four.)

   A. Verify the AS numbers.

   B. Verify that you have the proper interfaces enabled for EIGRP.

   C. Make sure there are no mismatched K values.

   D. Check your passive interface settings.

   E. Make sure your remote routers are not connected to the Internet.

   F. If authentication is configured, make sure all routers use different passwords.

16. You have two OSPF directly configured routers that are not forming an adjacency. What should you check? (Choose three.)

   A. Process ID

   B. Hello and dead timers

   C. Link cost

   D. Area

   E. IP address/subnet mask

17. When do two adjacent routers enter the 2WAY state?

   A. After both routers have received Hello information

   B. After they have exchanged topology databases

   C. When they connect only to a DR or BDR

   D. When they need to exchange RID information

18. Which type of LSAs are generated by ABRs and referred to as summary link advertisements (SLAs)?

   A. Type 1

   B. Type 2

   C. Type 3

   D. Type 4

   E. Type 5

19. Which of the following is *not* provided by the AH portion of IPsec?

   A. Integrity

   B. Confidentiality

   C. Authenticity

   D. Anti-replay

20. Which statement about GRE is not true?

   A. GRE is stateless and has no flow control.

   B. GRE has security.

   C. GRE has additional overhead for tunneled packets, at least 24 bytes.

   D. GRE uses a protocol-type field in the GRE header so any layer 3 protocol can be used through the tunnel.

21. Which of the following services provides the operating system and the network?

   A. IaaS

   B. PaaS

   C. SaaS

   D. None of the above

Answers to Assessment Test

1. B. To allow for the PVST+ to operate, there's a field inserted into the BPDU to accommodate the extended system ID so that PVST+ can have a root bridge configured on a per-STP instance. The extended system ID (VLAN ID) is a 12-bit field, and we can even see what this field is carrying via show spanning-tree command output. See Chapter 1 for more information.

2. A. Cisco's EtherChannel can bundle up to eight ports between switches in order to provide resiliency and more bandwidth between switches. See Chapter 1 for more information.

3. B, C, E. All the ports on both sides of every link must be configured exactly the same between switches or EtherChannel will not work. Speed, duplex, and allowed VLANs must match. See Chapter 1 for more information.

4. A, B. Southbound APIs (or device-to-control-plane interfaces) are used for communication between the controllers and network devices, which puts these interfaces between the control and data planes. See Chapter 8 for more information.

5. D. Class of Service (CoS) is a term to describe designated fields in a frame or packet header. How devices treat packets in your network depends on the field values. CoS is usually used with Ethernet frames and contains 3 bits. See Chapter 8 for more information.

6. C. When traffic exceeds the allocated rate, the policer can take one of two actions. It can either drop traffic or re-mark it to another class of service. The new class usually has a higher drop probability. See Chapter 8 for more information.

7. C, D, F. The SDN architecture slightly differs from the architecture of traditional networks. It comprises three stacked layers: data, control and application See Chapter 8 for more information.

8. C. NBAR is a layer 4 to layer 7 deep-packet inspection classifier. See Chapter 8 for more information.

9. B, D. Each stack of switches has a single IP address and is managed as a single object. This single IP management applies to activities such as fault detection, VLAN creation and modification, security, and QoS controls. Each stack has only one configuration file, which is distributed to each member in the stack. When you add a new switch to the stack, the master switch automatically configures the unit with the currently running IOS image and the configuration of the stack. You do not have to do anything to bring up the switch before it is ready to operate. See Chapter 8 for more information.

10. B. There is no IPv6 default gateway, which will be the link-local address of the router interface, sent to the host as a router advertisement. Until this host receives the router address, the host will communicate with IPv6 only on the local subnet. See Chapter 6 for more information.

11. D. The command show ipv6 neighbors provides the ARP cache on a router. See Chapter 6 for more information.

12. A. The state is STALE when the interface has not communicated within the neighbor reachable time frame. The next time the neighbor communicates, the state will be REACH. See Chapter 6 for more information.

13. C. There are two successor routes, so by default, EIGRP was load-balancing out s0/0 and s0/1. When s0/1 goes down, EIGRP will just keep forwarding traffic out the second link, s0/0. S0/1 will be removed from the routing table. See Chapter 3 for more information.

14. F. There isn't a lot to go on with the output, but the only commands that provide the FD and AD are `show ip eigrp topology` and `show ipv6 eigrp topology`. The addresses in the output are link-local IPv6 addresses, so our answer is the latter. See Chapter 3 for more information.

15. A, B, C, D. Cisco has documented steps, according to the objectives, that you must go through when troubleshooting an adjacency. See Chapter 3 for more information.

16. B, D, E. In order for two OSPF routers to create an adjacency, the hello and dead timers must match, and they must both be configured into the same area as well as be in the same subnet. See Chapter 6 for more information.

17. A. The process starts by sending out Hello packets. Every listening router will then add the originating router to the neighbor database. The responding routers will reply with all of their Hello information so that the originating router can add them to its own neighbor table. At this point, we will have reached the 2WAY state—only certain routers will advance beyond this. See Chapter 5 for more information.

18. C. Referred to as summary link advertisements (SLAs), Type 3 LSAs are generated by area border routers. These ABRs send Type 3 LSAs toward the area external to the one where they were generated. See Chapter 5 for more information.

19. B. AH checks the entire packet, but it doesn't offer any encryption services. See Chapter 7 for more information.

20. B. GRE is a generic tunnel protocol that has no built-in security. The rest of the options are correct for GRE tunnels. See Chapter 7 for more information.

21. B. Platform as a Service (PaaS) provides the operating system and the network by delivering a computing platform and solution stack. See Chapter 8 for more information.

CCNA®

ICND2

Study Guide

Third Edition

Chapter

1

Enhanced Switched Technologies

THE FOLLOWING ICND2 EXAM TOPICS ARE COVERED IN THIS CHAPTER:

✓ **1.0 LAN Switching Technologies**

- 1.1 Configure, verify, and troubleshoot VLANs (normal/extended range) spanning multiple switches

    - 1.1.a Access ports (data and voice)

    - 1.1.b Default VLAN

- 1.2 Configure, verify, and troubleshoot interswitch connectivity

    - 1.2.a Add and remove VLANs on a trunk

    - 1.2.b DTP and VTP (v1&v2)

    - 1.3 Configure, verify, and troubleshoot STP protocols

    - 1.3.a STP mode (PVST+ and RPVST+)

    - 1.3.b STP root bridge selection

- 1.4 Configure, verify, and troubleshoot STP-related optional features

    - 1.4.a PortFast

    - 1.4.b BPDU guard

- 1.5 Configure, verify, and troubleshoot (Layer 2/Layer 3) EtherChannel

    - 1.5.a Static

    - 1.5.b PAGP

    - 1.5.c LACP

- 1.7 Describe common access layer threat mitigation techniques

    - 1.7.c Nondefault native VLAN

✓ **2.0 Routing Technologies**

- 2.1 Configure, verify, and troubleshoot Inter-VLAN routing

    - 2.1.a Router on a stick

    - 2.1.b SVI

Long ago, a company called Digital Equipment Corporation (DEC) created the original version of *Spanning Tree Protocol (STP)*. The IEEE later created its own version of STP called 802.1d. Cisco has moved toward another industry standard in its newer switches called 802.1w. We'll explore both the old and new versions of STP in this chapter, but first, I'll define some important STP basics.

Routing protocols like RIP, EIGRP, and OSPF have processes for preventing loops from occurring at the Network layer, but if you have redundant physical links between your switches, these protocols won't do a thing to stop loops from occurring at the Data Link layer. That's exactly why STP was developed—to put an end to loop issues in a layer 2 switched network. It's also why we'll be thoroughly exploring the key features of this vital protocol as well as how it works within a switched network in this chapter.

After covering STP in detail, we'll move on to explore EtherChannel.

To find up-to-the-minute updates for this chapter, please see www.lammle .com/ccna or the book's web page at www.sybex.com/go/ccna.

VLAN Review

As you may remember from ICND1, configuring VLANs is actually pretty easy. It's just that figuring out which users you want in each VLAN is not, and doing that can eat up a lot of your time! But once you've decided on the number of VLANs you want to create and established which users you want to belong to each one, it's time to bring your first VLAN into the world.

To configure VLANs on a Cisco Catalyst switch, use the global config vlan command. In the following example, I'm going to demonstrate how to configure VLANs on the S1 switch by creating three VLANs for three different departments—again, remember that VLAN 1 is the native and management VLAN by default:

```
S1(config)#vlan ?
  WORD        ISL VLAN IDs 1-4094
  access-map  Create vlan access-map or enter vlan access-map command mode
  dot1q       dot1q parameters
  filter      Apply a VLAN Map
```

```
  group      Create a vlan group
  internal   internal VLAN
S1(config)#vlan 2
S1(config-vlan)#name Sales
S1(config-vlan)#vlan 3
S1(config-vlan)#name Marketing
S1(config-vlan)#vlan 4
S1(config-vlan)#name Accounting
S1(config-vlan)#^Z
S1#
```

In this output, you can see that you can create VLANs from 1 to 4094. But this is only mostly true. As I said, VLANs can really only be created up to 1001, and you can't use, change, rename, or delete VLANs 1 or 1002 through 1005 because they're reserved. The VLAN with numbers above 1005 are called extended VLANs and won't be saved in the database unless your switch is set to what is called VLAN Trunking Protocol (VTP) transparent mode. You won't see these VLAN numbers used too often in production. Here's an example of me attempting to set my S1 switch to VLAN 4000 when my switch is set to VTP server mode (the default VTP mode, which we'll talk about shortly):

```
S1#config t
S1(config)#vlan 4000
S1(config-vlan)#^Z
% Failed to create VLANs 4000
Extended VLAN(s) not allowed in current VTP mode.
%Failed to commit extended VLAN(s) changes.
```

After you create the VLANs that you want, you can use the show vlan command to check them out. But notice that, by default, all ports on the switch are in VLAN 1. To change the VLAN associated with a port, you need to go to each interface and specifically tell it which VLAN to be a part of.

 Remember that a created VLAN is unused until it is assigned to a switch port or ports and that all ports are always assigned in VLAN 1 unless set otherwise.

Once the VLANs are created, verify your configuration with the show vlan command (sh vlan for short):

```
S1#sh vlan

VLAN Name                             Status    Ports
---- -------------------------------- --------- -------------------------------
1    default                          active    Fa0/1, Fa0/2, Fa0/3, Fa0/4
                                                Fa0/5, Fa0/6, Fa0/7, Fa0/8
```

```
                                        Fa0/9, Fa0/10, Fa0/11, Fa0/12
                                        Fa0/13, Fa0/14, Fa0/19, Fa0/20
                                        Fa0/21, Fa0/22, Fa0/23, Gi0/1
                                        Gi0/2
2     Sales                  active
3     Marketing              active
4     Accounting             active
[output cut]
```

If you want to see which ports are assigned to a particular VLAN (for example, VLAN 200), you can obviously use the show vlan command as shown above, or you can use the show vlan id 200 command to get ports assigned only to VLAN 200.

This may seem repetitive, but it's important, and I want you to remember it: You can't change, delete, or rename VLAN 1 because it's the default VLAN and you just can't change that—period. It's also the native VLAN of all switches by default, and Cisco recommends that you use it as your management VLAN. If you're worried about security issues, then change the native VLAN! Basically, any ports that aren't specifically assigned to a different VLAN will be sent down to the native VLAN—VLAN 1.

In the preceding S1 output, you can see that ports Fa0/1 through Fa0/14, Fa0/19 through 23, and the Gi0/1 and Gi02 uplinks are all in VLAN 1. But where are ports 15 through 18? First, understand that the command show vlan only displays access ports, so now that you know what you're looking at with the show vlan command, where do you think ports Fa15–18 are? That's right! They are trunked ports. Cisco switches run a proprietary protocol called *Dynamic Trunk Protocol (DTP)*, and if there is a compatible switch connected, they will start trunking automatically, which is precisely where my four ports are. You have to use the show interfaces trunk command to see your trunked ports like this:

```
S1# show interfaces trunk
Port      Mode          Encapsulation  Status    Native vlan
Fa0/15    desirable     n-isl          trunking  1
Fa0/16    desirable     n-isl          trunking  1
Fa0/17    desirable     n-isl          trunking  1
Fa0/18    desirable     n-isl          trunking  1

Port      Vlans allowed on trunk
Fa0/15    1-4094
Fa0/16    1-4094
Fa0/17    1-4094
Fa0/18    1-4094

[output cut]
```

This output reveals that the VLANs from 1 to 4094 are allowed across the trunk by default. Another helpful command, which is also part of the Cisco exam objectives, is the show interfaces *interface* switchport command:

```
S1#sh interfaces fastEthernet 0/15 switchport
Name: Fa0/15
Switchport: Enabled
Administrative Mode: dynamic desirable
Operational Mode: trunk
Administrative Trunking Encapsulation: negotiate
Operational Trunking Encapsulation: isl
Negotiation of Trunking: On
Access Mode VLAN: 1 (default)
Trunking Native Mode VLAN: 1 (default)
Administrative Native VLAN tagging: enabled
Voice VLAN: none
[output cut]
```

The highlighted output shows us the administrative mode of dynamic desirable, that the port is a trunk port, and that DTP was used to negotiate the frame-tagging method of ISL. It also predictably shows that the native VLAN is the default of 1.

Now that we can see the VLANs created, we can assign switch ports to specific ones. Each port can be part of only one VLAN, with the exception of voice access ports. Using trunking, you can make a port available to traffic from all VLANs. I'll cover that next.

Assigning Switch Ports to VLANs

You configure a port to belong to a VLAN by assigning a membership mode that specifies the kind of traffic the port carries plus the number of VLANs it can belong to. You can also configure each port on a switch to be in a specific VLAN (access port) by using the interface switchport command. You can even configure multiple ports at the same time with the interface range command.

In the next example, I'll configure interface Fa0/3 to VLAN 3. This is the connection from the S3 switch to the host device:

```
S3#config t
S3(config)#int fa0/3
S3(config-if)#switchport ?
  access      Set access mode characteristics of the interface
  autostate   Include or exclude this port from vlan link up calculation
  backup      Set backup for the interface
  block       Disable forwarding of unknown uni/multi cast addresses
  host        Set port host
```

```
mode            Set trunking mode of the interface
nonegotiate     Device will not engage in negotiation protocol on this
                interface
port-security   Security related command
priority        Set appliance 802.1p priority
private-vlan    Set the private VLAN configuration
protected       Configure an interface to be a protected port
trunk           Set trunking characteristics of the interface
voice           Voice appliance attributes  voice
```

Well now, what do we have here? There's some new stuff showing up in our output now. We can see various commands—some that I've already covered, but no worries because I'm going to cover the access, mode, nonegotiate, and trunk commands very soon. Let's start with setting an access port on S1, which is probably the most widely used type of port you'll find on production switches that have VLANs configured:

```
S3(config-if)#switchport mode ?
    access        Set trunking mode to ACCESS unconditionally
  dot1q-tunnel    set trunking mode to TUNNEL unconditionally
  dynamic         Set trunking mode to dynamically negotiate access or trunk mode
  private-vlan    Set private-vlan mode
  trunk           Set trunking mode to TRUNK unconditionally


S3(config-if)#switchport mode access
S3(config-if)#switchport access vlan 3
```

By starting with the switchport mode access command, you're telling the switch that this is a nontrunking layer 2 port. You can then assign a VLAN to the port with the switchport access command. Remember, you can choose many ports to configure simultaneously with the interface range command.

Let's take a look at our VLANs now:

```
S3#show vlan
VLAN Name                     Status    Ports
---- ------------------------ --------- ------------------------------
1    default                  active    Fa0/4, Fa0/5, Fa0/6, Fa0/7
                                        Fa0/8, Fa0/9, Fa0/10, Fa0/11,
                                        Fa0/12, Fa0/13, Fa0/14, Fa0/19,
                                        Fa0/20, Fa0/21, Fa0/22, Fa0/23,
                                        Gi0/1,Gi0/2

2    Sales                    active
3    Marketing                active    Fa0/3
```

Notice that port Fa0/3 is now a member of VLAN 3. But, can you tell me where ports 1 and 2 are? And why aren't they showing up in the output of show vlan? That's right, because they are trunk ports!

We can also see this with the show interfaces interface switchport command:

```
S3#sh int fa0/3 switchport
Name: Fa0/3
Switchport: Enabled
Administrative Mode: static access
Operational Mode: static access
Administrative Trunking Encapsulation: negotiate
Negotiation of Trunking: Off
Access Mode VLAN: 3 (Marketing)
```

The highlighted output shows that Fa0/3 is an access port and a member of VLAN 3 (Marketing).

Before we move onto trunking and VTP, let's add a voice VLAN on our switch. When an IP phone is connected to a switch port, this port should have a voice VLAN associated with it. By creating a separate VLAN for voice traffic, which of course you would do, what happens when you have a PC or laptop that connects via Ethernet into an IP phone? The phone connects to the Ethernet port and into one port on the switch. You're now sending both voice and data to the single switch port.

All you need to do is add another VLAN to the same switch port like so to fix this issue and separate the data at the switch port into two VLANs:

```
S1(config)#vlan 10
S1(config-vlan)#name Voice
S1(config-vlan)#int g0/1
S1(config-if)#switchport voice vlan 10
```

That's it. Well, sort of. If you plugged devices into each VLAN port, they can only talk to other devices in the same VLAN. But as soon as you learn a bit more about trunking, we're going to enable inter-VLAN communication!

Configuring Trunk Ports

The 2960 switch only runs the IEEE 802.1q encapsulation method. To configure trunking on a FastEthernet port, use the interface command switchport mode trunk. It's a tad different on the 3560 switch.

The following switch output shows the trunk configuration on interfaces Fa0/15–18 as set to trunk:

```
S1(config)#int range f0/15-18
S1(config-if-range)#switchport trunk encapsulation dot1q
S1(config-if-range)#switchport mode trunk
```

If you have a switch that only runs the 802.1q encapsulation method, then you wouldn't use the encapsulation command as I did in the preceding output. Let's check out our trunk ports now:

```
S1(config-if-range)#do sh int f0/15 switchport
Name: Fa0/15
Switchport: Enabled
Administrative Mode: trunk
Operational Mode: trunk
Administrative Trunking Encapsulation: dot1q
Operational Trunking Encapsulation: dot1q
Negotiation of Trunking: On
Access Mode VLAN: 1 (default)
Trunking Native Mode VLAN: 1 (default)
Administrative Native VLAN tagging: enabled
Voice VLAN: none
```

Notice that port Fa0/15 is a trunk and running 802.1q. Let's take another look:

```
S1(config-if-range)#do sh int trunk
Port        Mode             Encapsulation  Status     Native vlan
Fa0/15      on               802.1q         trunking   1
Fa0/16      on               802.1q         trunking   1
Fa0/17      on               802.1q         trunking   1
Fa0/18      on               802.1q         trunking   1
Port        Vlans allowed on trunk
Fa0/15      1-4094
Fa0/16      1-4094
Fa0/17      1-4094
Fa0/18      1-4094
```

Take note of the fact that ports 15–18 are now in the trunk mode of on and the encapsulation is now 802.1q instead of the negotiated ISL. Here's a description of the different options available when configuring a switch interface:

switchport mode access   I discussed this in the previous section, but this puts the interface (access port) into permanent nontrunking mode and negotiates to convert the link into a nontrunk link. The interface becomes a nontrunk interface regardless of whether the neighboring interface is a trunk interface. The port would be a dedicated layer 2 access port.

switchport mode dynamic auto   This mode makes the interface able to convert the link to a trunk link. The interface becomes a trunk interface if the neighboring interface is set to trunk or desirable mode. The default is dynamic auto on a lot of Cisco switches, but that default trunk method is changing to dynamic desirable on most new models.

switchport mode dynamic desirable   This one makes the interface actively attempt to convert the link to a trunk link. The interface becomes a trunk interface if the neighboring interface is set to `trunk`, `desirable`, or `auto` mode. This is now the default switch port mode for all Ethernet interfaces on all new Cisco switches.

`switchport mode trunk`   Puts the interface into permanent trunking mode and negotiates to convert the neighboring link into a trunk link. The interface becomes a trunk interface even if the neighboring interface isn't a trunk interface.

`switchport nonegotiate`   Prevents the interface from generating DTP frames. You can use this command only when the interface switchport mode is access or trunk. You must manually configure the neighboring interface as a trunk interface to establish a trunk link.

 Dynamic Trunking Protocol (DTP) is used for negotiating trunking on a link between two devices as well as negotiating the encapsulation type of either 802.1q or ISL. I use the `nonegotiate` command when I want dedicated trunk ports; no questions asked.

To disable trunking on an interface, use the `switchport mode access` command, which sets the port back to a dedicated layer 2 access switch port.

Defining the Allowed VLANs on a Trunk

As I've mentioned, trunk ports send and receive information from all VLANs by default, and if a frame is untagged, it's sent to the management VLAN. Understand that this applies to the extended range VLANs too.

But we can remove VLANs from the allowed list to prevent traffic from certain VLANs from traversing a trunked link. I'll show you how you'd do that, but first let me again demonstrate that all VLANs are allowed across the trunk link by default:

```
S1#sh int trunk
[output cut]
Port        Vlans allowed on trunk
Fa0/15      1-4094
Fa0/16      1-4094
Fa0/17      1-4094
Fa0/18      1-4094
S1(config)#int f0/15
S1(config-if)#switchport trunk allowed vlan 4,6,12,15
S1(config-if)#do show int trunk
[output cut]
Port        Vlans allowed on trunk
Fa0/15      4,6,12,15
Fa0/16      1-4094
Fa0/17      1-4094
Fa0/18      1-4094
```

The preceding command affected the trunk link configured on S1 port Fa0/15, causing it to permit all traffic sent and received for VLANs 4, 6, 12, and 15. You can try to remove VLAN 1 on a trunk link, but it will still send and receive management data like CDP, DTP, and VTP, so what's the point?

To remove a range of VLANs, just use the hyphen:

```
S1(config-if)#switchport trunk allowed vlan remove 4-8
```

If by chance someone has removed some VLANs from a trunk link and you want to set the trunk back to default, just use this command:

```
S1(config-if)#switchport trunk allowed vlan all
```

Next, I want to show you how to configure a native VLAN for a trunk before we start routing between VLANs.

Changing or Modifying the Trunk Native VLAN

You can change the trunk port native VLAN from VLAN 1, which many people do for security reasons. To change the native VLAN, use the following command:

```
S1(config)#int f0/15
S1(config-if)#switchport trunk native vlan ?
  <1-4094>  VLAN ID of the native VLAN when this port is in trunking mode

S1(config-if)#switchport trunk native vlan 4
1w6d: %CDP-4-NATIVE_VLAN_MISMATCH: Native VLAN mismatch discovered on
FastEthernet0/15 (4), with S3 FastEthernet0/1 (1).
```

So we've changed our native VLAN on our trunk link to 4, and by using the show running-config command, I can see the configuration under the trunk link:

```
S1#sh run int f0/15
Building configuration...

Current configuration : 202 bytes
!
interface FastEthernet0/15
 description 1st connection to S3
 switchport trunk encapsulation dot1q
 switchport trunk native vlan 4
 switchport trunk allowed vlan 4,6,12,15
 switchport mode trunk
end

S1#!
```

Oops—wait a minute! You didn't think it would be this easy and would just start working, did you? Of course not! Here's the rub: If all switches don't have the same native VLAN configured on the given trunk links, then we'll start to receive this error, which happened immediately after I entered the command:

```
1w6d: %CDP-4-NATIVE_VLAN_MISMATCH: Native VLAN mismatch discovered
on FastEthernet0/15 (4), with S3 FastEthernet0/1 (1).
```

Actually, this is a good, noncryptic error, so either we can go to the other end of our trunk link(s) and change the native VLAN or we set the native VLAN back to the default to fix it. Here's how we'd do that:

```
S1(config-if)#no switchport trunk native vlan
1w6d: %SPANTREE-2-UNBLOCK_CONSIST_PORT: Unblocking FastEthernet0/15
on VLAN0004. Port consistency restored.
```

Now our trunk link is using the default VLAN 1 as the native VLAN. Just remember that all switches on a given trunk must use the same native VLAN or you'll have some serious management problems. These issues won't affect user data, just management traffic between switches. Now, let's mix it up by connecting a router into our switched network and configure inter-VLAN communication.

VLAN Trunking Protocol (VTP)

Cisco created this one too. The basic goals of *VLAN Trunking Protocol (VTP)* are to manage all configured VLANs across a switched internetwork and to maintain consistency throughout that network. VTP allows you to add, delete, and rename VLANs—information that is then propagated to all other switches in the VTP domain.

Here's a list of some of the cool features VTP has to offer:

- Consistent VLAN configuration across all switches in the network
- VLAN trunking over mixed networks, such as Ethernet to ATM LANE or even FDDI
- Accurate tracking and monitoring of VLANs
- Dynamic reporting of added VLANs to all switches in the VTP domain
- Adding VLANs using Plug and Play

Very nice, but before you can get VTP to manage your VLANs across the network, you have to create a VTP server (really, you don't need to even do that since all switches default to VTP server mode, but just make sure you have a server). All servers that need to share VLAN information must use the same domain name, and a switch can be in only one domain at a time. So basically, this means that a switch can share VTP domain information with other switches only if they're configured into the same VTP domain. You can use a VTP domain if you have more than one switch connected in a network, but if you've got all your switches in only one VLAN, you just don't need to use VTP. Do keep in mind that VTP information is sent between switches only via a trunk port.

Switches advertise VTP management domain information as well as a configuration revision number and all known VLANs with any specific parameters. But there's also something called *VTP transparent mode*. In it, you can configure switches to forward VTP information through trunk ports but not to accept information updates or update their VLAN databases.

If you've got sneaky users adding switches to your VTP domain behind your back, you can include passwords, but don't forget—every switch must be set up with the same password. And as you can imagine, this little snag can be a real hassle administratively!

Switches detect any added VLANs within a VTP advertisement and then prepare to send information on their trunk ports with the newly defined VLAN in tow. Updates are sent out as revision numbers that consist of summary advertisements. Anytime a switch sees a higher revision number, it knows the information it's getting is more current, so it will overwrite the existing VLAN database with the latest information.

You should know these four requirements for VTP to communicate VLAN information between switches:

- The VTP version must be set the same
- The VTP management domain name of both switches must be set the same.
- One of the switches has to be configured as a VTP server.
- Set a VTP password if used.

No router is necessary and is not a requirement. Now that you've got that down, we're going to delve deeper into the world of VTP with VTP modes and VTP pruning.

VTP Modes of Operation

Figure 1.1 shows you how a VTP server will update the connected VTP client's VLAN database when a change occurs in the VLAN database on the server.

FIGURE 1.1   VTP modes

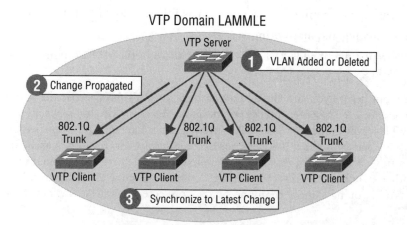

Server   This is the default mode for all Catalyst switches. You need at least one server in your VTP domain to propagate VLAN information throughout that domain. Also important: The switch must be in server mode to be able to create, add, and delete VLANs in a VTP domain. VLAN information has to be changed in server mode, and any change made to VLANs on a switch in server mode will be advertised to the entire VTP domain. In VTP server mode, VLAN configurations are saved in NVRAM on the switch.

Client   In client mode, switches receive information from VTP servers, but they also receive and forward updates, so in this way, they behave like VTP servers. The difference is that they can't create, change, or delete VLANs. Plus, none of the ports on a client switch can be added to a new VLAN before the VTP server notifies the client switch of the new VLAN and the VLAN exists in the client's VLAN database. Also good to know is that VLAN information sent from a VTP server isn't stored in NVRAM, which is important because it means that if the switch is reset or reloaded, the VLAN information will be deleted. Here's a hint: If you want a switch to become a server, first make it a client so it receives all the correct VLAN information, then change it to a server—so much easier!

So basically, a switch in VTP client mode will forward VTP summary advertisements and process them. This switch will learn about but won't save the VTP configuration in the running configuration, and it won't save it in NVRAM. Switches that are in VTP client mode will only learn about and pass along VTP information—that's it!

 Real World Scenario

So, When Do I Need to Consider Using VTP?

Here's a scenario for you. Bob, a senior network administrator at Acme Corporation in San Francisco, has about 25 switches all connected together, and he wants to configure VLANs to break up broadcast domains. When do you think he should start to consider using VTP?

If you answered that he should have used VTP the moment he had more than one switch and multiple VLANs, you're right. If you have only one switch, then VTP is irrelevant. It also isn't a player if you're not configuring VLANs in your network. But if you do have multiple switches that use multiple VLANs, you'd better configure your VTP server and clients, and you better do it right!

When you first bring up your switched network, verify that your main switch is a VTP server and that all the other ones are VTP clients. When you create VLANs on the main VTP server, all switches will receive the VLAN database.

If you have an existing switched network and you want to add a new switch, make sure to configure it as a VTP client before you install it. If you don't, it's possible—okay, highly probable—that your new little beauty will send out a new VTP database to all your other switches, effectively wiping out all your existing VLANs like a nuclear blast. No one needs that!

Transparent   Switches in transparent mode don't participate in the VTP domain or share its VLAN database, but they'll still forward VTP advertisements through any configured trunk links. They can create, modify, and delete VLANs because they keep their own database—one they keep secret from the other switches. Despite being kept in NVRAM, the VLAN database in transparent mode is actually only locally significant. The whole purpose of transparent mode is to allow remote switches to receive the VLAN database from a VTP Server configured switch through a switch that is not participating in the same VLAN assignments.

VTP only learns about normal-range VLANs, with VLAN IDs 1 to 1005; VLANs with IDs greater than 1005 are called extended-range VLANs and they're not stored in the VLAN database. The switch must be in VTP transparent mode when you create VLAN IDs from 1006 to 4094, so it would be pretty rare that you'd ever use these VLANs. One other thing: VLAN IDs 1 and 1002 to 1005 are automatically created on all switches and can't be removed.

VTP Pruning

VTP gives you a way to preserve bandwidth by configuring it to reduce the amount of broadcasts, multicasts, and unicast packets. This is called *pruning*. Switches enabled for VTP pruning send broadcasts only to trunk links that actually must have the information.

Here's what this means: If Switch A doesn't have any ports configured for VLAN 5 and a broadcast is sent throughout VLAN 5, that broadcast wouldn't traverse the trunk link to Switch A. By default, VTP pruning is disabled on all switches. Seems to me this would be a good default parameter. When you enable pruning on a VTP server, you enable it for the entire domain. By default, VLANs 2 through 1001 are pruning eligible, but VLAN 1 can never be pruned because it's an administrative VLAN. VTP pruning is supported with both VTP version 1 and version 2.

By using the show interface trunk command, we can see that all VLANs are allowed across a trunked link by default:

```
S1#sh int trunk

Port        Mode          Encapsulation  Status        Native vlan
Fa0/1       auto          802.1q         trunking      1
Fa0/2       auto          802.1q         trunking      1

Port        Vlans allowed on trunk
Fa0/1       1-4094
Fa0/2       1-4094

Port        Vlans allowed and active in management domain
Fa0/1       1
Fa0/2       1

Port        Vlans in spanning tree forwarding state and not pruned
```

```
Fa0/1      1
Fa0/2      none
S1#
```

Looking at the preceding output, you can see that VTP pruning is disabled by default. I'm going to go ahead and enable pruning. It only takes one command and it is enabled on your entire switched network for the listed VLANs. Let's see what happens:

```
S1#config t
S1(config)#int f0/1
S1(config-if)#switchport trunk ?
  allowed  Set allowed VLAN characteristics when interface is
  in trunking mode
  native   Set trunking native characteristics when interface
  is in trunking mode
  pruning  Set pruning VLAN characteristics when interface is
  in trunking mode
S1(config-if)#switchport trunk pruning ?
  vlan  Set VLANs enabled for pruning when interface is in
  trunking mode
S1(config-if)#switchport trunk pruning vlan 3-4
```

The valid VLANs that can be pruned are 2 to 1001. Extended-range VLANs (VLAN IDs 1006 to 4094) can't be pruned, and these pruning-ineligible VLANs can receive a flood of traffic.

Configuring VTP

All Cisco switches are configured to be VTP servers by default. To configure VTP, first you have to configure the domain name you want to use. And of course, once you configure the VTP information on a switch, you need to verify it.

When you create the VTP domain, you have a few options, including setting the VTP version, domain name, password, operating mode, and pruning capabilities of the switch. Use the vtp global configuration mode command to set all this information. In the following example, I'll set the S1 switch to vtp server, the VTP domain to Lammle, and the VTP password to todd:

```
S1#config t
S1#(config)#vtp mode server
Device mode already VTP SERVER.
S1(config)#vtp domain Lammle
Changing VTP domain name from null to Lammle
S1(config)#vtp password todd
```

```
Setting device VLAN database password to todd
S1(config)#do show vtp password
VTP Password: todd
S1(config)#do show vtp status
VTP Version                    : 2
Configuration Revision         : 0
Maximum VLANs supported locally : 255
Number of existing VLANs       : 8
VTP Operating Mode             : Server
VTP Domain Name                : Lammle
VTP Pruning Mode               : Disabled
VTP V2 Mode                    : Disabled
VTP Traps Generation           : Disabled
MD5 digest                     : 0x15 0x54 0x88 0xF2 0x50 0xD9 0x03 0x07
Configuration last modified by 192.168.24.6 at 3-14-93 15:47:32
Local updater ID is 192.168.24.6 on interface Vl1 (lowest numbered VLAN
interface found)
```

Please make sure you remember that all switches are set to VTP server mode by default, and if you want to change and distribute any VLAN information on a switch, you absolutely must be in VTP server mode. After you configure the VTP information, you can verify it with the show vtp status command as shown in the preceding output.

The preceding switch output shows the VTP Version, Configuration Revision, Maximum VLANs supported locally, Number of existing VLANs, VTP Operating Mode, VTP domain, the VTP domain, and the VTP password listed as an MD5 Digest. You can use show vtp password in privileged mode to see the password.

Troubleshooting VTP

You connect your switches with crossover cables, the lights go green on both ends, and you're up and running! Yeah—in a perfect world, right? Don't you wish it was that easy? Well, actually, it pretty much is—without VLANs, of course. But if you're using VLANs—and you definitely should be—then you need to use VTP if you have multiple VLANs configured in your switched network.

But here there be monsters: If VTP is not configured correctly, it (surprise!) will not work, so you absolutely must be capable of troubleshooting VTP. Let's take a look at a couple of configurations and solve the problems. Study the output from the two following switches:

```
SwitchA#sh vtp status
VTP Version                    : 2
Configuration Revision         : 0
Maximum VLANs supported locally : 64
```

```
Number of existing VLANs           : 7
VTP Operating Mode                 : Server
VTP Domain Name                    : Lammle
VTP Pruning Mode                   : Disabled
VTP V2 Mode                        : Disabled
VTP Traps Generation               : Disabled


SwitchB#sh vtp status
VTP Version                        : 2
Configuration Revision             : 1
Maximum VLANs supported locally    : 64
Number of existing VLANs           : 7
VTP Operating Mode                 : Server
VTP Domain Name                    : GlobalNet
VTP Pruning Mode                   : Disabled
VTP V2 Mode                        : Disabled
VTP Traps Generation               : Disabled
```

So what's happening with these two switches? Why won't they share VLAN information? At first glance, it seems that both servers are in VTP server mode, but that's not the problem. Servers in VTP server mode will share VLAN information using VTP. The problem is that they're in two different VTP *domains*. SwitchA is in VTP domain Lammle and SwitchB is in VTP domain GlobalNet. They will never share VTP information because the VTP domain names are configured differently.

Now that you know how to look for common VTP domain configuration errors in your switches, let's take a look at another switch configuration:

```
SwitchC#sh vtp status
VTP Version                        : 2
Configuration Revision             : 1
Maximum VLANs supported locally    : 64
Number of existing VLANs           : 7
VTP Operating Mode                 : Client
VTP Domain Name                    : Todd
VTP Pruning Mode                   : Disabled
VTP V2 Mode                        : Disabled
VTP Traps Generation               : Disabled
```

Here's what will happen when you have the preceding VTP configuration:

```
SwitchC(config)#vlan 50
VTP VLAN configuration not allowed when device is in CLIENT mode.
```

There you are just trying to create a new VLAN on SwitchC and what do you get for your trouble? A loathsome error! Why can't you create a VLAN on SwitchC? Well, the VTP domain name isn't the important thing in this example. What is critical here is the VTP *mode*. The VTP mode is client, and a VTP client cannot create, delete, or change VLANs, remember? VTP clients only keep the VTP database in RAM, and that's not saved to NVRAM. So, in order to create a VLAN on this switch, you've got to make the switch a VTP server first.

So to fix this problem, here's what you need to do:

```
SwitchC(config)#vtp mode server
Setting device to VTP SERVER mode
SwitchC(config)#vlan 50
SwitchC(config-vlan)#
```

Wait, we're not done. Now take a look at the output from these two switches and determine why SwitchB is not receiving VLAN information from SwitchA:

```
SwitchA#sh vtp status
VTP Version                    : 2
Configuration Revision         : 4
Maximum VLANs supported locally : 64
Number of existing VLANs       : 7
VTP Operating Mode             : Server
VTP Domain Name                : GlobalNet
VTP Pruning Mode               : Disabled
VTP V2 Mode                    : Disabled
VTP Traps Generation           : Disabled


SwitchB#sh vtp status
VTP Version                    : 2
Configuration Revision         : 14
Maximum VLANs supported locally : 64
Number of existing VLANs       : 7
VTP Operating Mode             : Server
VTP Domain Name                : GlobalNet
VTP Pruning Mode               : Disabled
VTP V2 Mode                    : Disabled
VTP Traps Generation           : Disabled
```

You may be tempted to say it's because they're both VTP servers, but that is not the problem. All your switches can be servers and they can still share VLAN information. As a matter of fact, Cisco actually suggests that all switches stay VTP servers and that you just make sure the switch you want to advertise VTP VLAN information has the highest revision number. If all switches are VTP servers, then all of the switches will save the VLAN database. But SwitchB isn't receiving VLAN information from SwitchA because SwitchB has a higher revision number than SwitchA. It's very important that you can recognize this problem.

There are a couple ways to go about resolving this issue. The first thing you could do is to change the VTP domain name on SwitchB to another name, then set it back to GlobalNet, which will reset the revision number to zero (0) on SwitchB. The second approach would be to create or delete VLANs on SwitchA until the revision number passes the revision number on SwitchB. I didn't say the second way was better; I just said it's another way to fix it!

Let's look at one more. Why is SwitchB not receiving VLAN information from SwitchA?

```
SwitchA#sh vtp status
VTP Version                    : 1
Configuration Revision         : 4
Maximum VLANs supported locally : 64
Number of existing VLANs       : 7
VTP Operating Mode             : Server
VTP Domain Name                : GlobalNet
VTP Pruning Mode               : Disabled
VTP V2 Mode                    : Disabled
VTP Traps Generation           : Disabled


SwitchB#sh vtp status
VTP Version                    : 2
Configuration Revision         : 3
Maximum VLANs supported locally : 64
Number of existing VLANs       : 5
VTP Operating Mode             : Server
VTP Domain Name                :
VTP Pruning Mode               : Disabled
VTP V2 Mode                    : Disabled
VTP Traps Generation           : Disabled
```

I know your first instinct is to notice that SwitchB doesn't have a domain name set and consider that the issue. That's not the problem! When a switch comes up, a VTP server with a domain name set will send VTP advertisements, and a new switch out of the box will configure itself using the advertisement with the received domain name and also download the VLAN database.

The problem with the above switches is that they are set to different VTP versions—but that still isn't the full problem.

By default, VTP operates in version 1. You can configure VTP version 2 if you want support for these features, which are not supported in version 1:

- Token Ring support—Hmmm…doesn't seem like much of a reason to go to version 2 today. Let's look at some other reasons.

- Unrecognized Type-Length-Value (TLV) support—A VTP server or client propagates configuration changes to its other trunks, even for TLVs it is not able to parse. The unrecognized TLV is saved in NVRAM when the switch is operating in VTP server mode.

- Version-Dependent Transparent Mode—In VTP version 1, a VTP transparent switch inspects VTP messages for the domain name and version and forwards a message only if the version and domain name match. Because VTP version 2 supports only one domain, it forwards VTP messages in transparent mode without inspecting the version and domain name.

- Consistency Checks—In VTP version 2, VLAN consistency checks (such as checking the consistency of VLAN names and values) are performed only when you enter new information through the CLI or SNMP. Consistency checks are not performed when new information is obtained from a VTP message or when information is read from NVRAM. If the MD5 digest on a received VTP message is correct, its information is accepted.

Wait! Nothing is that easy. Just set SwitchA to version 2 and we're up and running? Nope! The interesting thing about VTP version 2 is that if you set one switch in your network (VTP domain) to version 2, all switches would set their version to 2 automatically—very cool! So then what is the problem? SwitchA doesn't support VTP version 2, which is the actual answer to this question. Crazy! I think you can see that VTP will drive you to drink if you're not careful!

Okay, get a coffee, expresso or Mountain Dew and hold onto your hats—it's spanning tree time!

Spanning Tree Protocol (STP)

Spanning Tree Protocol (STP) achieves its primary objective of preventing network loops on layer 2 network bridges or switches by monitoring the network to track all links and shut down the redundant ones. STP uses the spanning-tree algorithm (STA) to first create a topology database and then search out and disable redundant links. With STP running, frames will be forwarded on only premium, STP-chosen links.

The Spanning Tree Protocol is a great protocol to use in networks like the one shown in Figure 1.2.

FIGURE 1.2   A switched network with switching loops

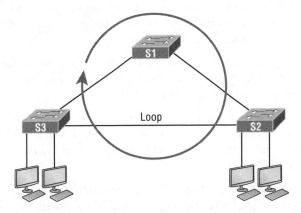

This is a switched network with a redundant topology that includes switching loops. Without some type of layer 2 mechanism in place to prevent a network loop, this network is vulnerable to nasty issues like broadcast storms, multiple frame copies, and MAC table thrashing! Figure 1.3 shows how this network would work with STP working on the switches.

FIGURE 1.3   A switched network with STP

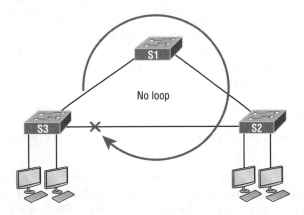

There a few types of spanning-tree protocols, but I'll start with the IEEE version 802.1d, which happens to be the default on all Cisco IOS switches.

Spanning-Tree Terms

Now, before I get into describing the details of how STP works within a network, it would be good for you to have these basic ideas and terms down first:

Root bridge   The *root bridge* is the bridge with the lowest and, therefore, the best bridge ID. The switches within the STP network elect a root bridge, which becomes the focal point in the network. All other decisions in the network, like which ports on the non-root bridges should be blocked or put in forwarding mode, are made from the perspective of the root bridge, and once it has been elected, all other bridges must create a single path to it. The port with the best path to the root bridge is called the root port.

Non-root bridges   These are all bridges that aren't the root bridge. Non-root bridges exchange BPDUs with all the other bridges and update the STP topology database on all switches. This prevents loops and helps defend against link failures.

BPDU   All switches exchange information to use for the subsequent configuration of the network. Each switch compares the parameters in the *Bridge Protocol Data Unit (BPDU)* that it sends to a neighbor with the parameters in the BPDU that it receives from other neighbors. Inside the BPDU is the bridge ID.

Bridge ID   The bridge ID is how STP keeps track of all the switches in the network. It's determined by a combination of the bridge priority, which is 32,768 by default on all Cisco switches, and the base MAC address. The bridge with the lowest bridge ID becomes the root bridge in the network. Once the root bridge is established, every other switch must make a single path to it. Most networks benefit by forcing a specific bridge or switch to be on the root bridge by setting its bridge priority lower than the default value.

Port cost   Port cost determines the best path when multiple links are used between two switches. The cost of a link is determined by the bandwidth of a link, and this path cost is the deciding factor used by every bridge to find the most efficient path to the root bridge.

Path cost   A switch may encounter one or more switches on its path to the root bridge, and there may be more than one possible path. All unique paths are analyzed individually, and a path cost is calculated for each unique path by adding the individual port costs encountered on the way to the root bridge.

Bridge Port Roles

STP uses roles to determine how a port on a switch will act within the spanning-tree algorithm.

Root port   The root port is the link with the lowest path cost to the root bridge. If more than one link connects to the root bridge, then a port cost is found by checking the bandwidth of each link. The lowest-cost port becomes the root port. When multiple links connect to the same device, the port connected to the lowest port number on the upstream switch will be the one that's used. The root bridge can never have a root port designation, while every other switch in a network must have one and only one root port.

Designated port   A *designated port* is one that's been determined to have the best (lowest) cost to get to on a given network segment, compared to other ports on that segment. A designated port will be marked as a forwarding port, and you can have only one forwarding port per network segment.

Non-designated port   A *non-designated port* is one with a higher cost than the designated port. These are basically the ones left over after the root ports and designated ports have been determined. Non-designated ports are put in blocking or discarding mode—they are not forwarding ports!

Forwarding port   A forwarding port forwards frames and will be either a root port or a designated port.

Blocked port   A blocked port won't forward frames in order to prevent loops. A blocked port will still always listen to BPDU frames from neighbor switches, but it will drop any and all other frames received and will never transmit a frame.

Alternate port   This corresponds to the blocking state of 802.1d and is a term used with the newer 802.1w (Rapid Spanning Tree Protocol). An alternative port is located on a switch connected to a LAN segment with two or more switches connected, and one of the other switches holds the designated port.

Backup port   This corresponds to the blocking state of 802.1d and is a term now used with the newer 802.1w. A backup port is connected to a LAN segment where another port on that switch is acting as the designated port.

Spanning-Tree Port States

Okay, so you plug your host into a switch port and the light turns amber and your host doesn't get a DHCP address from the server. You wait and wait and finally the light goes green after almost a full minute—that's an eternity in today's networks! This is the STA transitioning through the different port states verifying that you didn't just create a loop with the device you just plugged in. STP would rather time out your new host than allow a loop into the network because that would effectively bring your network to its knees. Let's talk about the transition states; then later in this chapter we'll talk about how to speed this process up.

The ports on a bridge or switch running IEEE 802.1d STP can transition through five different states:

Disabled (technically, not a transition state)   A port in the administratively disabled state doesn't participate in frame forwarding or STP. A port in the disabled state is virtually nonoperational.

Blocking   As I mentioned, a blocked port won't forward frames; it just listens to BPDUs. The purpose of the blocking state is to prevent the use of looped paths. All ports are in blocking state by default when the switch is powered up.

Listening   This port listens to BPDUs to make sure no loops occur on the network before passing data frames. A port in listening state prepares to forward data frames without populating the MAC address table.

Learning   The switch port listens to BPDUs and learns all the paths in the switched network. A port in learning state populates the MAC address table but still doesn't forward data frames. Forward delay refers to the time it takes to transition a port from listening to learning mode, or from learning to forwarding mode, which is set to 15 seconds by default and can be seen in the show spanning-tree output.

Forwarding   This port sends and receives all data frames on the bridged port. If the port is still a designated or root port at the end of the learning state, it will enter the forwarding state.

 Switches populate the MAC address table in learning and forwarding modes only.

Switch ports are most often in either the blocking or forwarding state. A forwarding port is typically the one that's been determined to have the lowest (best) cost to the root bridge. But when and if the network experiences a topology change due to a failed link or because someone has added in a new switch, you'll see the ports on a switch transitioning through listening and learning states.

As I said earlier, blocking ports is a strategy for preventing network loops. Once a switch determines the best path to the root bridge for its root port and any designated ports, all other redundant ports will be in blocking mode. Blocked ports can still receive BPDUs—they just don't send out any frames.

If a switch determines that a blocked port should become the designated or root port because of a topology change, it will go into listening mode and check all BPDUs it receives to make sure it won't create a loop once the port moves into forwarding mode.

Convergence

Convergence occurs when all ports on bridges and switches have transitioned to either forwarding or blocking modes. No data will be forwarded until convergence is complete. Yes—you read that right: When STP is converging, all host data stops transmitting through the switches! So if you want to remain on speaking terms with your network's users, or remain employed for any length of time, you must make sure that your switched network is physically designed really well so that STP can converge quickly!

Convergence is vital because it ensures that all devices have a coherent database. And making sure this happens efficiently will definitely require your time and attention. The original STP (802.1d) takes 50 seconds to go from blocking to forwarding mode by default and I don't recommend changing the default STP timers. You can adjust those timers for a large network, but the better solution is simply to opt out of using 802.1d at all! We'll get to the various STP versions in a minute.

Link Costs

Now that you know about the different port roles and states, you need to really understand all about path cost before we put this all together. Port cost is based on the speed of the link, and Table 1.1 breaks down the need-to-know path costs for you. Port cost is the cost of a single link, whereas path cost is the sum of the various port costs to the root bridge.

TABLE 1.1   IEEE STP link costs

Speed	Cost
10 Mb/s	100
100 Mb/s	19
1000 Mb/s	4
10,000 Mb/s	2

These costs will be used in the STP calculations to choose a single root port on each bridge. You absolutely need to memorize this table, but no worries—I'll guide you through lots of examples in this chapter to help you do that quite easily! Now it's time to take everything we've learned so far and put it all together.

Spanning-Tree Operations

Let's start neatly summarizing what you've learned so far using the simple three-switch network connected together as shown in Figure 1.4.

FIGURE 1.4   STP operations

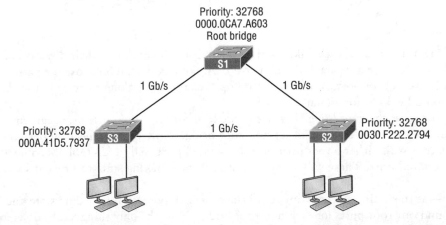

Basically, STP's job is to find all the links in the network and shut down any redundant ones, thereby preventing network loops from occurring. It achieves this by first electing a root bridge that will have all ports forwarding and will also act as a point of reference for all other devices within the STP domain. In Figure 1.4, S1 has been elected the root bridge based on bridge ID. Since the priorities are all equal to 32,768, we'll compare MAC addresses and find that the MAC address of S1 is lower than that of S2 and S3, meaning that S1 has a better bridge ID.

Once all switches agree on the root bridge, they must then determine their one and only root port—the single path to the root bridge. It's really important to remember that a bridge can go through many other bridges to get to the root, so it's not always the shortest path that will be chosen. That role will be given to the port that happens to offer the fastest, highest bandwidth. Figure 1.5 shows the root ports for both non-root bridges (the *RP* signifies a root port and the *F* signifies a designated forwarding port).

FIGURE 1.5 STP operations

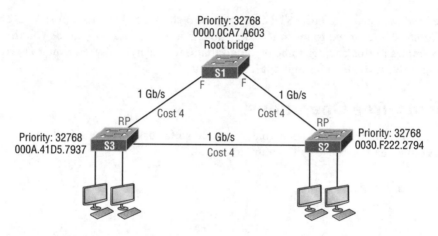

Looking at the cost of each link, it's clear why S2 and S3 are using their directly connected links, because a gigabit link has a cost of 4. For example, if S3 chose the path through S2 as its root port, we'd have to add up each port cost along the way to the root, which would be 4 + 4 for a total cost of 8.

Every port on the root bridge is a designated, or forwarding, port for a segment, and after the dust settles on all other non-root bridges, any port connection between switches that isn't either a root port or a designated port will predictably become a non-designated port. These will again be put into the blocking state to prevent switching loops.

Okay—at this point, we have our root bridge with all ports in forwarding state and we've found our root ports for each non-root bridge. Now the only thing left to do is to choose the one forwarding port on the segment between S2 and S3. Both bridges can't be forwarding on a segment because that's exactly how we would end up with loops. So, based on the bridge ID, the port with the best and lowest would become the only bridge forwarding on that segment, with the one having the highest, worst bridge ID put into blocking mode. Figure 1.6 shows the network after STP has converged.

FIGURE 1.6   STP operations

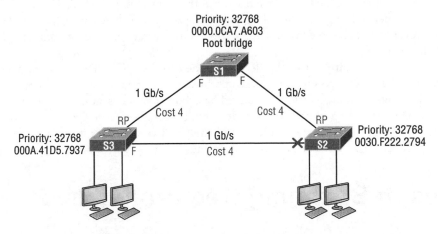

Since S3 had a lower bridge ID (better), S2's port went into blocking mode. Let's discuss the root bridge election process more completely now.

Selecting the Root Bridge

The bridge ID is used to elect the root bridge in the STP domain and to determine the root port for each of the remaining devices when there's more than one potential root port available because they have equal-cost paths. This key bridge ID is 8 bytes long and includes both the priority and the MAC address of the device, as illustrated in Figure 1.7. Remember—the default priority on all devices running the IEEE STP version is 32,768.

FIGURE 1.7   STP operations

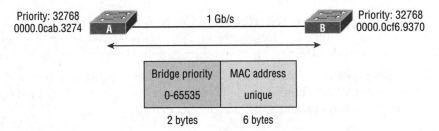

So, to determine the root bridge, you combine the priority of each bridge with its MAC address. If two switches or bridges happen to have the same priority value, the MAC address becomes the tiebreaker for figuring out which one has the lowest and, therefore, best ID. This means that because the two switches in Figure 1.7 are both using the default priority of 32,768, the MAC address will be the determining factor instead. And because Switch A's MAC address is 0000.0cab.3274 and Switch B's MAC address is 0000.0cf6.9370, Switch

A wins and will become the root bridge. A really easy way to figure out the lowest MAC address is to just start reading from the left toward the right until you find a lesser value. For Switch A, I only needed to get to 0000.0ca before stopping. Switch A wins since switch B is 0000.0cf. Never forget that the lower value is always the better one when it comes to electing a root bridge!

I want to point out that prior to the election of the root bridge, BPDUs are sent every 2 seconds out all active ports on a bridge/switch by default, and they're received and processed by all bridges. The root bridge is elected based on this information. You can change the bridge's ID by lowering its priority so that it will become a root bridge automatically. Being able to do that is important in a large switched network because it ensures that the best paths will actually be the ones chosen. Efficiency is always awesome in networking!

Types of Spanning-tree Protocols

There are several varieties of spanning-tree protocols in use today:

IEEE 802.1d   The original standard for bridging and STP, which is really slow but requires very little bridge resources. It's also referred to as Common Spanning Tree (CST).

PVST+ (Cisco default version)   Per-VLAN Spanning Tree+ (PVST+) is the Cisco proprietary enhancement for STP that provides a separate 802.1d spanning-tree instance for each VLAN. Know that this is just as slow as the CST protocol, but with it, we get to have multiple root bridges. This creates more efficiency of the links in the network, but it does use more bridge resources than CST does.

IEEE 802.1w   Also called Rapid Spanning Tree Protocol (RSTP), this iteration enhanced the BPDU exchange and paved the way for much faster network convergence, but it still only allows for one root bridge per network like CST. The bridge resources used with RSTP are higher than CST's but less than PVST+.

802.1s (MSTP)   IEEE standard that started out as Cisco propriety MISTP. Maps multiple VLANs into the same spanning-tree instance to save processing on the switch. It's basically a spanning-tree protocol that rides on top of another spanning-tree protocol.

Rapid PVST+   Cisco's version of RSTP that also uses PVST+ and provides a separate instance of 802.1w per VLAN. It gives us really fast convergence times and optimal traffic flow but predictably requires the most CPU and memory of all.

Common Spanning Tree

If you're running Common Spanning Tree (CST) in your switched network with redundant links, there will be an election to choose what STP considers to be the best root bridge for your network. That switch will also become the root for all VLANs in your network and all bridges in your network will create a single path to it. You can manually override this selection and pick whichever bridge you want if it makes sense for your particular network.

Figure 1.8 shows how a typical root bridge would look on your switched network when running CST.

FIGURE 1.8   Common STP example

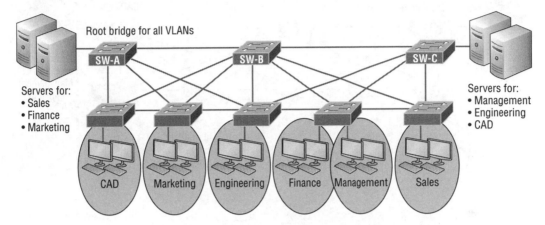

Notice that switch A is the root bridge for all VLANs even though it's really not the best path for some VLANs because all switches must make a single path to it! This is where Per-VLAN Spanning Tree+ (PVST+) comes into play. Because it allows for a separate instance of STP for each VLAN, it frees up the individual selection of the most optimal path.

Per-VLAN Spanning Tree+

PVST+ is a Cisco proprietary extension to 801.2d STP that provides a separate 802.1 spanning-tree instance for each VLAN configured on your switches. All of the Cisco proprietary extensions were created to improve convergence times, which is 50 seconds by default. Cisco IOS switches run 802.1d PVST+ by default, which means you'll have optimal path selection, but the convergence time will still be slow.

Creating a per-VLAN STP instance for each VLAN is worth the increased CPU and memory requirements, because it allows for per-VLAN root bridges. This feature allows the STP tree to be optimized for the traffic of each VLAN by allowing you to configure the root bridge in the center of each of them. Figure 1.9 shows how PVST+ would look in an optimized switched network with multiple redundant links.

This root bridge placement clearly enables faster convergence as well as optimal path determination. This version's convergence is really similar to 802.1 CST's, which has one instance of STP no matter how many VLANs you have configured on your network. The difference is that with PVST+, convergence happens on a per-VLAN basis, with each VLAN running its own instance of STP. Figure 1.9 shows us that we now have a nice, efficient root bridge selection for each VLAN.

FIGURE 1.9 PVST+ provides efficient root bridge selection.

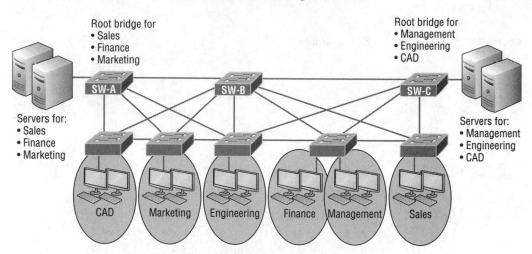

To allow for the PVST+ to operate, there's a field inserted into the BPDU to accommodate the extended system ID so that PVST+ can have a root bridge configured on a per-STP instance, shown in Figure 1.10. The bridge ID actually becomes smaller—only 4 bits—which means that we would configure the bridge priority in blocks of 4,096 rather than in increments of 1 as we did with CST. The extended system ID (VLAN ID) is a 12-bit field, and we can even see what this field is carrying via show spanning-tree command output, which I'll show you soon.

FIGURE 1.10 PVST+ unique bridge ID

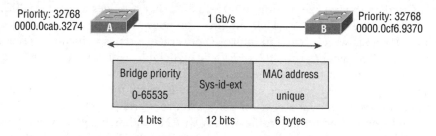

But still, isn't there a way we can do better than a 50-second convergence time? That's a really long time in today's world!

Rapid Spanning Tree Protocol 802.1w

Wouldn't it be wonderful to have a solid STP configuration running on your switched network, regardless of switch type, and still have all the features we just discussed built in and enabled on every one of your switches too? Rapid Spanning Tree Protocol (RSTP) serves up exactly this amazing capacity right to our networking table!

Cisco created proprietary extensions to "fix" all the sinkholes and liabilities the IEEE 802.1d standard threw at us, with the main drawback to them being they require extra configuration because they're Cisco proprietary. But RSTP, the new 802.1w standard, brings us most of the patches needed in one concise solution. Again, efficiency is golden!

RSTP, or IEEE 802.1w, is essentially an evolution of STP that allows for much faster convergence. But even though it does address all the convergence issues, it still only permits a single STP instance, so it doesn't help to take the edge off suboptimal traffic flow issues. And as I mentioned, to support that faster convergence, the CPU usage and memory demands are slightly higher than CST's. The good news is that Cisco IOS can run the Rapid PVST+ protocol—a Cisco enhancement of RSTP that provides a separate 802.1w spanning-tree instance for each VLAN configured within the network. But all that power needs fuel, and although this version addresses both convergence and traffic flow issues, it also demands the most CPU and memory of all solutions. And it's also good news that Cisco's newest switches don't have a problem with this protocol running on them.

 Keep in mind that Cisco documentation may say STP 802.1d and RSTP 802.1w, but it is referring to the PVST+ enhancement of each version.

Understand that RSTP wasn't meant to be something completely new and different. The protocol is more of an evolution than an innovation of the 802.1d standard, which offers faster convergence whenever a topology change occurs. Backward compatibility was a must when 802.1w was created.

So, RSTP helps with convergence issues that were the bane of traditional STP. Rapid PVST+ is based on the 802.1w standard in the same way that PVST+ is based on 802.1d. The operation of Rapid PVST+ is simply a separate instance of 802.1w for each VLAN. Here's a list to clarify how this all breaks down:

- RSTP speeds the recalculation of the spanning tree when the layer 2 network topology changes.

- It's an IEEE standard that redefines STP port roles, states, and BPDUs.

- RSTP is extremely proactive and very quick, so it doesn't need the 802.1d delay timers.

- RSTP (802.1w) supersedes 802.1d while remaining backward compatible.

- Much of the 802.1d terminology and most parameters remain unchanged.

- 802.1w is capable of reverting to 802.1d to interoperate with traditional switches on a per-port basis.

And to clear up confusion, there are also five terminology adjustments between 802.1d's five port states and 802.1w's, compared here, respectively:

802.1d State		802.1w State
Disabled	=	Discarding
Blocking	=	Discarding
Listening	=	Discarding
Learning	=	Learning
Forwarding	=	Forwarding

Make note of the fact that RSTP basically just goes from discarding to learning to forwarding, whereas 802.1d requires five states to transition.

The task of determining the root bridge, root ports, and designated ports hasn't changed from 802.1d to RSTP, and understanding the cost of each link is still key to making these decisions well. Let's take a look at an example of how to determine ports using the revised IEEE cost specifications in Figure 1.11.

FIGURE 1.11   RSTP example 1

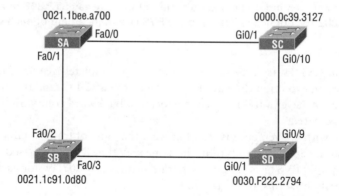

Can you figure out which is the root bridge? How about which port is the root and which ones are designated? Well, because SC has the lowest MAC address, it becomes the root bridge, and since all ports on a root bridge are forwarding designated ports, well, that's easy, right? Ports Gi0/1 and Gi0/10 become designated forwarding ports on SC.

But which one would be the root port for SA? To figure that out, we must first find the port cost for the direct link between SA and SC. Even though the root bridge (SC) has a Gigabit Ethernet port, it's running at 100 Mbps because SA's port is a 100-Mbps port, giving it a cost of 19. If the paths between SA and SC were both Gigabit Ethernet, their costs would only be 4, but because they're running 100 Mbps links instead, the cost jumps to a whopping 19!

Can you find SD's root port? A quick glance at the link between SC and SD tells us that's a Gigabit Ethernet link with a cost of 4, so the root port for SD would be its Gi0/9 port.

The cost of the link between SB and SD is also 19 because it's also a Fast Ethernet link, bringing the full cost from SB to SD to the root (SC) to a total cost of 19 + 4 = 23. If SB were to go through SA to get to SC, then the cost would be 19 + 19, or 38, so the root port of SB becomes the Fa0/3 port.

The root port for SA would be the Fa0/0 port since that's a direct link with a cost of 19. Going through SB to SD would be 19 + 19 + 4 = 42, so we'll use that as a backup link for SA to get to the root just in case we need to.

Now all we need is a forwarding port on the link between SA and SB. Because SA has the lowest bridge ID, Fa0/1 on SA wins that role. Also, the Gi0/1 port on SD would become a designated forwarding port. This is because the SB Fa0/3 port is a designed root port and you must have a forwarding port on a network segment! This leaves us with the Fa0/2 port on SB. Since it isn't a root port or designated forwarding port, it will be placed into blocking mode, which will prevent looks in our network.

Let's take a look at this example network when it has converged in Figure 1.12.

FIGURE 1.12   RSTP example 1 answer

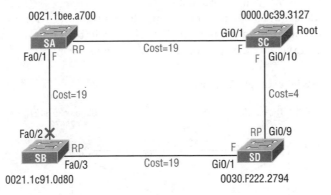

If this isn't clear and still seems confusing, just remember to always tackle this process following these three steps:

1. Find your root bridge by looking at bridge IDs.

2. Determine your root ports by finding the lowest path cost to the root bridge.

3. Find your designated ports by looking at bridge IDs.

As usual, the best way to nail this down is to practice, so let's explore another scenario, shown in Figure 1.13.

FIGURE 1.13 RSTP example 2

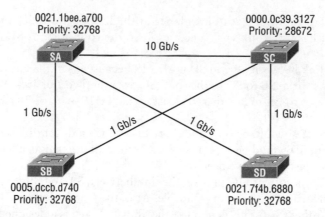

So which bridge is our root bridge? Checking priorities first tells us that SC is the root bridge, which means all ports on SC are designated forwarding ports. Now we need to find our root ports.

We can quickly see that SA has a 10-gigabit port to SC, so that would be a port cost of 2, and it would be our root port. SD has a direct Gigabit Ethernet port to SC, so that would be the root port for SD with a port cost of 4. SB's best path would also be the direct Gigabit Ethernet port to SC with a port cost of 4.

Now that we've determined our root bridge and found the three root ports we need, we've got to find our designated ports next. Whatever is left over simply goes into the discarding role. Let's take a look at Figure 1.14 and see what we have.

FIGURE 1.14 RSTP example 2, answer 1

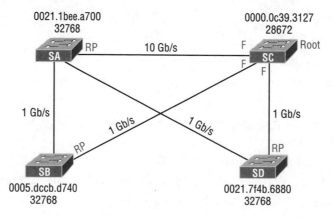

All right, it looks like there are two links to choose between to find one designated port per segment. Let's start with the link between SA and SD. Which one has the best bridge

ID? They're both running the same default priority, so by looking at the MAC address, we can see that SD has the better bridge ID (lower), so the SA port toward SD will go into a discarding role, or will it? The SD port will go into discarding mode, because the link from SA to the root has the lowest accumulated path costs to the root bridge, and that is used before the bridge ID in this circumstance. It makes sense to let the bridge with the fastest path to the root bridge be a designated forwarding port. Let's talk about this a little more in depth.

As you know, once your root bridge and root ports have been chosen, you're left with finding your designated ports. Anything left over goes into a discarding role. But how are the designated ports chosen? Is it just bridge ID? Here are the rules:

1. To choose the switch that will forward on the segment, we select the switch with the lowest accumulated path cost to the root bridge. We want the fast path to the root bridge.

2. If there is a tie on the accumulated path cost from both switches to the root bridge, then we'll use bridge ID, which was what we used in our previous example (but not with this latest RSTP example; not with a 10-Gigabit Ethernet link to the root bridge available!).

3. Port priorities can be set manually if we want a specific port chosen. The default priority is 32, but we can lower that if needed.

4. If there are two links between switches, and the bridge ID and priority are tied, the port with the lowest number will be chosen—for example, Fa0/1 would be chosen over Fa0/2.

Let's take a look at our answer now, but before we do, can you find the forwarding port between SA and SB? Take a look at Figure 1.15 for the answer.

FIGURE 1.15   RSTP example 2, answer 2

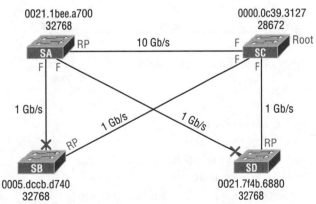

Again, to get the right answer to this question we're going to let the switch on the network segment with the lowest accumulated path cost to the root bridge forward on that segment. This is definitely SA, meaning the SB port goes into discarding role—not so hard at all!

802.1s (MSTP)

Multiple Spanning Tree Protocol (MSTP), also known as IEEE 802.ls, gives us the same fast convergence as RSTP but reduces the number of required STP instances by allowing us to map multiple VLANs with the same traffic flow requirements into the same spanning-tree instance. It essentially allows us to create VLAN sets and basically is a spanning-tree protocol that runs on top of another spanning-tree protocol.

So clearly, you would opt to use MSTP over RSTP when you've got a configuration involving lots of VLANs, resulting in CPU and memory requirements that would be too high otherwise. But there's no free lunch—though MSTP reduces the demands of Rapid PVST+, you've got to configure it correctly because MSTP does nothing by itself!

Modifying and Verifying the Bridge ID

To verify spanning tree on a Cisco switch, just use the command show spanning-tree. From its output, we can determine our root bridge, priorities, root ports, and designated and blocking/discarding ports.

Let's use the same simple three-switch network we used earlier as the base to play around with the configuration of STP. Figure 1.16 shows the network we'll work with in this section.

FIGURE 1.16   Our simple three-switch network

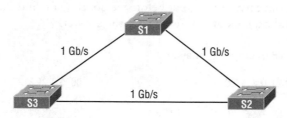

Let's start by taking a look at the output from S1:

```
S1#sh spanning-tree vlan 1
VLAN0001
  Spanning tree enabled protocol ieee
  Root ID    Priority    32769
             Address     0001.42A7.A603
             This bridge is the root
             Hello Time  2 sec  Max Age 20 sec  Forward Delay 15 sec

  Bridge ID  Priority    32769  (priority 32768 sys-id-ext 1)
             Address     0001.42A7.A603 him
```

```
                 Hello Time  2 sec  Max Age 20 sec  Forward Delay 15 sec
                 Aging Time  20

Interface        Role Sts Cost      Prio.Nbr Type
---------------- ---- --- --------- -------- --------------------------------
Gi1/1            Desg FWD 4         128.25   P2p
Gi1/2            Desg FWD 4         128.26   P2p
```

First, we can see that we're running the IEEE 802.1d STP version by default, and don't forget that this is really 802.1d PVST+! Looking at the output, we can see that S1 is the root bridge for VLAN 1. When you use this command, the top information is about the root bridge, and the Bridge ID output refers to the bridge you're looking at. In this example, they are one and the same. Notice the sys-id-ext 1 (for VLAN 1). This is the 12-bit PVST+ field that is placed into the BPDU so it can carry multiple-VLAN information. You add the priority and sys-id-ext to come up with the true priority for the VLAN. We can also see from the output that both Gigabit Ethernet interfaces are designated forwarding ports. You will not see a blocked/discarding port on a root bridge. Now let's take a look at S3's output:

```
S3#sh spanning-tree
VLAN0001
  Spanning tree enabled protocol ieee
  Root ID    Priority    32769
             Address     0001.42A7.A603
             Cost        4
             Port        26(GigabitEthernet1/2)
             Hello Time  2 sec  Max Age 20 sec  Forward Delay 15 sec

  Bridge ID  Priority    32769  (priority 32768 sys-id-ext 1)
             Address     000A.41D5.7937
             Hello Time  2 sec  Max Age 20 sec  Forward Delay 15 sec
             Aging Time  20

Interface        Role Sts Cost      Prio.Nbr Type
---------------- ---- --- --------- -------- --------------------------------
Gi1/1            Desg FWD 4         128.25   P2p
Gi1/2            Root FWD 4         128.26   P2p
```

Looking at the Root ID, it's easy to see that S3 isn't the root bridge, but the output tells us it's a cost of 4 to get to the root bridge and also that it's located out port 26 of the switch (Gi1/2). This tells us that the root bridge is one Gigabit Ethernet link away, which we already know is S1, but we can confirm this with the show cdp neighbors command:

```
Switch#sh cdp nei
Capability Codes: R - Router, T - Trans Bridge, B - Source Route Bridge
                  S - Switch, H - Host, I - IGMP, r - Repeater, P - Phone
Device ID    Local Intrfce   Holdtme   Capability   Platform   Port ID
S3           Gig 1/1         135           S         2960       Gig 1/1
S1           Gig 1/2         135           S         2960       Gig 1/1
```

That's how simple it is to find your root bridge if you don't have the nice figure as we do. Use the show spanning-tree command, find your root port, and then use the show cdp neighbors command. Let's see what S2's output has to tell us now:

```
S2#sh spanning-tree
VLAN0001
  Spanning tree enabled protocol ieee
  Root ID    Priority     32769
             Address      0001.42A7.A603
             Cost         4
             Port         26(GigabitEthernet1/2)
             Hello Time   2 sec  Max Age 20 sec  Forward Delay 15 sec

  Bridge ID  Priority     32769  (priority 32768 sys-id-ext 1)
             Address      0030.F222.2794
             Hello Time   2 sec  Max Age 20 sec  Forward Delay 15 sec
             Aging Time   20


Interface        Role Sts Cost     Prio.Nbr Type
---------------- ---- --- --------- -------- -------------------------------
Gi1/1            Altn BLK 4         128.25   P2p
Gi1/2            Root FWD 4         128.26   P2p
```

We're certainly not looking at a root bridge since we're seeing a blocked port, which is S2's connection to S3!

Let's have some fun by making S2 the root bridge for VLAN 2 and for VLAN 3. Here's how easy that is to do:

```
S2#sh spanning-tree vlan 2
VLAN0002
  Spanning tree enabled protocol ieee
  Root ID    Priority     32770
             Address      0001.42A7.A603
```

```
            Cost       4
            Port       26(GigabitEthernet1/2)
            Hello Time 2 sec  Max Age 20 sec  Forward Delay 15 sec

Bridge ID   Priority   32770  (priority 32768 sys-id-ext 2)
            Address    0030.F222.2794
            Hello Time 2 sec  Max Age 20 sec  Forward Delay 15 sec
            Aging Time 20

Interface        Role Sts Cost      Prio.Nbr Type
---------------- ---- --- --------- -------- --------------------------------
Gi1/1            Altn BLK 4         128.25   P2p
Gi1/2            Root FWD 4         128.26   P2p
```

We can see that the root bridge cost is 4, meaning that the root bridge is one gigabit link away. One more key factor I want to talk about before making S2 the root bridge for VLANs 2 and 3 is the sys-id-ext, which shows up as 2 in this output because this output is for VLAN 2. This sys-id-ext is added to the bridge priority, which in this case is 32768 + 2, which makes the priority 32770. Now that you understand what that output is telling us, let's make S2 the root bridge:

```
S2(config)#spanning-tree vlan 2 ?
  priority  Set the bridge priority for the spanning tree
  root      Configure switch as root
  <cr>
S2(config)#spanning-tree vlan 2 priority ?
  <0-61440>  bridge priority in increments of 4096
S2(config)#spanning-tree vlan 2 priority 16384
```

You can set the priority to any value from 0 through 61440 in increments of 4096. Setting it to zero (0) means that the switch will always be a root as long as it has a lower MAC address than another switch that also has its bridge ID set to 0. If you want to set a switch to be the root bridge for every VLAN in your network, then you have to change the priority for each VLAN, with 0 being the lowest priority you can use. But trust me—it's never a good idea to set all switches to a priority of 0!

Furthermore, you don't actually need to change priorities because there is yet another way to configure the root bridge. Take a look:

```
S2(config)#spanning-tree vlan 3 root ?
  primary    Configure this switch as primary root for this spanning tree
  secondary  Configure switch as secondary root
S2(config)#spanning-tree vlan 3 root primary
S3(config)#spanning-tree vlan 3 root secondary
```

Notice that you can set a bridge to either primary or secondary—very cool! If both the primary and secondary switches go down, then the next highest priority will take over as root.

Let's check to see if S2 is actually the root bridge for VLANs 2 and 3 now:

```
S2#sh spanning-tree vlan 2
VLAN0002
  Spanning tree enabled protocol ieee
  Root ID    Priority    16386
             Address     0030.F222.2794
             This bridge is the root
             Hello Time  2 sec  Max Age 20 sec  Forward Delay 15 sec

  Bridge ID  Priority    16386  (priority 16384 sys-id-ext 2)
             Address     0030.F222.2794
             Hello Time  2 sec  Max Age 20 sec  Forward Delay 15 sec
             Aging Time  20

Interface        Role Sts Cost      Prio.Nbr Type
---------------- ---- --- --------- -------- --------------------------------
Gi1/1            Desg FWD 4         128.25   P2p
Gi1/2            Desg FWD 4         128.26   P2p
```

Nice—S2 is the root bridge for VLAN 2, with a priority of 16386 (16384 + 2). Let's take a look to see the root bridge for VLAN 3. I'll use a different command for that this time. Check it out:

```
S2#sh spanning-tree summary
Switch is in pvst mode
Root bridge for: VLAN0002 VLAN0003
Extended system ID           is enabled
Portfast Default             is disabled
PortFast BPDU Guard Default  is disabled
Portfast BPDU Filter Default is disabled
Loopguard Default            is disabled
EtherChannel misconfig guard is disabled
UplinkFast                   is disabled
BackboneFast                 is disabled
Configured Pathcost method used is short

Name                  Blocking Listening Learning Forwarding STP Active
--------------------- -------- --------- -------- ---------- ----------
VLAN0001                     1         0        0          1          2
```

VLAN0002	0	0	0	2	2
VLAN0003	0	0	0	2	2
----------------------	--------	---------	--------	----------	----------
3 vlans	1	0	0	5	6

The preceding output tells us that S2 is the root for the two VLANs, but we can see we have a blocked port for VLAN 1 on S2, so it's not the root bridge for VLAN 1. This is because there's another bridge with a better bridge ID for VLAN 1 than S2's.

One last burning question: How do you enable RSTP on a Cisco switch? Well, doing that is actually the easiest part of this chapter! Take a look:

```
S2(config)#spanning-tree mode rapid-pvst
```

Is that really all there is to it? Yes, because it's a global command, not per VLAN. Let's verify we're running RSTP now:

```
S2#sh spanning-tree
VLAN0001
  Spanning tree enabled protocol rstp
  Root ID    Priority    32769
             Address     0001.42A7.A603
             Cost        4
             Port        26(GigabitEthernet1/2)
             Hello Time  2 sec  Max Age 20 sec  Forward Delay 15 sec
[output cut
S2#sh spanning-tree summary
Switch is in rapid-pvst mode
Root bridge for: VLAN0002 VLAN0003
```

Looks like we're set! We're running RSTP, S1 is our root bridge for VLAN 1, and S2 is the root bridge for VLANs 2 and 3. I know this doesn't seem hard, and it really isn't, but you still need to practice what we've covered so far in this chapter to really get your skills solid!

Spanning-Tree Failure Consequences

Clearly, there will be consequences when a routing protocol fails on a single router, but mainly, you'll just lose connectivity to the networks directly connected to that router, and it usually does not affect the rest of your network. This definitely makes it easier to troubleshoot and fix the issue!

There are two failure types with STP. One of them causes the same type of issue I mentioned with a routing protocol; when certain ports have been placed in a blocking state they should be forwarding on a network segment instead. This situation makes the network segment unusable, but the rest of the network will still be working. But what happens when blocked ports are placed into forwarding state when they should be blocking? Let's work through this second failure issue now, using the same layout we used in the last section. Let's start with Figure 1.17 and then find out what happens when STP fails. Squeamish readers be warned—this isn't pretty!

Looking at Figure 1.17, what do you think will happen if SD transitions its blocked port to the forwarding state?

FIGURE 1.17 STP stopping loops

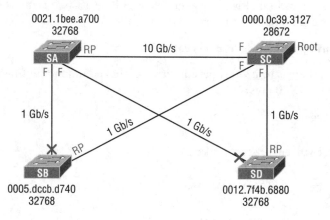

Clearly, the consequences to the entire network will be pretty devastating! Frames that already had a destination address recorded in the MAC address table of the switches are forwarded to the port they're associated with; however, any broadcast, multicast, and unicasts not in the CAM are now in an endless loop. Figure 1.18 shows us the carnage—when you see all the lights on each port blinking super-fast amber/green, this means serious errors are occurring, and lots of them!

FIGURE 1.18 STP failure

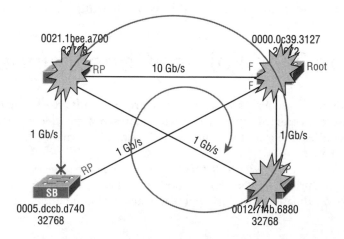

As frames begin building up on the network, the bandwidth starts getting saturated. The CPU percentage goes way up on the switches until they'll just give up and stop working completely, and all this within a few seconds!

Here is a list of the problems that will occur in a failed STP network that you must be aware of and you must be able to find in your production network—and of course, you must know them to meet the exam objectives:

- The load on all links begins increasing and more and more frames enter the loop. Remember, this loop affects all the other links in the network because these frames are always flooded out all ports. This scenario is a little less dire if the loop occurs within a single VLAN. In that case, the snag will be isolated to ports only in that VLAN membership, plus all trunk links that carry information for that VLAN.

- If you have more than one loop, traffic will increase on the switches because all the circling frames actually get duplicated. Switches basically receive a frame, make a copy of it, and send it out all ports. And they do this over and over and over again with the same frame, as well as for any new ones!

- The MAC address table is now completely unstable. It no longer knows where any source MAC address hosts are actually located because the same source address comes in via multiple ports on the switch.

- With the overwhelmingly high load on the links and the CPUs, now possibly at 100% or close to that, the devices become unresponsive, making it impossible to troubleshoot—it's a terrible thing!

At this point your only option is to systematically remove every redundant link between switches until you can find the source of the problem. And don't freak because, eventually, your ravaged network will calm down and come back to life after STP converges. Your fried switches will regain consciousness, but the network will need some serious therapy, so you're not out of the woods yet!

Now is when you start troubleshooting to find out what caused the disaster in the first place. A good strategy is to place the redundant links back into your network one at a time and wait to see when a problem begins to occur. You could have a failing switch port, or even a dead switch. Once you've replaced all your redundant links, you need to carefully monitor the network and have a back-out plan to quickly isolate the problem if it reoccurs. You don't want to go through this again!

You're probably wondering how to prevent these STP problems from ever darkening your doorstep in the first place. Well, just hang on, because after the next section, I'll tell you all about EtherChannel, which can stop ports from being placed in the blocked/discarding state on redundant links to save the day! But before we add more links to our switches and then bundle them, let's talk about PortFast.

PortFast and BPDU Guard

If you have a server or other devices connected into your switch that you're totally sure won't create a switching loop if STP is disabled, you can use a Cisco proprietary extension to the 802.1d standard called PortFast on these ports. With this tool, the port won't spend the usual 50 seconds to come up into forwarding mode while STP is converging, which is what makes it so cool.

Since ports will transition from blocking to forwarding state immediately, PortFast can prevent our hosts from being potentially unable to receive a DHCP address due to STP's slow convergence. If the host's DHCP request times out, or if every time you plug a host in you're just tired of looking at the switch port being amber for almost a minute before it transitions to forwarding state and turns green, PortFast can really help you out!

Figure 1.19 illustrates a network with three switches, each with a trunk to each of the others and a host and server off the S1 switch.

FIGURE 1.19   PortFast

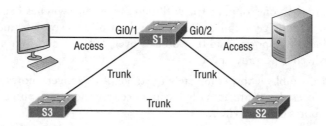

We can use PortFast on the ports on S1 to help them transition to the STP forwarding state immediately upon connecting to the switch.

Here are the commands, first from global config mode—they're pretty simple:

```
S1(config)#spanning-tree portfast ?
  bpdufilter  Enable portfast bdpu filter on this switch
  bpduguard   Enable portfast bpdu guard on this switch
  default     Enable portfast by default on all access ports
```

If you were to type spanning-tree portfast default, you would enable all nontrunking ports with PortFast. From interface mode, you can be more specific, which is the better way to go:

```
S1(config-if)#spanning-tree portfast ?
  disable  Disable portfast for this interface
  trunk    Enable portfast on the interface even in trunk mode
  <cr>
```

From interface mode you can actually configure PortFast on a trunk port, but you would do that only if the port connects to a server or router, not to another switch, so we won't use that here. So let's take a look at the message I get when I turn on PortFast on interface Gi0/1:

```
S1#config t
S1#config)#int range gi0/1 - 2
```

```
S1(config-if)#spanning-tree portfast
%Warning: portfast should only be enabled on ports connected to a single
 host. Connecting hubs, concentrators, switches, bridges, etc... to this
 interface  when portfast is enabled, can cause temporary bridging loops.
 Use with CAUTION

%Portfast has been configured on GigabitEthernet0/1 but will only
 have effect when the interface is in a non-trunking mode.
```

PortFast is enabled on port Gi0/1 and Gi0/2, but notice that you get a pretty long message that's essentially telling you to be careful. This is because when using PortFast, you definitely don't want to create a network loop by plugging another switch or hub into a port that's also configured with PortFast! Why? Because if you let this happen, even though the network may still sort of work, data will pass super slowly, and worse, it could take you a really long time to find the source of the problem, making you very unpopular. So proceed with caution!

At this juncture, you would be happy to know that there are some safeguard commands to have handy when using PortFast just in case someone causes a loop in a port that's configured with PortFast enabled. Let's talk about a really key safeguard command now.

BPDU Guard

If you turn on PortFast for a switch port, it's a really good idea to turn on BPDU Guard as well. In fact, it's such a great idea, I personally feel that it should be enabled by default whenever a port is configured with PortFast!

This is because if a switch port that has PortFast enabled receives a BPDU on that port, it will place the port into error disabled (shutdown) state, effectively preventing anyone from accidentally connecting another switch or hub port into a switch port configured with PortFast. Basically, you're preventing (guarding) your network from being severely crippled or even brought down. So let's configure our S1 interface, which is already configured with PortFast, with BPDU Guard now—it's easy!

Here's how to set it globally:

```
S1(config)# spanning-tree portfast bpduguard default
```

And specifically on an interface:

```
S1(config-if)#spanning-tree bpduguard enable
```

It's important to know that you would only configure this command on your access layer switches—switches where users are directly connected.

Real World Scenario

Hedging My Bets Created Bad Switch Ports during the Super Bowl

A junior admin called me frantically telling me all switch ports had just gone bad on the core switch, which was located at the data center where I was lead consultant for a data center upgrade. Now these things happen, but keep in mind that I just happened to be at a Super Bowl party having a great time watching my favorite team play in the "Big One" when I received this call! So I took a deep breath to refocus. I needed to find out some key information to determine just how bad the situation really was, and my client was in as big of a hurry as I was to get to a solution!

First I asked the junior admin exactly what he did. Of course, he said, "Nothing, I swear!" I figured that's what he'd say, so I pressed him for more info and finally asked for stats on the switch. The admin told me that all the ports on the 10/100/1000 line card went amber at the same time—finally some information I could use! I confirmed that, as suspected, these ports trunked to uplink distribution switches. Wow—this was not good!

At this point, though, I found it hard to believe that all 24 ports would suddenly go bad, but it's possible, so I asked if he had a spare card to try. He told me that he had already put in the new card but the same thing was still happening. Well, it's not the card, or the ports, but maybe something happened with the other switches. I knew there were a lot of switches involved, so someone must have screwed something up to make this catas-trophe happen! Or, maybe the fiber distribution closet went down somehow? If so, how? Was there a fire in the closet or something? Some serious internal shenanigans would be the only answer if that were the cause!

So remaining ever patient (because, to quote Dr. House, "Patients lie"), I again had to ask the admin exactly what he did, and sure enough, he finally admitted that he tried to plug his personal laptop into the core switch so he could watch the Super Bowl, and he quickly added, "...but that's it, I didn't do anything else!" I'll skip over the fact that this guy was about to have the ugliest Monday ever, but something still didn't make sense, and here's why.

Knowing that the ports on that card would all connect to distribution switches, I config-ured the ports with PortFast so they wouldn't have to transition through the STP process. And because I wanted to make sure no one plugged a switch into any of those ports, I enabled BPDU Guard on the entire line card.

But a host would not bring down those ports, so I asked him if he had plugged in the lap-top directly or used something in between. He admitted that he had indeed used another switch because, turns out, there were lots of people from the office who wanted to plug into the core switch and watch the game too. Was he kidding me? The security policy wouldn't allow connecting from their offices, so wouldn't you think they'd consider the core even more off-limits? Some people!

But wait... This doesn't explain all ports turning amber, because only the one he plugged into should be doing that. It took me a second, but I figured out what he did and finally got him to confess. When he plugged the switch in, the port turned amber so he thought it went bad. So what do think he did? Well, if at first you don't succeed, try, try again, and that's just what he did—he actually kept trying ports—all 24 of them to be exact! Now that's what I call determined!

Sad to say, I got back to the party in time just to watch my team lose in the last few minutes! A dark day, indeed!

EtherChannel

Know that almost all Ethernet networks today will typically have multiple links between switches because this kind of design provides redundancy and resiliency. On a physical design that includes multiple links between switches, STP will do its job and put a port or ports into blocking mode. In addition to that, routing protocols like OSPF and EIGRP could see all these redundant links as individual ones, depending on the configuration, which can mean an increase in routing overhead.

We can gain the benefits from multiple links between switches by using port channeling. EtherChannel is a port channel technology that was originally developed by Cisco as a switch-to-switch technique for grouping several Fast Ethernet or Gigabit Ethernet ports into one logical channel.

Also important to note is that once your port channel (EtherChannel) is up and working, layer 2 STP and layer 3 routing protocols will treat those bundled links as a single one, which would stop STP from performing blocking. An additional nice result is that because the routing protocols now only see this as a single link, a single adjacency across the link can be formed—elegant!

Figure 1.20 shows how a network would look if we had four connections between switches, before and after configuring port channels.

FIGURE 1.20   Before and after port channels

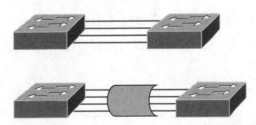

Now as usual, there's the Cisco version and the IEEE version of port channel negotiation protocols to choose from—take your pick. Cisco's version is called Port Aggregation Protocol (PAgP), and the IEEE 802.3ad standard is called Link Aggregation Control Protocol (LACP). Both versions work equally well, but the way you configure each is slightly different. Keep in mind that both PAgP and LACP are negotiation protocols and that EtherChannel can actually be statically configured without PAgP or LACP. Still, it's better to use one of these protocols to help with compatibility issues as well as to manage link additions and failures between two switches.

Cisco EtherChannel allows us to bundle up to eight ports active between switches. The links must have the same speed, duplex setting, and VLAN configuration—in other words, you can't mix interface types and configurations into the same bundle.

There are a few differences in configuring PAgP and LACP, but first, let's go over some terms so you don't get confused:

Port channeling   Refers to combining two to eight Fast Ethernet or two Gigabit Ethernet ports together between two switches into one aggregated logical link to achieve more bandwidth and resiliency.

EtherChannel   Cisco's proprietary term for port channeling.

PAgP   This is a Cisco proprietary port channel negotiation protocol that aids in the automatic creation for EtherChannel links. All links in the bundle must match the same parameters (speed, duplex, VLAN info), and when PAgP identifies matched links, it groups the links into an EtherChannel. This is then added to STP as a single bridge port. At this point, PAgP's job is to send packets every 30 seconds to manage the link for consistency, any link additions, and failures.

LACP (802.3ad)   This has the exact same purpose as PAgP, but it's nonproprietary so it can work between multi-vendor networks.

channel-group   This is a command on Ethernet interfaces used to add the specified interface to a single EtherChannel. The number following this command is the port channel ID.

interface port-channel   Here's a command that creates the bundled interface. Ports can be added to this interface with the channel-group command. Keep in mind that the interface number must match the group number.

Now let's see if you can make some sense out of all these terms by actually configuring something!

Configuring and Verifying Port Channels

Let's use Figure 1.21 for our simple example of how to configure port channels.

FIGURE 1.21   EtherChannel example

You can enable your `channel-group` for each channel by setting the channel mode for each interface to either `active` or `passive` if using LACP. When a port is configured in `passive` mode, it will respond to the LACP packets it receives, but it won't initiate an LACP negotiation. When a port is configured for `active` mode, the port initiates negotiations with other ports by sending LACP packets.

Let me show you a simple example of configuring port channels and then verifying them. First I'll go to global configuration mode and create a port channel interface, and then I'll add this port channel to the physical interfaces.

Remember, all parameters and configurations of the ports must be the same, so I'll start by trunking the interfaces before I configure EtherChannel, like this:

```
S1(config)#int range g0/1 - 2
S1(config-if-range)#switchport trunk encapsulation dot1q
S1(config-if-range)#switchport mode trunk
```

All ports in your bundles must be configured the same, so I'll configure both sides with the same trunking configuration. Now I can assign these ports to a bundle:

```
S1(config-if-range)#channel-group 1 mode ?
  active     Enable LACP unconditionally
  auto       Enable PAgP only if a PAgP device is detected
  desirable  Enable PAgP unconditionally
  on         Enable Etherchannel only
  passive    Enable LACP only if a LACP device is detected
S1(config-if-range)#channel-group 1 mode active
S1(config-if-range)#exit
```

To configure the IEEE nonproprietary LACP, I'll use the `active` or `passive` command; if I wanted to use Cisco's PAgP, I'd use the `auto` or `desirable` command. You can't mix and match these on either end of the bundle, and really, it doesn't matter which one you use in a pure Cisco environment, as long as you configure them the same on both ends (setting the mode to on would be statically configuring your EtherChannel bundle).

At this point in the configuration, I'd have to set the mode to `active` on the S2 interfaces if I wanted the bundle to come up with LACP because, again, all parameters must be the same on both ends of the link. Let's configure our port channel interface, which was created when we used the channel-group command:

```
S1(config)#int port-channel 1
S1(config-if)#switchport trunk encapsulation dot1q
S1(config-if)#switchport mode trunk
S1(config-if)#switchport trunk allowed vlan 1,2,3
```

Notice that I set the same trunking method under the port channel interface as I did the physical interfaces, as well as VLAN information too. Nicely, all command performed under the port-channel are inherited at the interface level, so you can just easily configure the port-channel with all parameters.

Time to configure the interfaces, channel groups, and port channel interface on the S2 switch:

```
S2(config)#int range g0/13 - 14
S2(config-if-range)#switchport trunk encapsulation dot1q
S2(config-if-range)#switchport mode trunk
S2(config-if-range)#channel-group 1 mode active
S2(config-if-range)#exit
S2(config)#int port-channel 1
S2(config-if)#switchport trunk encapsulation dot1q
S2(config-if)#switchport mode trunk
S2(config-if)#switchport trunk allowed vlan 1,2,3
```

On each switch, I configured the ports I wanted to bundle with the same configuration, then created the port channel. After that, I added the ports into the port channel with the channel-group command.

Remember, for LACP we'll use either active/active on each side of the bundle or active/passive, but you can't use passive/passive. Same goes for PAgP; you can use desirable/desirable or auto/desirable but not auto/auto.

Let's verify our EtherChannel with a few commands. We'll start with the show etherchannel port-channel command to see information about a specific port channel interface:

```
S2#sh etherchannel port-channel
                Channel-group listing:
                ----------------------


Group: 1
----------
                Port-channels in the group:
                ---------------------------


Port-channel: Po1     (Primary Aggregator)
------------

Age of the Port-channel   = 00d:00h:46m:49s
Logical slot/port    = 2/1        Number of ports = 2
GC                   = 0x00000000       HotStandBy port = null
Port state           = Port-channel
Protocol             =   LACP
Port Security        = Disabled
```

```
Ports in the Port-channel:

Index  Load   Port   EC state         No of bits
------+------+------+-----------------+-----------
  0     00    Gig0/2  Active              0
  0     00    Gig0/1  Active              0
Time since last port bundled:    00d:00h:46m:47s    Gig0/1
S2#
```

Notice that we have one group and that we're running the IEEE LACP version of port channeling. We're in `Active` mode, and that `Port-channel: Po1` interface has two physical interfaces. The heading `Load` is not the load over the interfaces, it's a hexadecimal value that decides which interface will be chosen to specify the flow of traffic.

The `show etherchannel summary` command displays one line of information per port channel:

```
S2#sh etherchannel summary
Flags:  D - down        P - in port-channel
        I - stand-alone s - suspended
        H - Hot-standby (LACP only)
        R - Layer3      S - Layer2
        U - in use      f - failed to allocate aggregator
        u - unsuitable for bundling
        w - waiting to be aggregated
        d - default port


Number of channel-groups in use: 1
Number of aggregators:           1

Group  Port-channel  Protocol     Ports
------+-------------+-----------+--------------------------------------------


1      Po1(SU)         LACP   Gig0/1(P) Gig0/2(P)
```

This command shows that we have one group, that we're running LACP, and Gig0/1 and Gig0/2 or (P), which means these ports are `in port-channel` mode. This command isn't really all that helpful unless you have multiple channel groups, but it does tell us our group is working well!

Layer 3 EtherChannel

One last item to discuss before we finish this chapter and that is layer 3 EtherChannel. You'd use layer 3 EtherChannel when connecting a switch to multiple ports on a router, for example. It's important to understand that you wouldn't put IP addresses under the physical interfaces of the router, instead you'd actually add the IP address of the bundle under the logical port-channel interface.

Here is an example on how to create the logical port channel 1 and assign 20.2.2.2 as its IP address:

```
Router#config t
Router(config)#int port-channel 1
Router(config-if)#ip address 20.2.2.2 255.255.255.0
```

Now we need to add the physical ports into port channel 1:

```
Router(config-if)#int range g0/0-1
Router(config-if-range)#channel-group 1
GigabitEthernet0/0 added as member-1 to port-channel1
GigabitEthernet0/1 added as member-2 to port-channel1
```

Now let's take a look at the running-config. Notice there are no IP addresses under the physical interface of the router:

```
!
interface Port-channel1
 ip address 20.2.2.2 255.255.255.0
 load-interval 30
!
 interface GigabitEthernet0/0
 no ip address
 load-interval 30
 duplex auto
 speed auto
 channel-group 1
!
 interface GigabitEthernet0/1
 no ip address
 load-interval 30
 duplex auto
 speed auto
 channel-group 1
```

Summary

This chapter was all about switching technologies, with a particular focus on the Spanning Tree Protocol (STP) and its evolution to newer versions like RSTP and then Cisco's PVST+.

You learned about the problems that can occur if you have multiple links between bridges (switches) and the solutions attained with STP.

I also talked about and demonstrated issues that can occur if you have multiple links between bridges (switches), plus how to solve these problems by using the Spanning Tree Protocol (STP).

I covered a detailed configuration of Cisco's Catalyst switches, including verifying the configuration, setting the Cisco STP extensions, and changing the root bridge by setting a bridge priority.

Finally, we discussed, configured, and verified the EtherChannel technology that helps us bundle multiple links between switches.

Exam Essentials

Understand the main purpose of the Spanning Tree Protocol in a switched LAN.   The main purpose of STP is to prevent switching loops in a network with redundant switched paths.

Remember the states of STP.   The purpose of the blocking state is to prevent the use of looped paths. A port in listening state prepares to forward data frames without populating the MAC address table. A port in learning state populates the MAC address table but doesn't forward data frames. A port in forwarding state sends and receives all data frames on the bridged port. Also, a port in the disabled state is virtually nonoperational.

Remember the command `show spanning-tree`.   You must be familiar with the command `show spanning-tree` and how to determine the root bridge of each VLAN. Also, you can use the `show spanning-tree summary` command to help you get a quick glimpse of your STP network and root bridges.

Understand what PortFast and BPDU Guard provide.   PortFast allows a port to transition to the forwarding state immediately upon a connection. Because you don't want other switches connecting to this port, BPDU Guard will shut down a PortFast port if it receives a BPDU.

Understand what EtherChannel is and how to configure it.   EtherChannel allows you to bundle links to get more bandwidth, instead of allowing STP to shut down redundant ports. You can configure Cisco's PAgP or the IEEE version, LACP, by creating a port channel interface and assigning the port channel group number to the interfaces you are bundling.

Written Lab 1

You can find the answers to this lab in Appendix A, "Answers to Written Labs."

Write the answers to the following questions:

1. Which of the following is Cisco proprietary: LACP or PAgP?

2. What command will show you the STP root bridge for a VLAN?

3. What standard is RSTP PVST+ based on?

4. Which protocol is used in a layer 2 network to maintain a loop-free network?

5. Which proprietary Cisco STP extension would put a switch port into error disabled mode if a BPDU is received on this port?

6. You want to configure a switch port to not transition through the STP port states but to go immediately to forwarding mode. What command will you use on a per-port basis?

7. What command will you use to see information about a specific port channel interface?

8. What command can you use to set a switch so that it will be the root bridge for VLAN 3 over any other switch?

9. You need to find the VLANs for which your switch is the root bridge. What two commands can you use?

10. What are the two modes you can set with LACP?

Hands-on Labs

In this section, you will configure and verify STP, as well as configure PortFast and BPDU Guard, and finally, bundle links together with EtherChannel.

Note that the labs in this chapter were written to be used with real equipment using 2960 switches. However, you can use the free LammleSim IOS version simulator or Cisco's Packet Tracer to run through these labs.

The labs in this chapter are as follows:

Lab 1.1: Verifying STP and Finding Your Root Bridge

Lab 1.2: Configuring and Verifying Your Root Bridge

Lab 1.3: Configuring PortFast and BPDU Guard

Lab 1.4: Configuring and Verifying EtherChannel

We'll use the following illustration for all four labs:

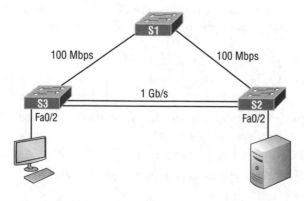

Hands-on Lab 1.1: Verifying STP and Finding Your Root Bridge

This lab will assume that you have added VLANs 2 and 3 to each of your switches and all of your links are trunked.

1. From one of your switches, use the show spanning-tree vlan 2 command. Verify the output.

```
S3#sh spanning-tree vlan 2
VLAN0002
  Spanning tree enabled protocol ieee
  Root ID    Priority    32770
             Address     0001.C9A5.8748
             Cost        19
             Port        1(FastEthernet0/1)
             Hello Time  2 sec  Max Age 20 sec  Forward Delay 15 sec

  Bridge ID  Priority    32770  (priority 32768 sys-id-ext 2)
             Address     0004.9A04.ED97
             Hello Time  2 sec  Max Age 20 sec  Forward Delay 15 sec
             Aging Time  20

Interface        Role Sts Cost      Prio.Nbr Type
---------------- ---- --- --------- -------- -------------------------------
Fa0/1            Root FWD 19        128.1    P2p
Fa0/2            Desg FWD 19        128.2    P2p
Gi1/1            Altn BLK 4         128.25   P2p
Gi1/2            Altn BLK 4         128.26   P2p
```

Notice that S3 is not the root bridge, so to find your root bridge, just follow the root port and see what bridge is connected to that port. Port Fa0/1 is the root port with a cost of 19, which means the switch that is off the Fa0/1 port is the root port connecting to the root bridge because it is a cost of 19, meaning one Fast Ethernet link away.

2. Find the bridge that is off of Fa0/1, which will be our root.

```
S3#sh cdp neighbors
Capability Codes: R - Router, T - Trans Bridge, B - Source Route Bridge
                  S - Switch, H - Host, I - IGMP, r - Repeater, P - Phone
Device ID    Local Intrfce  Holdtme   Capability   Platform   Port ID
S1           Fas 0/1        158           S        2960       Fas 0/1
S2           Gig 1/1        151           S        2960       Gig 1/1
```

```
S2              Gig 1/2         151        S       2960      Gig 1/2
S3#
```

Notice that S1 is connected to the local interface Fa0/1, so let's go to S1 and verify our root bridge.

3. Verify the root bridge for each of the three VLANs. From S1, use the show spanning-tree summary command.

```
S1#sh spanning-tree summary
Switch is in pvst mode
Root bridge for: default VLAN0002 VLAN0003
Extended system ID            is enabled
Portfast Default              is disabled
PortFast BPDU Guard Default   is disabled
Portfast BPDU Filter Default  is disabled
Loopguard Default             is disabled
EtherChannel misconfig guard  is disabled
UplinkFast                    is disabled
BackboneFast                  is disabled
Configured Pathcost method used is short


Name              Blocking Listening Learning Forwarding STP Active
----------------- -------- --------- -------- ---------- ----------
VLAN0001              0         0        0         2          2
VLAN0002              0         0        0         2          2
VLAN0003              0         0        0         2          2


----------------- -------- --------- -------- ---------- ----------
3 vlans               0         0        0         6          6

S1#
```

Notice that S1 is the root bridge for all three VLANs.

4. Make note of all your root bridges, for all three VLANs, if you have more than one root bridge.

Hands-on Lab 1.2: Configuring and Verifying Your Root Bridge

This lab will assume you have performed Lab 1 and now know who your root bridge is for each VLAN.

1. Go to one of your non-root bridges and verify the bridge ID with the show spanning-tree vlan command.

    ```
    S3#sh spanning-tree vlan 1
    VLAN0001
      Spanning tree enabled protocol ieee
      Root ID    Priority    32769
                 Address     0001.C9A5.8748
                 Cost        19
                 Port        1(FastEthernet0/1)
                 Hello Time  2 sec  Max Age 20 sec  Forward Delay 15 sec

      Bridge ID  Priority    32769  (priority 32768 sys-id-ext 1)
                 Address     0004.9A04.ED97
                 Hello Time  2 sec  Max Age 20 sec  Forward Delay 15 sec
                 Aging Time  20

    Interface        Role Sts Cost      Prio.Nbr Type
    ---------------- ---- --- --------- -------- -----------------------------
    Fa0/1            Root FWD 19        128.1    P2p
    Fa0/2            Desg FWD 19        128.2    P2p
    Gi1/1            Altn BLK 4         128.25   P2p
    Gi1/2            Altn BLK 4         128.26   P2p
    ```

    Notice that this bridge is not the root bridge for VLAN 1 and the root port is Fa0/1 with a cost of 19, which means the root bridge is directly connected one Fast Ethernet link away.

2. Make one of your non-root bridges the root bridge for VLAN 1. Use priority 16,384, which is lower than the 32,768 of the current root.

    ```
    S3(config)#spanning-tree vlan 1 priority ?
      <0-61440>  bridge priority in increments of 4096
    S3(config)#spanning-tree vlan 1 priority 16384
    ```

3. Verify the root bridge for VLAN 1.

    ```
    S3#sh spanning-tree vlan 1
    VLAN0001
      Spanning tree enabled protocol ieee
      Root ID    Priority    16385
                 Address     0004.9A04.ED97
                 This bridge is the root
                 Hello Time  2 sec  Max Age 20 sec  Forward Delay 15 sec
    ```

```
Bridge ID  Priority    16385  (priority 16384 sys-id-ext 1)
           Address     0004.9A04.ED97
           Hello Time  2 sec  Max Age 20 sec  Forward Delay 15 sec
           Aging Time  20

Interface        Role Sts Cost      Prio.Nbr Type
---------------- ---- --- --------- -------- -------------------------------
Fa0/1            Desg FWD 19        128.1    P2p
Fa0/2            Desg FWD 19        128.2    P2p
Gi1/1            Desg FWD 4         128.25   P2p
Gi1/2            Desg FWD 4         128.26   P2p
```

Notice that this bridge is indeed the root and all ports are in Desg FWD mode.

Hands-on Lab 1.3: Configuring PortFast and BPDU Guard

This lab will have you configure ports on switches S3 and S2 to allow the PC and server to automatically go into forward mode when they connect into the port.

1. Connect to your switch that has a host connected and enable PortFast for the interface.

```
S3#config t
S3(config)#int fa0/2
S3(config-if)#spanning-tree portfast
%Warning: portfast should only be enabled on ports connected to a single
host. Connecting hubs, concentrators, switches, bridges, etc... to this
interface  when portfast is enabled, can cause temporary bridging loops.
Use with CAUTION

%Portfast has been configured on FastEthernet0/2 but will only
have effect when the interface is in a non-trunking mode.
```

2. Verify that the switch port will be shut down if another switch Ethernet cable plugs into this port.

```
S3(config-if)#spanning-tree bpduguard enable
```

3. Verify your configuration with the show running-config command.

```
!
interface FastEthernet0/2
 switchport mode trunk
 spanning-tree portfast
 spanning-tree bpduguard enable
!
```

Hands-on Lab 1.4: Configuring and Verifying EtherChannel

This lab will have you configure the Cisco EtherChannel PAgP version on the switches used in this lab. Because I have preconfigured the switches, I have set up the trunks on all inter-switch ports. We'll use the Gigabit Ethernet ports between switches S3 and S2.

1. Configure the S3 switch with EtherChannel by creating a port channel interface.

   ```
   S3#config t
   S3(config)#inter port-channel 1
   ```

2. Configure the ports to be in the bundle with the channel-group command.

   ```
   S3(config-if)#int range g1/1 - 2
   S3(config-if-range)#channel-group 1 mode ?
     active      Enable LACP unconditionally
     auto        Enable PAgP only if a PAgP device is detected
     desirable   Enable PAgP unconditionally
     on          Enable Etherchannel only
     passive     Enable LACP only if a LACP device is detected
   S3(config-if-range)#channel-group 1 mode desirable
   ```

   I chose the PAgP desirable mode for the S3 switch.

3. Configure the S2 switch with EtherChannel, using the same parameters as S3.

   ```
   S2#config t
   S2(config)#interface port-channel 1
   S2(config-if)#int rang g1/1 - 2
   S2(config-if-range)#channel-group 1 mode desirable
   %LINK-5-CHANGED: Interface Port-channel 1, changed state to up

   %LINEPROTO-5-UPDOWN: Line protocol on Interface Port-channel 1, changed state
   to up
   ```

   Pretty simple, really. Just a couple of commands.

4. Verify with the show etherchannel port-channel command.

   ```
   S3#sh etherchannel port-channel
                 Channel-group listing:
                 ----------------------

   Group: 1
   ----------
                 Port-channels in the group:
                 ---------------------------
   ```

```
Port-channel: Po1
------------

Age of the Port-channel   = 00d:00h:06m:43s
Logical slot/port  = 2/1      Number of ports = 2
GC                 = 0x00000000      HotStandBy port = null
Port state         = Port-channel
Protocol           =   PAGP
Port Security      = Disabled

Ports in the Port-channel:

Index   Load   Port    EC state           No of bits
------+------+------+------------------+-----------
  0     00    Gig1/1  Desirable-Sl         0
  0     00    Gig1/2  Desirable-Sl         0
Time since last port bundled:   00d:00h:01m:30s   Gig1/2
```

5. Verify with the show etherchannel summary command.

```
S3#sh etherchannel summary
Flags:  D - down       P - in port-channel
        I - stand-alone s - suspended
        H - Hot-standby (LACP only)
        R - Layer3     S - Layer2
        U - in use     f - failed to allocate aggregator
        u - unsuitable for bundling
        w - waiting to be aggregated
        d - default port

Number of channel-groups in use: 1
Number of aggregators:           1

Group  Port-channel  Protocol    Ports
------+-------------+-----------+--------------------------------

1      Po1(SU)         PAgP   Gig1/1(P) Gig1/2(P)
S3#
```

Review Questions

 The following questions are designed to test your understanding of this chapter's material. For more information on how to get additional questions, please see www.lammle.com/ccna.

You can find the answers to these questions in Appendix B, "Answers to Review Questions."

1. You receive the following output from a switch:

```
S2#sh spanning-tree
VLAN0001
  Spanning tree enabled protocol rstp
  Root ID    Priority    32769
             Address     0001.42A7.A603
             Cost        4
             Port        26(GigabitEthernet1/2)
             Hello Time  2 sec  Max Age 20 sec  Forward Delay 15 sec
[output cut]
```

   Which are true regarding this switch? (Choose two.)
   A. The switch is a root bridge.
   B. The switch is a non-root bridge.
   C. The root bridge is four switches away.
   D. The switch is running 802.1w.
   E. The switch is running STP PVST+.

2. You have configured your switches with the `spanning-tree vlan x root primary` and `spanning-tree vlan x root secondary` commands. Which of the following tertiary switch will take over if both switches fail?
   A. A switch with priority 4096
   B. A switch with priority 8192
   C. A switch with priority 12288
   D. A switch with priority 20480

3. Which of the following would you use to find the VLANs for which your switch is the root bridge? (Choose two.)
   A. `show spanning-tree`
   B. `show root all`
   C. `show spanning-tree port root VLAN`
   D. `show spanning-tree summary`

4. You want to run the new 802.1w on your switches. Which of the following would enable this protocol?

    A. `Switch(config)#spanning-tree mode rapid-pvst`

    B. `Switch#spanning-tree mode rapid-pvst`

    C. `Switch(config)#spanning-tree mode 802.1w`

    D. `Switch#spanning-tree mode 802.1w`

5. Which of the following is a layer 2 protocol used to maintain a loop-free network?

    A. VTP

    B. STP

    C. RIP

    D. CDP

6. Which statement describes a spanning-tree network that has converged?

    A. All switch and bridge ports are in the forwarding state.

    B. All switch and bridge ports are assigned as either root or designated ports.

    C. All switch and bridge ports are in either the forwarding or blocking state.

    D. All switch and bridge ports are either blocking or looping.

7. Which of the following modes enable LACP EtherChannel? (Choose two.)

    A. On

    B. Prevent

    C. Passive

    D. Auto

    E. Active

    F. Desirable

8. Which of the following are true regarding RSTP? (Choose three.)

    A. RSTP speeds the recalculation of the spanning tree when the layer 2 network topology changes.

    B. RSTP is an IEEE standard that redefines STP port roles, states, and BPDUs.

    C. RSTP is extremely proactive and very quick, and therefore it absolutely needs the 802.1 delay timers.

    D. RSTP (802.1w) supersedes 802.1d while remaining proprietary.

    E. All of the 802.1d terminology and most parameters have been changed.

    F. 802.1w is capable of reverting to 802.1d to interoperate with traditional switches on a per-port basis.

9. What does BPDU Guard perform?

    A. Makes sure the port is receiving BPDUs from the correct upstream switch.

    B. Makes sure the port is not receiving BPDUs from the upstream switch, only the root.

    C. If a BPDU is received on a BPDU Guard port, PortFast is used to shut down the port.

    D. Shuts down a port if a BPDU is seen on that port.

10. How many bits is the `sys-id-ext` field in a BPDU?

    A. 4

    B. 8

    C. 12

    D. 16

11. There are four connections between two switches running RSTP PVST+ and you want to figure out how to achieve higher bandwidth without sacrificing the resiliency that RSTP provides. What can you configure between these two switches to achieve higher bandwidth than the default configuration is already providing?

    A. Set PortFast and BPDU Guard, which provides faster convergence.

    B. Configure unequal cost load balancing with RSTP PVST+.

    C. Place all four links into the same EtherChannel bundle.

    D. Configure PPP and use multilink.

12. In which circumstance are multiple copies of the same unicast frame likely to be transmitted in a switched LAN?

    A. During high-traffic periods

    B. After broken links are reestablished

    C. When upper-layer protocols require high reliability

    D. In an improperly implemented redundant topology

13. You want to configure LACP. Which do you need to make sure are configured exactly the same on all switch interfaces you are using? (Choose three.)

    A. Virtual MAC address

    B. Port speeds

    C. Duplex

    D. PortFast enabled

    E. VLAN information

14. Which of the following modes enable PAgP EtherChannel? (Choose two.)

    A. On

    B. Prevent

    C. Passive

    D. Auto

    E. Active

    F. Desirable

15. For this question, refer to the following illustration. SB's RP to the root bridge has failed.

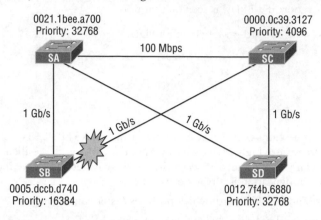

What is the new cost for SB to make a single path to the root bridge?

   A. 4

   B. 8

   C. 23

   D. 12

16. Which of the following would put switch interfaces into EtherChannel port number 1, using LACP? (Choose two.)

   A. `Switch(config)#interface port-channel 1`

   B. `Switch(config)#channel-group 1 mode active`

   C. `Switch#interface port-channel 1`

   D. `Switch(config-if)#channel-group 1 mode active`

17. Which two commands would guarantee your switch to be the root bridge for VLAN 30? (Choose two.)

   A. `spanning-tree vlan 30 priority 0`

   B. `spanning-tree vlan 30 priority 16384`

   C. `spanning-tree vlan 30 root guarantee`

   D. `spanning-tree vlan 30 root primary`

18. Why does Cisco use its proprietary extension of PVST+ with STP and RSTP?

   A. Root bridge placement enables faster convergence as well as optimal path determination.

   B. Non-root bridge placement clearly enables faster convergence as well as optimal path determination.

    C. PVST+ allows for faster discarding of non-IP frames.

    D. PVST+ is actually an IEEE standard called 802.1w.

19. Which are states in 802.1d? (Choose all that apply.)

    A. Blocking

    B. Discarding

    C. Listening

    D. Learning

    E. Forwarding

    F. Alternate

20. Which of the following are roles in STP? (Choose all that apply.)

    A. Blocking

    B. Discarding

    C. Root

    D. Non-designated

    E. Forwarding

    F. Designated

Chapter 2

Network Device Management and Security

THE FOLLOWING ICND2 EXAM TOPICS ARE COVERED IN THIS CHAPTER:

✓ **1.7** **Describe common access layer threat mitigation techniques**

- 1.7.a 802.1x

- 1.7.b DHCP snooping

✓ **4.0** **Infrastructure Services**

✓ **4.1** **Configure, verify, and troubleshoot basic HSRP**

- 4.1.a Priority

- 4.1.b Preemption

- 4.1.c Version

✓ **5.0** **Infrastructure Maintenance**

✓ **5.1** **Configure and verify device-monitoring protocols**

- 5.1.a SNMPv2

- 5.1.b SNMPv3

✓ **5.4** **Describe device management using AAA with TACACS+ and RADIUS**

We're going to start this chapter by discussing how to mitigate threats at the access layer using various security techniques.

Keeping our discussion on security, we're then going to turn our attention to external authentication with authentication, authorization, and accounting (AAA) of our network devices using RADIUS and TACACS+.

Next, we're going to look at Simple Network Management Protocol (SNMP) and the type of alerts sent to the network management station (NMS).

Last, I'm going to show you how to integrate redundancy and load-balancing features into your network elegantly with the routers that you likely have already. Acquiring some overpriced load-balancing device just isn't always necessary because knowing how to properly configure and use Hot Standby Router Protocol (HSRP) can often meet your needs instead.

To find up-to-the-minute updates for this chapter, please see www.lammle .com/ccna or the book's web page at www.sybex.com/go/ccna.

Mitigating Threats at the Access Layer

The Cisco hierarchical model can help you design, implement, and maintain a scalable, reliable, cost-effective hierarchical internetwork.

The access layer controls user and workgroup access to internetwork resources and is also sometimes referred to as the desktop layer. The network resources most users need at this layer will be available locally because the distribution layer handles any traffic for remote services.

The following are some of the functions to be included at the access layer:

- Continued (from the distribution layer) use of access control and policies

- Creation of separate collision domains (microsegmentation/switches)

- Workgroup connectivity into the distribution layer

- Device connectivity

- Resiliency and security services

- Advanced technology capabilities (voice/video, PoE, port-security, etc.)

- Interfaces like Gigabit or FastEthernet switching frequently seen in the access layer

Since the access layer is both the point at which user devices connect to the network and the connection point between the network and client device, protecting it plays an important role in protecting other users, applications, and the network itself from attacks.

Here are some of the ways to protect the access layer (also shown in Figure 2.1):

FIGURE 2.1   Mitigating threats at the access layer

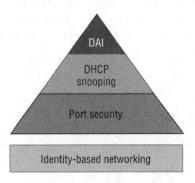

Port security   You're already very familiar with port security (or you should be!), but restricting a port to a specific set of MAC addresses is the most common way to defend the access layer.

DHCP snooping   DHCP snooping is a layer 2 security feature that validates DHCP messages by acting like a firewall between untrusted hosts and trusted DHCP servers.

In order to stop rogue DHCP servers in the network, switch interfaces are configured as trusted or untrusted, where trusted interfaces allow all types of DHCP messages and untrusted interfaces allow only requests. Trusted interfaces are interfaces that connect to a DHCP server or are an uplink toward the DHCP server, as shown in Figure 2.2.

FIGURE 2.2   DHCP snooping and DAI

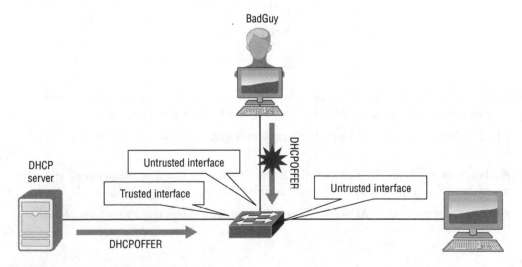

With DHCP snooping enabled, a switch also builds a DHCP snooping binding database, where each entry includes the MAC and IP address of the host as well as the DHCP lease time, binding type, VLAN, and interface. Dynamic ARP inspection also uses this DHCP snooping binding database.

Dynamic ARP inspection (DAI)   DAI, used with DHCP snooping, tracks IP-to-MAC bindings from DHCP transactions to protect against ARP poisoning (which is an attacker trying to have your traffic be sent to him instead of to your valid destination). DHCP snooping is required in order to build the MAC-to-IP bindings for DAI validation.

Identity-based networking   Identity-based networking is a concept that ties together several authentication, access control, and user policy components in order to provide users with the network services you want them to have.

In the past, for a user to connect to the Finance services, for example, a user had to be plugged into the Finance LAN or VLAN. However, with user mobility as one of the core requirements of modern networks, this is no longer practical, nor does it provide sufficient security.

Identity-based networking allows you to verify users when they connect to a switch port by authenticating them and placing them in the right VLAN based on their identity. Should any users fail to pass the authentication process, their access can be rejected, or they might be simply put in a guest VLAN. Figure 2.3 shows this process.

FIGURE 2.3   Identity-based networking

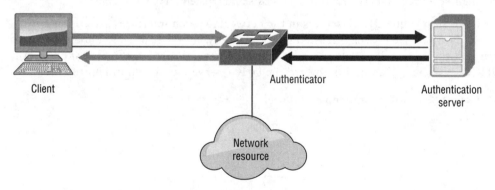

The IEEE 802.1x standard allows you to implement identity-based networking on wired and wireless hosts by using client/server access control. There are three roles:

Client   Also referred to as a supplicant, this software runs on a client that is 802.1x compliant.

Authenticator   Typically a switch, this controls physical access to the network and is a proxy between the client and the authentication server.

Authentication server (RADIUS)   This is a server that authenticates each client before making available any services.

External Authentication Options

Of course we only want authorized IT folks to have administrative access to our network devices such as routers and switches, and in a small to medium-sized network, just using local authentication is sufficient.

However, if you have hundreds of devices, managing administrative connectivity would be nearly impossible since you'd have to configure local authentication on each device by hand, and if you changed just one password, it can take hours to update your network.

Since maintaining the local database for each network device for the size of the network is usually not feasible, you can use an external AAA server that will manage all user and administrative access needs for an entire network.

The two most popular options for external AAA are RADIUS and TACACS+, both covered next.

RADIUS

Remote Authentication Dial-In User Service, or RADIUS, was developed by the Internet Engineering Task Force—the IETF—and is basically a security system that works to guard the network against unauthorized access. RADIUS, which uses only UDP, is an open standard implemented by most major vendors, and it's one of the most popular types of security servers around because it combines authentication and authorization services into a single process. So after users are authenticated, they are then authorized for network services.

RADIUS implements a client/server architecture, where the typical client is a router, switch, or AP and the typical server is a Windows or Unix device that's running RADIUS software.

The authentication process has three distinct stages:

1. The user is prompted for a username and password.

2. The username and encrypted password are sent over the network to the RADIUS server.

3. The RADIUS server replies with one of the following:

Response	Meaning
Accept	The user has been successfully authenticated.
Reject	The username and password are not valid.
Challenge	The RADIUS server requests additional information.
Change Password	The user should select a new password.

It's important to remember that RADIUS encrypts only the password in the access-request packet from the client to the server. The remainder of the packet is unencrypted.

Configuring RADIUS

To configure a RADIUS server for console and VTY access, first you need to enable AAA services in order to configure all the AAA commands. Configure the `aaa new-model` command in the global configuration mode.

```
Router(config)# aaa new-model
```

The `aaa new-model` command immediately applies local authentication to all lines and interfaces (except `line con 0`). So, to avoid being locked out of the router or switch, you should define a local username and password before starting the AAA configuration.

Now, configure a local user:

```
Router(config)#username Todd password Lammle
```

Creating this user is super important because you can then use this same locally created user if the external authentication server fails! If you don't create this and you can't get to the server, you're going to end up doing a password recovery.

Next, configure a RADIUS server using any name and the RADIUS key that is configured on the server.

```
Router(config)#radius server SecureLogin
Router(config-radius-server)#address ipv4 10.10.10.254
Router(config-radius-server)#key MyRadiusPassword
```

Now, add your newly created RADIUS server to an AAA group of any name.

```
Router(config)#aaa group server radius MyRadiusGroup
Router(config-sg-radius)#server name SecureLogin
```

Last, configure this newly created group to be used for AAA login authentication. If the RADIUS server fails, the fallback to local authentication should be set.

```
Router(config)# aaa authentication login default group MyRadiusGroup local
```

TACACS+

Terminal Access Controller Access Control System (TACACS+) is also a security server that's Cisco proprietary and uses TCP. It's really similar in many ways to RADIUS; however, it does all that RADIUS does and more, including multiprotocol support.

TACACS+ was developed by Cisco Systems, so it's specifically designed to interact with Cisco's AAA services. If you're using TACACS+, you have the entire menu of AAA features available to you—and it handles each security aspect separately, unlike RADIUS:

- Authentication includes messaging support in addition to login and password functions.

- Authorization enables explicit control over user capabilities.

- Accounting supplies detailed information about user activities.

Configuring TACACS+

This is pretty much identical to the RADIUS configuration.

To configure a TACACS+ server for console and VTY access, first you need to enable AAA services in order to configure all the AAA commands. Configure the `aaa new-model` command in the global configuration mode (if it isn't already enabled).

```
Router(config)# aaa new-model
```

Now, configure a local user if you haven't already.

```
Router(config)#username Todd password Lammle
```

Next, configure a TACACS+ server using any name and the key that is configured on the server.

```
Router(config)#radius server SecureLoginTACACS+
Router(config-radius-server)#address ipv4 10.10.10.254
Router(config-radius-server)#key MyTACACS+Password
```

Now, add your newly created TACACS+ server to a AAA group of any name.

```
Router(config)#aaa group server radius MyTACACS+Group
Router(config-sg-radius)#server name SecureLoginTACACS+
```

Last configure this newly created group to be used for AAA login authentication. If the TACACS+ server fails, the fallback to local authentication should be set.

```
Router(config)# aaa authentication login default group MyTACACS+Group local
```

SNMP

Although *Simple Network Management Protocol (SNMP)* certainly isn't the oldest protocol ever, it's still pretty old, considering it was created way back in 1988 (RFC 1065)!

SNMP is an Application layer protocol that provides a message format for agents on a variety of devices to communicate with network management stations (NMSs)—for example, Cisco Prime or HP Openview. These agents send messages to the NMS station, which then either reads or writes information in the database that's stored on the NMS and called a management information base (MIB).

The NMS periodically queries or polls the SNMP agent on a device to gather and analyze statistics via GET messages. End devices running SNMP agents would send an SNMP trap to the NMS if a problem occurs. This is demonstrated in Figure 2.4.

FIGURE 2.4   SNMP GET and TRAP messages

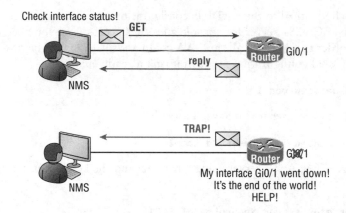

Admins can also use SNMP to provide some configurations to agents as well, called SET messages. In addition to polling to obtain statistics, SNMP can be used for analyzing information and compiling the results in a report or even a graph. Thresholds can be used to trigger a notification process when exceeded. Graphing tools are used to monitor the CPU statistics of Cisco devices like a core router. The CPU should be monitored continuously and the NMS can graph the statistics. Notification will be sent when any threshold you've set has been exceeded.

SNMP has three versions, with version 1 being rarely, if ever, implemented today. Here's a summary of these three versions:

SNMPv1   Supports plaintext authentication with community strings and uses only UDP.

SNMPv2c   Supports plaintext authentication with community strings with no encryption but provides GET BULK, which is a way to gather many types of information at once and minimize the number of GET requests. It offers a more detailed error message reporting method called INFORM, but it's not more secure than v1. It uses UDP even though it can be configured to use TCP.

SNMPv3   Supports strong authentication with MD5 or SHA, providing confidentiality (encryption) and data integrity of messages via DES or DES-256 encryption between agents and managers. GET BULK is a supported feature of SNMPv3, and this version also uses TCP.

Management Information Base (MIB)

With so many kinds of devices and so much data that can be accessed, there needed to be a standard way to organize this plethora of data, so MIB to the rescue! A *management information base (MIB)* is a collection of information that's organized hierarchically and can be accessed by protocols like SNMP. RFCs define some common public variables, but most organizations define their own private branches along with basic SNMP standards. Organizational IDs (OIDs) are laid out as a tree with different levels assigned by different organizations, with top-level MIB OIDs belonging to various standards organizations.

Vendors assign private branches in their own products. Let's take a look at Cisco's OIDs, which are described in words or numbers to locate a particular variable in the tree, as shown in Figure 2.5.

FIGURE 2.5 Cisco's MIB OIDs

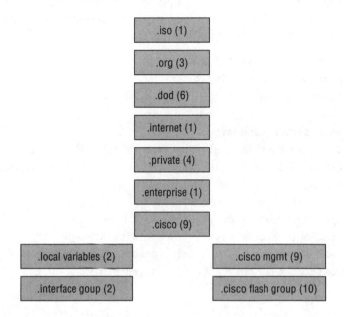

Luckily, you don't need to memorize the OIDs in Figure 2.5 for the Cisco exams!

To obtain information from the MIB on the SNMP agent, you can use several different operations:

- GET: This operation is used to get information from the MIB to an SNMP agent.

- SET: This operation is used to get information to the MIB from an SNMP manager.

- WALK: This operation is used to list information from successive MIB objects within a specified MIB.

- TRAP: This operation is used by the SNMP agent to send a triggered piece of information to the SNMP manager.

- INFORM: This operation is the same as a trap, but it adds an acknowledgment that a trap does not provide.

Configuring SNMP

Configuring SNMP is a pretty straightforward process for which you only need a few commands. These five steps are all you need to run through to configure a Cisco device for SNMP access:

1. Configure where the traps are to be sent.

2. Enable SNMP read-write access to the router.

3. Configure SNMP contact information.

4. Configure SNMP location.

5. Configure an ACL to restrict SNMP access to the NMS hosts.

The only required configuration is the IP address of the NMS station and the community string (which acts as a password or authentication string) because the other three are optional. Here's an example of a typical SNMP router configuration:

```
Router(config)#snmp-server host 1.2.3.4
Router(config)#snmp-server community ?
  WORD  SNMP community string

Router(config)#snmp-server community Todd ?
  <1-99>       Std IP accesslist allowing access with this community string
  <1300-1999>  Expanded IP accesslist allowing access with this community
               string
  WORD         Access-list name
  ipv6         Specify IPv6 Named Access-List
  ro           Read-only access with this community string
  rw           Read-write access with this community string
  view         Restrict this community to a named MIB view
  <cr>

Router(config)#snmp-server community Todd rw
Router(config)#snmp-server location Boulder
Router(config)#snmp-server contact Todd Lammle
Router(config)#ip access-list standard Protect_NMS_Station
Router(config-std-nacl)#permit host 192.168.10.254
```

Entering the snmp-server command enables SNMPv1 on the Cisco device.

You can enter the ACL directly in the SNMP configuration to provide security, using either a number or a name. Here is an example:

```
Router(config)#snmp-server community Todd Protect_NMS_Station rw
```

Notice that even though there's a boatload of configuration options under SNMP, you only really need to work with a few of them to configure a basic SNMP trap setup on a router. First, I set the IP address of the NMS station where the router will send the traps; then I chose the community name of Todd with RW access (read-write), which means the NMS will be able to retrieve and modify MIB objects from the router. Location and contact information comes in really handy for troubleshooting the configuration. Make sure you understand that the ACL protects the NMS from access, not the devices with the agents!

Let's define the SNMP read and write options.

Read-only Gives authorized management stations read access to all objects in the MIB except the community strings and doesn't allow write access

Read-write Gives authorized management stations read and write access to all objects in the MIB but doesn't allow access to the community strings

Next we'll explore a Cisco proprietary method of configuring redundant default gateways for hosts.

Client Redundancy Issues

If you're wondering how you can possibly configure a client to send data off its local link when its default gateway router has gone down, you've targeted a key issue because the answer is that, usually, you can't! Most host operating systems just don't allow you to change data routing. Sure, if a host's default gateway router goes down, the rest of the network will still converge, but it won't share that information with the hosts. Take a look at Figure 2.6 to see what I am talking about. There are actually two routers available to forward data for the local subnet, but the hosts know about only one of them. They learn about this router when you provide them with the default gateway either statically or through DHCP.

FIGURE 2.6   Default gateway

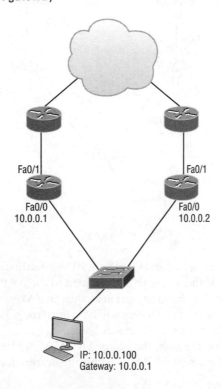

IP: 10.0.0.100
Gateway: 10.0.0.1

This begs the question: Is there another way to use the second active router? The answer is a bit complicated, but bear with me. There is a feature that's enabled by default on Cisco routers called Proxy Address Resolution Protocol (Proxy ARP). Proxy ARP enables hosts, which have no knowledge of routing options, to obtain the MAC address of a gateway router that can forward packets for them.

You can see how this happens in Figure 2.7. If a Proxy ARP–enabled router receives an ARP request for an IP address that it knows isn't on the same subnet as the requesting host, it will respond with an ARP reply packet to the host. The router will give its own local MAC address—the MAC address of its interface on the host's subnet—as the destination MAC address for the IP address that the host is seeking to be resolved. After receiving the destination MAC address, the host will then send all the packets to the router, not knowing that what it sees as the destination host is really a router. The router will then forward the packets toward the intended host.

FIGURE 2.7 Proxy ARP

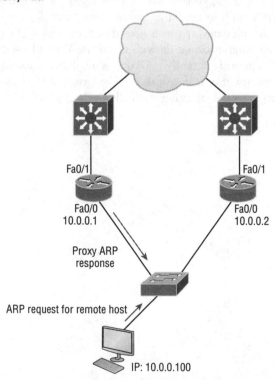

So with Proxy ARP, the host device sends traffic as if the destination device were located on its own network segment. If the router that responded to the ARP request fails, the source host continues to send packets for that destination to the same MAC address. But because they're being sent to a failed router, the packets will be sent to the other router on the network that is also responding to ARP requests for remote hosts.

After the time-out period on the host, the proxy ARP MAC address ages out of the ARP cache. The host can then make a new ARP request for the destination and get the address of another proxy ARP router. Still, keep in mind that the host cannot send packets off of its subnet during the failover time. This isn't exactly a perfect situation, so there has to be a better way, right? Well, there is, and that's precisely where redundancy protocols come to the rescue!

Introducing First Hop Redundancy Protocols (FHRPs)

First hop redundancy protocols (FHRPs) work by giving you a way to configure more than one physical router to appear as if they were only a single logical one. This makes client configuration and communication easier because you can simply configure a single default gateway and the host machine can use its standard protocols to communicate. *First hop* is a reference to the default router being the first router, or first router hop, through which a packet must pass.

So how does a redundancy protocol accomplish this? The protocols I'm going to describe to you do this basically by presenting a virtual router to all of the clients. The virtual router has its own IP and MAC addresses. The virtual IP address is the address that's configured on each of the host machines as the default gateway. The virtual MAC address is the address that will be returned when an ARP request is sent by a host. The hosts don't know or care which physical router is actually forwarding the traffic, as you can see in Figure 2.8.

FIGURE 2.8   FHRPs use a virtual router with a virtual IP address and virtual MAC address.

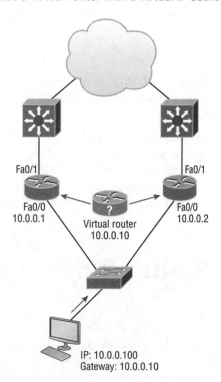

It's the responsibility of the redundancy protocol to decide which physical router will actively forward traffic and which one will be placed on standby in case the active router fails. Even if the active router fails, the transition to the standby router will be transparent to the hosts because the virtual router, which is identified by the virtual IP and MAC addresses, is now used by the standby router. The hosts never change default gateway information, so traffic keeps flowing.

> Fault-tolerant solutions provide continued operation in the event of a device failure, and load-balancing solutions distribute the workload over multiple devices.

There are three important redundancy protocols, but only HSRP is covered on the CCNA objectives now:

Hot Standby Router Protocol (HSRP)   HSRP is by far Cisco's favorite protocol ever! Don't buy just one router; buy up to eight routers to provide the same service, and keep seven as backup in case of failure! HSRP is a Cisco proprietary protocol that provides a redundant gateway for hosts on a local subnet, but this isn't a load-balanced solution. HSRP allows you to configure two or more routers into a standby group that shares an IP address and MAC address and provides a default gateway. When the IP and MAC addresses are independent from the routers' physical addresses (on a virtual interface, not tied to a specific interface), HSRP can swap control of an address if the current forwarding and active router fails. But there is actually a way you can sort of achieve load balancing with HSRP—by using multiple VLANs and designating a specific router active for one VLAN, then an alternate router as active for the other VLAN via trunking. This still isn't a true load-balancing solution and it's not nearly as solid as what you can achieve with GLBP!

Virtual Router Redundancy Protocol (VRRP)   Also provides a redundant—but again, not load-balanced—gateway for hosts on a local subnet. It's an open standard protocol that functions almost identically to HSRP.

Gateway Load Balancing Protocol (GLBP)   For the life of me I can't figure out how GLBP isn't a CCNA objective anymore! GLBP doesn't just stop at providing us with a redundant gateway; it's a true load-balancing solution for routers. GLBP allows a maximum of four routers in each forwarding group. By default, the active router directs the traffic from hosts to each successive router in the group using a round-robin algorithm. The hosts are directed to send their traffic toward a specific router by being given the MAC address of the next router in line to be used.

Hot Standby Router Protocol (HSRP)

Again, HSRP is a Cisco proprietary protocol that can be run on most, but not all, of Cisco's router and multilayer switch models. It defines a standby group, and each standby group that you define includes the following routers:

- Active router
- Standby router
- Virtual router
- Any other routers that maybe attached to the subnet

The problem with HSRP is that with it, only one router is active and two or more routers just sit there in standby mode and won't be used unless a failure occurs—not very cost effective or efficient! Figure 2.9 shows how only one router is used at a time in an HSRP group.

The standby group will always have at least two routers participating in it. The primary players in the group are the one active router and one standby router that communicate to each other using multicast Hello messages. The Hello messages provide all of the required communication for the routers. The Hellos contain the information required to accomplish the election that determines the active and standby router positions. They also hold the key to the failover process. If the standby router stops receiving Hello packets from the active router, it then takes over the active router role, as shown in Figure 2.9 and Figure 2.10.

FIGURE 2.9   HSRP active and standby routers

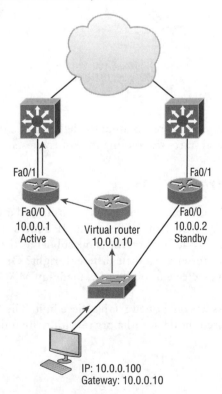

FIGURE 2.10   Example of HSRP active and standby routers swapping interfaces

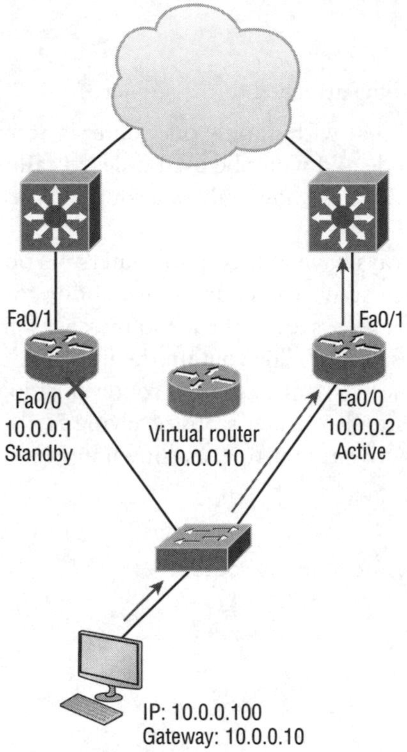

As soon as the active router stops responding to Hellos, the standby router automatically becomes the active router and starts responding to host requests.

Virtual MAC Address

A virtual router in an HSRP group has a virtual IP address and a virtual MAC address. So where does that virtual MAC come from? The virtual IP address isn't that hard to figure out; it just has to be a unique IP address on the same subnet as the hosts defined in the configuration. But MAC addresses are a little different, right? Or are they? The answer is yes—sort of. With HSRP, you create a totally new, made-up MAC address in addition to the IP address.

The HSRP MAC address has only one variable piece in it. The first 24 bits still identify the vendor who manufactured the device (the organizationally unique identifier, or OUI).

The next 16 bits in the address tell us that the MAC address is a well-known HSRP MAC address. Finally, the last 8 bits of the address are the hexadecimal representation of the HSRP group number.

Let me clarify all this with an example of what an HSRP MAC address would look like:

```
0000.0c07.ac0a
```

- The first 24 bits (0000.0c) are the vendor ID of the address; in the case of HSRP being a Cisco protocol, the ID is assigned to Cisco.

- The next 16 bits (07.ac) are the well-known HSRP ID. This part of the address was assigned by Cisco in the protocol, so it's always easy to recognize that this address is for use with HSRP.

- The last 8 bits (0a) are the only variable bits and represent the HSRP group number that you assign. In this case, the group number is 10 and converted to hexadecimal when placed in the MAC address, where it becomes the 0a that you see.

You can see this displayed with every MAC address added to the ARP cache of every router in the HSRP group. There will be the translation from the IP address to the MAC address, as well as the interface on which it's located.

HSRP Timers

Before we get deeper into the roles that each of the routers can have in an HSRP group, I want to define the HSRP timers for HSRP to function because they ensure communication between the routers, and if something goes wrong, they allow the standby router to take over. The HSRP timers include *hello*, *hold*, *active*, and *standby*.

Hello timer   The hello timer is the defined interval during which each of the routers send out Hello messages. Their default interval is 3 seconds and they identify the state that each router is in. This is important because the particular state determines the specific role of each router and, as a result, the actions each will take within the group. Figure 2.11 shows the Hello messages being sent and the router using the hello timer to keep the network flowing in case of a failure.

This timer can be changed, and people used to avoid doing so because it was thought that lowering the hello value would place an unnecessary load on the routers. That isn't true with most of the routers today; in fact, you can configure the timers in milliseconds, meaning the failover time can be in milliseconds! Still, keep in mind that increasing the value will make the standby router wait longer before taking over for the active router when it fails or can't communicate.

FIGURE 2.11   HSRP Hellos

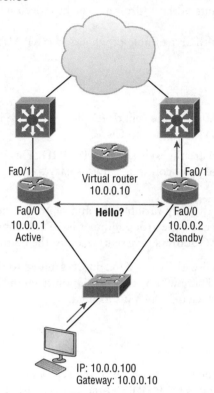

Hold timer   The hold timer specifies the interval the standby router uses to determine whether the active router is offline or out of communication. By default, the hold timer is 10 seconds, roughly three times the default for the hello timer. If one timer is changed for some reason, I recommend using this multiplier to adjust the other timers too. By setting the hold timer at three times the hello timer, you ensure that the standby router doesn't take over the active role every time there's a short break in communication.

Active timer   The active timer monitors the state of the active router. The timer resets each time a router in the standby group receives a Hello packet from the active router. This timer expires based on the hold time value that's set in the corresponding field of the HSRP Hello message.

Standby timer   The standby timer is used to monitor the state of the standby router. The timer resets anytime a router in the standby group receives a Hello packet from the standby router and expires based on the hold time value that's set in the respective Hello packet.

⊕ **Real World Scenario**

Large Enterprise Network Outages with FHRPs

Years ago when HSRP was all the rage, and before VRRP and GLBP, enterprises used hundreds of HSRP groups. With the hello timer set to 3 seconds and a hold time of 10 seconds, these timers worked just fine and we had great redundancy with our core routers.

However, as we've seen in the last few years and certainly will see in the future, 10 seconds is now a lifetime! Some of my customers have been complaining with the failover time and loss of connectivity to their virtual server farm.

So lately I've been changing the timers to well below the defaults. Cisco had changed the timers so you could use sub-second times for failover. Because these are multicast packets, the overhead that is seen on a current high-speed network is almost nothing.

The hello timer is typically set to 200 msec and the hold time is 700 msec. The command is as follows:

```
(config-if)#Standby 1 timers msec 200 msec 700
```

This almost ensures that not even a single packet is lost when there is an outage.

Group Roles

Each of the routers in the standby group has a specific function and role to fulfill. The three main roles are as virtual router, active router, and standby router. Additional routers can also be included in the group.

Virtual router   As its name implies, the virtual router is not a physical entity. It really just defines the role that's held by one of the physical routers. The physical router that communicates as the virtual router is the current active router. The virtual router is nothing more than a separate IP address and MAC address to which packets are sent.

Active router   The active router is the physical router that receives data sent to the virtual router address and routes it onward to its various destinations. As I mentioned, this router accepts all the data sent to the MAC address of the virtual router in addition to the data that's been sent to its own physical MAC address. The active router processes the data that's being forwarded and will also answer any ARP requests destined for the virtual router's IP address.

Standby router   The standby router is the backup to the active router. Its job is to monitor the status of the HSRP group and quickly take over packet-forwarding responsibilities if the active router fails or loses communication. Both the active and standby routers transmit Hello messages to inform all other routers in the group of their role and status.

Other routers   An HSRP group can include additional routers, which are members of the group but don't take the primary roles of either active or standby states. These routers monitor the Hello messages sent by the active and standby routers to ensure that an active and standby router exists for the HSRP group that they belong to. They will forward data that's specifically addressed to their own IP addresses, but they will never forward data addressed to the virtual router unless elected to the active or standby state. These routers send "speak" messages based on the hello timer interval that informs other routers of their position in an election.

Interface Tracking

By now, you probably understand why having a virtual router on a LAN is a great idea. You also know why it's a very good thing that the active router can change dynamically, giving us much needed redundancy on our inside network. But what about the links to the upstream network or the Internet connection off of those HSRP-enabled routers? And how will the inside hosts know if an outside interface goes down or if they are sending packets to an active router that can't route to a remote network? Key questions and HSRP do provide a solution for them; it's called interface tracking.

Figure 2.12 shows how HSRP-enabled routers can keep track of the interface status of the outside interfaces and how they can switch the inside active router as needed to keep the inside hosts from losing connectivity upstream.

FIGURE 2.12   Interface tracking setup

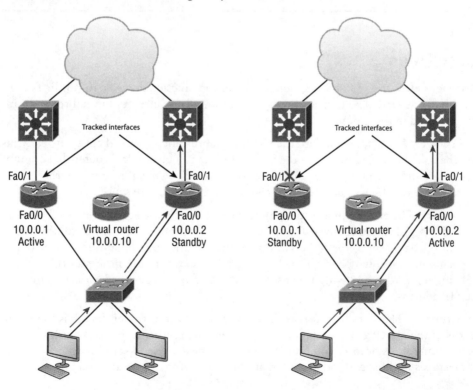

If the outside link of the active router goes down, the standby router will take over and become the active router. There is a default priority of 100 on routers configured with an HSRP interface, and if you raise this priority (we'll do this in a minute), it means your router has a higher priority to become the active router. The reason I am bringing this up now is because when a tracked interface goes down, it decrements the priority of this router.

Configuring and Verifying HSRP

Configuring and verifying the different FHRPs can be pretty simple, especially regarding the Cisco objectives, but as with most technologies, you can quickly get into advanced configurations and territory with the different FHRPs if you're not careful, so I'll show you exactly what you need to know.

The Cisco objectives don't cover much about the configuration of FHRPs, but verification and troubleshooting is important, so I'll use a simple configuration on two routers here. Figure 2.13 shows the network I'll use to demonstrate HSRP.

FIGURE 2.13   HSRP configuration and verification

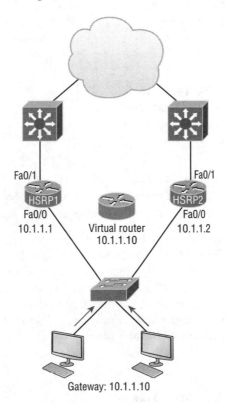

This is a simple configuration for which you really need only one command: `standby` *group* `ip` *virtual_ip*. After using this single mandatory command, I'll name the group and set the interface on router HSRP1 so it wins the election and becomes the active router by default.

```
HSRP1#config t
HSRP1(config)#int fa0/0
HSRP1(config-if)#standby ?
  <0-255>        group number
  authentication Authentication
  delay          HSRP initialisation delay
  ip             Enable HSRP and set the virtual IP address
  mac-address    Virtual MAC address
  name           Redundancy name string
  preempt        Overthrow lower priority Active routers
  priority       Priority level
  redirect       Configure sending of ICMP Redirect messages with an HSRP
                 virtual IP address as the gateway IP address
  timers         Hello and hold timers
  track          Priority tracking
  use-bia        HSRP uses interface's burned in address
  version        HSRP version

HSRP1(config-if)#standby 1 ip 10.1.1.10
HSRP1(config-if)#standby 1 name HSRP_Test
HSRP1(config-if)#standby 1 priority ?
  <0-255>  Priority value

HSRP1(config-if)#standby 1 priority 110
000047: %HSRP-5-STATECHANGE: FastEthernet0/0 Grp 1 state Speak -> Standby
000048: %HSRP-5-STATECHANGE: FastEthernet0/0 Grp 1 state Standby -> Active110
```

There are quite a few commands available to use in an advanced setting with the standby command, but we'll stick with the simple commands that follow the Cisco objectives. First, I numbered the group (1), which must be the same on all routers sharing HSRP duties; then I added the virtual IP address shared by all routers in the HSRP group. Optionally, I named the group and then set the priority of HSRP1 to 110, and I left HSRP2 to a default of 100. The router with the highest priority will win the election to become the active router. Let's configure the HSRP2 router now:

```
HSRP2#config t
HSRP2(config)#int fa0/0
HSRP2(config-if)#standby 1 ip 10.1.1.10
HSRP2(config-if)#standby 1 name HSRP_Test
```

```
*Jun 23 21:40:10.699:%HSRP-5-STATECHANGE:FastEthernet0/0 Grp 1 state
Speak -> Standby
```

I really only needed the first command—naming it was for administrative purposes only. Notice that the link came up and HSRP2 became the standby router because it had the lower priority of 100 (the default). Make a note that this priority comes into play only if both routers were to come up at the same time. This means that HSRP2 would be the active router, regardless of the priority, if it comes up first.

Let's take a look at the configurations with the show standby and show standby brief commands:

```
HSRP1(config-if)#do show standby
FastEthernet0/0 - Group 1
  State is Active
    2 state changes, last state change 00:03:40
  Virtual IP address is 10.1.1.10
  Active virtual MAC address is 0000.0c07.ac01
    Local virtual MAC address is 0000.0c07.ac01 (v1 default)
  Hello time 3 sec, hold time 10 sec
    Next hello sent in 1.076 secs
  Preemption disabled
  Active router is local
  Standby router is 10.1.1.2, priority 100 (expires in 7.448 sec)
  Priority 110 (configured 110)
  IP redundancy name is "HSRP_Test" (cfgd)

HSRP1(config-if)#do show standby brief
                     P indicates configured to preempt.
                     |
Interface   Grp Prio P State   Active       Standby      Virtual IP
Fa0/0        1   110  Active   local        10.1.1.2     10.1.1.10
```

Notice the group number in each output—it's a key troubleshooting spot! Each router must be configured in the same group or they won't work. Also, you can see the virtual MAC and configured virtual IP address, as well as the hello time of 3 seconds. The standby and virtual IP addresses are also displayed.

HSRP2's output tells us that it's in standby mode:

```
HSRP2(config-if)#do show standby brief
                     P indicates configured to preempt.
                     |
Interface   Grp Prio P State   Active       Standby      Virtual IP
Fa0/0        1   100    Standby 10.1.1.1     local        10.1.1.10
HRSP2(config-if)#
```

Notice so far that you have seen HSRP states of active and standby, but watch what happens when I disable Fa0/0:

```
HSRP1#config t
HSRP1(config)#interface Fa0/0
HSRP1(config-if)#shutdown
*Nov 20 10:06:52.369: %HSRP-5-STATECHANGE: Ethernet0/0 Grp 1 state Active ->
Init
```

The HSRP went into Init state, meaning it's trying to initialize with a peer. The possible interface states for HSRP are shown in Table 2.1.

TABLE 2.1   HSRP states

State	Definition
Initial (INIT)	This is the state at the start. This state indicates that HSRP does not run. This state is entered through a configuration change or when an interface first becomes available.
Learn	The router has not determined the virtual IP address and has not yet seen an authenticated Hello message from the active router. In this state, the router still waits to hear from the active router.
Listen	The router knows the virtual IP address, but the router is neither the active router nor the standby router. It listens for Hello messages from those routers.
Speak	The router sends periodic Hello messages and actively participates in the election of the active and/or standby router. A router cannot enter speak state unless the router has the virtual IP address.
Standby	The router is a candidate to become the next active router and sends periodic Hello messages. With the exclusion of transient conditions, there is, at most, one router in the group in standby state.
Active	The router currently forwards packets that are sent to the group virtual MAC address. The router sends periodic Hello messages. With the exclusion of transient conditions, there must be, at most, one router in active state in the group.

There is one other command that I want to cover. If you're studying and want to understand HSRP, you should learn to use this debug command and have your active and standby routers move. You'll really get to see what is going on.

```
HSRP2#debug standby
*Sep 15 00:07:32.344:HSRP:Fa0/0 Interface UP
*Sep 15 00:07:32.344:HSRP:Fa0/0 Initialize swsb, Intf state Up
*Sep 15 00:07:32.344:HSRP:Fa0/0 Starting minimum intf delay (1 secs)
*Sep 15 00:07:32.344:HSRP:Fa0/0 Grp 1 Set virtual MAC 0000.0c07.ac01
type: v1 default
*Sep 15 00:07:32.344:HSRP:Fa0/0 MAC hash entry 0000.0c07.ac01, Added
Fa0/0 Grp 1 to list
*Sep 15 00:07:32.348:HSRP:Fa0/0 Added 10.1.1.10 to hash table
*Sep 15 00:07:32.348:HSRP:Fa0/0 Grp 1 Has mac changed? cur 0000.0c07.ac01
new 0000.0c07.ac01
*Sep 15 00:07:32.348:HSRP:Fa0/0 Grp 1 Disabled -> Init
*Sep 15 00:07:32.348:HSRP:Fa0/0 Grp 1 Redundancy "hsrp-Fa0/0-1" state
Disabled -> Init
*Sep 15 00:07:32.348:HSRP:Fa0/0 IP Redundancy "hsrp-Fa0/0-1" added
*Sep 15 00:07:32.348:HSRP:Fa0/0 IP Redundancy "hsrp-Fa0/0-1" update,
Disabled -> Init
*Sep 15 00:07:33.352:HSRP:Fa0/0 Intf min delay expired
*Sep 15 00:07:39.936:HSRP:Fa0/0 Grp 1 MAC addr update Delete from SMF
0000.0c07.ac01
*Sep 15 00:07:39.936:HSRP:Fa0/0 Grp 1 MAC addr update Delete from SMF
0000.0c07.ac01
*Sep 15 00:07:39.940:HSRP:Fa0/0 ARP reload
```

HSRP Load Balancing

As you know, HSRP doesn't really perform true load balancing, but it can be configured to use more than one router at a time for use with different VLANs. This is different from the true load balancing that's possible with GLBP, which I'll demonstrate in a minute, but HSRP still performs a load-balancing act of sorts. Figure 2.14 shows how load balancing would look with HSRP.

How can you get two HSRP routers active at the same time? Well for the same subnet with this simple configuration, you can't, but if you trunk the links to each router, they'll run and be configured with a "router on a stick" (ROAS) configuration. This means that each router can be the default gateway for different VLANs, but you still can have only one active router per VLAN. Typically, in a more advanced setting you won't use HSRP for load balancing; you'll use GLBP, but you can do load-sharing with HSRP, and that is the topic of an objective, so we'll remember that, right? It comes in handy because it prevents situations where a single point of failure causes traffic interruptions. This HSRP feature improves network resilience by allowing for load-balancing and redundancy capabilities between subnets and VLANs.

FIGURE 2.14 HSRP load balancing per VLAN

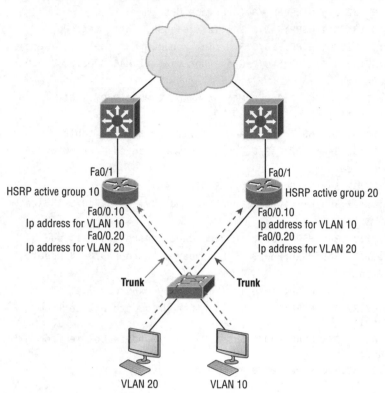

HSRP Troubleshooting

Besides HSRP verification, the troubleshooting of HSRP is the Cisco objective hotspot, so let's go through this.

Most of your HSRP misconfiguration issues can be solved by checking the output of the show standby command. In the output, you can see the active IP and the MAC address, the timers, the active router, and more, as shown earlier in the verification section.

There are several possible misconfigurations of HSRP, but these are what you need to pay attention to for your CCNA:

Different HSRP virtual IP addresses configured on the peers Console messages will notify you about this, of course, but if you configure it this way and the active router fails, the standby router takes over with a virtual IP address, which is different than the one used previously, and different than the one configured as the default-gateway address for end devices, so your hosts stop working, which defeats the purpose of a FHRP.

Different HSRP groups configured on the peers This misconfiguration leads to both peers becoming active, and you'll start receiving duplicate IP address warnings. It seems like this would be easy to troubleshoot, but the next issue has the same warnings.

Different HSRP versions configured on the peers or ports blocked HSRP comes in two versions, 1 and 2. If there is a version mismatch, both routers will become active and you'll again have duplicate IP address warnings.

In version 1, HSRP messages are sent to the multicast IP address 224.0.0.2 and UDP port 1985. HSRP version 2 uses the multicast IP address 224.0.0.102 and UDP port 1985. These IP addresses and ports need to be permitted in the inbound access lists. If the packets are blocked, the peers will not see each other and there will be no HSRP redundancy.

Summary

I started this chapter by discussing how to mitigate security threats at the access layer and then also discussed external authentication for our network devices for ease of management.

SNMP is an Application layer protocol that provides a message format for agents on a variety of devices to communicate to network management stations (NMSs). I discussed the basic information you need to use syslog and SNMP, that is, configuration and verification.

Last, I showed you how to integrate redundancy and load-balancing features into your network elegantly with the routers that you likely have already. HSRP is Cisco proprietary; acquiring some overpriced load-balancing device just isn't always necessary because knowing how to properly configure and use Hot Standby Router Protocol (HSRP) can often meet your needs instead.

Exam Essentials

Understand how to mitigate threats at the access layer. You can mitigate threats at the access layer by using port security, DHCP snooping, dynamic ARP inspection, and identity-based networking.

Understand TACACS+ and RADIUS. TACACS+ is Cisco proprietary, uses TCP, and can separate services. RADIUS is an open standard, uses UDP, and cannot separate services.

Remember the differences between SNMPv2 and SNMPv3. SNMPv2 uses UDP but can use TCP; however, v2 still sends data to the NMS station in clear text, exactly like SNMPv1, plus SNMPv2 implemented GETBULK and INFORM messages. SNMPv3 uses TCP and authenticates users, plus it can use ACLs in the SNMP strings to protect the NMS station from unauthorized use.

Understand FHRPs, especially HSRP.   The FHRPs are HSRP, VRRP, and GLBP, with HSRP and GLBP being Cisco proprietary.

Remember the HSRP virtual address.   The HSRP MAC address has only one variable piece in it. The first 24 bits still identify the vendor who manufactured the device (the organizationally unique identifier, or OUI). The next 16 bits in the address tell us that the MAC address is a well-known HSRP MAC address. Finally, the last 8 bits of the address are the hexadecimal representation of the HSRP group number.

Let me clarify all this with an example of what an HSRP MAC address would look like:

```
0000.0c07.ac0a
```

Written Lab 2

You can find the answers to this lab in Appendix A, "Answers to Written Labs."

1. Which operation used by SNMP is the same as a trap but adds an acknowledgment that a trap does not provide?

2. Which operation is used by SNMP to get information from the MIB to an SNMP agent?

3. Which operation used by the SNMP agent to send a triggered piece of information to the SNMP manager?

4. Which operation is used to get information to the MIB from an SNMP manager?

5. This operation is used to list information from successive MIB objects within a specified MIB.

6. You have different HSRP virtual IP addresses configured on peers. What is the result?

7. You configure HSRP on peers with different group numbers. What is the result?

8. You configure your HSRP peers with different versions (v1 and v2). What is the result?

9. What is the multicast and port number used for both HSRP versions 1 and 2?

10. The two most popular options for external AAA are what, and which one of them is Cisco proprietary?

Review Questions

The following questions are designed to test your understanding of this chapter's material. For more information on how to get additional questions, please see www.lammle.com/ccna.

You can find the answers to these questions in Appendix B, "Answers to Review Questions."

1. How can you efficiently restrict the read-only function of a requesting SNMP management station based on the IP address?

    A. Place an ACL on the logical control plane.

    B. Place an ACL on the line when configuring the RO community string.

    C. Place an ACL on the VTY line.

    D. Place an ACL on all router interfaces.

2. What is the default priority setting on an HSRP router?

    A. 25

    B. 50

    C. 100

    D. 125

3. Which of the following commands will enable AAA on a router?

    A. `aaa enable`

    B. `enable aaa`

    C. `new-model aaa`

    D. `aaa new-model`

4. Which of the following will mitigate access layer threats? (Choose two.)

    A. Port security

    B. Access lists

    C. Dynamic ARP inspection

    D. AAA

5. Which of the following is not true about DHCP snooping?

    A. DHCP snooping validates DHCP messages received from untrusted sources and filters out invalid messages.

    B. DHCP snooping builds and maintains the DHCP snooping binding database, which contains information about untrusted hosts with leased IP addresses.

    C. DHCP snooping rate-limits DHCP traffic from trusted and untrusted sources.

    D. DHCP snooping is a layer 2 security feature that acts like a firewall between hosts.

6. Which of the following are true about TACACS+? (Choose two.)

    A. TACACS+ is a Cisco proprietary security mechanism.

    B. TACACS+ uses UDP.

    C. TACACS+ combines authentication and authorization services as a single process—after users are authenticated, they are also authorized.

    D. TACACS+ offers multiprotocol support.

7. Which of the following is not true about RADIUS?

    A. RADIUS is an open standard protocol.

    B. RADIUS separates AAA services.

    C. RADIUS uses UDP.

    D. RADIUS encrypts only the password in the access-request packet from the client to the server. The remainder of the packet is unencrypted.

8. A switch is configured with the `snmp-server community Cisco RO` command running SNMPv2c. An NMS is trying to communicate to this router via SNMP, so what can be performed by the NMS? (Choose two.)

    A. The NMS can only graph obtained results.

    B. The NMS can graph obtained results and change the hostname of the router.

    C. The NMS can only change the hostname of the router.

    D. The NMS can use GETBULK and return many results.

9. What is true regarding any type of FHRP?

    A. The FHRP supplies hosts with routing information.

    B. The FHRP is a routing protocol.

    C. The FHRP provides default gateway redundancy.

    D. The FHRP is only standards-based.

10. Which of the following are HSRP states? (Choose two.)

    A. INIT

    B. Active

    C. Established

    D. Idle

11. Which command configures an interface to enable HSRP with the virtual router IP address 10.1.1.10?

    A. `standby 1 ip 10.1.1.10`

    B. `ip hsrp 1 standby 10.1.1.10`

    C. `hsrp 1 ip 10.1.1.10`

    D. `standby 1 hsrp ip 10.1.1.10`

12. Which command displays the status of all HSRP groups on a Cisco router or layer 3 switch?

   A. `show ip hsrp`

   B. `show hsrp`

   C. `show standby hsrp`

   D. `show standby`

   E. `show hsrp groups`

13. Two routers are part of a HSRP standby group and there is no priority configured on the routers for the HSRP group. Which of the statements below is correct?

   A. Both routers will be in the active state.

   B. Both routers will be in the standby state.

   C. Both routers will be in the listen state.

   D. One router will be active, the other standby.

14. Which of the following statement is true about the HSRP version 1 Hello packet?

   A. HSRP Hello packets are sent to multicast address 224.0.0.5.

   B. HSRP RP Hello packets are sent to multicast address 224.0.0.2 with TCP port 1985.

   C. HSRP Hello packets are sent to multicast address 224.0.0.2 with UDP port 1985.

   D. HSRP Hello packets are sent to multicast address 224.0.0.10 with UDP port 1986.

15. Routers HSRP1 and HSRP2 are in HSRP group 1. HSRP1 is the active router with a priority of 120 and HSRP2 has the default priority. When HSRP1 reboots, HSRP2 will become the active router. Once HSRP1 comes back up, which of the following statements will be true? (Choose two.)

   A. HSRP1 will become the active router.

   B. HSRP2 will stay the active router.

   C. HSRP1 will become the active router if it is also configured to preempt.

   D. Both routers will go into speak state.

16. What is the multicast address and port number used for HSRP version 2?

   A. 224.0.0.2, UDP port 1985

   B. 224.0.0.2, TCP port 1985

   C. 224.0.0.102, UDP port 1985

   D. 224.0.0.102, TCP port 1985

17. Which is true regarding SNMP? (Choose two.)

   A. SNMPv2c offers more security than SNMPv1.

   B. SNMPv3 uses TCP and introduced the GETBULK operation.

   C. SNMPv2c introduced the INFORM operation.

   D. SNMPv3 provides the best security of the three versions.

18. You want to configure RADIUS so your network devices have external authentication, but you also need to make sure you can fall back to local authentication. Which command will you use?

A. `aaa authentication login local group MyRadiusGroup`

B. `aaa authentication login group MyRadiusGroup fallback local`

C. `aaa authentication login default group MyRadiusGroup external local`

D. `aaa authentication login default group MyRadiusGroup local`

19. Which is true about DAI?

A. It must use TCP, BootP, and DHCP snooping in order to work.

B. DHCP snooping is required in order to build the MAC-to-IP bindings for DAI validation.

C. DAI is required in order to build the MAC-to-IP bindings, which protect against man-in-the-middle attacks.

D. DAI tracks ICMP-to-MAC bindings from DHCP.

20. The IEEE 802.1x standard allows you to implement identity-based networking on wired and wireless hosts by using client/server access control. There are three roles. Which of the following are these three roles?

A. Client

B. Forwarder

C. Security access control

D. Authenticator

E. Authentication server

Chapter

3

Enhanced IGRP

THE FOLLOWING ICND2 EXAM TOPICS ARE COVERED IN THIS CHAPTER:

✓ **2.0 Routing Technologies**

- 2.2 Compare and contrast distance vector and link-state routing protocols

- 2.3 Compare and contrast interior and exterior routing protocols

- 2.6 Configure, verify, and troubleshoot EIGRP for IPv4 (excluding authentication, filtering, manual summarization, redistribution, stub)

- 2.7 Configure, verify, and troubleshoot EIGRP for IPv6 (excluding authentication, filtering, manual summarization, redistribution, stub

Enhanced Interior Gateway Routing Protocol (EIGRP) is a Cisco protocol that runs on Cisco routers and on some Cisco switches. In this chapter, I'll cover the many features and functions of EIGRP, with an added focus on the unique way that it discovers, selects, and advertises routes.

EIGRP has a number of features that make it especially useful within large, complex networks. A real standout among these is its support of VLSM, which is crucial to its ultra-efficient scalability. EIGRP even includes benefits gained through other common protocols like OSPF and RIPv2, such as the ability to create route summaries at any location you choose.

I'll also cover key EIGRP configuration details and give you examples of each, as well as demonstrate the various commands required to verify that EIGRP is working properly. Finally, I'll wrap up the chapter by showing you how to configure and verify EIGRPv6. I promise that after you get through it, you'll agree that EIGRPv6 is truly the easiest part of this chapter!

To find up-to-the-minute updates for this chapter, please see www.lammle.com/ccna or the book's web page at www.sybex.com/go/ccna.

EIGRP Features and Operations

EIGRP is a classless, distance-vector protocol that uses the concept of an autonomous system to describe a set of contiguous routers that run the same routing protocol and share routing information; it also includes the subnet mask in its route updates. This is a very big deal because by advertising subnet information, this robust protocol enables us to use VLSM and permits summarization to be included within the design of EIGRP networks.

EIGRP is sometimes referred to as a *hybrid routing protocol* or an *advanced distance-vector protocol* because it has characteristics of both distance-vector and some link-state protocols. For example, EIGRP doesn't send link-state packets like OSPF does. Instead, it sends traditional distance-vector updates that include information about networks plus the cost of reaching them from the perspective of the advertising router.

EIGRP has link-state characteristics as well—it synchronizes network topology information between neighbors at startup and then sends specific updates only when topology changes occur (bounded updates). This particular feature is a huge advancement over RIP and is a big reason that EIGRP works so well in very large networks.

EIGRP has a default hop count of 100, with a maximum of 255, but don't let this confuse you because EIGRP doesn't rely on hop count as a metric like RIP does. In

EIGRP-speak, hop count refers to how many routers an EIGRP route update packet can go through before it will be discarded, which limits the size of the autonomous system (AS). So don't forget that this isn't how metrics are calculated with EIGRP!

There are a bunch of powerful features that make EIGRP a real standout from other protocols. Here's a list of some of the major ones:

- Support for IP and IPv6 (and some other useless routed protocols) via protocol-dependent modules
- Considered classless (same as RIPv2 and OSPF)
- Support for VLSM/CIDR
- Support for summaries and discontiguous networks
- Efficient neighbor discovery
- Communication via Reliable Transport Protocol (RTP)
- Best path selection via Diffusing Update Algorithm (DUAL)
- Reduced bandwidth usage with bounded updates
- No broadcasts

 Cisco refers to EIGRP as a distance-vector routing protocol but also as an advanced distance-vector or even a hybrid routing protocol.

Neighbor Discovery

Before EIGRP routers can exchange routes with each other, they must become neighbors, and there are three conditions that must be met before this can happen, as shown in Figure 3.1.

FIGURE 3.1 EIGRP neighbor discovery

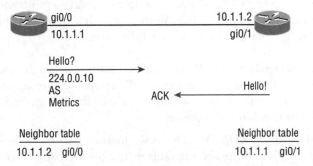

And these three things will be exchanged with directly connected neighbors:

- Hello or ACK received
- AS numbers match
- Identical metrics (K values)

Link-state protocols often use Hello messages to establish who their neighbors are because they usually don't send out periodic route updates but still need a way to help neighbors know when a new peer has arrived or an old one has gone down. And because Hellos are also used to maintain neighbor relationships, it follows that EIGRP routers must also continuously receive Hellos from their neighbors.

But EIGRP routers that belong to different ASs don't automatically share routing information and, therefore, don't become neighbors. This factor is really helpful operating in larger networks because it reduces the amount of route information propagated through a specific AS. But it also means that manual redistribution can sometimes be required between different ASs as a result. Because metrics play a big role in choosing between the five possible factors to be evaluated when choosing the best possible route, it's important that all EIGRP neighbors agree on how a specific route is chosen. This is vital because the calculations on one router depend upon the calculations of its neighbors.

Hellos between EIGRP routers are set to 5 seconds by default. Another timer that's related to the *hello timer* is the *hold timer*. The hold timer determines the amount of time a router is willing to wait to get a Hello from a neighbor before declaring it dead. Once a neighbor is declared dead, it's removed from the neighbor table and all routes that depended upon it are recalculated. Interestingly, the hold timer configuration doesn't determine how long a router waits before it declares neighbors dead; it establishes how long the router will tell others to wait before they can declare it dead. This means that the hold timers on neighboring routers don't need to match because they only tell the others how long to wait.

The only time EIGRP advertises its entire information is when it discovers a new neighbor and forms a relationship or adjacency with it by exchanging Hello packets. When this happens, both neighbors then advertise their complete information to one another. After each has learned its neighbor's routes, only changes to the routing table will be propagated.

During each EIGRP session running on a router, a neighbor table is created in which the router stores information about all routers known to be directly connected neighbors. Each neighboring router's IP address, hold time interval, *smooth round-trip timer (SRTT)*, and queue information are all kept in this table. It's an important reference used to establish that topology changes have occurred that neighboring routers need to know about.

To sum this all up, remember that EIGRP routers receive their neighbors' updates and store them in a local topology table that contains all known routes from all known neighbors and serves as the raw material from which the best routes are selected.

Let's define some terms before we move on:

Reported/advertised distance (RD/AD)   This is the metric of a remote network, as reported by a neighbor. It's also the routing table metric of the neighbor and is the same as the second number in parentheses as displayed in the topology table. The first number is the administrative distance, and I'll discuss more about these values in a minute. In Figure 3.2, routers SF and NY are both advertising the path to network 10.0.0.0 to the Corp router, but the cost through SF to network 10.0.0.0 is less than NY.

FIGURE 3.2   Advertised distance

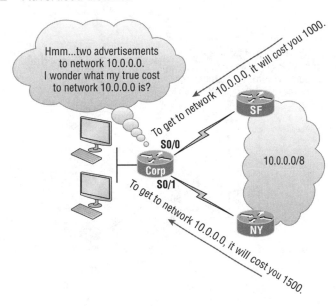

We're not done yet because the Corp router still needs to calculate its cost to each neighbor.

Feasible distance (FD)   This is the best metric among all paths to a remote network, including the metric to the neighbor that's advertising the remote network. The route with the lowest FD is the route that you'll find in the routing table because it's considered the best path. The metric of a feasible distance is calculated using the metric reported by the neighbor that's referred to as the reported or advertised distance plus the metric to the neighbor reporting the route. In Figure 3.3, the Corp router will have the path through router SF to network 10.0.0.0 in the routing table since it's the lowest feasible distance. It's the lowest true cost from end to end.

Take a look at an EIGRP route that's been injected into a routing table and find the FD listed in the entry.

```
D    10.0.0.0/8 [90/2195456] via 172.16.10.2, 00:27:06,Serial0/0
```

First, the D means Dual, and it's an EIGRP injected route and the route used by EIGRP to forward traffic to the 10.0.0.0 network via its neighbor, 172.16.10.2. But that's not what I want to focus on right now. See the [90/2195456] entry in the line? The first number (90) is the administrative distance (AD), which is not to be confused with advertised distance (AD), which is why a lot of people call it the reported distance! The second number, is the feasible distance (FD), or the entire cost for this router to get to network 10.0.0.0. To sum this up, the neighbor router sends a reported, or advertised, distance (RD/AD) for network 10.0.0.0, and EIGRP calculates the cost to get to that neighbor and then adds those two numbers together to get the FD, or total cost.

FIGURE 3.3   Feasible distance

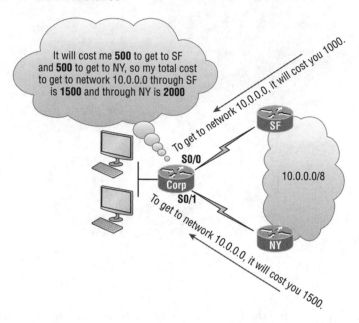

Neighbor table   Each router keeps state information about adjacent neighbors. When a newly discovered neighbor is found, its address and interface are recorded and the information is held in the neighbor table, stored in RAM. Sequence numbers are used to match acknowledgments with update packets. The last sequence number received from the neighbor is recorded so that out-of-order packets can be detected. We'll get into this more, later in the chapter, when we look at the neighbor table and find out how it's useful for troubleshooting links between neighbor routers.

Topology table   The topology table is populated by the neighbor table and the Diffusing Update Algorithm (DUAL) calculates the best loop-free path to each remote network. It contains all destinations advertised by neighboring routers, holding each destination address and a list of neighbors that have advertised the destination. For each neighbor, the advertised metric (distance), which comes only from the neighbor's routing table, is recorded, as well as the FD. The best path to each remote network is copied and placed in the routing table and then IP will use this route to forward traffic to the remote network. The path copied to the routing table is called a successor router—think "successful" to help you remember. The path with a good, but less desirable, cost will be entered in the topology table as a backup link and called the feasible successor. Let's talk more about these terms now.

The neighbor and topology tables are stored in RAM and maintained through the use of Hello and update packets. While the routing table is also stored in RAM, the information stored in the routing table is gathered only from the topology table.

Feasible successor (FS)   So a feasible successor is basically an entry in the topology table that represents a path that's inferior to the successor route(s). An FS is defined as a path whose advertised distance is less than the feasible distance of the current successor and considered a backup route. EIGRP will keep up to 32 feasible successors in the topology table in 15.0 code but only up to 16 in previous IOS versions, which is still a lot! Only the path with the best metric—the successor—is copied and placed in the routing table. The show ip eigrp topology command will display all the EIGRP feasible successor routes known to the router.

A feasible successor is a backup route and is stored in the topology table. A successor route is stored in the topology table and is copied and placed in the routing table.

Successor   A successor route—again, think "successful"—is the best route to a remote network. A successor route is the lowest cost to a destination and stored in the topology table along with everything else. However, this particular best route is copied and placed in the routing table so IP can use it to get to the remote network. The successor route is backed up by a feasible successor route, which is also stored in the topology table, if there's one available. The routing table contains only successor routes; the topology table contains successor and feasible successor routes.

Figure 3.4 illustrates that the SF and NY routers each have subnets of the 10.0.0.0 network and the Corp router has two paths to get to this network.

FIGURE 3.4   The tables used by EIGRP

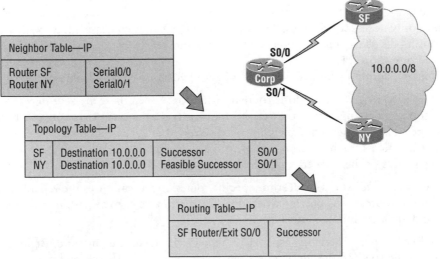

As shown in Figure 3.4, there are two paths to network 10.0.0.0 that can be used by the Corp router. EIGRP picks the best path and places it in the routing table, but if both links have equal-cost paths, EIGRP would load-balance between them—up to four links, by default. By using the successor, and having feasible successors in the topology table as backup links, the network can converge instantly and updates to any neighbor make up the only traffic sent from EIGRP—very clean!

Reliable Transport Protocol (RTP)

EIGRP depends on a proprietary protocol, called *Reliable Transport Protocol (RTP)*, to manage the communication of messages between EIGRP-speaking routers. As the name suggests, reliability is a key concern of this protocol, so Cisco designed this mechanism, which leverages multicasts and unicasts, to ensure that updates are delivered quickly and that data reception is tracked accurately.

But how does this really work? Well, when EIGRP sends multicast traffic, it uses the Class D address 224.0.0.10, and each EIGRP router knows who its neighbors are. For each multicast it sends out, a list is built and maintained that includes all the neighbors who have replied. If a router doesn't get a reply from a neighbor via the multicast, EIGRP will then try using unicasts to resend the same data. If there's no reply from a neighbor after 16 unicast attempts, that neighbor will then be declared dead. This process is often referred to as *reliable multicast*.

Routers keep track of the information they send by assigning a sequence number to each packet that enables them to identify old, redundant information and data that's out of sequence. You'll get to actually see this information in the neighbor table coming up when we get into configuring EIGRP.

Remember, EIGRP is all about topology changes and updates, making it the quiet, performance-optimizing protocol it is. Its ability to synchronize routing databases at startup time, while maintaining the consistency of databases over time, is achieved quietly by communicating only necessary changes. The downside here is that you can end up with a corrupted routing database if any packets have been permanently lost or if packets have been mishandled out of order!

Here's a description of the five different types of packets used by EIGRP:

Update   An *Update packet* contains route information. When these are sent in response to metric or topology changes, they use reliable multicasts. In the event that only one router needs an update, like when a new neighbor is discovered, it's sent via unicasts. Keep in mind that the unicast method still requires an acknowledgment, so updates are always reliable regardless of their underlying delivery mechanism.

Query   A *Query packet* is a request for specific routes and always uses the reliable multicast method. Routers send queries when they realize they've lost the path to a particular network and are searching for alternatives.

Reply   A *Reply packet* is sent in response to a query via the unicast method. Replies either include a specific route to the queried destination or declare that there's no known route.

Hello   A *Hello packet* is used to discover EIGRP neighbors and is sent via unreliable multicast, meaning it doesn't require an acknowledgment.

ACK   An *ACK packet* is sent in response to an update and is always unicast. ACKs are never sent reliably because this would require another ACK sent for acknowledgment, which would just create a ton of useless traffic!

It's helpful to think of all these different packet types like envelopes. They're really just types of containers that EIGRP routers use to communicate with their neighbors. What's really interesting is the actual content envelopes these communications and the procedures that guide their conversations, and that's what we'll be exploring next!

Diffusing Update Algorithm (DUAL)

I mentioned that EIGRP uses *Diffusing Update Algorithm (DUAL)* for selecting and maintaining the best path to each remote network. DUAL allows EIGRP to carry out these vital tasks:

- Figure out a backup route if there's one available.
- Support variable length subnet masks (VLSMs).
- Perform dynamic route recoveries.
- Query neighbors for unknown alternate routes.
- Send out queries for an alternate route.

Quite an impressive list, but what really makes DUAL so great is that it enables EIGRP to converge amazingly fast! The key to the speed is twofold: First, EIGRP routers maintain a copy of all of their neighbors' routes to refer to for calculating their own cost to each remote network. So if the best path goes down, all it often takes to find another one is a quick scan of the topology table looking for a feasible successor. Second, if that quick table survey doesn't work out, EIGRP routers immediately ask their neighbors for help finding the best path. It's exactly this, ahem, DUAL strategy of reliance upon, and the leveraging of, other routers' information that accounts for the algorithm's "diffusing" character. Unlike other routing protocols where the change is propagated through the entire network, EIGRP bounded updates are propagated only as far as needed.

Three critical conditions must be met for DUAL to work properly:

- Neighbors are discovered or noted as dead within a finite time.
- All transmitted messages are received correctly.
- All changes and messages are processed in the order in which they're detected.

As you already know, the Hello protocol ensures the rapid detection of new or dead neighbors, and RTP provides a reliable method of conveying and sequencing messages. Based upon this solid foundation, DUAL can then select and maintain information about the best paths. Let's check further into the process of route discovery and maintenance next.

Route Discovery and Maintenance

The hybrid nature of EIGRP is fully revealed in its approach to route discovery and maintenance. Like many link-state protocols, EIGRP supports the concept of neighbors that are formally discovered via a Hello process and whose state is monitored thereafter. And like many distance-vector protocols, EIGRP uses the routing-by-rumor approach, which implies that many routers within an AS never actually hear about a route update firsthand. Instead, these devices rely on "network gossip" to hear about neighbors and their respective status via another router that may have also gotten the info from yet another router and so on.

Given all of the information that EIGRP routers have to collect, it follows that they must have a place to store it, and they do this in the tables I referred to earlier in this chapter. As you know, EIGRP doesn't depend on just one table—it actually uses three of them to store important information about its environment:

Neighbor table   Contains information about the specific routers with whom neighbor relationships have been formed. It also displays information about the Hello transmit interval and queue counts for unaccounted Hello acknowledgment.

Topology table   Stores the route advertisements received from each neighbor. All routes in the AS are stored in the topology table, both successors and feasible successors.

Route table   Stores the routes that are currently in use to make local routing decisions. Anything in the routing table is considered a successor route.

We'll explore more of EIGRP's features in greater detail soon, beginning with a look at the metrics associated with particular routes. After that, I'll cover the decision-making process that's used to select the best routes, and then we'll review the procedures followed when routes change.

Configuring EIGRP

I know what you're thinking! "We're going to jump in to configuring EIGRP already when I've heard how complex it is?" No worries here—what I'm about to show is basic, and I know you won't have a problem with it at all! We're going to start with the easy part of EIGRP, and by configuring it on our little internetwork, you'll learn a lot more this way than you would if I just continued explaining more at this point. After we've completed the initial configuration, we'll fine-tune it and have fun experimenting with it throughout this chapter!

Okay, there are two modes for entering EIGRP commands: router configuration mode and interface configuration mode. In router configuration mode, we'll enable the protocol, determine which networks will run EIGRP, and set global factors. When in interface configuration mode, we'll customize summaries and bandwidth.

To initiate an EIGRP session on a router, I'll use the `router eigrp` command followed by our network's AS number. After that, we'll enter the specific numbers of the networks that we want to connect to the router using the `network` command followed by the network number. This is pretty straightforward stuff—if you can configure RIP, then you can configure EIGRP!

Just so you know, we'll use the same network I used in the previous CCENT routing chapters, but I'm going to connect more networks so we can look deeper into EIGRP. With that, I'm going to enable EIGRP for autonomous system 20 on our Corp router connected to four networks.

Figure 3.5 shows the network we'll be configuring throughout this chapter and the next chapter. Here's the Corp configuration:

FIGURE 3.5   Configuring our little internetwork with EIGRP

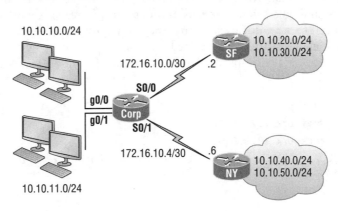

```
Corp#config t
Corp(config)#router eigrp 20
Corp(config-router)#network 172.16.0.0
Corp(config-router)#network 10.0.0.0
```

Remember, just as we would when configuring RIP, we need to use the classful network address, which is all subnet and host bits turned off. This is another thing that makes EIGRP so great: it has the complexity of a link-state protocol running in the background and the same easy configuration process used for RIP!

 Understand that the AS number is irrelevant—that is, as long as all routers use the same number! You can use any number from 1 to 65,535.

But wait, the EIGRP configuration can't be that easy, can it? A few simple EIGRP commands and my network just works? Well, it can be and usually is, but not always. Remember the wildcards you learned about in your access list configurations in your preparation for the Cisco exam? Let's say, for example, that we wanted to advertise all the directly connected networks with EIGRP off the Corp router. By using the command network 10.0.0.0, we can effectively advertise to all subnets within that classful network; however, take a look at this configuration now:

```
Corp#config t
Corp(config)#router eigrp 20
Corp(config-router)#network 10.10.11.0 0.0.0.255
Corp(config-router)#network 172.16.10.0 0.0.0.3
Corp(config-router)#network 172.16.10.4 0.0.0.3
```

This configuration should look pretty familiar to you because by now you should have a solid understanding of how wildcards are configured. This configuration will advertise the network connected to g0/1 on the Corp router as well as the two WAN links. Still, all we accomplished with this configuration was to stop the g0/0 interface from being placed into the EIGRP process, and unless you have tens of thousands of networks worldwide, then there is really no need to use wildcards because they don't provide any other administrative purpose other than what I've already described.

Now let's take a look at the simple configuration needed for the SF and NY routers in our internetwork:

```
SF(config)#router eigrp 20
SF(config-router)#network 172.16.0.0
SF(config-router)#network 10.0.0.0
000060:&#x00025;DUAL-5-NBRCHANGE:IP-EIGRP(0) 20:Neighbor 172.16.10.1
(Serial0/0/0) is up:
new adjacency


NY(config)#router eigrp 20
NY(config-router)#network 172.16.0.0
NY(config-router)#network 10.0.0.0
*Jun 26 02:41:36:%DUAL-5-NBRCHANGE:IP-EIGRP(0) 20:Neighbor 172.16.10.5
(Serial0/0/1) is up: new adjacency
```

Nice and easy—or is it? We can see that the SF and NY router created an adjacency to the Corp router, but are they actually sharing routing information? To find out, let's take a look at the number that I pointed out as the autonomous system (AS) number in the configuration.

EIGRP uses ASs to identify the group of routers that will share route information. Only routers that have the same AS share routes. The range of values we can use to create an AS with EIGRP is 1–65535:

```
Corp(config)#router eigrp ?
  <1-65535>  Autonomous System
  WORD       EIGRP Virtual-Instance Name
Corp(config)#router eigrp 20
```

Notice that I could have used any number from 1 to 65,535, but I chose to use 20 because it just felt good at the time. As long as all routers use the same number, they'll create an adjacency. Okay, now the AS makes sense, but it looks like I can type a word in the place of the AS number, and I can! Let's take a look at the configuration:

```
Corp(config)#router eigrp Todd
Corp(config-router)#address-family ipv4 autonomous-system 20
Corp(config-router-af)#network 10.0.0.0
Corp(config-router-af)#network 172.16.0.0
```

What I just showed you is not part of the Cisco exam objectives, but it's also not really necessary for any IPv4 routing configuration in your network. The previous configuration examples I've gone through so far in this chapter covers the objectives and work just fine, but I included this last configuration example because it's now an option in IOS 15.0 code.

VLSM Support and Summarization

Being one of the more sophisticated classless routing protocols, EIGRP supports using variable length subnet masks. This is good because it allows us to conserve address space by using subnet masks that map to specific host requirements in a much better way. Being able to use 30-bit subnet masks for the point-to-point networks that I configured in our internetwork is a great example. Plus, because the subnet mask is propagated with every route update, EIGRP also supports the use of discontiguous subnets, giving us greater administrative flexibility when designing a network IP address scheme. Another versatile feature is that EIGRP allows us to use and place route summaries at strategically optimal locations throughout the EIGRP network to reduce the size of the routing table.

Keep in mind that EIGRP automatically summarizes networks at their classful boundaries and supports the manual creation of summaries at any and all EIGRP routers. This is usually a good thing, but by checking out the routing table in the Corp router, you can see the possible complications that auto-summarization can cause:

```
Corp#sh ip route
[output cut]
     172.16.0.0/16 is variably subnetted, 3 subnets, 2 masks
C       172.16.10.4/30 is directly connected, Serial0/1
C       172.16.10.0/30 is directly connected, Serial0/0
D       172.16.0.0/16 is a summary, 00:01:37, Null0
     10.0.0.0/8 is variably subnetted, 3 subnets, 2 masks
C       10.10.10.0/24 is directly connected, GigabitEthernet0/0
D       10.0.0.0/8 is a summary, 00:01:19, Null0
C       10.10.11.0/24 is directly connected, GigabitEthernet0/1
```

Now this just doesn't look so good—both 172.16.0.0 and 10.0.0.0/8 are being advertised as summary routes injected by EIGRP, but we have multiple subnets in the 10.0.0.0/8 classful network address, so how would the Corp router know how to route to a specific network like 10.10.20.0? The answer is, it wouldn't. Let's see why in Figure 3.6.

The networks we're using make up what is considered a discontinuous network because we have the 10.0.0.0/8 network subnetted across a different class of address, the 172.16.0.0 network, with 10.0.0.0/8 subnets on both sides of the WAN links.

You can see that the SF and NY routers will both create an automatic summary of 10.0.0.0/8 and then inject it into their routing tables. This is a common problem, and an important one that Cisco really wants you to understand (by including it in the objectives)! With this type of topology, disabling automatic summarization is definitely the better option. Actually, it's the only option if we want this network to work.

FIGURE 3.6 Discontiguous networks

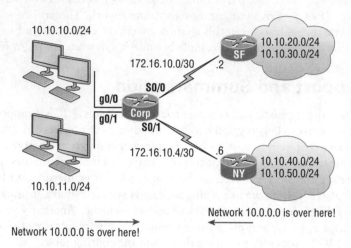

Let's take a look at the routing tables on the NY and SF routers to find out what they're seeing:

```
SF>sh ip route
[output cut]
     172.16.0.0/16 is variably subnetted, 3 subnets, 3 masks
C        172.16.10.0/30 is directly connected, Serial0/0/0
D        172.16.10.0/24 [90/2681856] via 172.16.10.1, 00:54:58, Serial0/0/0
D        172.16.0.0/16 is a summary, 00:55:12, Null0
     10.0.0.0/8 is variably subnetted, 3 subnets, 2 masks
D        10.0.0.0/8 is a summary, 00:54:58, Null0
C        10.10.20.0/24 is directly connected, FastEthernet0/0
C        10.10.30.0/24 is directly connected, Loopback0
SF>


NY>sh ip route
[output cut]
     172.16.0.0/16 is variably subnetted, 2 subnets, 2 masks
C        172.16.10.4/30 is directly connected, Serial0/0/1
D        172.16.0.0/16 is a summary, 00:55:56, Null0
     10.0.0.0/8 is variably subnetted, 3 subnets, 2 masks
D        10.0.0.0/8 is a summary, 00:55:26, Null0
C        10.10.40.0/24 is directly connected, FastEthernet0/0
C        10.10.50.0/24 is directly connected, Loopback0
NY>ping 10.10.10.1
Type escape sequence to abort.
```

```
Sending 5, 100-byte ICMP Echos to 10.10.10.1, timeout is 2 seconds:
.....
Success rate is 0 percent (0/5)
NY>
```

The confirmed answer is that our network isn't working because we're discontiguous and our classful boundaries are auto-summarizing. We can see that EIGRP is injecting summary routes into both the SF and NY routing tables.

We need to advertise our subnets in order to make this work, and here's how we make that happen, starting with the Corp router:

```
Corp#config t
Corp(config)#router eigrp 20
Corp(config-router)#no auto-summary
Corp(config-router)#
*Feb 25 18:29:30%DUAL-5-NBRCHANGE:IP-EIGRP(0) 20:Neighbor 172.16.10.6
(Serial0/1)
 is resync: summary configured
*Feb 25 18:29:30%DUAL-5-NBRCHANGE:IP-EIGRP(0) 20:Neighbor 172.16.10.2
(Serial0/0)
 is resync: summary configured
Corp(config-router)#
```

Okay—our network still isn't working because the other routers are still sending a summary. So let's configure the SF and NY routers to advertise subnets:

```
SF#config t
SF(config)#router eigrp 20
SF(config-router)#no auto-summary
SF(config-router)#
000090:%DUAL-5-NBRCHANGE:IP-EIGRP(0) 20:Neighbor 172.16.10.1 (Serial0/0/0) is
resync: summary configured


NY#config t
NY(config)#router eigrp 20
NY(config-router)#no auto-summary
NY(config-router)#
*Jun 26 21:31:08%DUAL-5-NBRCHANGE:IP-EIGRP(0) 20:Neighbor 172.16.10.5
(Serial0/0/1)
is resync: summary configured
```

Let's take a look at the Corp router's output now:

```
Corp(config-router)#do show ip route
[output cut]
```

```
        172.16.0.0/30 is subnetted, 2 subnets
C       172.16.10.4 is directly connected, Serial0/1
C       172.16.10.0 is directly connected, Serial0/0
        10.0.0.0/24 is subnetted, 6 subnets
C       10.10.10.0 is directly connected, GigabitEthernet0/0
C       10.10.11.0 is directly connected, GigabitEthernet0/1
D       10.10.20.0 [90/3200000] via 172.16.10.2, 00:00:27, Serial0/0
D       10.10.30.0 [90/3200000] via 172.16.10.2, 00:00:27, Serial0/0
D       10.10.40.0 [90/2297856] via 172.16.10.6, 00:00:29, Serial0/1
D       10.10.50.0 [90/2297856] via 172.16.10.6, 00:00:30, Serial0/1
Corp# ping 10.10.20.1

Type escape sequence to abort.
Sending 5, 100-byte ICMP Echos to 10.10.20.1, timeout is 2 seconds:
!!!!!
Success rate is 100 percent (5/5), round-trip min/avg/max = 1/2/4 ms
```

Wow, what a difference compared to the previous routing table output! We can see all the subnets now. It would be hard to justify using auto-summarization today. If you want to summarize, it should definitely be done manually. Always typing in no auto-summary under RIPv2 and EIGRP is common practice today.

The new 15.x code auto-summarization feature is disabled by default, as it should be. But don't think that discontiguous networks and disabling auto-summary are no longer topics in the Cisco exam objectives, because they most certainly are! When troubleshooting EIGRP on the exam, verify the code version, and if it is 15.x code, then you can assume that auto-summary is not a problem.

Controlling EIGRP Traffic

But what if you need to stop EIGRP from working on a specific interface? Maybe it's a connection to your ISP, or where we didn't want to have the g0/0 interface be part of the EIGRP process as in our earlier example. All you need to do is to flag the interface as passive, and to do this from an EIGRP session, just use this command:

```
passive-interface interface-type interface-number
```

This works because the interface-type portion defines the type of interface and the interface-number portion defines the number of the interface. The following command makes interface serial 0/0 into a passive interface:

```
Corp(config)#router eigrp 20
Corp(config-router)#passive-interface g0/0
```

What we've accomplished here is to prevent this interface from sending or reading received Hello packets so that it will no longer form adjacencies or send or receive route information. But this still won't stop EIGRP from advertising the subnet of this interface out all other interfaces without using wildcards. This really illustrates the reason you must understand why and when to use wildcards as well as what the `passive-interface` command does. This knowledge really helps you to make an informed decision on which command you need to use to meet your specific business requirements!

 The impact of the `passive-interface` command depends upon the routing protocol under which the command is issued. For example, on an interface running RIP, the `passive-interface` command will prohibit sending route updates but will permit receiving them. An RIP router with a passive interface will still learn about the networks advertised by other routers. This is different from EIGRP, where an interface configured with the `passive-interface` command will neither send nor read received Hellos.

Typically, EIGRP neighbors use multicast to exchange routing updates. You can change this by specifically telling the router about a particular neighbor, which will ensure that unicast packets will only be used for the routing updates with that specific neighbor. To take advantage of this feature, apply the `neighbor` command and execute it under the EIGRP process.

I'm going to configure the Corp router with information about routers SF and NY:

```
Corp(config)#router eigrp 20
Corp(config-router)#neighbor 172.16.10.2
Corp(config-router)#neighbor 172.16.10.6
```

Understand that you don't need to use the preceding commands to create neighbor relationships, but they're available if you need them.

EIGRP Metrics

Unlike many other protocols that use a single element to compare routes and select the best possible path, EIGRP uses a combination of these four factors:

- *Bandwidth*
- *Delay*
- *Load*
- *Reliability*

It's worth noting that there's a fifth element, *maximum transmission unit (MTU)*, which has never been used in EIGRP metrics calculations though it's still a required parameter in some EIGRP-related commands—especially those involving redistribution. The value of the MTU element represents the smallest MTU value encountered along the path to the destination network.

Also good to know is that there's a mathematical formula that combines the four main elements to create a single value representing just how good a given route actually is. The higher the metric associated with it, the less desirable the route. Here's that formula:

$$metric = [K_1 \times Bandwidth + (K_2 \times Bandwidth)/(256 - Load) + K_3 \times Delay] \times [K_5/(Reliability + K_4)]$$

The formula's components break down like this:

- By default, $K_1 = 1$, $K_2 = 0$, $K_3 = 1$, $K_4 = 0$, $K_5 = 0$.
- *Delay* equals the sum of all the delays of the links along the path.
  - *Delay* = [Delay in 10s of microseconds] × 256.
- *Bandwidth* is the lowest bandwidth of the links along the path.
  - *Bandwidth* = [10000000 / (bandwidth in Kbps)] × 256.
- By default, *metric* = lowest bandwidth along path + sum of all delays along path.

If necessary, you can adjust the constant K values on a per-interface basis, but I would recommend that you only do this under the direction of the Cisco Technical Assistance Center (TAC). Metrics are tuned to change the manner in which routes are calculated. The K values can be seen with a show ip protocols output:

```
Corp#sh ip protocols
*** IP Routing is NSF aware ***

Routing Protocol is "eigrp 1"
  Outgoing update filter list for all interfaces is not set
  Incoming update filter list for all interfaces is not set
  Default networks flagged in outgoing updates
  Default networks accepted from incoming updates
  EIGRP-IPv4 Protocol for AS(1)
    Metric weight K1=1, K2=0, K3=1, K4=0, K5=0
```

Notice that that the K1 and K3 values are enabled by default—for example, K1 = 1. Table 3.1 shows the relationship between each constant and the metric it affects.

Each constant is used to assign a weight to a specific variable, meaning that when the metric is calculated, the algorithm will assign a greater importance to the specified metric. This is very cool because it means that by assigning a weight, you get to specify the factor that's most important to you. For example, if bandwidth is your priority, you would assign K1 to weight it accordingly, but if delay is totally unacceptable, then K3 would be assigned a greater weight. A word of caution though: Always remember that any changes to the default values could result in instability and convergence problems, particularly if delay or reliability values are constantly changing! But if you're looking for something to do on a rainy Saturday, it's an interesting experiment to pass some time and gain some nice networking insight!

TABLE 3.1 Metric association of K values

Constant	Metric
K1	Bandwidth (B_e)
K2	Load (utilization on path)
K3	Delay (D_c)
K4	Reliability (r)
K5	MTU

Maximum Paths and Hop Count

By default, EIGRP can provide equal-cost load balancing across up to 4 links. RIP and OSPF do this too. But you can have EIGRP actually load-balance across up to 32 links with 15.0 code (equal or unequal) by using the following command:

```
Corp(config)#router eigrp 10
Corp(config-router)#maximum-paths ?
  <1-32>  Number of paths
```

As I mentioned, pre–15.0 code routers allowed up to 16 paths to remote networks, which is still a lot!

EIGRP has a default maximum hop count of 100 for route update packets, but it can be set up to 255. Chances are you wouldn't want to ever change this, but if you did, here is how you would do it:

```
Corp(config)#router eigrp 10
Corp(config-router)#metric maximum-hops ?
  <1-255>  Hop count
```

As you can see from this router output, EIGRP can be set to a maximum of 255 hops. Even though it doesn't use hop count in the path metric calculation, it still uses the maximum hop count to limit the scope of the AS.

Route Selection

Now that you've got a good idea how EIGRP works and also how easy it actually is to configure, it's probably clear that determining the best path simply comes down to seeing which one gets awarded the lowest metric. But it's not the winning path that really sets EIGRP apart from other protocols. You know that EIGRP stores route information from its neighbors in its topology table and that as long as a given neighbor remains alive, it will rarely throw out anything it has learned from that neighbor. This makes EIGRP able to flag the best routes in its topology table for positioning in its local routing table, enabling it to flag the next-best routes as alternatives if the best route goes down.

In Figure 3.7, you can see that I added another Fast Ethernet link between the SF and NY routers. This will give us a great opportunity to play with the topology and routing tables!

FIGURE 3.7   EIGRP route selection process

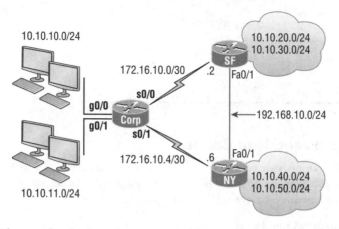

First, let's take another look at the routing table on the Corp router before I bring up the new interfaces:

```
172.16.0.0/30 is subnetted, 2 subnets
C        172.16.10.4 is directly connected, Serial0/1
C        172.16.10.0 is directly connected, Serial0/0
     10.0.0.0/24 is subnetted, 6 subnets
C        10.10.10.0 is directly connected, GigabitEthernet0/0
C        10.10.11.0 is directly connected, GigabitEthernet0/1
D        10.10.20.0 [90/3200000] via 172.16.10.2, 00:00:27, Serial0/0
D        10.10.30.0 [90/3200000] via 172.16.10.2, 00:00:27, Serial0/0
D        10.10.40.0 [90/2297856] via 172.16.10.6, 00:00:29, Serial0/1
D        10.10.50.0 [90/2297856] via 172.16.10.6, 00:00:30, Serial0/1
```

We can see the three directly connected interfaces as well as the other four networks injected into the routing table by EIGRP. Now I'll add the network 192.168.10.0/24 between the SF and NY routers, then enable the interfaces.

And let's check out the routing table of the Corp router now that I've configured that link:

```
D    192.168.10.0/24 [90/2172416] via 172.16.10.6, 00:04:27, Serial0/1
 172.16.0.0/30 is subnetted, 2 subnets
C        172.16.10.4 is directly connected, Serial0/1
C        172.16.10.0 is directly connected, Serial0/0
     10.0.0.0/24 is subnetted, 6 subnets
```

```
C        10.10.10.0 is directly connected, GigabitEthernet0/0
C        10.10.11.0 is directly connected, GigabitEthernet0/1
D        10.10.20.0 [90/3200000] via 172.16.10.2, 00:00:27, Serial0/0
D        10.10.30.0 [90/3200000] via 172.16.10.2, 00:00:27, Serial0/0
D        10.10.40.0 [90/2297856] via 172.16.10.6, 00:00:29, Serial0/1
D        10.10.50.0 [90/2297856] via 172.16.10.6, 00:00:30, Serial0/1
```

Okay—that's weird. The only thing different I see is one path to the 192.168.10.0/24 network listed first. Glad it is there, which means that we can route to that network. Notice that we can reach the network from the Serial0/1 interface, but what happened to my link to the SF router—shouldn't we have an advertisement from that router and be load-balancing? Let's take a look the topology table to find out what's going on:

```
Corp#sh ip eigrp topology
IP-EIGRP Topology Table for AS(20)/ID(10.10.11.1)

Codes: P - Passive, A - Active, U - Update, Q - Query, R - Reply,
       r - reply Status, s - sia Status

P 10.10.10.0/24, 1 successors, FD is 128256
        via Connected, GigbitEthernet0/0
P 10.10.11.0/24, 1 successors, FD is 128256
        via Connected, GigbitEthernet0/1
P 10.10.20.0/24, 1 successors, FD is 2300416
        via 172.16.10.6 (2300416/156160), Serial0/1
        via 172.16.10.2 (3200000/128256), Serial0/0
P 10.10.30.0/24, 1 successors, FD is 2300416
        via 172.16.10.6 (2300416/156160), Serial0/1
        via 172.16.10.2 (3200000/128256), Serial0/0
P 10.10.40.0/24, 1 successors, FD is 2297856
        via 172.16.10.6 (2297856/128256), Serial0/1
        via 172.16.10.2 (3202560/156160), Serial0/0
P 10.10.50.0/24, 1 successors, FD is 2297856
        via 172.16.10.6 (2297856/128256), Serial0/1
        via 172.16.10.2 (3202560/156160), Serial0/0
P 192.168.10.0/24, 1 successors, FD is 2172416
        via 172.16.10.6 (2172416/28160), Serial0/1
        via 172.16.10.2 (3074560/28160), Serial0/0
P 172.16.10.4/30, 1 successors, FD is 2169856
        via Connected, Serial0/1
P 172.16.10.0/30, 1 successors, FD is 3072000
        via Connected, Serial0/0
```

Okay, we can see there are two paths to the 192.168.10.0/24 network, but it's using the next hop of 172.16.10.6 (NY) because the feasible distance (FD) is less! The advertised distance from both routers is 28160, but the cost to get to each router via the WAN links is not the same. This means the FD is not the same, meaning we're not load-balancing by default.

Both WAN links are a T1, so this should have load-balanced by default, but EIGRP has determined that it costs more to go through SF than through NY. Since EIGRP uses bandwidth and delay of the line to determine the best path, we can use the show interfaces command to verify our stats like this:

```
Corp#sh int s0/0
Serial0/0 is up, line protocol is up
  Hardware is PowerQUICC Serial
  Description: <<Connection to CR1>>
  Internet address is 172.16.10.1/30
  MTU 1500 bytes, BW 1000 Kbit, DLY 20000 usec,
     reliability 255/255, txload 1/255, rxload 1/255
  Encapsulation HDLC, loopback not set Keepalive set (10 sec)

Corp#sh int s0/1
Serial0/1 is up, line protocol is up
  Hardware is PowerQUICC Serial
  Internet address is 172.16.10.5/30
  MTU 1500 bytes, BW 1544 Kbit, DLY 20000 usec,
     reliability 255/255, txload 1/255, rxload 1/255
  Encapsulation HDLC, loopback not set Keepalive set (10 sec)
```

I highlighted the statistics that EIGRP uses to determine the metrics to a next-hop router: MTU, bandwidth, delay, reliability, and load, with bandwidth and delay enabled by default. We can see that the bandwidth on the Serial0/0 interface is set to 1000 Kbit, which is not the default bandwidth. Serial0/1 is set to the default bandwidth of 1544 Kbit.

Let's set the bandwidth back to the default on the s0/0 interface and we should start load-balancing to the 192.168.10.0 network. I'll just use the no bandwidth command, which will set it back to its default of 1544 Mbps:

```
Corp#config t
Corp(config)#int s0/0
Corp(config-if)#no bandwidth
Corp(config-if)#^Z
```

Now let's take a look at the topology table and see if we're equal.

```
Corp#sh ip eigrp topo | section 192.168.10.0
P 192.168.10.0/24, 2 successors, FD is 2172416
        via 172.16.10.2 (2172416/28160), Serial0/0
        via 172.16.10.6 (2172416/28160), Serial0/1
```

Since the topology tables can get really huge in most networks, the show ip eigrp topology | section *network* command comes in handy because it allows us to see information about the network we want to look into in a couple of lines.

Let's use the show ip route *network* command and check out what is going on there:

```
Corp#sh ip route 192.168.10.0
Routing entry for 192.168.10.0/24
  Known via "eigrp 20", distance 90, metric 2172416, type internal
  Redistributing via eigrp 20
  Last update from 172.16.10.2 on Serial0/0, 00:05:18 ago
  Routing Descriptor Blocks:
  * 172.16.10.6, from 172.16.10.6, 00:05:18 ago, via Serial0/1
      Route metric is 2172416, traffic share count is 1
      Total delay is 20100 microseconds, minimum bandwidth is 1544 Kbit
      Reliability 255/255, minimum MTU 1500 bytes
      Loading 1/255, Hops 1
    172.16.10.2, from 172.16.10.2, 00:05:18 ago, via Serial0/0
      Route metric is 2172416, traffic share count is 1
      Total delay is 20100 microseconds, minimum bandwidth is 1544 Kbit
      Reliability 255/255, minimum MTU 1500 bytes
      Loading 1/255, Hops 1
```

Lots of detail about our routes to the 192.168.10.0 network! The Corp route has two equal-cost links to the 192.168.10.0 network. And to reveal load balancing even better, we'll just use the plain, ever useful show ip route command:

```
Corp#sh ip route
[output cut]
D    192.168.10.0/24 [90/2172416] via 172.16.10.6, 00:05:35, Serial0/1
                     [90/2172416] via 172.16.10.2, 00:05:35, Serial0/0
```

Now we can see that there are two successor routes to the 192.168.10.0 network. Pretty sweet! But in the routing table, there's one path to 192.168.20.0 and 192.168.30.0, with the link between the SF and NY routers being feasible successors. And it's the same with the 192.168.40.0 and 192.168.50.0 networks. Let's take a look at the topology table to examine this more closely:

```
Corp#sh ip eigrp topology
IP-EIGRP Topology Table for AS(20)/ID(10.10.11.1)

Codes: P - Passive, A - Active, U - Update, Q - Query, R - Reply,
       r - reply Status, s - sia Status

P 10.10.10.0/24, 1 successors, FD is 128256
        via Connected, GigabitEthernet0/0
```

```
P 10.10.11.0/24, 1 successors, FD is 128256
        via Connected, GigabitEthernet0/1
P 10.10.20.0/24, 1 successors, FD is 2297856
        via 172.16.10.2 (2297856/128256), Serial0/0
        via 172.16.10.6 (2300416/156160), Serial0/1
P 10.10.30.0/24, 1 successors, FD is 2297856
        via 172.16.10.2 (2297856/128256), Serial0/0
        via 172.16.10.6 (2300416/156160), Serial0/1
P 10.10.40.0/24, 1 successors, FD is 2297856
        via 172.16.10.6 (2297856/128256), Serial0/1
        via 172.16.10.2 (2300416/156160), Serial0/0
P 10.10.50.0/24, 1 successors, FD is 2297856
        via 172.16.10.6 (2297856/128256), Serial0/1
        via 172.16.10.2 (2300416/156160), Serial0/0
P 192.168.10.0/24, 2 successors, FD is 2172416
        via 172.16.10.2 (2172416/28160), Serial0/0
        via 172.16.10.6 (2172416/28160), Serial0/1
P 172.16.10.4/30, 1 successors, FD is 2169856
        via Connected, Serial0/1
P 172.16.10.0/30, 1 successors, FD is 2169856
        via Connected, Serial0/0
```

It is nice that we can see that we have a successor and a feasible successor to each network, so we know that EIGRP is doing its job. Let's take a close look at the links to 10.10.20.0 now and dissect what it's telling us:

```
P 10.10.20.0/24, 1 successors, FD is 2297856
        via 172.16.10.2 (2297856/128256), Serial0/0
        via 172.16.10.6 (2300416/156160), Serial0/1
```

Okay—first, we can see that it's passive (P), which means that it has found all the usable paths to the network 10.10.20.0 and is happy! If we see active (A), that means that EIGRP is not happy at all and is querying its neighbors for a new path to that network. The (2297856/128256) is the FD/AD, meaning that the SF router is advertising the 10.10.20.0 network as a cost of 128256, which is the AD. The Corp router adds the bandwidth and delay of the line to get to the SF router and then adds that number to the AD (128256) to come up with a total cost (FD) of 2297856 to get to network 10.10.20.0.

 WARNING   To become a CCNA R/S, you must understand how to read a topology table!

Unequal-Cost Load Balancing

As with all routing protocols running on Cisco routers, EIGRP automatically supports load balancing over four equal-cost routes and can be configured to support up to 32 equal-cost paths with IOS 15.0 code. As you know, previous IOS versions supported up to 16. I've mentioned this a few times in this chapter already, but I want to show you how to configure unequal-cost load balancing with EIGRP. First let's take a look at the Corp router by typing in the show ip protocols command:

```
Corp#sh ip protocols
Routing Protocol is "eigrp 20"
  Outgoing update filter list for all interfaces is not set
  Incoming update filter list for all interfaces is not set
  Default networks flagged in outgoing updates
  Default networks accepted from incoming updates
  EIGRP metric weight K1=1, K2=0, K3=1, K4=0, K5=0
  EIGRP maximum hopcount 100
  EIGRP maximum metric variance 1
  Redistributing: eigrp 20
  EIGRP NSF-aware route hold timer is 240s
  Automatic network summarization is not in effect
  Maximum path: 4
  Routing for Networks:
    10.0.0.0
    172.16.0.0
  Routing Information Sources:
    Gateway         Distance      Last Update
    (this router)         90      19:15:10
    172.16.10.6          90      00:25:38
    172.16.10.2          90      00:25:38
  Distance: internal 90 external 170
```

The variance 1 means equal-path load balancing with the maximum paths set to 4 by default. Unlike most other protocols, EIGRP also supports unequal-cost load balancing through the use of the variance parameter.

To clarify, let's say the parameter has been set to a variance of 2. This would effectively load-balance traffic across the best route plus any route with a feasible distance of up to twice as large. But still keep in mind that load balancing occurs in proportion with and relative to the cost of the route, meaning that more traffic would travel across the best route than the suboptimal one.

Let's configure the variance on the Corp router and see if we can load-balance across our feasible successors now:

```
Corp# config t
Corp(config)#router eigrp 20
Corp(config-router)#variance 2
Corp(config-router)#
*Feb 26 22:24:24:IP-EIGRP(Default-IP-Routing-Table:20):route installed for
10.10.20.0
*Feb 26 22:24:24:IP-EIGRP(Default-IP-Routing-Table:20):route installed for
10.10.20.0
*Feb 26 22:24:24:IP-EIGRP(Default-IP-Routing-Table:20):route installed for
10.10.30.0
*Feb 26 22:24:24:IP-EIGRP(Default-IP-Routing-Table:20):route installed for
10.10.30.0
*Feb 26 22:24:24:IP-EIGRP(Default-IP-Routing-Table:20):route installed for
10.10.40.0
*Feb 26 22:24:24:IP-EIGRP(Default-IP-Routing-Table:20):route installed for
10.10.40.0
*Feb 26 22:24:24:IP-EIGRP(Default-IP-Routing-Table:20):route installed for
10.10.50.0
*Feb 26 22:24:24:IP-EIGRP(Default-IP-Routing-Table:20):route installed for
10.10.50.0
*Feb 26 22:24:24:IP-EIGRP(Default-IP-Routing-Table:20):route installed for
192.168.10.0
*Feb 26 22:24:24:IP-EIGRP(Default-IP-Routing-Table:20):route installed for
192.168.10.0
Corp(config-router)#do show ip route
[output cut]
D    192.168.10.0/24 [90/2172416] via 172.16.10.6, 00:00:18, Serial0/1
                     [90/2172416] via 172.16.10.2, 00:00:18, Serial0/0
     172.16.0.0/30 is subnetted, 2 subnets
C       172.16.10.4 is directly connected, Serial0/1
C       172.16.10.0 is directly connected, Serial0/0
     10.0.0.0/24 is subnetted, 6 subnets
C       10.10.10.0 is directly connected, GigabitEthernet0/0
C       10.10.11.0 is directly connected, GigabitEthernet0/1
D       10.10.20.0 [90/2300416] via 172.16.10.6, 00:00:18, Serial0/1
                   [90/2297856] via 172.16.10.2, 00:00:19, Serial0/0
D       10.10.30.0 [90/2300416] via 172.16.10.6, 00:00:19, Serial0/1
                   [90/2297856] via 172.16.10.2, 00:00:19, Serial0/0
D       10.10.40.0 [90/2297856] via 172.16.10.6, 00:00:19, Serial0/1
                   [90/2300416] via 172.16.10.2, 00:00:19, Serial0/0
```

```
D       10.10.50.0 [90/2297856] via 172.16.10.6, 00:00:20, Serial0/1
                   [90/2300416] via 172.16.10.2, 00:00:20, Serial0/0
Corp(config-router)#
```

Nice—it worked! Now we have two paths to each remote network in the routing table, even though the feasible distances to each route aren't equal. Don't forget that unequal load balancing is not enabled by default and that you can perform load balancing through paths that have up to 128 times worse metrics than the successor route!

Split Horizon

Split horizon is enabled on interfaces by default, which means that if a route update is received on an interface from a neighbor router, this interface will not advertise those networks back out to the neighbor router who sent them. Let's take a look at an interface and then go through an example:

```
Corp#sh ip int s0/0
Serial0/0 is up, line protocol is up
  Internet address is 172.16.10.1/24
  Broadcast address is 255.255.255.255
  Address determined by setup command
  MTU is 1500 bytes
  Helper address is not set
  Directed broadcast forwarding is disabled
  Multicast reserved groups joined: 224.0.0.10
  Outgoing access list is not set
  Inbound  access list is not set
  Proxy ARP is enabled
  Local Proxy ARP is disabled
  Security level is default
  Split horizon is enabled
[output cut]
```

Okay—we can see that split horizon is enabled by default. But what does this really mean? Most of the time it's more helpful than harmful, but let's check out our internetwork in Figure 3.8 so I can really explain what split horizon is doing.

Notice that the SF and NY routers are each advertising their routes to the Corp router. Now, let's see what the Corp router sends back to each router in Figure 3.9.

Can you see that the Corp router is not advertising back out the advertised networks that it received on each interface? This is saving the SF and NY routers from receiving the incorrect route information that they could possibly get to their own network through the Corp router, which we know is wrong.

FIGURE 3.8 Split horizon in action, part 1

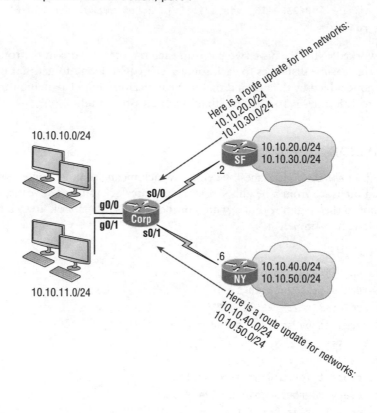

FIGURE 3.9 Split horizon in action, part 2

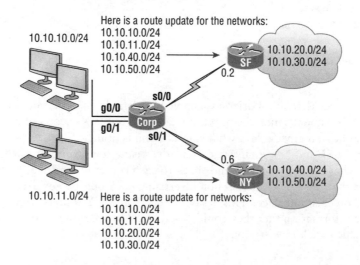

So how can this cause a problem? After all, it seems reasonable not to send misinformation back to an originating router, right? You'll see this create a problem on point-to-multipoint links, such as Frame Relay, when multiple remote routers connect to a single interface at the Corp location. We can use logical interfaces, called subinterfaces, which I'll tell you all about in Chapter 7, "Wide Area Networks," to solve the split horizon issue on a point-to-multipoint interface.

Verifying and Troubleshooting EIGRP

Even though EIGRP usually runs smoothly and is relatively low maintenance, there are several commands you need to memorize for using on a router that can be super helpful when troubleshooting EIGRP! I've already shown you a few of them, but I'm going to demonstrate all the tools you'll need to verify and troubleshoot EIGRP now. Table 3.2 contains all of the commands you need to know for verifying that EIGRP is functioning well and offers a brief description of what each command does.

TABLE 3.2   EIGRP troubleshooting commands

Command	Description/Function
show ip eigrp neighbors	Shows all EIGRP neighbors, their IP addresses, and the retransmit interval and queue counts for the adjacent routers
show ip eigrp interfaces	Lists the interfaces on which the router has actually enabled EIGRP
show ip route eigrp	Shows EIGRP entries in the routing table
show ip eigrp topology	Shows entries in the EIGRP topology table
show ip eigrp traffic	Shows the packet count for EIGRP packets sent and received
show ip protocols	Shows information about the active protocol sessions

When troubleshooting an EIGRP problem, it's always a good idea to start by getting an accurate map of the network, and the best way to do that is by using the show ip eigrp neighbors command to find out who your directly connected neighbors are. This command shows all adjacent routers that share route information within a given AS. If neighbors are missing, check the configuration, AS number, and link status on both routers to verify that the protocol has been configured correctly.

Let's execute the command on the Corp router:

Corp#**sh ip eigrp neighbors**
IP-EIGRP neighbors for process 20

H	Address	Interface	Hold	Uptime	SRTT	RTO	Q	Seq
			(sec)		(ms)		Cnt	Num
1	172.16.10.2	Se0/0	11	03:54:25	1	200	0	127
0	172.16.10.6	Se0/1	11	04:14:47	1	200	0	2010

Here's a breakdown of the important information we can see in the preceding output:

- H indicates the order in which the neighbor was discovered.

- Hold time in seconds is how long this router will wait for a Hello packet to arrive from a specific neighbor.

- The Uptime value indicates how long the neighbor relationship has been established.

- The SRTT field is the smooth round-trip timer and represents how long it takes to complete a round-trip from this router to its neighbor and back. This value delimits how long to wait after a multicast for a reply from this neighbor. As mentioned earlier, the router will attempt to establish communication via unicasts if it doesn't receive a reply.

- The time between multicast attempts is specified by the Retransmission Time Out (RTO) field, which is based upon the SRTT values.

- The Q value tells us if there are any outstanding messages in the queue. We can make a mental note that there's a problem if we see consistently large values here!

- Finally, the Seq field shows the sequence number of the last update from that neighbor, which is used to maintain synchronization and avoid duplicate messages or their out-of-sequence processing.

The neighbors command is a great command, but we can get local status of our router by also using the show ip eigrp interface command like this:

Corp#**sh ip eigrp interfaces**
IP-EIGRP interfaces for process 20

Interface	Peers	Xmit Queue Un/Reliable	Mean SRTT	Pacing Time Un/Reliable	Multicast Flow Timer	Pending Routes
Gi0/0	0	0/0	0	0/1	0	0
Se0/1	1	0/0	1	0/15	50	0
Se0/0	1	0/0	1	0/15	50	0
Gi0/1	0	0/0	0	0/1	0	0

Corp#**sh ip eigrp interface detail s0/0**
IP-EIGRP interfaces for process 20

Interface	Peers	Xmit Queue Un/Reliable	Mean SRTT	Pacing Time Un/Reliable	Multicast Flow Timer	Pending Routes
Se0/0	1	0/0	1	0/15	50	0

```
   Hello interval is 5 sec
   Next xmit serial <none>
   Un/reliable mcasts: 0/0  Un/reliable ucasts: 21/26
   Mcast exceptions: 0  CR packets: 0  ACKs suppressed: 9
   Retransmissions sent: 0  Out-of-sequence rcvd: 0
   Authentication mode is not set
```

The first command, show ip eigrp interfaces, lists all interfaces for which EIGRP is enabled as well as those the router is currently sending Hello messages to in an attempt to find new EIGRP neighbors. The show ip eigrp interface detail *interface* command lists more details per interface, including the local router's own Hello interval. Understand that you can use these commands to verify that all your interfaces are within the AS process used by EIGRP, but also note that the passive interfaces won't show up in these outputs. So be sure to also check to see if an interface has been configured as passive if is not present in the outputs.

Okay, if all neighbors are present, then verify the routes learned. By executing the show ip route eigrp command, you're given a quick picture of the routes in the routing table. If a certain route doesn't appear in the routing table, you need to verify its source. If the source is functioning properly, then check the topology table.

The routing table according to Corp looks like this:

```
D     192.168.10.0/24 [90/2172416] via 172.16.10.6, 02:29:09, Serial0/1
                      [90/2172416] via 172.16.10.2, 02:29:09, Serial0/0
      172.16.0.0/30 is subnetted, 2 subnets
C        172.16.10.4 is directly connected, Serial0/1
C        172.16.10.0 is directly connected, Serial0/0
      10.0.0.0/24 is subnetted, 6 subnets
C        10.10.10.0 is directly connected, Loopback0
C        10.10.11.0 is directly connected, Loopback1
D        10.10.20.0 [90/2300416] via 172.16.10.6, 02:29:09, Serial0/1
                    [90/2297856] via 172.16.10.2, 02:29:10, Serial0/0
D        10.10.30.0 [90/2300416] via 172.16.10.6, 02:29:10, Serial0/1
                    [90/2297856] via 172.16.10.2, 02:29:10, Serial0/0
D        10.10.40.0 [90/2297856] via 172.16.10.6, 02:29:10, Serial0/1
                    [90/2300416] via 172.16.10.2, 02:29:10, Serial0/0
D        10.10.50.0 [90/2297856] via 172.16.10.6, 02:29:11, Serial0/1
                    [90/2300416] via 172.16.10.2, 02:29:11, Serial0/0
```

You can see here that most EIGRP routes are referenced with a D and that their administrative distance is 90. Remember that the [90/2300416] represents AD/FD, and in the preceding output, EIGRP is performing equal- and unequal-cost load balancing between two links to our remote networks.

We can see this by looking closer at two different networks. Pay special attention to the FD of each output:

```
Corp#sh ip route | section 192.168.10.0
D    192.168.10.0/24 [90/2172416] via 172.16.10.6, 01:15:44, Serial0/1
                     [90/2172416] via 172.16.10.2, 01:15:44, Serial0/0
```

The preceding output shows equal-cost load balancing, and here's our unequal-cost load balancing in action:

```
Corp#sh ip route | section 10.10.50.0
D    10.10.50.0 [90/2297856] via 172.16.10.6, 01:16:16, Serial0/1
                [90/2300416] via 172.16.10.2, 01:16:16, Serial0/0
```

We can get the topology table displayed for us via the show ip eigrp topology command. If the route is in the topology table but not in the routing table, it's a pretty safe assumption that there's a problem between the topology database and the routing table. After all, there must be a good reason the topology database isn't adding the route into the routing table, right? We discussed this issue in detail earlier in the chapter, and it's oh so important!

Corp's topology table looks like this:

```
P 10.10.10.0/24, 1 successors, FD is 128256
        via Connected, GigabitEthernet0/0
P 10.10.11.0/24, 1 successors, FD is 128256
        via Connected, GigabitEthernet0/1
P 10.10.20.0/24, 1 successors, FD is 2297856
        via 172.16.10.2 (2297856/128256), Serial0/0
        via 172.16.10.6 (2300416/156160), Serial0/1
P 10.10.30.0/24, 1 successors, FD is 2297856
        via 172.16.10.2 (2297856/128256), Serial0/0
        via 172.16.10.6 (2300416/156160), Serial0/1
P 10.10.40.0/24, 1 successors, FD is 2297856
        via 172.16.10.6 (2297856/128256), Serial0/1
        via 172.16.10.2 (2300416/156160), Serial0/0
P 10.10.50.0/24, 1 successors, FD is 2297856
        via 172.16.10.6 (2297856/128256), Serial0/1
        via 172.16.10.2 (2300416/156160), Serial0/0
P 192.168.10.0/24, 2 successors, FD is 2172416
        via 172.16.10.2 (2172416/28160), Serial0/0
        via 172.16.10.6 (2172416/28160), Serial0/1
P 172.16.10.4/30, 1 successors, FD is 2169856
        via Connected, Serial0/1
P 172.16.10.0/30, 1 successors, FD is 2169856
        via Connected, Serial0/0
```

Notice that every route in this output is preceded by a P, which shows that these routes are in a *passive state*. This is good because routes in the active state indicate that the router has lost its path to this network and is searching for a replacement. Each entry also reveals the feasible distance, or FD, to each remote network as well as the next-hop neighbor through which packets will travel to this destination. Each entry also has two numbers in brackets, with the first indicating the feasible distance and the second, the advertised distance to a remote network.

Again, here's our equal- and unequal-cost load-balancing output shown in the topology table:

```
Corp#sh ip eigrp top | section 192.168.10.0
P 192.168.10.0/24, 2 successors, FD is 2172416
        via 172.16.10.2 (2172416/28160), Serial0/0
        via 172.16.10.6 (2172416/28160), Serial0/1
```

The preceding output shows equal-cost load balancing, and here is our unequal-cost load balancing in action:

```
Corp#sh ip eigrp top | section 10.10.50.0
P 10.10.50.0/24, 1 successors, FD is 2297856
        via 172.16.10.6 (2297856/128256), Serial0/1
        via 172.16.10.2 (2300416/156160), Serial0/0
```

The command show ip eigrp traffic enables us to see if updates are being sent. If the counters for EIGRP input and output packets don't increase, it means that no EIGRP information is being sent between peers. The following output indicates that the Corp router is experiencing normal traffic:

```
Corp#show ip eigrp traffic
IP-EIGRP Traffic Statistics for process 200
  Hellos sent/received: 2208/2310
  Updates sent/received: 184/183
  Queries sent/received: 17/4
  Replies sent/received: 4/18
  Acks sent/received: 62/65
  Input queue high water mark 2, 0 drops
```

All of the packet types I talked about in the section on RTP are represented in the output of this command. And we can't forget the always useful troubleshooting command show ip protocols. Here's the output the Corp router gives us after using it:

```
Routing Protocol is "eigrp 20"
  Outgoing update filter list for all interfaces is not set
  Incoming update filter list for all interfaces is not set
  Default networks flagged in outgoing updates
  Default networks accepted from incoming updates
```

```
EIGRP metric weight K1=1, K2=0, K3=1, K4=0, K5=0
EIGRP maximum hopcount 100
EIGRP maximum metric variance 2
Redistributing: eigrp 20
EIGRP NSF-aware route hold timer is 240s
Automatic network summarization is not in effect
Maximum path: 4
Routing for Networks:
   10.0.0.0
   172.16.0.0
Routing Information Sources:
   Gateway         Distance      Last Update
   (this router)         90      04:23:51
   172.16.10.6           90      02:30:48
   172.16.10.2           90      02:30:48
Distance: internal 90 external 170
```

In this output, we can see that EIGRP is enabled for autonomous system 20 and that the K values are set to their defaults. The variance is 2, so both equal- and unequal-cost load balancing is happening here. Automatic summarization has been turned off. We can also see that EIGRP is advertising two classful networks and that it sees two neighbors.

The show ip eigrp events command displays a log of every EIGRP event: when routes are injected and removed from the routing table and when EIGRP adjacencies are reset or fail. This information is so helpful in determining if there are routing instabilities in the network! Be advised that this command can result in quite a flood of information even for really simple configurations like ours. To demonstrate, here's the output the Corp router divulged after I used it:

```
Corp#show ip eigrp events
Event information for AS 20:
1    22:24:24.258 Metric set: 172.16.10.0/30 2169856
2    22:24:24.258 FC sat rdbmet/succmet: 2169856 0
3    22:24:24.258 FC sat nh/ndbmet: 0.0.0.0 2169856
4    22:24:24.258 Find FS: 172.16.10.0/30 2169856
5    22:24:24.258 Metric set: 172.16.10.4/30 2169856
6    22:24:24.258 FC sat rdbmet/succmet: 2169856 0
7    22:24:24.258 FC sat nh/ndbmet: 0.0.0.0 2169856
8    22:24:24.258 Find FS: 172.16.10.4/30 2169856
9    22:24:24.258 Metric set: 192.168.10.0/24 2172416
10   22:24:24.258 Route install: 192.168.10.0/24 172.16.10.2
11   22:24:24.258 Route install: 192.168.10.0/24 172.16.10.6
12   22:24:24.254 FC sat rdbmet/succmet: 2172416 28160
13   22:24:24.254 FC sat nh/ndbmet: 172.16.10.6 2172416
```

```
14    22:24:24.254 Find FS: 192.168.10.0/24 2172416
15    22:24:24.254 Metric set: 10.10.50.0/24 2297856
16    22:24:24.254 Route install: 10.10.50.0/24 172.16.10.6
17    22:24:24.254 FC sat rdbmet/succmet: 2297856 128256
18    22:24:24.254 FC sat nh/ndbmet: 172.16.10.6 2297856
19    22:24:24.254 Find FS: 10.10.50.0/24 2297856
20    22:24:24.254 Metric set: 10.10.40.0/24 2297856
21    22:24:24.254 Route install: 10.10.40.0/24 172.16.10.6
22    22:24:24.250 FC sat rdbmet/succmet: 2297856 128256
--More--
```

Troubleshooting Example with EIGRP

Throughout this chapter I've covered many of the problems that commonly occur with EIGRP and how to verify and troubleshoot these issues. Make sure you clearly understand what I have shown you so far in this chapter so you're prepared to answer any question the Cisco exam could possibly throw at you!

Just to make sure you're solidly armed with all the skills you need to ace the exam as well as successfully administer a network, I'm going to provide even more examples about verifying EIGRP. We'll be dealing with mostly the same commands and problems we've already covered, but this is so important, and the best way to get this all nailed down is to practice troubleshooting an EIGRP network as much as possible!

With that, after you've configured EIGRP, you would first test connectivity to the remote network by using the Ping program. If that fails, you need to check whether the directly connected router is in the neighbor table.

Here are some key things to look for if neighbors haven't formed an adjacency:

- Interfaces between the devices are down.
- The two routers have mismatching EIGRP autonomous system numbers.
- Proper interfaces are not enabled for the EIGRP process.
- An interface is configured as passive.
- The K values are mismatched.
- EIGRP authentication is misconfigured.

Also, if the adjacency is up but you're not receiving remote network updates, there may be a routing problem, likely caused by these issues:

- The proper networks aren't being advertised under the EIGRP process.
- An access list is blocking the advertisements from remote networks.
- Automatic summary is causing confusion in your discontiguous network.

Let's use Figure 3.10 as our example network and run through some troubleshooting scenarios. I've preconfigured the routers with IP addresses, and without having to try too hard, I also snuck in a few snags for us to find and fix. Let's see what we're facing.

FIGURE 3.10 Troubleshooting scenario

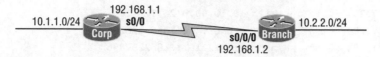

A good place to start is by checking to see if we have an adjacency with show ip eigrp neighbors and show ip eigrp interfaces. It's also smart to see what information the show ip eigrp topology command reveals:

Corp#**sh ip eigrp neighbors**
IP-EIGRP neighbors for process 20
Corp#

Corp#**sh ip eigrp interfaces**
IP-EIGRP interfaces for process 20

Interface	Peers	Xmit Queue Un/Reliable	Mean SRTT	Pacing Time Un/Reliable	Multicast Flow Timer	Pending Routes
Se0/1	0	0/0	0	0/15	50	0
Fa0/0	0	0/0	0	0/1	0	0
Se0/0	0	0/0	0	0/15	50	0

Corp#**sh ip eigrp top**
IP-EIGRP Topology Table for AS(20)/ID(10.10.11.1)

Codes: P - Passive, A - Active, U - Update, Q - Query, R - Reply,
       r - reply Status, s - sia Status

P 10.1.1.0/24, 1 successors, FD is 28160
        via Connected, FastEthernet0/0

Alright—we can see by looking at the neighbor and the interface as well as the topology table command that our LAN is up on the Corp router but the serial link isn't working between routers because we don't have an adjacency. From the show ip eigrp interfaces command, we can establish that EIGRP is running on all interfaces, so that means our network statements under the EIGRP process are probably correct, but we'll verify that later.

Let's move on by checking into our Physical and Data Link status with the show ip int brief command because maybe there's a physical problem between routers:

Corp#**sh ip int brief**
Interface	IP-Address	OK? Method Status	Protocol

```
FastEthernet0/0          10.1.1.1        YES manual up                      up
Serial0/0                192.168.1.1     YES manual up                      up
FastEthernet0/1          unassigned      YES manual administratively down down
Serial0/1                172.16.10.5     YES manual administratively down down
Corp#
Corp#sh protocols s0/0
Serial0/0 is up, line protocol is up
  Internet address is 192.168.1.1/30
```

Well, since the Serial0/0 interface shows the correct IP address and the status is up/up, it means we have a good Data Link connection between routers, so it's not a physical link issue between the routers, which is good! Notice I also used the show protocols command, which gave me the subnet mask for the link. Remember, the information obtained via the two commands gives us only layer 1 and layer 2 status and doesn't mean we can ping across the link. In other words, we might have a layer 3 issue, so let's check the Branch router with the same commands:

```
Branch#sh ip int brief
Interface               IP-Address      OK? Method Status            Protocol
FastEthernet0/0         10.2.2.2        YES manual up                      up
FastEthernet0/1         unassigned      YES manual administratively down down
Serial0/0/0             192.168.1.2     YES manual up                      up
Serial0/0/1             unassigned      YES unset  administratively down down
Branch#sh proto s0/0/0
Serial0/0/0 is up, line protocol is up
  Internet address is 192.168.1.2/30
```

Okay, well, we can see that our IP address and mask are correct, and that the link shows up/up, so we're looking pretty good! Let's try to ping from the Corp router to the Branch router now:

```
Corp#ping 192.168.1.2

Type escape sequence to abort.
Sending 5, 100-byte ICMP Echos to 192.168.1.2, timeout is 2 seconds:
!!!!!
Success rate is 100 percent (5/5), round-trip min/avg/max = 1/3/4 ms
```

Now because that was successful, we've ruled out layer 1, 2, or 3 issues between routers at this point! Since everything seems to be working between the routers, except

EIGRP, checking our EIGRP configurations is our next move. Let's start with the show ip protocols command:

```
Corp#sh ip protocols
Routing Protocol is "eigrp 20"
  Outgoing update filter list for all interfaces is not set
  Incoming update filter list for all interfaces is not set
  Default networks flagged in outgoing updates
  Default networks accepted from incoming updates
  EIGRP metric weight K1=1, K2=0, K3=1, K4=0, K5=0
  EIGRP maximum hopcount 100
  EIGRP maximum metric variance 2
  Redistributing: eigrp 20
  EIGRP NSF-aware route hold timer is 240s
  Automatic network summarization is in effect
  Maximum path: 4
  Routing for Networks:
    10.0.0.0
    172.16.0.0
    192.168.1.0
Passive Interface(s):
    FastEthernet0/1
  Routing Information Sources:
    Gateway          Distance      Last Update
    (this router)         90       20:51:48
    192.168.1.2          90       00:22:58
    172.16.10.6          90       01:58:46
    172.16.10.2          90       01:59:52
  Distance: internal 90 external 170
```

This output shows us we're using AS 20, that we don't have an access-list filter list set on the routing tables, and that our K values are set to default. We can see that we're routing for the 10.0.0.0, 172.16.0.0, and 192.168.1.0 networks and that we have a passive interface on interface FastEthernet0/1. We don't have an interface configured for the 172.16.0.0 network, which means that this entry is an extra network statement under EIGRP. But that won't hurt anything, so this is not causing our issue. Last, the passive interface is not causing a problem with this network either, because we're not using interface Fa0/1. Still, keep in mind that when troubleshooting, it's always good to see if there are any interfaces set to passive.

Let's see what the show interfaces command will tell us:

```
Corp#sh interfaces s0/0
Serial0/0 is up, line protocol is up
  Hardware is PowerQUICC Serial
  Description: <<Connection to Branch>>
```

```
Internet address is 192.168.1.1/30
MTU 1500 bytes, BW 1544 Kbit, DLY 20000 usec,
   reliability 255/255, txload 1/255, rxload 1/255
Encapsulation HDLC, loopback not set
[output cut]
```

Looks like our statistics are set to defaults, so nothing really pops as a problem here. But remember when I covered the steps to check if there is no adjacency back at the beginning of this section? In case you forgot, here's a list of things to investigate:

- The interface between the devices are down.

- The two routers have mismatching EIGRP autonomous system numbers.

- The proper interfaces aren't enabled for the EIGRP process.

- An interface is configured as passive.

- K values are mismatched.

- EIGRP authentication is misconfigured.

Okay, our interfaces are not down, our AS number matches, layer 3 is working between routers, all the interfaces show up under the EIGRP process, and none of our needed interfaces are passive, so now we'll have to look even deeper into the EIGRP configuration to uncover the problem.

Since the Corp router has the basic default configurations, we need to check the Branch router's EIGRP configuration:

```
Branch#sh ip protocols
Routing Protocol is "eigrp 20"
  Outgoing update filter list for all interfaces is 10
  Incoming update filter list for all interfaces is not set
  Default networks flagged in outgoing updates
  Default networks accepted from incoming updates
  EIGRP metric weight K1=1, K2=0, K3=0, K4=0, K5=0
  EIGRP maximum hopcount 100
  EIGRP maximum metric variance 1
  Redistributing: eigrp 20
  EIGRP NSF-aware route hold timer is 240s
  Automatic network summarization is not in effect
  Maximum path: 4
  Routing for Networks:
    10.0.0.0
    192.168.1.0
  Routing Information Sources:
    Gateway         Distance      Last Update
    192.168.1.1           90      00:27:09
  Distance: internal 90 external 170
```

This router has the correct AS—always check this first—and we're routing for the correct networks. But I see two possible snags here, do you? First, the outgoing ACL filter list is set, but the metrics are not set to default. Remember, just because an ACL is set doesn't mean it's automatically giving you grief. Second, the K values must match, and we know these values are not matching the Corp router!

Let's take a look at the Branch interface statistics to see what else might be wrong:

```
Branch>sh int s0/0/0
Serial0/0/0 is up, line protocol is up
  Hardware is GT96K Serial
  Internet address is 192.168.1.2/30
  MTU 1500 bytes, BW 512 Kbit, DLY 30000 usec,
     reliability 255/255, txload 1/255, rxload 1/255
  Encapsulation HDLC, loopback not set
[output cut]
```

Aha! The bandwidth and delay are not set to their defaults and don't match the directly connected Corp router. Let's start by changing those back to the default and see if that fixes our problem:

```
Branch#config t
Branch(config)#int s0/0/0
Branch(config-if)#no bandwidth
Branch(config-if)#no delay
```

And let's check out our stats now to see if we're back to defaults:

```
Branch#sh int s0/0/0
Serial0/0/0 is up, line protocol is up
  Hardware is GT96K Serial
  Internet address is 192.168.1.2/30
  MTU 1500 bytes, BW 1544 Kbit, DLY 20000 usec,
     reliability 255/255, txload 1/255, rxload 1/255
  Encapsulation HDLC, loopback not set
[output cut]
```

The bandwidth and delay are now at the defaults, so let's check our adjacencies next:

```
Corp#sh ip eigrp neighbors
IP-EIGRP neighbors for process 20
```

Okay, so it wasn't the bandwidth and delay settings because our adjacency didn't come up, so let's set our K values back to default like this:

```
Branch#config t
Branch(config)#router eigrp 20
```

```
Branch(config-router)#metric weights 0 1 0 1 0 0
Branch(config-router)#do sho ip proto
Routing Protocol is "eigrp 20"
  Outgoing update filter list for all interfaces is 10
  Incoming update filter list for all interfaces is not set
  Default networks flagged in outgoing updates
  Default networks accepted from incoming updates
  EIGRP metric weight K1=1, K2=0, K3=1, K4=0, K5=0
[output cut]
```

I know this probably seems a little complicated at first, but it's something you shouldn't have to do much, if ever. Remember, there are five K values, so why 6 numbers? The first number listed is type of service (ToS), so always just set that to 0, which means you must type in six numbers as shown in my configuration example. After we chose the default of 0 first, the default K values are then 1 0 1 0 0, which is bandwidth and delay enabled. Let's check our adjacency now:

```
Corp#sh ip eigrp neighbors
IP-EIGRP neighbors for process 20
H    Address              Interface        Hold Uptime    SRTT    RTO  Q   Seq
                                           (sec)          (ms)         Cnt Num
0    192.168.1.2          Se0/0            14   00:02:09   7       200  0   18
```

Bam! There we go! Looks like mismatched K values were our problem. Now let's just check to make sure we can ping from end to end and we're done:

```
Corp#ping 10.2.2.2

Type escape sequence to abort.
Sending 5, 100-byte ICMP Echos to 10.2.2.2, timeout is 2 seconds:
.....
Success rate is 0 percent (0/5)
Corp#
```

Rats! It looks like even though we have our adjacency, we still can't reach our remote network. Next step? Let's see what the routing table shows us:

```
Corp#sh ip route
[output cut]

     10.0.0.0/8 is variably subnetted, 2 subnets, 2 masks
C       10.1.1.0/24 is directly connected, FastEthernet0/0
D       10.0.0.0/8 is a summary, 00:18:55, Null0
     192.168.1.0/24 is variably subnetted, 2 subnets, 2 masks
C       192.168.1.0/30 is directly connected, Serial0/0
D       192.168.1.0/24 is a summary, 00:18:55, Null0
```

The problem is screamingly clear now because I went through this in detail throughout this chapter. But just in case you still can't find it, let's look at the show ip protocols command output:

```
Routing Protocol is "eigrp 20"
  Outgoing update filter list for all interfaces is not set
  Incoming update filter list for all interfaces is not set
  Default networks flagged in outgoing updates
  Default networks accepted from incoming updates
  EIGRP metric weight K1=1, K2=0, K3=1, K4=0, K5=0
  EIGRP maximum hopcount 100
  EIGRP maximum metric variance 2
  Redistributing: eigrp 20
  EIGRP NSF-aware route hold timer is 240s
  Automatic network summarization is in effect
  Automatic address summarization:
    192.168.1.0/24 for FastEthernet0/0
      Summarizing with metric 2169856
    10.0.0.0/8 for Serial0/0
      Summarizing with metric 28160
 [output cut]
```

By looking at the Figure 5.10, you should have noticed right away that we had a discontiguous network. This means that unless they are running 15.0 IOS code, the routers will auto-summarize, so we need to disable auto-summary:

```
Branch(config)#router eigrp 20
Branch(config-router)#no auto-summary
008412:%DUAL-5-NBRCHANGE:IP-EIGRP(0) 20:Neighbor 192.168.1.1 (Serial0/0/0) is
resync:
peer graceful-restart

Corp(config)#router eigrp 20
Corp(config-router)#no auto-summary
Corp(config-router)#
*Feb 27 19:52:54:%DUAL-5-NBRCHANGE: IP-EIGRP(0) 20:Neighbor 192.168.1.2
(Serial0/0)
 is resync: summary configured
*Feb 27 19:52:54.177:IP-EIGRP(Default-IP-Routing-Table:20):10.1.1.0/24 - do
advertise
 out Serial0/0
*Feb 27 19:52:54:IP-EIGRP(Default-IP-Routing-Table:20):Int 10.1.1.0/24 metric
2816
```

```
0 - 25600 2560
*Feb 27 19:52:54:IP-EIGRP(Default-IP-Routing-Table:20):192.168.1.0/30 - do
advertise out Serial0/0
*Feb 27 19:52:54:IP-EIGRP(Default-IP-Routing-Table:20):192.168.1.0/24 - do
advertise out Serial0/0
*Feb 27 19:52:54:IP-EIGRP(Default-IP-Routing-Table:20):Int 192.168.1.0/24 metric
4294967295 - 0 4294967295
*Feb 27 19:52:54:IP-EIGRP(Default-IP-Routing-Table:20):10.0.0.0/8 - do advertise
 out Serial0/0
Corp(config-router)#
*Feb 27 19:52:54:IP-EIGRP(Default-IP-Routing-Table:20):Int 10.0.0.0/8 metric
4294967295 - 0 4294967295
*Feb 27 19:52:54:IP-EIGRP(Default-IP-Routing-Table:20):Processing incoming REPLY
packet
*Feb 27 19:52:54:IP-EIGRP(Default-IP-Routing-Table:20):Int 192.168.1.0/24 M
4294967295 - 1657856 4294967295 SM 4294967295 - 1657856 4294967295
*Feb 27 19:52:54:IP-EIGRP(Default-IP-Routing-Table:20):Int 10.0.0.0/8 M
4294967295 - 25600 4294967295 SM 4294967295 - 25600 4294967295
*Feb 27 19:52:54:IP-EIGRP(Default-IP-Routing-Table:20):Processing incoming
UPDATE packet
```

Finally the Corp looks happy, so it looks like we're good to go! Let's just check our routing table to be sure:

```
Corp#sh ip route
[output cut]
     10.0.0.0/24 is subnetted, 1 subnets
C       10.1.1.0 is directly connected, FastEthernet0/0
     192.168.1.0/30 is subnetted, 1 subnets
C       192.168.1.0 is directly connected, Serial0/0
```

What the heck? How can this be! We saw all those updates on the Corp console, right? Let's check the configuration of EIGRP by looking at the active configuration on the Branch router:

```
Branch#sh run
[output cut]
!
router eigrp 20
 network 10.0.0.0
 network 192.168.1.0
 distribute-list 10 out
 no auto-summary
!
```

We can see that the access list is set outbound on the routing table of the Branch router. This may be preventing us from receiving the updates from remote networks! Let's see what the ACL 10 list is doing:

```
Branch#sh access-lists
Standard IP access list 10
    10 deny   any (40 matches)
    20 permit any
```

Now who in the world would stick an access list like this on a router? This ACL says to deny every packet, which makes the second line of the ACL irrelevant since every single packet will match the first line! This has got to be the source of our troubles, so let's remove that list and see if the Corp router starts working:

```
Branch#config t
Branch(config)#router eigrp 20
Branch(config-router)#no distribute-list 10 out
```

Okay, with that ugly thing gone, let's check to see if we're receiving our remote networks now:

```
Corp#sh ip route
[output cut]
     10.0.0.0/24 is subnetted, 2 subnets
D       10.2.2.0 [90/2172416] via 192.168.1.2, 00:00:24, Serial0/0
C       10.1.1.0 is directly connected, FastEthernet0/0
     192.168.1.0/30 is subnetted, 1 subnets
C       192.168.1.0 is directly connected, Serial0/0
Corp#
Corp#ping 10.2.2.2

Type escape sequence to abort.
Sending 5, 100-byte ICMP Echos to 10.2.2.2, timeout is 2 seconds:
!!!!!
Success rate is 100 percent (5/5), round-trip min/avg/max = 1/3/4 ms
Corp#
```

Clear skies! We're up and running. We had mismatched K values, discontiguous networking, and a nasty ACL on our routing table. For the CCNA R/S objectives, always check for an ACL on the actual interface as well, not just in the routing table. It could be set on the interface or routing table, either one, or both! And never forget to check for passive interfaces when troubleshooting a routing protocol issue!

All of these commands are seriously powerful tools in the hands of a savvy professional faced with the task of troubleshooting myriad network issues. I could go on and on about the profusion of information these commands can generate and how well they can equip us to solve virtually every networking ill, but that would be way outside the scope of this book. Even so, I have no doubt that the foundation I've given you here will prove practical and valuable for certification purposes as well as for working in the real networking world.

Simple Troubleshooting EIGRP for the CCNA

Let's do one more troubleshooting scenario. You have two routers not forming an adjacency. What would you do first? Well, we went through a lot in this chapter, but let me make it super easy for you when you're troubleshooting on the CCNA exam.

All you need to do is perform a show running-config on each router. That's it! I can then fix anything regarding EIGRP. Remember that dynamic routing is all about the router you are looking at—it's not important to be looking at another router's configuration to get EIGRP correct on the router you're configuring as long as you know your AS number.

Let's look at each router's configuration and determine what the problem is—no network figure needed here because this is all about the router you're looking at.

Here is the first router's configuration:

```
R1#sh run
Building configuration...

Current configuration : 737 bytes
!
version 15.1
!
interface Loopback0
 ip address 10.1.1.1 255.255.255.255
int FastEthernet0/0
 ip address 192.168.16.1 255.255.255.0
int Serial1/1
 ip address 192.168.13.1 255.255.255.0
 bandwidth 1000
int Serial1/3
 ip address 192.168.12.1 255.255.255.0
!
router eigrp 1
 network 192.168.12.0
 network 192.168.13.0
 network 192.168.16.0
```

Here is the neighbor router's configuration:

```
R2#sh run
Building configuration...
```

```
Current configuration : 737 bytes
!
version 15.1
!
interface Loopback0
 ip address 10.2.2.2 255.255.255.255
interface Loopback1
 ip address 10.5.5.5 255.255.255.255
interface Loopback2
 ip address 10.5.5.55 255.255.255.255
int FastEthernet0/0
 ip address 192.168.123.2 255.255.255.0
int Serial2/1
 ip address 192.168.12.2 255.255.255.0
!
router eigrp 2
 network 10.2.2.2 0.0.0.0
 network 192.168.12.0
 network 192.168.123.0
```

Can you see the problems? Pretty simple. First, notice that we're running 15.1 code so we don't need to worry about discontiguous networks or need to configure the no auto-summary command. One thing down!

Now, let's look at each interface and either remember or write down the network numbers under each interface, including the loopback interfaces. Once we do that we can then make sure our EIGRP configuration is correct.

Here is the new configuration for R1:

```
R1#config t
R1(config)#router eigrp 1
R1(config-router)#network 10.1.1.1 0.0.0.0
```

That's it! I just added the missing network statement from the loopback0 interface under the EIGRP process; all the other networks were already under the EIGRP process. We're golden on R1. Let's fix R2 now:

```
R2#config t
R2(config)#no router eigrp 2
R2(config)#router eigrp 1
R2(config-router)#network 10.2.2.2 0.0.0
R2(config-router)#network 10.5.5.5 0.0.0.0
R2(config-router)#network 10.5.5.55 0.0.0.0
R2(config-router)#network 192.168.123.0
R2(config-router)#network 192.168.12.0
```

Notice I started by deleting the wrong AS number—they have to match! I then created another EIGRP process using AS 1 and then added all the networks found under every interface, including the loopback interfaces.

It's that easy! Just perform a Show running-config on each router, add any missing networks found under each interface to the EIGRP process, make sure the AS numbers match, and you're set!

Now it's time to relax a bit as we move into the easiest part of this chapter, seriously—not joking! You still need to pay attention though.

EIGRPv6

As I was just saying, welcome to the easiest part of the chapter! Of course, I only mostly mean that, and here's why: I talked about IPv6 in the earlier ICND1 chapters, and in order to continue on with this section of the chapter, you need to have that vital, foundational part of IPv6 down solidly before you dare to dwell here! If you do, you're pretty much set and this will all be pretty simple for you.

EIGRPv6 works much the same way as its IPv4 predecessor does—most of the features that EIGRP provided before EIGRPv6 will still be available.

EIGRPv6 is still an advanced distance-vector protocol that has some link-state features. The neighbor discovery process using Hellos still happens, and it still provides reliable communication with Reliable Transport Protocol that gives us loop-free fast convergence using the Diffusing Update Algorithm (DUAL).

Hello packets and updates are sent using multicast transmission, and as with RIPng, EIGRPv6's multicast address stayed almost the same. In IPv4 it was 224.0.0.10; in IPv6, it's FF02::A (A = 10 in hexadecimal notation).

But clearly, there are key differences between the two versions. Most notably the use of the pesky network command is gone, so it's hard to make a mistake with EIGRPv6. Also, the network and interface to be advertised must be enabled from interface configuration mode with one simple command.

But you still have to use the router configuration mode to enable the routing protocol in EIGRPv6 because the routing process must be literally enabled like an interface with the no shutdown command—interesting! However, the 15.0 code does enable this by default, so this command actually may or may not be needed.

Here's an example of enabling EIGRPv6 on the Corp router:

```
Corp(config)#ipv6 unicast-routing
Corp(config)#ipv6 router eigrp 10
```

The 10 in this case is still the AS number. The prompt changes to (config-rtr), and from here, just initiate a no shutdown if needed:

```
Corp(config-rtr)#no shutdown
```

Other options also can be configured in this mode, like redistribution and router ID (RID). So now, let's go to the interface and enable IPv6:

```
Corp(config-if)#ipv6 eigrp 10
```

The 10 in the interface command again references the AS number that was enabled in the configuration mode.

Figure 3.11 shows the layout we've been using throughout this chapter, only with IPv6 addresses now assigned to interfaces. I used the EUI-64 option on each interface so each router assigned itself an IPv6 address after I typed in the 64-bit network/subnet address.

FIGURE 3.11 Configuring EIGRPv6 on our internetwork

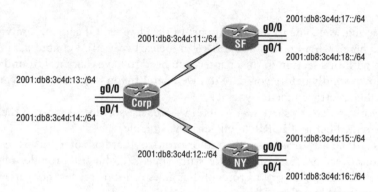

We'll start with the Corp router. Really, all we need to know in order to enable EIGRPv6 are which interfaces we're using and want to advertise our networks.

```
Corp#config t
Corp(config)#ipv6 router eigrp 10
Corp(config-rtr)#no shut
Corp(config-rtr)#router-id 1.1.1.1
Corp(config-rtr)#int s0/0/0
Corp(config-if)#ipv6 eigrp 10
Corp(config-if)#int s0/0/1
Corp(config-if)#ipv6 eigrp 10
Corp(config-if)#int g0/0
Corp(config-if)#ipv6 eigrp 10
Corp(config-if)#int g0/1
Corp(config-if)#ipv6 eigrp 10
```

I had erased and reloaded the routers before I started this EIGRPv6 section of the chapter. What this means is that there were no 32-bit addresses on the router in order to create the RID for EIGRP, so I had to set it under the IPv6 router global command, which is the same command used with EIGRP and EIGRPv6. Unlike with OSPF, the RID isn't that important, and it can actually be the same address on every router. You just can't get away with doing this with OSPF! The configuration for EIGRPv6 was pretty straightforward because unless you type the AS number wrong, it's pretty hard to screw this up!

Okay, let's configure the SF and NY routers now, and then we'll verify our networks:

```
SF#config t
SF(config)#ipv6 router eigrp 10
SF(config-rtr)#no shut
SF(config-rtr)#router-id 2.2.2.2
SF(config-rtr)#int s0/0/0
SF(config-if)#ipv6 eigrp 10
SF(config-if)#int g0/0
SF(config-if)#ipv6 eigrp 10
SF(config-if)#int g0/1
SF(config-if)#ipv6 eigrp 10


NY#config t
NY(config)#ipv6 router eigrp 10
NY(config-rtr)#no shut
NY(config-rtr)#router-id 3.3.3.3
NY(config-rtr)#int s0/0/0
NY(config-if)#ipv6 eigrp 10
NY(config-if)#int g0/0
NY(config-if)#ipv6 eigrp 10
NY(config-if)#int g0/1
```

Since we configured EIGRPv6 on a per-interface basis, no worries about having to use the passive-interface command. This is because if we don't enable the routing protocol on an interface, it's just not part of the EIGRPv6 process. We can see which interfaces are part of the EIGRPv6 process with the show ipv6 eigrp interfaces command like this:

```
Corp#sh ipv6 eigrp interfaces
IPv6-EIGRP interfaces for process 10
                     Xmit Queue   Mean   Pacing Time   Multicast    Pending
Interface    Peers   Un/Reliable  SRTT   Un/Reliable   Flow Timer   Routes
Se0/0/0        1        0/0       1236       0/10           0          0
Se0/0/1        1        0/0       1236       0/10           0          0
Gig0/1         0        0/0       1236       0/10           0          0
Gig0/0         0        0/0       1236       0/10           0          0
Corp#
```

Looks great so far—all the interfaces we want in our AS are listed, so we're looking good for our Corp's local configuration. Now it's time to check if our adjacencies came up with the show ipv6 eigrp neighbors command:

```
Corp#sh ipv6 eigrp neighbors
IPv6-EIGRP neighbors for process 10
H   Address                   Interface    Hold   Uptime    SRTT   RTO   Q   Seq
                                           (sec)            (ms)       Cnt  Num
0   Link-local address:       Se0/0/0      10     00:01:40  40     1000  0   11
    FE80::201:C9FF:FED0:3301
1   Link-local address:       Se0/0/1      14     00:01:24  40     1000  0   11
    FE80::209:7CFF:FE51:B401
```

It's great that we can see neighbors listed off of each serial interface, but do you notice something missing from the preceding output? That's right, the actual IPv6 network/subnet addresses of the links aren't listed in the neighbor table! Only the link-local addresses are used for forming EIGRP neighbor adjacencies. With IPv6, neighbor interfaces and next-hop addresses are always link-local.

We can verify our configuration with the show ip protocols command:

```
Corp#sh ipv6 protocols
IPv6 Routing Protocol is "connected"
IPv6 Routing Protocol is "static
IPv6 Routing Protocol is "eigrp  10 "
  EIGRP metric weight K1=1, K2=0, K3=1, K4=0, K5=0
  EIGRP maximum hopcount 100
  EIGRP maximum metric variance 1
  Interfaces:
    Serial0/0/0
    Serial0/0/1
    GigabitEthernet0/0
    GigabitEthernet0/1
Redistributing: eigrp 10
  Maximum path: 16
  Distance: internal 90 external 170
```

You can verify the AS number from this output, but be sure to verify your K values, variance, and interfaces too. Remember that the AS number and interfaces are the first factors to check when troubleshooting.

The topology table lists all feasible routes in the network, so this output can be rather long, but let's see what this shows us:

```
Corp#sh ipv6 eigrp topology
IPv6-EIGRP Topology Table for AS 10/ID(1.1.1.1)

Codes: P - Passive, A - Active, U - Update, Q - Query, R - Reply,
       r - Reply status
```

```
P 2001:DB8:C34D:11::/64, 1 successors, FD is 2169856
        via Connected, Serial0/0/0
P 2001:DB8:C34D:12::/64, 1 successors, FD is 2169856
        via Connected, Serial0/0/1
P 2001:DB8:C34D:14::/64, 1 successors, FD is 2816
        via Connected, GigabitEthernet0/1
P 2001:DB8:C34D:13::/64, 1 successors, FD is 2816
        via Connected, GigabitEthernet0/0
P 2001:DB8:C34D:17::/64, 1 successors, FD is 2170112
        via FE80::201:C9FF:FED0:3301 (2170112/2816), Serial0/0/0
P 2001:DB8:C34D:18::/64, 1 successors, FD is 2170112
        via FE80::201:C9FF:FED0:3301 (2170112/2816), Serial0/0/0
P 2001:DB8:C34D:15::/64, 1 successors, FD is 2170112
        via FE80::209:7CFF:FE51:B401 (2170112/2816), Serial0/0/1
P 2001:DB8:C34D:16::/64, 1 successors, FD is 2170112
        via FE80::209:7CFF:FE51:B401 (2170112/2816), Serial0/0/1
```

Since we only have eight networks in our internetwork, we can see all eight networks in the topology table, which clearly is as it should be. I've highlighted a couple of things I want to discuss, and the first is that you need to be able to read and understand a topology table. This includes understanding which routes are directly connected and which are being advertised via neighbors. The via Connected shows us our directly connected networks. The second item I want to show you is (2170112/2816), which is the FD/AD, and by the way, it's no different than if you're working with IPv4.

So let's wrap up this chapter by taking a look at a routing table:

```
Corp#sh ipv6 route eigrp
IPv6 Routing Table - 13 entries
Codes: C - Connected, L - Local, S - Static, R - RIP, B - BGP
       U - Per-user Static route, M - MIPv6
       I1 - ISIS L1, I2 - ISIS L2, IA - ISIS interarea, IS - ISIS summary
       O - OSPF intra, OI - OSPF inter, OE1 - OSPF ext 1, OE2 - OSPF ext 2
       ON1 - OSPF NSSA ext 1, ON2 - OSPF NSSA ext 2
       D - EIGRP, EX - EIGRP external
C   2001:DB8:C34D:11::/64 [0/0]
    via ::, Serial0/0/0
L   2001:DB8:C34D:11:230:A3FF:FE36:B101/128 [0/0]
    via ::, Serial0/0/0
C   2001:DB8:C34D:12::/64 [0/0]
    via ::, Serial0/0/1
L   2001:DB8:C34D:12:230:A3FF:FE36:B102/128 [0/0]
    via ::, Serial0/0/1
```

```
C    2001:DB8:C34D:13::/64 [0/0]
       via ::, GigabitEthernet0/0
L    2001:DB8:C34D:13:2E0:F7FF:FEDA:7501/128 [0/0]
       via ::, GigabitEthernet0/0
C    2001:DB8:C34D:14::/64 [0/0]
       via ::, GigabitEthernet0/1
L    2001:DB8:C34D:14:2E0:F7FF:FEDA:7502/128 [0/0]
       via ::, GigabitEthernet0/1
D    2001:DB8:C34D:15::/64 [90/2170112]
       via FE80::209:7CFF:FE51:B401, Serial0/0/1
D    2001:DB8:C34D:16::/64 [90/2170112]
       via FE80::209:7CFF:FE51:B401, Serial0/0/1
D    2001:DB8:C34D:17::/64 [90/2170112]
       via FE80::201:C9FF:FED0:3301, Serial0/0/0
D    2001:DB8:C34D:18::/64 [90/2170112]
       via FE80::201:C9FF:FED0:3301, Serial0/0/0
L    FF00::/8 [0/0]
       via ::, Null0
```

I highlighted the EIGRPv6 injected routes that were injected into the routing table. It's important to notice that in order for IPv6 to get to a remote network, the router uses the next-hop link-local address. Do you see that in the table? For example, via FE80::209:7CFF:FE51:B401, Serial0/0/1 is the link-local address of the NY router.

See? I told you it was easy!

Summary

It's true that this chapter has been pretty extensive, so let's briefly recap what we covered in it. EIGRP, the main focus of the chapter, is a hybrid of link-state routing and typically referred to as an advanced distance-vector protocol. It allows for unequal-cost load balancing, controlled routing updates, and formal neighbor adjacencies called relationships to be formed.

EIGRP uses the capabilities of the Reliable Transport Protocol (RTP) to communicate between neighbors and utilizes the Diffusing Update Algorithm (DUAL) to compute the best path to each remote network.

We also covered the configuration of EIGRP and explored a number of troubleshooting commands plus key ways and means to help solve some common networking issues.

Moving on, EIGRP facilitates unequal-cost load balancing, controlled routing updates, and formal neighbor adjacencies.

I also went over the configuration of EIGRP and explored a number of troubleshooting commands as well as taking you through a highly informative scenario that will not only help you to ace the exam, it will help you confront and overcome many troubleshooting issues common to today's internetworks!

Finally, I went over the easiest topic at the end of this long chapter: EIGRPv6. Easy to understand, configure, and verify!

Exam Essentials

Know EIGRP features.   EIGRP is a classless, advanced distance-vector protocol that supports IP and now IPv6. EIGRP uses a unique algorithm, called DUAL, to maintain route information and uses RTP to communicate with other EIGRP routers reliably.

Know how to configure EIGRP.   Be able to configure basic EIGRP. This is configured the same as RIP with classful addresses.

Know how to verify EIGRP operation.   Know all of the EIGRP show commands and be familiar with their output and the interpretation of the main components of their output.

Be able to read an EIGRP topology table.   Understand which are successors, which are feasible successors, and which routes will become successors if the main successor fails.

You must be able to troubleshoot EIGRP.   Go through the EIGRP troubleshooting scenario and make sure you understand to look for the AS number, ACLs, passive interfaces, variance, and other factors.

Be able to read an EIGRP neighbor table.   Understand the output of the show ip eigrp neighbor command.

Understand how to configure EIGRPv6.   To configure EIGRPv6, first create the autonomous system from global configuration mode and perform a no shutdown. Then enable EIGRPv6 on each interface individually.

Written Lab 3

You can find the answers to this lab in Appendix A, "Answers to Written Labs."

1. What is the command to enable EIGRPv6 from global configuration mode?
2. What is the EIGRPv6 multicast address?
3. True/False: Each router within an EIGRP domain must use different AS numbers.
4. If you have two routers with various K values assigned, what will this do to the link?
5. What type of EIGRP interface will neither send nor receive Hello packets?
6. Which type of EIGRP route entry describes a feasible successor?

Hands-on Labs

In this section, you will use the following network and add EIGRP and EIGRPv6 routing.

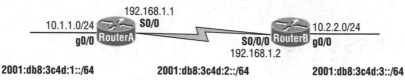

The first lab requires you to configure two routers for EIGRP and then view the configuration. In the last lab, you will be asked to enable EIGRPv6 routing on the same network. Note that the labs in this chapter were written to be used with real equipment—real cheap equipment, that is. I wrote these labs with the cheapest, oldest routers I had lying around so you can see that you don't need expensive gear to get through some of the hardest labs in this book. However, you can use the free LammleSim IOS version simulator or Cisco's Packet Tracer to run through these labs.

The labs in this chapter are as follows:

Lab 3.1: Configuring and Verifying EIGRP

Lab 3.2: Configuring and Verifying EIGRPv6

Hands-on Lab 3.1: Configuring and Verifying EIGRP

This lab will assume you have configured the IP addresses on the interfaces as shown in the preceding diagram.

1. Implement EIGRP on RouterA.

   ```
   RouterA#conf t
   Enter configuration commands, one per line.
     End with CNTL/Z.
   RouterA(config)#router eigrp 100
   RouterA(config-router)#network 192.168.1.0
   RouterA(config-router)#network 10.0.0.0
   RouterA(config-router)#^Z
   RouterA#
   ```

2. Implement EIGRP on RouterB.

   ```
   RouterB#conf t
   Enter configuration commands, one per line.
     End with CNTL/Z.
   RouterB(config)#router eigrp 100
   ```

```
RouterB(config-router)#network 192.168.1.0
RouterA(config-router)#network 10.0.0.0
RouterB(config-router)#exit
RouterB#
```

3. Display the topology table for RouterA.
    ```
    RouterA#show ip eigrp topology
    ```

4. Display the routing table for RouterA.
    ```
    RouterA #show ip route
    ```

5. Display the neighbor table for RouterA.
    ```
    RouterA show ip eigrp neighbor
    ```

6. Type the command on each router to fix the routing problem. You did see a problem, didn't you? Yes, the network is discontiguous.
    ```
    RouterA#config t
    RouterA(config)#router eigrp 100
    RouterA(config-router)#no auto-summary

    RouterB#config t
    RouterA(config)#router eigrp 100
    RouterA(config-router)#no auto-summary
    ```

7. Verify your routes with the show ip route command.

Hands-on Lab 3.2: Configuring and Verifying EIGRPv6

This lab will assume you configured the IPv6 address as shown in the diagram preceding Lab 5.1.

1. Implement EIGRPv6 on RouterA with AS 100.
    ```
    RouterA#config t
    RouterA (config)#ipv6 router eigrp 100
    RouterA (config-rtr)#no shut
    RouterA (config-rtr)#router-id 2.2.2.2
    RouterA (config-rtr)#int s0/0
    RouterA (config-if)#ipv6 eigrp 100
    RouterA (config-if)#int g0/0
    RouterA (config-if)#ipv6 eigrp 100
    ```

2. Implement EIGRP on RouterB.
    ```
    RouterA#config t
    RouterB(config)#ipv6 router eigrp 100
    ```

```
RouterB(config-rtr)#no shut
RouterB(config-rtr)#router-id 2.2.2.2
RouterB(config-rtr)#int s0/0
RouterB(config-if)#ipv6 eigrp 100
RouterB(config-if)#int g0/0
RouterB(config-if)#ipv6 eigrp 100
```

3. Display the topology table RouterA.
    ```
    RouterA#show ipv6 eigrp topology
    ```

4. Display the routing table for RouterA.
    ```
    RouterA #show ipv6 route
    ```

5. Display the neighbor table for RouterA.
    ```
    RouterA show ipv6 eigrp neighbor
    ```

Review Questions

The following questions are designed to test your understanding of this chapter's material. For more information on how to get additional questions, please see www.lammle.com/ccna.

You can find the answers to these questions in Appendix B, "Answers to Review Questions."

1. There are three possible routes for a router to reach a destination network. The first route is from OSPF with a metric of 782. The second route is from RIPv2 with a metric of 4. The third is from EIGRP with a composite metric of 20514560. Which route will be installed by the router in its routing table?

    A. RIPv2

    B. EIGRP

    C. OSPF

    D. All three

2. Which EIGRP information is held in RAM and maintained through the use of Hello and update packets? (Choose two.)

    A. Neighbor table

    B. STP table

    C. Topology table

    D. DUAL table

3. What will be the reported distance to a downstream neighbor router for the 10.10.30.0 network, with the neighbor adding the cost to find the true FD?

    ```
    P 10.10.30.0/24, 1 successors, FD is 2297856
            via 172.16.10.2 (2297856/128256), Serial0/0
    ```

    A. Four hops

    B. 2297856

    C. 128256

    D. EIGRP doesn't use reported distances.

4. Where are EIGRP successor routes stored?

    A. In the routing table only

    B. In the neighbor table only

    C. In the topology table only

    D. In the routing table and the neighbor table

E. In the routing table and the topology table

F. In the topology table and the neighbor table

5. Which command will display all the EIGRP feasible successor routes known to a router?

A. `show ip routes *`

B. `show ip eigrp summary`

C. `show ip eigrp topology`

D. `show ip eigrp adjacencies`

E. `show ip eigrp neighbors detail`

6. Which of the following commands are used when routing with EIGRP or EIGRPv6? (Choose three.)

A. `network 10.0.0.0`

B. `eigrp router-id`

C. `variance`

D. `router eigrp`

E. `maximum-paths`

7. Serial0/0 goes down. How will EIGRP send packets to the 10.1.1.0 network?

```
Corp#show ip eigrp topology
[output cut]
P 10.1.1.0/24, 2 successors, FD is 2681842
          via 10.1.2.2 (2681842/2169856), Serial0/0
          via 10.1.3.1 (2973467/2579243), Serial0/2
          via 10.1.3.3 (2681842/2169856), Serial0/1
```

A. EIGRP will put the 10.1.1.0 network into active mode.

B. EIGRP will drop all packets destined for 10.1.1.0.

C. EIGRP will just keep sending packets out s0/1.

D. EIGRP will use s0/2 as the successor and keep routing to 10.1.1.0.

8. What command do you use to enable EIGRPv6 on an interface?

A. `router eigrp as`

B. `ip router eigrp as`

C. `router eigrpv6 as`

D. `ipv6 eigrp as`

9. What command was typed in to have these two paths to network 10.10.50.0 in the routing table?

```
D        10.10.50.0 [90/2297856] via 172.16.10.6, 00:00:20, Serial0/1
                     [90/6893568] via 172.16.10.2, 00:00:20, Serial0/0
```

    A. maximum-paths 2

    B. variance 2

    C. variance 3

    D. maximum-hops 2

10. A route to network 10.10.10.0 goes down. How does EIGRP respond in the local routing table? (Choose two.)

    A. It sends a poison reverse with a maximum hop of 16.

    B. If there is a feasible successor, that is copied and placed into the routing table.

    C. If a feasible successor is not found, a query will be sent to all neighbors asking for a path to network 10.10.10.0.

    D. EIGRP will broadcast out all interfaces that the link to network 10.10.10.0 is down and that it is looking for a feasible successor.

11. You need the IP address of the devices with which the router has established an adjacency. Also, the retransmit interval and the queue counts for the adjacent routers need to be checked. What command will display the required information?

    A. show ip eigrp adjacency

    B. show ip eigrp topology

    C. show ip eigrp interfaces

    D. show ip eigrp neighbors

12. For some reason, you cannot establish an adjacency relationship on a common Ethernet link between two routers. Looking at the output shown here, what are the causes of the problem? (Choose two.)

```
RouterA##show ip protocols
Routing Protocol is "eigrp 20"
  Outgoing update filter list for all interfaces is not set
  Incoming update filter list for all interfaces is not set
  Default networks flagged in outgoing updates
  Default networks accepted from incoming updates
  EIGRP metric weight K1=1, K2=0, K3=1, K4=0, K5=0

RouterB##show ip protocols
Routing Protocol is "eigrp 220"
  Outgoing update filter list for all interfaces is not set
  Incoming update filter list for all interfaces is not set
  Default networks flagged in outgoing updates
  Default networks accepted from incoming updates
  EIGRP metric weight K1=1, K2=1, K3=1, K4=0, K5=0
```

    A. EIGRP is running on RouterA and OSPF is running on RouterB.

    B. There is an ACL set on the routing protocol.

    C. The AS numbers don't match.

    D. There is no default network accepted from incoming updates.

    E. The K values don't match.

    F. There is a passive interface set.

13. Which are true regarding EIGRP successor routes? (Choose two.)

    A. A successor route is used by EIGRP to forward traffic to a destination.

    B. Successor routes are saved in the topology table to be used if the primary route fails.

    C. Successor routes are flagged as "active" in the routing table.

    D. A successor route may be backed up by a feasible successor route.

    E. Successor routes are stored in the neighbor table following the discovery process.

14. The remote RouterB router has a directly connected network of 10.255.255.64/27. Which two of the following EIGRP network statements could you use so this directly connected network will be advertised under the EIGRP process? (Choose two.)

    A. `network 10.255.255.64`

    B. `network 10.255.255.64 0.0.0.31`

    C. `network 10.255.255.64 0.0.0.0`

    D. `network 10.255.255.64 0.0.0.15`

15. RouterA and RouterB are connected via their Serial 0/0 interfaces, but they have not formed an adjacency. Based on the following output, what could be the problem?

```
RouterA#sh ip protocols
Routing Protocol is "eigrp 220"
  Outgoing update filter list for all interfaces is not set
  Incoming update filter list for all interfaces is not set
  Default networks flagged in outgoing updates
  Default networks accepted from incoming updates
  EIGRP metric weight K1=1, K2=0, K3=1, K4=0, K5=0
  EIGRP maximum hopcount 100
  EIGRP maximum metric variance 2
  Redistributing: eigrp 220
  EIGRP NSF-aware route hold timer is 240s
  Automatic network summarization is in effect
  Maximum path: 4
  Routing for Networks:
    10.0.0.0
    172.16.0.0
    192.168.1.0
  Routing Information Sources:
    Gateway          Distance      Last Update
    (this router)          90      20:51:48
    192.168.1.2            90      00:22:58
    172.16.10.6           90      01:58:46
    172.16.10.2           90      01:59:52
  Distance: internal 90 external 170
```

```
RouterB#sh ip protocols
Routing Protocol is "eigrp 220"
  Outgoing update filter list for all interfaces is not set
  Incoming update filter list for all interfaces is not set
  Default networks flagged in outgoing updates
  Default networks accepted from incoming updates
  EIGRP metric weight K1=1, K2=0, K3=1, K4=0, K5=0
  EIGRP maximum hopcount 100
  EIGRP maximum metric variance 2
  Redistributing: eigrp 220
  EIGRP NSF-aware route hold timer is 240s
  Automatic network summarization is in effect
  Maximum path: 4
  Routing for Networks:
    10.0.0.0
    172.16.0.0
    192.168.1.0
Passive Interface(s):
    Serial0/0
  Routing Information Sources:
    Gateway         Distance      Last Update
    (this router)        90       20:51:48
    192.168.1.2          90       00:22:58
    172.16.10.6          90       01:58:46
    172.16.10.2          90       01:59:52
  Distance: internal 90 external 170
```

A. The metric K values don't match.

B. The AS numbers don't match.

C. There is a passive interface on RouterB.

D. There is an ACL set on RouterA.

16. How many paths will EIGRPv6 load-balance by default?

A. 16

B. 32

C. 4

D. None

17. What would your configurations be on RouterB based on the illustration? (Choose two.)

A. (config)#router eigrp 10

B. (config)#ipv6 router eigrp 10

C. (config)#ipv6 router 2001:db8:3c4d:15::/64

D. (config-if)#ip eigrp 10

E. (config-if)#ipv6 eigrp 10

F. (config-if)#ipv6 router eigrp 10

18. RouterA has a feasible successor not shown in the following output. Based on what you can learn from the output, which one of the following will be the successor for 2001:db8:c34d:18::/64 if the current successor fails?

via FE80::201:C9FF:FED0:3301 (29110112/33316), Serial0/0/0

via FE80::209:7CFF:FE51:B401 (4470112/42216), Serial0/0/1

via FE80::209:7CFF:FE51:B401 (2170112/2816), Serial0/0/2

A. Serial0/0/0

B. Serial0/0/1

C. Serial0/0/2

D. There is no feasible successor.

19. You have router output as shown in the following illustrations with routers running IOS 12.4. However, the two networks are not sharing routing table route entries. What is the problem?

```
RouterA#sh ip protocols
Routing Protocol is "eigrp 930"
  Outgoing update filter list for all interfaces is not set
  Incoming update filter list for all interfaces is not set
  Default networks flagged in outgoing updates
  Default networks accepted from incoming updates
  EIGRP metric weight K1=1, K2=0, K3=1, K4=0, K5=0
  EIGRP maximum hopcount 100
  EIGRP maximum metric variance 2
  Redistributing: eigrp 930
  EIGRP NSF-aware route hold timer is 240s
  Automatic network summarization is in effect
  Automatic address summarization:
    192.168.1.0/24 for FastEthernet0/0
      Summarizing with metric 2169856
    10.0.0.0/8 for Serial0/0
      Summarizing with metric 28160
 [output cut]

RouterB#sh ip protocols
Routing Protocol is "eigrp 930"
  Outgoing update filter list for all interfaces is not set
  Incoming update filter list for all interfaces is not set
  Default networks flagged in outgoing updates
  Default networks accepted from incoming updates
  EIGRP metric weight K1=1, K2=0, K3=1, K4=0, K5=0
  EIGRP maximum hopcount 100
  EIGRP maximum metric variance 3
  Redistributing: eigrp 930
  EIGRP NSF-aware route hold timer is 240s
  Automatic network summarization is in effect
  Maximum path: 4
  Routing for Networks:
    10.0.0.0
    192.168.1.0
Passive Interface(s):
    Serial0/0
  Routing Information Sources:
    Gateway         Distance      Last Update
    (this router)         90      20:51:48
    192.168.1.2          90      00:22:58
    172.16.10.6          90      01:58:46
    172.16.10.2          90      01:59:52
Distance: internal 90 external 170
```

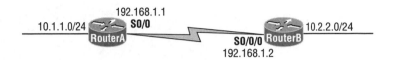

A. The variances don't match between routers.

B. The metrics are not valid between neighbors.

C. There is a discontiguous network.

D. There is a passive interface on RouterB.

E. An ACL is set on the router.

20. Which should you look for when troubleshooting an adjacency? (Choose four.)

A. Verify the AS numbers.

B. Verify that you have the proper interfaces enabled for EIGRP.

C. Make sure there are no mismatched K values.

D. Check your passive interface settings.

E. Make sure your remote routers are not connected to the Internet.

F. If authentication is configured, make sure all routers use different passwords.

Chapter

4

Open Shortest Path First (OSPF)

THE FOLLOWING ICND1 EXAM TOPICS ARE COVERED IN THIS CHAPTER:

✓ **2.0 Routing Technologies**

✓ **2.2 Compare and contrast distance vector and link-state routing protocols**

✓ **2.3 Compare and contrast interior and exterior routing protocols**

✓ **2.4 Configure, verify, and troubleshoot single area and multiarea OSPFv2 for IPv4 (excluding authentication, filtering, manual summarization, redistribution, stub, virtual-link, and LSAs)**

✓ **2.5 Configure, verify, and troubleshoot single area and multiarea OSPFv3 for IPv6 (excluding authentication, filtering, manual summarization, redistribution, stub, virtual-link, and LSAs)**

Open Shortest Path First (OSPF) is by far the most popular and important routing protocol in use today—so important, I'm devoting this entire chapter to it! Sticking with the same approach we've adhered to throughout this book, we'll begin with the basics by completely familiarizing you with key OSPF terminology. Once we've covered that thoroughly, I'll guide you through OSPF's internal operation and then move on to tell you all about OSPF's many advantages over RIP.

This chapter is going to be more than chock full of vitally important information and it's also going to be really exciting because together, we'll explore some seriously critical factors and issues innate to implementing OSPF! I'll walk you through exactly how to implement single-area OSPF in a variety of networking environments and then demonstrate some great techniques you'll need to verify that everything is configured correctly and running smoothly.

To find up-to-the-minute updates for this chapter, please see www.lammle.com/ccna or the book's web page at www.sybex.com/go/ccna.

Open Shortest Path First (OSPF) Basics

Open Shortest Path First is an open standard routing protocol that's been implemented by a wide variety of network vendors, including Cisco. And it's that open standard characteristic that's the key to OSPF's flexibility and popularity.

Most people opt for OSPF, which works by using the Dijkstra algorithm to initially construct a shortest path tree and follows that by populating the routing table with the resulting best paths. EIGRP's convergence time may be blindingly fast, but OSPF isn't that far behind, and its quick convergence is another reason it's a favorite. Another two great advantages OSPF offers are that it supports multiple, equal-cost routes to the same destination and, like EIGRP, it also supports both IP and IPv6 routed protocols.

Here's a list that summarizes some of OSPF's best features:

- Allows for the creation of areas and autonomous systems
- Minimizes routing update traffic
- Is highly flexible, versatile, and scalable
- Supports VLSM/CIDR

- Offers an unlimited hop count
- Is open standard and supports multi-vendor deployment

Because OSPF is the first link-state routing protocol that most people run into, it's a good idea to size it up against more traditional distance-vector protocols like RIPv2 and RIPv1. Table 4.1 presents a nice comparison of all three of these common protocols.

TABLE 4.1 OSPF and RIP comparison

Characteristic	OSPF	RIPv2	RIPv1
Type of protocol	Link state	Distance vector	Distance vector
Classless support	Yes	Yes	No
VLSM support	Yes	Yes	No
Auto-summarization	No	Yes	Yes
Manual summarization	Yes	Yes	No
Noncontiguous support	Yes	Yes	No
Route propagation	Multicast on change	Periodic multicast	Periodic broadcast
Path metric	Bandwidth	Hops	Hops
Hop count limit	None	15	15
Convergence	Fast	Slow	Slow
Peer authentication	Yes	Yes	No
Hierarchical network requirement	Yes (using areas)	No (flat only)	No (flat only)
Updates	Event triggered	Periodic	Periodic
Route computation	Dijkstra	Bellman-Ford	Bellman-Ford

I want you know that OSPF has many features beyond the few I've listed in Table 4.1, and all of them combine to produce a fast, scalable, robust protocol that's also flexible enough to be actively deployed in a vast array of production networks!

One of OSPF's most useful traits is that its design is intended to be hierarchical in use, meaning that it allows us to subdivide the larger internetwork into smaller internetworks called areas. It's a really powerful feature that I recommend using, and I promise to show you how to do that later in the chapter.

Here are three of the biggest reasons to implement OSPF in a way that makes full use of its intentional, hierarchical design:

- To decrease routing overhead

- To speed up convergence

- To confine network instability to single areas of the network

Because free lunches are invariably hard to come by, all this wonderful functionality predictably comes at a price and doesn't exactly make configuring OSPF any easier. But no worries—we'll crush it!

Let's start by checking out Figure 4.1, which shows a very typical, yet simple OSPF design. I really want to point out the fact that some routers connect to the backbone—called area 0—the backbone area. OSPF absolutely must have an area 0, and all other areas should connect to it except for those connected via virtual links, which are beyond the scope of this book. A router that connects other areas to the backbone area within an AS is called an *area border router (ABR)*, and even these must have at least one of their interfaces connected to area 0.

FIGURE 4.1   OSPF design example. An OSPF hierarchical design minimizes routing table entries and keeps the impact of any topology changes contained within a specific area.

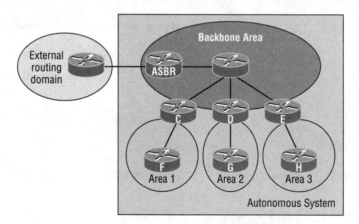

OSPF runs great inside an autonomous system, but it can also connect multiple autonomous systems together. The router that connects these ASs is called an *autonomous system boundary router (ASBR)*. Ideally, your aim is to create other areas of networks to help keep route updates to a minimum, especially in larger networks. Doing this also keeps problems from propagating throughout the network, effectively isolating them to a single area.

But let's pause here to cover some key OSPF terms that are really essential for you to nail down before we move on any further.

OSPF Terminology

Imagine being given a map and compass with no prior concept of east, west, north or south—not even what rivers, mountains, lakes, or deserts are. I'm guessing that without any ability to orient yourself in a basic way, your cool, new tools wouldn't help you get anywhere but completely lost, right? This is exactly why we're going to begin exploring OSPF by getting you solidly acquainted with a fairly long list of terms before setting out from base camp into the great unknown! Here are those vital terms to commit to memory now:

Link   A *link* is a network or router interface assigned to any given network. When an interface is added to the OSPF process, it's considered to be a link. This link, or interface, will have up or down state information associated with it as well as one or more IP addresses.

Router ID   The *router ID (RID)* is an IP address used to identify the router. Cisco chooses the router ID by using the highest IP address of all configured loopback interfaces. If no loopback interfaces are configured with addresses, OSPF will choose the highest IP address out of all active physical interfaces. To OSPF, this is basically the "name" of each router.

Neighbor   *Neighbors* are two or more routers that have an interface on a common network, such as two routers connected on a point-to-point serial link. OSPF neighbors must have a number of common configuration options to be able to successfully establish a neighbor relationship, and all of these options must be configured exactly the same way:

- Area ID
- Stub area flag
- Authentication password (if using one)
- Hello and Dead intervals

Adjacency   An *adjacency* is a relationship between two OSPF routers that permits the direct exchange of route updates. Unlike EIGRP, which directly shares routes with all of its neighbors, OSPF is really picky about sharing routing information and will directly share routes only with neighbors that have also established adjacencies. And not all neighbors will become adjacent—this depends upon both the type of network and the configuration of the routers. In multi-access networks, routers form adjacencies with designated and backup designated routers. In point-to-point and point-to-multipoint networks, routers form adjacencies with the router on the opposite side of the connection.

Designated router   A *designated router (DR)* is elected whenever OSPF routers are connected to the same broadcast network to minimize the number of adjacencies formed and to publicize received routing information to and from the remaining routers on the broadcast network or link. Elections are won based upon a router's priority level, with the one having the highest priority becoming the winner. If there's a tie, the router ID will be used to break it. All routers on the shared network will establish adjacencies with the DR and the BDR, which ensures that all routers' topology tables are synchronized.

Backup designated router   A *backup designated router (BDR)* is a hot standby for the DR on broadcast, or multi-access, links. The BDR receives all routing updates from OSPF adjacent routers but does not disperse LSA updates.

Hello protocol   The OSPF Hello protocol provides dynamic neighbor discovery and maintains neighbor relationships. Hello packets and Link State Advertisements (LSAs) build and maintain the topological database. Hello packets are addressed to multicast address 224.0.0.5.

Neighborship database   The *neighborship database* is a list of all OSPF routers for which Hello packets have been seen. A variety of details, including the router ID and state, are maintained on each router in the neighborship database.

Topological database   The *topological database* contains information from all of the Link State Advertisement packets that have been received for an area. The router uses the information from the topology database as input into the Dijkstra algorithm that computes the shortest path to every network.

   LSA packets are used to update and maintain the topological database.

Link State Advertisement   A *Link State Advertisement (LSA)* is an OSPF data packet containing link-state and routing information that's shared among OSPF routers. An OSPF router will exchange LSA packets only with routers to which it has established adjacencies.

OSPF areas   An *OSPF area* is a grouping of contiguous networks and routers. All routers in the same area share a common area ID. Because a router can be a member of more than one area at a time, the area ID is associated with specific interfaces on the router. This would allow some interfaces to belong to area 1 while the remaining interfaces can belong to area 0. All of the routers within the same area have the same topology table. When configuring OSPF with multiple areas, you've got to remember that there must be an area 0 and that this is typically considered the backbone area. Areas also play a role in establishing a hierarchical network organization—something that really enhances the scalability of OSPF!

Broadcast (multi-access)   *Broadcast (multi-access) networks* such as Ethernet allow multiple devices to connect to or access the same network, enabling a *broadcast* ability in which a single packet is delivered to all nodes on the network. In OSPF, a DR and BDR must be elected for each broadcast multi-access network.

Nonbroadcast multi-access   *Nonbroadcast multi-access (NBMA)* networks are networks such as Frame Relay, X.25, and Asynchronous Transfer Mode (ATM). These types of networks allow for multi-access without broadcast ability like Ethernet. NBMA networks require special OSPF configuration to function properly.

Point-to-point   *Point-to-point* refers to a type of network topology made up of a direct connection between two routers that provides a single communication path. The point-to-point connection can be physical—for example, a serial cable that directly connects two routers—or logical, where two routers thousands of miles apart are connected by a circuit in a Frame Relay network. Either way, point-to-point configurations eliminate the need for DRs or BDRs.

Point-to-multipoint   *Point-to-multipoint* refers to a type of network topology made up of a series of connections between a single interface on one router and multiple destination routers. All interfaces on all routers share the point-to-multipoint connection and belong to the same network. Point-to-multipoint networks can be further classified according to whether they support broadcasts or not. This is important because it defines the kind of OSPF configurations you can deploy.

All of these terms play a critical role when you're trying to understand how OSPF actually works, so again, make sure you're familiar with each of them. Having these terms down will enable you to confidently place them in their proper context as we progress on our journey through the rest of this chapter!

OSPF Operation

Fully equipped with your newly acquired knowledge of the terms and technologies we just covered, it's now time to delve into how OSPF discovers, propagates, and ultimately chooses routes. Once you know how OSPF achieves these tasks, you'll understand how OSPF operates internally really well.

OSPF operation is basically divided into these three categories:

- Neighbor and adjacency initialization
- LSA flooding
- SPF tree calculation

The beginning neighbor/adjacency formation stage is a very big part of OSPF operation. When OSPF is initialized on a router, the router allocates memory for it, as well as for the maintenance of both neighbor and topology tables. Once the router determines which interfaces have been configured for OSPF, it will then check to see if they're active and begin sending Hello packets as shown in Figure 4.2.

FIGURE 4.2   The Hello protocol

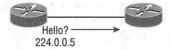

The Hello protocol is used to discover neighbors, establish adjacencies, and maintain relationships with other OSPF routers. Hello packets are periodically sent out of each enabled OSPF interface and in environments that support multicast.

The address used for this is 224.0.0.5, and the frequency with which Hello packets are sent out depends upon the network type and topology. Broadcast and point-to-point networks send Hellos every 10 seconds, whereas non-broadcast and point-to-multipoint networks send them every 30 seconds.

LSA Flooding

LSA flooding is the method OSPF uses to share routing information. Via Link State Updates (LSU's) packets, LSA information containing link-state data is shared with all OSPF routers within an area. The network topology is created from the LSA updates, and flooding is used so that all OSPF routers have the same topology map to make SPF calculations with.

Efficient flooding is achieved through the use of a reserved multicast address: 224.0.0.5 (AllSPFRouters). LSA updates, which indicate that something in the topology has changed, are handled a bit differently. The network type determines the multicast address used for sending updates. Table 4.2 contains the multicast addresses associated with LSA flooding. Point-to-multipoint networks use the adjacent router's unicast IP address.

TABLE 4.2   LSA update multicast addresses

Network Type	Multicast Address	Description
Point-to-point	224.0.0.5	AllSPFRouters
Broadcast	224.0.0.6	AllDRouters
Point-to-multipoint	NA	NA

Once the LSA updates have been flooded throughout the network, each recipient must acknowledge that the flooded update has been received. It's also important for recipients to validate the LSA update.

SPF Tree Calculation

Within an area, each router calculates the best/shortest path to every network in that same area. This calculation is based upon the information collected in the topology database and an algorithm called shortest path first (SPF). Picture each router in an area constructing a tree—much like a family tree—where the router is the root and all other networks are arranged along the branches and leaves. This is the shortest-path tree used by the router to insert OSPF routes into the routing table.

It's important to understand that this tree contains only networks that exist in the same area as the router itself does. If a router has interfaces in multiple areas, then separate trees will be constructed for each area. One of the key criteria considered during the route selection process of the SPF algorithm is the metric or cost of each potential path to a network. But this SPF calculation doesn't apply to routes from other areas.

OSPF Metrics

OSPF uses a metric referred to as *cost*. A cost is associated with every outgoing interface included in an SPF tree. The cost of the entire path is the sum of the costs of the outgoing interfaces along the path. Because cost is an arbitrary value as defined in RFC 2338, Cisco had to implement its own method of calculating the cost for each OSPF-enabled interface. Cisco uses a simple equation of $10^8/bandwidth$, where *bandwidth* is the configured bandwidth for the interface. Using this rule, a 100 Mbps Fast Ethernet interface would have a default OSPF cost of 1 and a 1,000 Mbps Ethernet interface would have a cost of 1.

Important to note is that this value can be overridden with the `ip ospf cost` command. The cost is manipulated by changing the value to a number within the range of 1 to 65,535. Because the cost is assigned to each link, the value must be changed on the specific interface you want to change the cost on.

 Cisco bases link cost on bandwidth. Other vendors may use other metrics to calculate a given link's cost. When connecting links between routers from different vendors, you'll probably have to adjust the cost to match another vendor's router because both routers must assign the same cost to the link for OSPF to work properly.

Configuring OSPF

Configuring basic OSPF isn't as simple as configuring RIP and EIGRP, and it can get really complex once the many options that are allowed within OSPF are factored in. But that's okay because you really only need to focus on basic, single-area OSPF configuration at this point. Coming up, I'll show you how to configure single-area OSPF.

The two factors that are foundational to OSPF configuration are enabling OSPF and configuring OSPF areas.

Enabling OSPF

The easiest and also least scalable way to configure OSPF is to just use a single area. Doing this requires a minimum of two commands.

The first command used to activate the OSPF routing process is as follows:

```
Router(config)#router ospf ?
<1-65535> Process ID
```

A value in the range from 1 to 65,535 identifies the OSPF process ID. It's a unique number on this router that groups a series of OSPF configuration commands under a specific running process. Different OSPF routers don't have to use the same process ID to communicate. It's a purely local value that doesn't mean a lot, but you still need to remember that it cannot start at 0; it has to start at a minimum of 1.

You can have more than one OSPF process running simultaneously on the same router if you want, but this isn't the same as running multi-area OSPF. The second process will maintain an entirely separate copy of its topology table and manage its communications independently of the first one and you use it when you want OSPF to connect multiple ASs together. Also, because the Cisco exam objectives only cover single-area OSPF with each router running a single OSPF process, that's what we'll focus on in this book.

The OSPF process ID is needed to identify a unique instance of an OSPF database and is locally significant.

Configuring OSPF Areas

After identifying the OSPF process, you need to identify the interfaces that you want to activate OSPF communications on as well as the area in which each resides. This will also configure the networks you're going to advertise to others.

Here's an example of a basic OSPF configuration for you, showing our second minimum command needed, the network command:

```
Router#config t
Router(config)#router ospf 1
Router(config-router)#network 10.0.0.0 0.255.255.255 area ?
  <0-4294967295>  OSPF area ID as a decimal value
  A.B.C.D         OSPF area ID in IP address format
Router(config-router)#network 10.0.0.0 0.255.255.255 area 0
```

The areas can be any number from 0 to 4.2 billion. Don't get these numbers confused with the process ID, which ranges from 1 to 65,535.

Remember, the OSPF process ID number is irrelevant. It can be the same on every router on the network, or it can be different—doesn't matter. It's locally significant and just enables the OSPF routing on the router.

The arguments of the network command are the network number (10.0.0.0) and the wildcard mask (0.255.255.255). The combination of these two numbers identifies the interfaces that OSPF will operate on and will also be included in its OSPF LSA advertisements. Based on my sample configuration, OSPF will use this command to find any interface on the router configured in the 10.0.0.0 network and will place any interface it finds into area 0.

Notice that you can create about 4.2 billion areas! In reality, a router wouldn't let you create that many, but you can certainly name them using the numbers up to 4.2 billion. You can also label an area using an IP address format.

Let me stop here a minute to give you a quick explanation of wildcards: A 0 octet in the wildcard mask indicates that the corresponding octet in the network must match exactly. On the other hand, a 255 indicates that you don't care what the corresponding octet is in the network number. A network and wildcard mask combination of 1.1.1.1 0.0.0.0 would match an interface configured exactly with 1.1.1.1 only, and nothing else. This is really useful if you want to activate OSPF on a specific interface in a very clear and simple way. If you insist on matching a range of networks, the network and wildcard mask combination of 1.1.0.0 0.0.255.255 would match any interface in the range of 1.1.0.0 to 1.1.255.255. Because of this, it's simpler and safer to stick to using wildcard masks of 0.0.0.0 and identify each OSPF interface individually. Once configured, they'll function exactly the same—one way really isn't better than the other.

The final argument is the area number. It indicates the area to which the interfaces identified in the network and wildcard mask portion belong. Remember that OSPF routers will become neighbors only if their interfaces share a network that's configured to belong to the same area number. The format of the area number is either a decimal value from the range 0 to 4,294,967,295 or a value represented in standard dotted-decimal notation. For example, area 0.0.0.0 is a legitimate area and is identical to area 0.

Wildcard Example

Before getting down to configuring our network, let's take a quick peek at a more complex OSPF network configuration to find out what our OSPF network statements would be if we were using subnets and wildcards.

In this scenario, you have a router with these four subnets connected to four different interfaces:

- 192.168.10.64/28
- 192.168.10.80/28
- 192.168.10.96/28
- 192.168.10.8/30

All interfaces need to be in area 0, so it seems to me the easiest configuration would look like this:

```
Test#config t
Test(config)#router ospf 1
Test(config-router)#network 192.168.10.0 0.0.0.255 area 0
```

I'll admit that the preceding example is actually pretty simple, but easy isn't always best—especially when dealing with OSPF! So even though this is an easy-button way to configure OSPF, it doesn't make good use of its capabilities and what fun is that? Worse yet, the objectives aren't very likely to present something this simple for you! So let's create a separate network statement for each interface using the subnet numbers and wildcards. Doing that would look something like this:

```
Test#config t
Test(config)#router ospf 1
Test(config-router)#network 192.168.10.64 0.0.0.15 area 0
Test(config-router)#network 192.168.10.80 0.0.0.15 area 0
Test(config-router)#network 192.168.10.96 0.0.0.15 area 0
Test(config-router)#network 192.168.10.8 0.0.0.3 area 0
```

Wow, now that's a different looking config! Truthfully, OSPF would work exactly the same way as it would with the easy configuration I showed you first—but unlike the easy configuration, this one covers the objectives!

And although this looks a bit complicated, trust me, it really isn't. All you need for clarity is to fully understand your block sizes! Just remember that when configuring wildcards, they're always one less than the block size. A /28 is a block size of 16, so we would add our network statement using the subnet number and then add a wildcard of 15 in the interesting octet. For the /30, which is a block size of 4, we would go with a wildcard of 3. Once you practice this a few times, it gets really easy. And do practice because we'll deal with them again when we get to access lists later on!

Let's use Figure 4.3 as an example and configure that network with OSPF using wildcards to make sure you have a solid grip on this. The figure shows a three-router network with the IP addresses of each interface.

FIGURE 4.3 Sample OSPF wildcard configuration

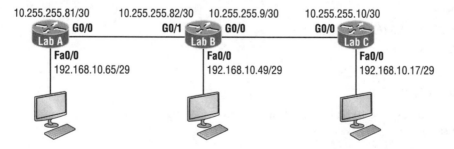

The very first thing you need to be able to do is to look at each interface and determine the subnet that the addresses are in. Hold on, I know what you're thinking: "Why don't I just use the exact IP addresses of the interface with the 0.0.0.0 wildcard?" Well, you can, but we're paying attention to Cisco exam objectives here, not just what's easiest, remember?

The IP addresses for each interface are shown in the figure. The Lab_A router has two directly connected subnets: 192.168.10.64/29 and 10.255.255.80/30. Here's the OSPF configuration using wildcards:

```
Lab_A#config t
Lab_A(config)#router ospf 1
Lab_A(config-router)#network 192.168.10.64 0.0.0.7 area 0
Lab_A(config-router)#network 10.255.255.80 0.0.0.3 area 0
```

The Lab_A router is using a /29, or 255.255.255.248, mask on the Fa0/0 interface. This is a block size of 8, which is a wildcard of 7. The G0/0 interface is a mask of 255.255.255.252—block size of 4, with a wildcard of 3. Notice that I typed in the network number, not the interface number. You can't configure OSPF this way if you can't look at the IP address and slash notation and then figure out the subnet, mask, and wildcard, can you? So don't take your exam until you can do this.

Here are other two configurations to help you practice:

```
Lab_B#config t
Lab_B(config)#router ospf 1
Lab_B(config-router)#network 192.168.10.48 0.0.0.7 area 0
Lab_B(config-router)#network 10.255.255.80 0.0.0.3 area 0
Lab_B(config-router)#network 10.255.255.8 0.0.0.3 area 0

Lab_C#config t
Lab_C(config)#router ospf 1
Lab_C(config-router)#network 192.168.10.16 0.0.0.7 area 0
Lab_C(config-router)#network 10.255.255.8 0.0.0.3 area 0
```

As I mentioned with the Lab_A configuration, you've got to be able to determine the subnet, mask, and wildcard just by looking at the IP address and mask of an interface. If you can't do that, you won't be able to configure OSPF using wildcards as I just demonstrated. So go over this until you're really comfortable with it!

Configuring Our Network with OSPF

Now we get to have some fun! Let's configure our internetwork with OSPF using just area 0. OSPF has an administrative distance of 110, but let's remove RIP while we're at it because I don't want you to get in the habit of having RIP running on your network.

There's a bunch of different ways to configure OSPF, and as I said, the simplest and easiest is to use the wildcard mask 0.0.0.0. But I want to demonstrate that we can configure each router differently with OSPF and still come up with the exact same result. This is one reason why OSPF is more fun and challenging than other routing protocols—it gives us all a lot more ways to screw things up, which automatically provides a troubleshooting opportunity! We'll use our network as shown in Figure 4.4 to configure OSPF, and by the way, notice I added a new router!

FIGURE 4.4 Our new network layout

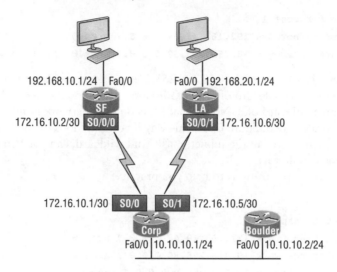

Corp

Here's the Corp router's configuration:

```
Corp#sh ip int brief
Interface       IP-Address    OK? Method Status                 Protocol
FastEthernet0/0 10.10.10.1    YES manual up                     up
Serial0/0       172.16.10.1   YES manual up                     up
FastEthernet0/1 unassigned    YES unset  administratively down down
Serial0/1       172.16.10.5   YES manual up                     up
Corp#config t
Corp(config)#no router rip
Corp(config)#router ospf 132
Corp(config-router)#network 10.10.10.1 0.0.0.0 area 0
Corp(config-router)#network 172.16.10.1 0.0.0.0 area 0
Corp(config-router)#network 172.16.10.5 0.0.0.0 area 0
```

Alright—it looks like we have a few things to talk about here. First, I removed RIP and then added OSPF. Why did I use OSPF 132? It really doesn't matter—the number is irrelevant. I guess it just felt good to use 132. But notice that I started with the show ip int brief command, just like when I was configuring RIP. I did this because it's always important to verify exactly what you are directly connected to. Doing this really helps prevent typos!

The network commands are pretty straightforward. I typed in the IP address of each interface and used the wildcard mask of 0.0.0.0, which means that the IP address must precisely match each octet. This is actually one of those times where easier is better, so just do this:

```
Corp(config)#router ospf 132
Corp(config-router)#network 172.16.10.0 0.0.0.255 area 0
```

Nice—there's only one line instead of two for the 172.16.10.0 network! I really want you to understand that OSPF will work the same here no matter which way you configure the network statement. Now, let's move on to SF. To simplify things, we're going to use our same sample configuration.

SF

The SF router has two directly connected networks. I'll use the IP addresses on each interface to configure this router.

```
SF#sh ip int brief
Interface     IP-Address     OK? Method Status                Protocol
FastEthernet0/0  192.168.10.1    YES manual up                    up
FastEthernet0/1  unassigned      YES unset  administratively down down
Serial0/0/0      172.16.10.2     YES manual up                    up
Serial0/0/1      unassigned      YES unset  administratively down down
SF#config t
SF(config)#no router rip
SF(config)#router ospf 300
SF(config-router)#network 192.168.10.1 0.0.0.0 area 0
SF(config-router)#network 172.16.10.2 0.0.0.0 area 0
*Apr 30 00:25:43.810: %OSPF-5-ADJCHG: Process 300, Nbr 172.16.10.5 on
Serial0/0/0 from LOADING to FULL, Loading Done
```

Here, all I did was to first disable RIP, turn on OSPF routing process 300, and then I added my two directly connected networks. Now let's move on to LA!

LA

We're going to give some attention to the LA router that's directly connected to two networks:

```
LA#sh ip int brief
Interface     IP-Address     OK? Method Status                Protocol
FastEthernet0/0 192.168.20.1    YES manual up                    up
```

```
FastEthernet0/1 unassigned    YES unset  administratively down down
Serial0/0/0     unassigned    YES unset  administratively down down
Serial0/0/1     172.16.10.6   YES manual up                     up
LA#config t
LA(config)#router ospf 100
LA(config-router)#network 192.168.20.0 0.0.0.255 area 0
LA(config-router)#network 172.16.0.0 0.0.255.255 area 0
*Apr 30 00:56:37.090: %OSPF-5-ADJCHG: Process 100, Nbr 172.16.10.5 on
Serial0/0/1 from LOADING to FULL, Loading Done
```

Remember that when you're configuring dynamic routing, using the show ip int brief command first will make it all so much easier!

And don't forget, I can use any process ID I want, as long as it's a value from 1 to 65,535, because it doesn't matter if all routers use the same process ID. Also, notice that I used different wildcards in this example. Doing this works really well too.

Okay, I want you to think about something for a second before we move onto more advanced OSPF topics: What if the Fa0/1 interface of the LA router was connected to a link that we didn't need OSPF running on, as shown in Figure 4.5?

FIGURE 4.5   Adding a non-OSPF network to the LA router

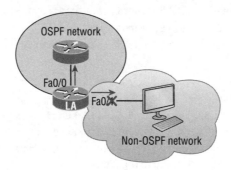

You've seen this before because I demonstrated this already back in the RIP section. We can use the same command that we did under that routing process here as well! Take a look:

```
LA(config)#router ospf 100
LA(config-router)#passive-interface fastEthernet 0/1
```

Even though this is pretty simple, you've really got to be careful before you configure this command on your router! I added this command as an example on interface Fa0/1, which happens to be an interface we're not using in this network because I want OSPF to work on my other router's interfaces.

Now it's time to configure our Corp router to advertise a default route to the SF and LA routers because doing so will make our lives a lot easier. Instead of having to configure all our routers with a default route, we'll only configure one router and then advertise that this router is the one that holds the default route—elegant!

In Figure 4.4, keep in mind that, for now, the corporate router is connected to the Internet off of Fa0/0. We'll create a default route toward this imaginary Internet and then tell the other routers that this is the route they'll use to get to the Internet. Here is the configuration:

```
Corp#config t
Corp(config)#ip route 0.0.0.0 0.0.0.0 Fa0/0
Corp(config)#router ospf 1
Corp(config-router)#default-information originate
```

Now, let's check and see if our other routers have received this default route from the Corp router:

```
SF#show ip route
[output cut]
E1 - OSPF external type 1, E2 - OSPF external type 2
[output cut]
O*E2 0.0.0.0/0 [110/1] via 172.16.10.1, 00:01:54, Serial0/0/0
SF#
```

Sure enough—the last line in the SF router shows that it received the advertisement from the Corp router regarding the fact that the corporate router is the one holding the default route out of the AS.

But hold on a second! I need to configure our new router into my lab to create the example network we'll use from here on. Here's the configuration of the new router that I connected to the same network that the Corp router is connected to via the Fa0/0 interface:

```
Router#config t
Router(config)#hostname Boulder
Boulder(config)#int f0/0
Boulder(config-if)#ip address 10.10.10.2 255.255.255.0
Boulder(config-if)#no shut
*Apr  6 18:01:38.007: %LINEPROTO-5-UPDOWN: Line protocol on Interface
FastEthernet0/0, changed state to up
Boulder(config-if)#router ospf 2
Boulder(config-router)#network 10.0.0.0 0.255.255.255 area 0
*Apr  6 18:03:27.267: %OSPF-5-ADJCHG: Process 2, Nbr 223.255.255.254 on
FastEthernet0/0 from LOADING to FULL, Loading Done
```

This is all good, but I need to make sure that you don't follow my example to a tee because here, I just quickly brought a router up without setting my passwords first. I can get away with this only because I am in a nonproduction network, so don't do this in the real world where security is key!

Anyway, now that I have my new router nicely connected with a basic configuration, we're going to move on to cover loopback interfaces, how to set the router ID (RID) used with OSPF, and finally, how to verify OSPF.

OSPF and Loopback Interfaces

It's really vital to configure loopback interfaces when using OSPF. In fact, Cisco suggests using them whenever you configure OSPF on a router for stability purposes.

Loopback interfaces are logical interfaces, which means they're virtual, software-only interfaces, not actual, physical router interfaces. A big reason we use loopback interfaces with OSPF configurations is because they ensure that an interface is always active and available for OSPF processes.

Loopback interfaces also come in very handy for diagnostic purposes as well as for OSPF configuration. Understand that if you don't configure a loopback interface on a router, the highest active IP address on a router will become that router's RID during bootup! Figure 4.6 illustrates how routers know each other by their router ID.

FIGURE 4.6   OSPF router ID (RID)

The RID is not only used to advertise routes, it's also used to elect the designated router (DR) and the backup designated router (BDR). These designated routers create adjacencies when a new router comes up and exchanges LSAs to build topological databases.

By default, OSPF uses the highest IP address on any active interface at the moment OSPF starts up to determine the RID of the router. But this behavior can be overridden via a logical interface. Remember—the highest IP address of any logical interface will always become a router's RID!

Now it's time to show you how to configure these logical loopback interfaces and how to verify them, as well as verify RIDs.

Configuring Loopback Interfaces

Configuring loopback interfaces rocks mostly because it's the easiest part of OSPF configuration, and we all need a break about now—right? So hang on—we're in the home stretch!

First, let's see what the RID is on the Corp router with the show ip ospf command:

```
Corp#sh ip ospf
 Routing Process "ospf 1" with ID 172.16.10.5
[output cut]
```

Okay, we can see that the RID is 172.16.10.5—the Serial0/1 interface of the router. So let's configure a loopback interface using a completely different IP addressing scheme:

```
Corp(config)#int loopback 0
*Mar 22 01:23:14.206: %LINEPROTO-5-UPDOWN: Line protocol on Interface
  Loopback0, changed state to up
Corp(config-if)#ip address 172.31.1.1 255.255.255.255
```

The IP scheme really doesn't matter here, but each one being in a separate subnet does! By using the /32 mask, we can use any IP address we want as long as the addresses are never the same on any two routers.

Let's configure the other routers now:

```
SF#config t
SF(config)#int loopback 0
*Mar 22 01:25:11.206: %LINEPROTO-5-UPDOWN: Line protocol on Interface
  Loopback0, changed state to up
SF(config-if)#ip address 172.31.1.2 255.255.255.255
```

Here's the configuration of the loopback interface on LA:

```
LA#config t
LA(config)#int loopback 0
*Mar 22 02:21:59.686: %LINEPROTO-5-UPDOWN: Line protocol on Interface
  Loopback0, changed state to up
LA(config-if)#ip address 172.31.1.3 255.255.255.255
```

I'm pretty sure you're wondering what the IP address mask of 255.255.255.255 (/32) means and why we don't just use 255.255.255.0 instead. While it's true that either mask works, the /32 mask is called a host mask and works fine for loopback interfaces. It also allows us to save subnets. Notice how I was able to use 172.31.1.1, .2, .3, and .4? If I didn't use the /32, I'd have to use a separate subnet for each and every router—not good!

One important question to answer before we move on is did we actually change the RIDs of our router by setting the loopback interfaces? Let's find out by taking a look at the Corp's RID:

```
Corp#sh ip ospf
 Routing Process "ospf 1" with ID 172.16.10.5
```

What happened here? You would think that because we set logical interfaces, the IP addresses under them would automatically become the RID of the router, right? Well, sort of, but only if you do one of two things: either reboot the router or delete OSPF and re-create the database on your router. Neither is all that great an option, so try to remember to create your logical interfaces before you start OSPF routing. That way, the loopback interface would always become your RID straight away!

With all this in mind, I'm going with rebooting the Corp router because it's the easier of the two options I have right now.

Now let's look and see what our RID is:

```
Corp#sh ip ospf
 Routing Process "ospf 1" with ID 172.31.1.1
```

That did the trick! The Corp router now has a new RID, so I guess I'll just go ahead and reboot all my routers to get their RIDs reset to our logical addresses. But should I really do that?

Maybe not because there is *one* other way. What do you think about adding a new RID for the router right under the router ospf *process-id* command instead? Sounds good, so I'd say let's give that a shot! Here's an example of doing that on the Corp router:

```
Corp#config t
Corp(config)#router ospf 1
Corp(config-router)#router-id 223.255.255.254
Reload or use "clear ip ospf process" command, for this to take effect
Corp(config-router)#do clear ip ospf process
Reset ALL OSPF processes? [no]: yes
*Jan 16 14:20:36.906: %OSPF-5-ADJCHG: Process 1, Nbr 192.168.20.1
on Serial0/1 from FULL to DOWN, Neighbor Down: Interface down
or detached
*Jan 16 14:20:36.906: %OSPF-5-ADJCHG: Process 1, Nbr 192.168.10.1
on Serial0/0 from FULL to DOWN, Neighbor Down: Interface down
or detached
*Jan 16 14:20:36.982: %OSPF-5-ADJCHG: Process 1, Nbr 192.168.20.1
on Serial0/1 from LOADING to FULL, Loading Done
*Jan 16 14:20:36.982: %OSPF-5-ADJCHG: Process 1, Nbr 192.168.10.1
on Serial0/0 from LOADING to FULL, Loading Done
Corp(config-router)#do sh ip ospf
 Routing Process "ospf 1" with ID 223.255.255.254
```

Now look at that—it worked! We changed the RID without reloading the router! But wait—remember, we set a logical loopback interface earlier. Does that mean the loopback interface will win over the router-id command? Well, we can see our answer...
A loopback interface will *not* override the router-id command, and we don't have to reboot the router to make it take effect as the RID!

So this process follows this hierarchy:

1. Highest active interface by default.

2. Highest logical interface overrides a physical interface.

3. The router-id overrides the interface and loopback interface.

The only thing left now is to decide whether you want to advertise the loopback interfaces under OSPF. There are pros and cons to using an address that won't be advertised versus using an address that will be. Using an unadvertised address saves on real IP address space, but the address won't appear in the OSPF table, which means you can't ping it.

So basically, what you're faced with here is a choice that equals a trade-off between the ease of debugging the network and conservation of address space—what to do? A really tight strategy is to use a private IP address scheme as I did. Do this and all will be well!

Now that we've configured all the routers with OSPF, what's next? Miller time? Nope—not yet. It's that verification thing again. We still have to make sure that OSPF is really working, and that's exactly what we're going to do next.

Verifying OSPF Configuration

There are several ways to verify proper OSPF configuration and operation, so next, I'm going to demonstrate the various OSPF show commands you need to know in order to achieve this. We're going to start by taking a quick look at the routing table of the Corp router.

First, let's issue a show ip route command on the Corp router:

```
O    192.168.10.0/24 [110/65] via 172.16.10.2, 1d17h, Serial0/0
     172.131.0.0/32 is subnetted, 1 subnets
    172.131.0.0/32 is subnetted, 1 subnets
C       172.131.1.1 is directly connected, Loopback0
     172.16.0.0/30 is subnetted, 4 subnets
C       172.16.10.4 is directly connected, Serial0/1
L       172.16.10.5/32 is directly connected, Serial0/1
C       172.16.10.0 is directly connected, Serial0/0
L       172.16.10.1/32 is directly connected, Serial0/0
O    192.168.20.0/24 [110/65] via 172.16.10.6, 1d17h, Serial0/1
     10.0.0.0/24 is subnetted, 2 subnets
C       10.10.10.0 is directly connected, FastEthernet0/0
L       10.10.10.1/32 is directly connected, FastEthernet0/0
```

The Corp router shows only two dynamic routes for the internetwork, with the O representing OSPF internal routes. The Cs are clearly our directly connected networks, and our two remote networks are showing up too—nice! Notice the 110/65, which is our administrative distance/metric.

Now that's a really sweet-looking OSPF routing table! It's important to make it easier to troubleshoot and fix an OSPF network, which is why I always use the show ip int brief command when configuring my routing protocols. It's very easy to make little mistakes with OSPF, so keep your eyes on the details!

It's time to show you all the OSPF verification commands that you need in your toolbox for now.

The *show ip ospf* Command

The show ip ospf command is what you'll need to display OSPF information for one or all OSPF processes running on the router. Information contained therein includes the router ID, area information, SPF statistics, and LSA timer information. Let's check out the output from the Corp router:

```
Corp#sh ip ospf
 Routing Process "ospf 1" with ID 223.255.255.254
 Start time: 00:08:41.724, Time elapsed: 2d16h
 Supports only single TOS(TOS0) routes
 Supports opaque LSA
 Supports Link-local Signaling (LLS)
 Supports area transit capability
 Router is not originating router-LSAs with maximum metric
 Initial SPF schedule delay 5000 msecs
 Minimum hold time between two consecutive SPFs 10000 msecs
 Maximum wait time between two consecutive SPFs 10000 msecs
 Incremental-SPF disabled
 Minimum LSA interval 5 secs
 Minimum LSA arrival 1000 msecs
 LSA group pacing timer 240 secs
 Interface flood pacing timer 33 msecs
 Retransmission pacing timer 66 msecs
 Number of external LSA 0. Checksum Sum 0x000000
 Number of opaque AS LSA 0. Checksum Sum 0x000000
 Number of DCbitless external and opaque AS LSA 0
 Number of DoNotAge external and opaque AS LSA 0
 Number of areas in this router is 1. 1 normal 0 stub 0 nssa
 Number of areas transit capable is 0
 External flood list length 0
 IETF NSF helper support enabled
```

```
Cisco NSF helper support enabled
   Area BACKBONE(0)
       Number of interfaces in this area is 3
       Area has no authentication
       SPF algorithm last executed 00:11:08.760 ago
       SPF algorithm executed 5 times
       Area ranges are
       Number of LSA 6. Checksum Sum 0x03B054
       Number of opaque link LSA 0. Checksum Sum 0x000000
       Number of DCbitless LSA 0
       Number of indication LSA 0
       Number of DoNotAge LSA 0
       Flood list length 0
```

Notice the router ID (RID) of 223.255.255.254, which is the highest IP address configured on the router. Hopefully, you also noticed that I set the RID of the corporate router to the highest IP address available with IPv4.

The *show ip ospf database* Command

Using the show ip ospf database command will give you information about the number of routers in the internetwork (AS) plus the neighboring router's ID—the topology database I mentioned earlier. Unlike the show ip eigrp topology command, this command reveals the OSPF routers, but not each and every link in the AS like EIGRP does.

The output is broken down by area. Here's a sample output, again from Corp:

Corp#**sh ip ospf database**

```
                OSPF Router with ID (223.255.255.254) (Process ID 1)
Router Link States (Area 0)

Link ID          ADV Router       Age       Seq#       Checksum Link count
10.10.10.2       10.10.10.2       966       0x80000001 0x007162 1
172.31.1.4       172.31.1.4       885       0x80000002 0x00D27E 1
192.168.10.1     192.168.10.1     886       0x8000007A 0x00BC95 3
192.168.20.1     192.168.20.1     1133      0x8000007A 0x00E348 3
223.255.255.254 223.255.255.254 925        0x8000004D 0x000B90 5


                Net Link States (Area 0)

Link ID          ADV Router       Age       Seq#       Checksum
10.10.10.1       223.255.255.254 884        0x80000002 0x008CFE
```

You can see all the routers and the RID of each router—the highest IP address on each of them. For example, the link ID and ADV router of my new Boulder router shows up twice: once with the directly connected IP address (10.10.10.2) and as the RID that I set under the OSPF process (172.31.1.4).

The router output shows the link ID—remember that an interface is also a link—and the RID of the router on that link under the ADV router, or advertising router.

The *show ip ospf interface* Command

The show ip ospf interface command reveals all interface-related OSPF information. Data is displayed about OSPF information for all OSPF-enabled interfaces or for specified interfaces. I'll highlight some of the more important factors for you. Check it out:

```
Corp#sh ip ospf int f0/0
FastEthernet0/0 is up, line protocol is up
  Internet Address 10.10.10.1/24, Area 0
  Process ID 1, Router ID 223.255.255.254, Network Type BROADCAST, Cost: 1
  Transmit Delay is 1 sec, State DR, Priority 1
  Designated Router (ID) 223.255.255.254, Interface address 10.10.10.1
  Backup Designated router (ID) 172.31.1.4, Interface address 10.10.10.2
  Timer intervals configured, Hello 10, Dead 40, Wait 40, Retransmit 5
    oob-resync timeout 40
    Hello due in 00:00:08
  Supports Link-local Signaling (LLS)
  Cisco NSF helper support enabled
  IETF NSF helper support enabled
  Index 3/3, flood queue length 0
  Next 0x0(0)/0x0(0)
  Last flood scan length is 1, maximum is 1
  Last flood scan time is 0 msec, maximum is 0 msec
  Neighbor Count is 1, Adjacent neighbor count is 1
    Adjacent with neighbor 172.31.1.  Suppress hello for 0 neighbor(s)
```

So this command has given us the following information:

- Interface IP address
- Area assignment
- Process ID
- Router ID
- Network type
- Cost
- Priority

- DR/BDR election information (if applicable)
- Hello and Dead timer intervals
- Adjacent neighbor information

The reason I used the show ip ospf interface f0/0 command is because I knew that there would be a designated router elected on the FastEthernet broadcast multi-access network between our Corp and Boulder routers. The information that I highlighted is all very important, so make sure you've noted it! A good question to ask you here is what are the Hello and Dead timers set to by default?

What if you type in the show ip ospf interface command and receive this response:

```
Corp#sh ip ospf int f0/0
%OSPF: OSPF not enabled on FastEthernet0/0
```

This error occurs when OSPF is enabled on the router, but not the interface. When this happens, you need to check your network statements because it means that the interface you're trying to verify is not in your OSPF process!

The *show ip ospf neighbor* Command

The show ip ospf neighbor command is super-useful because it summarizes the pertinent OSPF information regarding neighbors and the adjacency state. If a DR or BDR exists, that information will also be displayed. Here's a sample:

```
Corp#sh ip ospf neighbor
```

Neighbor ID	Pri	State	Dead Time	Address	Interface
172.31.1.4	1	FULL/BDR	00:00:34	10.10.10.2	FastEthernet0/0
192.168.20.1	0	FULL/ -	00:00:31	172.16.10.6	Serial0/1
192.168.10.1	0	FULL/ -	00:00:32	172.16.10.2	Serial0/0

 Real World Scenario

An Admin Connects Two Disparate Routers Together with OSPF and the Link between them Never Comes Up

Quite a few years ago, an admin called me in a panic because he couldn't get OSPF working between two routers, one of which was an older router that they needed to use while they were waiting for their new router to be shipped to them.

OSPF can be used in a multi-vendor network, so he was confused as to why this wasn't working. He turned on RIP and it worked, so he was super confused with why OSPF was

> not creating adjacencies. I had him use the show ip ospf interface command to look at the link between the two routers and sure enough, the hello and dead timers didn't match. I had him configure the mismatched parameters so they would match, but it still wouldn't create an adjacency. Looking more closely at the show ip ospf interface command, I noticed the cost did not match! Cisco calculated the bandwidth differently than the other vendor. Once I had him configure both as the same value, the link came up! Always remember, just because OSPF can be used in a multi-vendor network does not mean it will work out of the box!

This is a critical command to understand because it's extremely useful in production networks. Let's take a look at the Boulder router output:

```
Boulder>sh ip ospf neighbor

Neighbor ID      Pri   State    Dead Time   Address        Interface
223.255.255.254   1    FULL/DR  00:00:31    10.10.10.1     FastEthernet0/0
```

Here we can see that since there's an Ethernet link (broadcast multi-access) on the link between the Boulder and the Corp router, there's going to be an election to determine who will be the designated router (DR) and who will be the backup designated router (BDR). We can see that the Corp became the designated router, and it won because it had the highest IP address on the network—the highest RID.

Now the reason that the Corp connections to SF and LA don't have a DR or BDR listed in the output is that by default, elections don't happen on point-to-point links and they show FULL/ - . But we can still determine that the Corp router is fully adjacent to all three routers from its output.

The *show ip protocols* Command

The show ip protocols command is also highly useful, whether you're running OSPF, EIGRP, RIP, BGP, IS-IS, or any other routing protocol that can be configured on your router. It provides an excellent overview of the actual operation of all currently running protocols!

Check out the output from the Corp router:

```
Corp#sh ip protocols
Routing Protocol is "ospf 1"
  Outgoing update filter list for all interfaces is not set
  Incoming update filter list for all interfaces is not set
  Router ID 223.255.255.254
```

```
   Number of areas in this router is 1. 1 normal 0 stub 0 nssa
   Maximum path: 4
   Routing for Networks:
     10.10.10.1 0.0.0.0 area 0
     172.16.10.1 0.0.0.0 area 0
     172.16.10.5 0.0.0.0 area 0
  Reference bandwidth unit is 100 mbps
   Routing Information Sources:
     Gateway          Distance       Last Update
     192.168.10.1         110        00:21:53
     192.168.20.1         110        00:21:53
  Distance: (default is 110) Distance: (default is 110)
```

From looking at this output, you can determine the OSPF process ID, OSPF router ID, type of OSPF area, networks and areas configured for OSPF, and the OSPF router IDs of neighbors—that's a lot. It's super-efficient!

Summary

This chapter gave you a great deal of information about OSPF. It's really difficult to include everything about OSPF because so much of it falls outside the scope of this chapter and book, but I've given you a few tips here and there, so you're good to go—as long as you make sure you've got what I presented to you dialed in, that is!

I talked about a lot of OSPF topics, including terminology, operations, and configuration as well as verification and monitoring.

Each of these topics encompasses quite a bit of information—the terminology section just scratched the surface of OSPF. But you've got the goods you really need for your studies. Finally, I gave you a tight survey of commands highly useful for observing the operation of OSPF so you can verify that things are moving along as they should. So eat it all up, and you're set!

Exam Essentials

Compare OSPF and RIPv1. OSPF is a link-state protocol that supports VLSM and classless routing; RIPv1 is a distance-vector protocol that does not support VLSM and supports only classful routing.

Know how OSPF routers become neighbors and/or adjacent. OSPF routers become neighbors when each router sees the other's Hello packets and the timers match between routers.

Be able to configure single-area OSPF. A minimal single-area configuration involves only two commands: router ospf *process-id* and network *x.x.x.x y.y.y.y area Z*.

Be able to verify the operation of OSPF. There are many show commands that provide useful details on OSPF, and it is useful to be completely familiar with the output of each: show ip ospf, show ip ospf database, show ip ospf interface, show ip ospf neighbor, and show ip protocols.

Written Lab 4

You can find the answers to this lab in Appendix A, "Answers to Written Labs."

1. Write the command that will enable the OSPF process 101 on a router.
2. Write the command that will display details of all OSPF routing processes enabled on a router.
3. Write the command that will display interface-specific OSPF information.
4. Write the command that will display all OSPF neighbors.
5. Write the command that will display all different OSPF route types that are currently known by the router.
6. Which parameter or parameters are used to calculate OSPF cost in Cisco routers?
7. Two routers are not forming an adjacency. What are all the reasons that OSPF will not form this adjacency with the neighbor router?
8. Which command is used to display the collection of OSPF link states?
9. What is the default administrative distance of OSPF?
10. What is the default to which hello and dead timers are set?

Hands-on Labs

In this section, you will use the following network and add OSPF routing.

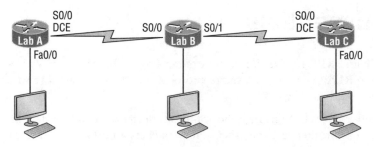

The first lab (Lab 4.1) requires you to configure three routers for OSPF and then view the configuration. Note that the labs in this chapter were written to be used with real equipment—but they can be used with any router simulator. You can replace the WAN links with Ethernet links if you want to.

The labs in this chapter are as follows:

Lab 4.1: Enabling the OSPF Process

Lab 4.2: Configuring OSPF Interfaces

Lab 4.3: Verifying OSPF Operation

Table 4.3 shows our IP addresses for each router (each interface uses a /24 mask).

TABLE 4.3 Our IP addresses

Router	Interface	IP address
Lab_A	Fa0/0	172.16.10.1
Lab_A	S0/0	172.16.20.1
Lab_B	S0/0	172.16.20.2
Lab_B	S0/1	172.16.30.1
Lab_C	S0/0	172.16.30.2
Lab_C	Fa0/0	172.16.40.1

Hands-on Lab 4.1: Enabling the OSPF Process

This is the first mandatory step in OSPF configuration.

1. Enable OSPF process 100 on Lab_A:

```
Lab_A#conf t
Enter configuration commands, one per line.
  End with CNTL/Z.
Lab_A (config)#router ospf 100
Lab_A (config-router)#^Z
```

2. Enable OSPF process 101 on Lab_B:

```
Lab_B#conf t
Enter configuration commands, one per line.
  End with CNTL/Z.
```

```
Lab_B (config)#router ospf 101
Lab_B (config-router)#^Z
```

3. Enable OSPF process 102 on Lab_C:

```
Lab_C#conf t
Enter configuration commands, one per line.
  End with CNTL/Z.
Lab_C (config)#router ospf 102
Lab_C (config-router)#^Z
```

Hands-on Lab 4.2: Configuring OSPF Interfaces

The second mandatory step in OSPF is adding your network statements.

1. Configure the LAN and the network between Lab_A and Lab_B. Assign it to area 0.

```
Lab_A#conf t
Enter configuration commands, one per line.
  End with CNTL/Z.
Lab_A (config)#router ospf 100
Lab_A (config-router)#network 172.16.10.1 0.0.0.0 area 0
Lab_A (config-router)#network 172.16.20.1 0.0.0.0 area 0
Lab_A (config-router)#^Z
Lab_A #
```

2. Configure the networks on the Lab_B router. Assign them to area 0.

```
Lab_B#conf t
Enter configuration commands, one per line.
  End with CNTL/Z.
Lab_B(config)#router ospf 101
Lab_B(config-router)#network 172.16.20.2 0.0.0.0 area 0
Lab_B(config-router)#network 172.16.30.1 0.0.0.0 area 0
Lab_B(config-router)#^Z
Lab_B #
```

3. Configure the networks on the Lab_C router. Assign them to area 0.

```
Lab_C#conf t
Enter configuration commands, one per line.
  End with CNTL/Z.
Lab_C(config)#router ospf 102
Lab_C(config-router)#network 172.16.30.2 0.0.0.0 area 0
```

```
Lab_C(config-router)#network 172.16.40.1 0.0.0.0 area 0
Lab_C(config-router)#^Z
Lab_C#
```

Hands-on Lab 4.3: Verifying OSPF Operation

You need to be able to verify what you configure.

1. Execute a show ip ospf neighbors command from the Lab_A router and view the results.

   ```
   Lab_A#sho ip ospf neighbors
   ```

2. Execute a show ip route command to verify that all other routers are learning all routes.

   ```
   Lab_A#sho ip route
   ```

3. Execute a show ip protocols command to verify OSPF information.

   ```
   Lab_A#sho ip protocols
   ```

4. Execute a show ip OSPF command to verify your RID.

   ```
   Lab_A#sho ip ospf
   ```

5. Execute a show ip ospf interface f0/0 command to verify your timers.

   ```
   Lab_A#sho ip ospf int f0/0
   ```

Review Questions

You can find the answers to these questions in Appendix B, "Answers to Review Questions."

1. There are three possible routes for a router to reach a destination network. The first route is from OSPF with a metric of 782. The second route is from RIPv2 with a metric of 4. The third is from EIGRP with a composite metric of 20514560. Which route will be installed by the router in its routing table?

   A. RIPv2

   B. EIGRP

   C. OSPF

   D. All three

2. In the accompanying diagram, which of the routers must be ABRs? (Choose all that apply.)

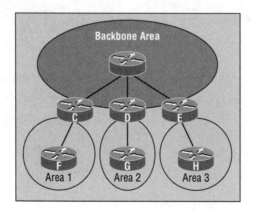

   A. C

   B. D

   C. E

   D. F

   E. G

   F. H

3. Which of the following describe the process identifier that is used to run OSPF on a router? (Choose two.)

   A. It is locally significant.

   B. It is globally significant.

   C. It is needed to identify a unique instance of an OSPF database.

   D. It is an optional parameter required only if multiple OSPF processes are running on the router.

   E. All routes in the same OSPF area must have the same process ID if they are to exchange routing information.

4. All of the following must match for two OSPF routers to become neighbors except which?

   A. Area ID

   B. Router ID

   C. Stub area flag

   D. Authentication password if using one

5. In the diagram, by default what will be the router ID of Lab_B?

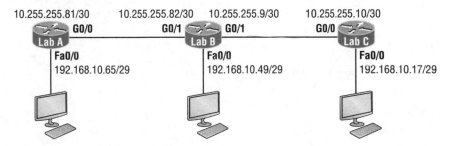

   A. 10.255.255.82

   B. 10.255.255.9

   C. 192.168.10.49

   D. 10.255.255.81

6. You get a call from a network administrator who tells you that he typed the following into his router:

```
Router(config)#router ospf 1
Router(config-router)#network 10.0.0.0 255.0.0.0 area 0
```

   He tells you he still can't see any routes in the routing table. What configuration error did the administrator make?

   A. The wildcard mask is incorrect.

   B. The OSPF area is wrong.

    C.   The OSPF process ID is incorrect.

    D.   The AS configuration is wrong.

7.   Which of the following statements is true with regard to the output shown?

```
Corp#sh ip ospf neighbor
Neighbor ID     Pri   State      Dead Time   Address       Interface
172.31.1.4       1    FULL/BDR   00:00:34    10.10.10.2    FastEthernet0/0
192.168.20.1     0    FULL/ -    00:00:31    172.16.10.6   Serial0/1
192.168.10.1     0    FULL/ -    00:00:32    172.16.10.2   Serial0/0
```

    A.   There is no DR on the link to 192.168.20.1.

    B.   The Corp router is the BDR on the link to 172.31.1.4.

    C.   The Corp router is the DR on the link to 192.168.20.1.

    D.   The link to 192.168.10.1 is Active.

8.   What is the administrative distance of OSPF?

    A.   90

    B.   100

    C.   120

    D.   110

9.   In OSPF, Hellos are sent to what IP address?

    A.   224.0.0.5

    B.   224.0.0.9

    C.   224.0.0.10

    D.   224.0.0.1

10.   What command generated the following output?

```
172.31.1.4       1    FULL/BDR   00:00:34    10.10.10.2    FastEthernet0/0
192.168.20.1     0    FULL/ -    00:00:31    172.16.10.6   Serial0/1
192.168.10.1     0    FULL/ -    00:00:32    172.16.10.2   Serial0/0
```

    A.   `show ip ospf neighbor`

    B.   `show ip ospf database`

    C.   `show ip route`

    D.   `show ip ospf interface`

11.   Updates addressed to 224.0.0.6 are destined for which type of OSPF router?

    A.   DR

    B.   ASBR

C. ABR

D. All OSPF routers

12. For some reason, you cannot establish an adjacency relationship on a common Ethernet link between two routers. Looking at this output, what is the cause of the problem?

```
RouterA#
Ethernet0/0 is up, line protocol is up
  Internet Address 172.16.1.2/16, Area 0
  Process ID 2, Router ID 172.126.1.2, Network Type BROADCAST, Cost: 10
  Transmit Delay is 1 sec, State DR, Priority 1
  Designated Router (ID) 172.16.1.2, interface address 172.16.1.1
  No backup designated router on this network
  Timer intervals configured, Hello 5, Dead 20, Wait 20, Retransmit 5


RouterB#
Ethernet0/0 is up, line protocol is up
  Internet Address 172.16.1.1/16, Area 0
  Process ID 2, Router ID 172.126.1.1, Network Type BROADCAST, Cost: 10
  Transmit Delay is 1 sec, State DR, Priority 1
  Designated Router (ID) 172.16.1.1, interface address 172.16.1.2
  No backup designated router on this network
  Timer intervals configured, Hello 10, Dead 40, Wait 40, Retransmit 5
```

A. The OSPF area is not configured properly.

B. The priority on RouterA should be set higher.

C. The cost on RouterA should be set higher.

D. The Hello and Dead timers are not configured properly.

E. A backup designated router needs to be added to the network.

F. The OSPF process ID numbers must match.

13. In the work area, match each OSPF term (by line) to its definition.

Designated router	Contains only the best routes
Topological database	Elected on broadcast networks
Hello protocol	Contains all routes learned
Routing table	Provides dynamic neighbor discovery

14. Type the command that will disable OSPF on the Fa0/1 interface under the routing process. Write only the command and not the prompt.

15. Which two of the following commands will place network 10.2.3.0/24 into area 0? (Choose two.)

A. `router eigrp 10`

B. `router ospf 10`

C. `router rip`

D. `network 10.0.0.0`

E. `network 10.2.3.0 255.255.255.0 area 0`

F. `network 10.2.3.0 0.0.0.255 area0`

G. `network 10.2.3.0 0.0.0.255 area 0`

16. Given the following output, which statement or statements can be determined to be true? (Choose all that apply.)

```
RouterA2# show ip ospf neighbor

Neighbor ID Pri State Dead Time Address Interface
192.168.23.2 1 FULL/BDR 00:00:29 10.24.4.2 FastEthernet1/0
192.168.45.2 2 FULL/BDR 00:00:24 10.1.0.5 FastEthernet0/0
192.168.85.1 1 FULL/- 00:00:33 10.6.4.10 Serial0/1
192.168.90.3 1 FULL/DR 00:00:32 10.5.5.2 FastEthernet0/1
192.168.67.3 1 FULL/DR 00:00:20 10.4.9.20 FastEthernet0/2
192.168.90.1 1 FULL/BDR 00:00:23 10.5.5.4 FastEthernet0/1
<<output omitted>>
```

A. The DR for the network connected to Fa0/0 has an interface priority higher than 2.

B. This router (A2) is the BDR for subnet 10.1.0.0.

C. The DR for the network connected to Fa0/1 has a router ID of 10.5.5.2.

D. The DR for the serial subnet is 192.168.85.1.

17. What are three reasons for creating OSPF in a hierarchical design? (Choose three.)

A. To decrease routing overhead

B. To speed up convergence

C. To confine network instability to single areas of the network

D. To make configuring OSPF easier

18. Type the command that produced the following output. Write only the command and not the prompt.

```
FastEthernet0/0 is up, line protocol is up
  Internet Address 10.10.10.1/24, Area 0
  Process ID 1, Router ID 223.255.255.254, Network Type BROADCAST, Cost:
1 Transmit Delay is 1 sec, State DR, Priority 1
  Designated Router (ID) 223.255.255.254, Interface address 10.10.10.1
```

```
Backup Designated router (ID) 172.31.1.4, Interface address 10.10.10.2
Timer intervals configured, Hello 10, Dead 40, Wait 40, Retransmit 5
   oob-resync timeout 40
   Hello due in 00:00:08
 Supports Link-local Signaling (LLS)
 Cisco NSF helper support enabled
 IETF NSF helper support enabled
 Index 3/3, flood queue length 0
 Next 0x0(0)/0x0(0)
 Last flood scan length is 1, maximum is 1
 Last flood scan time is 0 msec, maximum is 0 msec
 Neighbor Count is 1, Adjacent neighbor count is 1
   Adjacent with neighbor 172.31.1.  Suppress hello for 0 neighbor(s)
```

19. A(n) _____ is an OSPF data packet containing link-state and routing information that is shared among OSPF routers.

    A. LSA

    B. TSA

    C. Hello

    D. SPF

20. If routers in a single area are configured with the same priority value, what value does a router use for the OSPF router ID in the absence of a loopback interface?

    A. The lowest IP address of any physical interface

    B. The highest IP address of any physical interface

    C. The lowest IP address of any logical interface

    D. The highest IP address of any logical interface

Chapter

5

Multi-Area OSPF

THE FOLLOWING ICND2 EXAM TOPICS ARE COVERED IN THIS CHAPTER:

✓ **2.0   Routing Technologies**

✓ **2.2   Compare and contrast distance vector and link-state routing protocols**

✓ **2.3   Compare and contrast interior and exterior routing protocols**

✓ **2.4   Configure, verify, and troubleshoot single area and multiarea OSPFv2 for IPv4 (excluding authentication, filtering, manual summarization, redistribution, stub, virtual-link, and LSAs)**

✓ **2.5   Configure, verify, and troubleshoot single area and multiarea OSPFv3 for IPv6 (excluding authentication, filtering, manual summarization, redistribution, stub, virtual-link, and LSAs)**

We'll begin this chapter by focusing on the scalability constraints of an Open Shortest Path First (OSPF) network with a single area and move on from there to explore the concept of multi-area OSPF as a solution to these scalability limitations.

I'll also identify and introduce you to the various categories of routers used in multi-area configurations, including backbone routers, internal routers, area border routers (ABRs), and autonomous system boundary routers (ASBRs).

The functions of different OSPF Link-State Advertisements (LSAs) are absolutely crucial for you to understand for success in taking the Cisco exam, so I'll go into detail about the types of LSAs used by OSPF as well as the Hello protocol and different neighbor states when an adjacency is taking place.

And because troubleshooting is always a vital skill to have, I'll guide you through the process with a collection of show commands that can be effectively used to monitor and troubleshoot a multi-area OSPF implementation. Finally, I'll end the chapter with the easiest part: configuring and verifying OSPFv3.

To find up-to-the-minute updates for this chapter, please see www.lammle .com/ccna or the book's web page at www.sybex.com/go/ccna.

OSPF Scalability

At this point, and before you read this chapter, be sure that you have the foundation of single-area OSPF down pat. I'm sure you remember OSPF's significant advantage over distance-vector protocols like RIP, due to OSPF's ability to represent an entire network within its link-state database, which dramatically reduces the time required for convergence!

But what does a router actually go through to give us this great performance? Each router recalculates its database every time there's a topology change. If you have numerous routers in an area, they'll clearly have lots of links. Every time a link goes up or down, an LSA Type 1 packet is advertised, forcing all of the routers in the same area to recalculate their shortest path first (SPF) tree. Predictably, this kind of heavy lifting requires a ton of CPU overhead. On top of that, each router must hold the entire link-state database that represents the topology of the entire network, which results in considerable memory overhead. As if all that weren't enough, each router also holds a complete copy of the routing table, adding more to the already heavy overhead burden on memory. And keep in mind that the number of entries in the routing table can be much greater than the number of networks in the routing table because there are typically multiple routes to the same remote networks!

Considering these OSPF factors, it's easy to imagine that in a really large network, single-area OSPF presents some serious scalability challenges, as shown in Figure 5.1. We'll move on in a bit to compare the single-area OSPF network in that illustration to our multi-area networks.

FIGURE 5.1 OSPF single-area network: All routers flood the network with link-state information to all other routers within the same area.

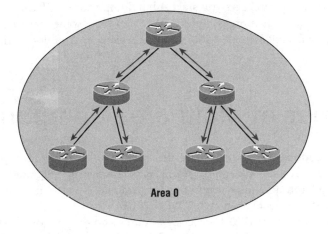

Single-area OSPF design places all routers into a single OSPF area, which results in many LSAs being processed on every router.

Fortunately, OSPF allows us to take a large OSPF topology and break it down into multiple, more manageable areas, as illustrated in Figure 5.2.

FIGURE 5.2 OSPF multi-area network: All routers flood the network only within their area.

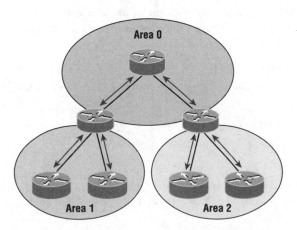

Just take a minute to think about the advantages of this hierarchical approach. First, routers that are internal to a defined area don't need to worry about having a link-state database for the entire network because they need one for only their own areas. This factor seriously reduces memory overhead! Second, routers that are internal to a defined area now have to recalculate their link-state database only when there's a topology change within their given area. Topology changes in one area won't cause global OSPF recalculations, further reducing processor overhead. Finally, because routes can be summarized at area boundaries, the routing tables on each router just don't need to be nearly as huge as they would be in a single-area environment!

But of course there's a catch: As you start subdividing your OSPF topology into multiple areas, the configuration gets more complex, so we'll explore some strategic ways to finesse the configuration plus look at some cool tricks for effectively troubleshooting multi-area OSPF networks.

Categories of Multi-area Components

In the following sections, I'm going to cover the various roles that routers play in a multi-area OSPF network. You'll find routers serving as backbone routers, internal routers, area border routers, and autonomous system boundary routers. I'll also introduce you to the different types of advertisements used in an OSPF network.

Link-State Advertisements (LSAs) describe a router and the networks that are connected to it by sending the LSAs to neighbor routers. Routers exchange LSAs and learn the complete topology of the network until all routers have the exact same topology database. After the topology database is built, OSPF uses the Dijkstra algorithm to find the best path to each remote network and places only the best routes into the routing table.

Adjacency Requirements

Once neighbors have been identified, adjacencies must be established so that routing (LSA) information can be exchanged. There are two steps required to change a neighboring OSPF router into an adjacent OSPF router:

1. Two-way communication (achieved via the Hello protocol)

2. Database synchronization, which consists of three packet types being exchanged between routers:

    ▪ Database Description (DD) packets

    ▪ Link-State Request (LSR) packets

    ▪ Link-State Update (LSU) packets

Once database synchronization is complete, the two routers are considered adjacent. This is how adjacency is achieved, but you need to know when an adjacency will occur.

It's important to remember that neighbors will not form an adjacency if the following do not match:

- Area ID
- Subnet
- Hello and dead timers
- Authentication (if configured)

When adjacencies form depends on the network type. If the link is point-to-point, the two neighbors will become adjacent if the Hello packet information for both routers is configured properly. On broadcast multi-access networks, adjacencies are formed only between the OSPF routers on the network and the DR and BDR.

OSPF Router Roles

Routers within a multi-area OSPF network fall into different categories. Check out Figure 5.3 to see the various roles that routers can play.

FIGURE 5.3   Router roles: Routers within an area are called internal routers.

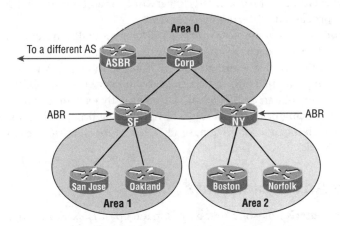

Notice that there are four routers that are part of area 0: the Corp router, SF and NY, and the autonomous system border router (ASBR). When configuring multi-area OSPF, one area must be called area 0, referred to as the *backbone area*. All other areas must connect to area 0. The four routers are referred to as the backbone routers, which are any routers that exist either partially or completely in OSPF area 0.

Another key distinction about the SF and NY routers connecting to other areas is that they have interfaces in more than one area. This makes them *area border routers (ABRs)* because in addition to having an interface in area 0, SF has an interface in area 1 and NY has an interface in area 2.

An ABR is a router that belongs to more than one OSPF area. It maintains information from all directly connected areas in its topology table but doesn't share the topological details from one area with the other. But it will forward routing information from one area to the other. The key concept here is that an ABR separates the LSA flooding zone, is a primary point for area address summarization, and typically has the source default route, all while maintaining the link-state database (LSDB) for each area it's connected to.

> Remember that a router can play more than one role. In Figure 5.3, SF and NY are both backbone routers and area border routers.

Let's turn our focus to the San Jose and Oakland routers. You can see that all interfaces on both of these routers reside only in area 1. Because all of San Jose's and Oakland's interfaces are internal to a single area, they're called internal routers. An *internal router* is any router with all of its interfaces included as members of the same area. This also applies to the Boston and Norfolk routers and their relationship to area 2. The Corp router is internal to area 0.

Finally, the ASBR is unique among all routers in our example because of its connection to an external *autonomous system (AS)*. When an OSPF network is connected to an EIGRP network, a *Border Gateway Protocol (BGP)* network, or a network running any other external routing process, it's referred to as an AS.

An *autonomous system boundary router (ASBR)* is an OSPF router with at least one interface connected to an external network or different AS. A network is considered external if a route received is from a routing protocol other than OSPF. An ASBR is responsible for injecting route information learned via the external network into OSPF.

I want to point out that an ASBR doesn't automatically exchange routing information between its OSPF routing process and the external routing process that it's connected to. These routes are exchanged through a method called *route redistribution*, which is beyond the scope of this book.

Link-State Advertisements

You know that a router's link-state database is made up of *Link-State Advertisements (LSAs)*. But just as there are several OSPF router categories to remember, there are also various types of LSAs to keep in mind—five of them, to be exact. These LSA classifications may not seem important at first, but you'll see why they are when we cover how the various types of OSPF areas operate. Let's start by exploring the different types of LSAs that Cisco uses:

Type 1 LSA   Referred to as a *router link advertisement (RLA)*, or just router LSA, a *Type 1 LSA* is sent by every router to other routers in its area. This advertisement contains the status of a router's link in the area to which it is connected. If a router is connected to multiple areas, then it will send separate Type 1 LSAs for each of the areas it's connected to. Type 1 LSAs contain the router ID (RID), interfaces, IP information, and current interface state. For example, in the network in Figure 5.4, router SF will send an LSA Type 1 advertisement for its interface into area 0 and a separate LSA Type 1 advertisement for its interfaces into area 1 describing the state of its links. The same will happen with the other routers in Figure 5.4.

FIGURE 5.4   Type 1 Link-State Advertisements

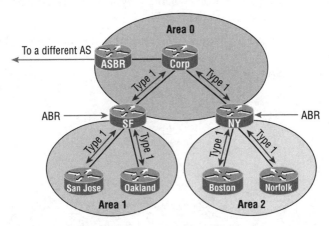

Type 1: Here is the status of my links!

Type 2 LSA   Referred to as a *network link advertisement (NLA)*, a *Type 2 LSA* is generated by designated routers (DRs). Remember that a designated router is elected to represent other routers in its network, and it establishes adjacencies with them. The DR uses a Type 2 LSA to send out information about the state of other routers that are part of the same network. Note that the Type 2 LSA is flooded to all routers that are in the same area as the one containing the specific network but not to any outside of that area. These updates contain the DR and BDR IP information.

Type 3 LSA   Referred to as a *summary link advertisement (SLA)*, a *Type 3 LSA* is generated by area border routers. These ABRs send Type 3 LSAs toward the area external to the one where they were generated. The Type 3 LSA advertises networks, and these LSAs advertise *inter-area routes* to the backbone area (area 0). Advertisements contain the IP information and RID of the ABR that is advertising an LSA Type 3.

The word *summary* often invokes images of a summarized network address that hides the details of many small subnets within the advertisement of a single large one. But in OSPF, summary link advertisements don't necessarily contain network summaries. Unless the administrator manually creates a summary, the full list of individual networks available within an area will be advertised by the SLAs.

Type 4 LSA   *Type 4 LSAs* are generated by area border routers. These ABRs send a Type 4 LSA toward the area external to the one in which they were generated. These are also summary LSAs like Type 3, but Type 4 are specifically used to inform the rest of the OSPF areas how to get to the ASBR.

Type 5 LSA   Referred to as *AS external link advertisements*, a *Type 5 LSA* is sent by autonomous system boundary routers to advertise routes that are external to the OSPF autonomous system and are flooded everywhere. A Type 5 LSA is generated for each individual external network advertised by the ASBR.

Figure 5.5 shows how each LSA type would be used in a multi-area OSPF network.

FIGURE 5.5   Basic LSA types

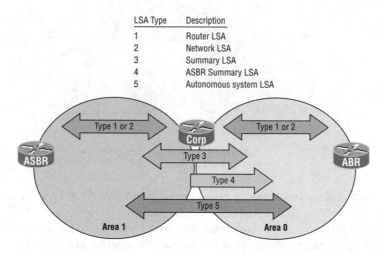

It's important to understand the different LSA types and how they work. Looking at Figure 5.5, you can see that Type 1 and 2 are flooded between routers in their same area. Type 3 LSAs from the Corp router (which is an ABR and maintains the LSDB for each area it is connected to) will summarize information learned from area 1 into area 0 and vice versa. The ASBR will flood Type 5 LSAs into area 1, and the Corp router will then flood Type 4 LSAs into area 0, telling all routers how to get to the ASBR, basically becoming a proxy ASBR.

OSPF Hello Protocol

The Hello protocol provides a lot of information to neighbors. The following is communicated between neighbors, by default, every 10 seconds:

Router ID (RID)   This is the highest active IP address on the router. The highest loopback IP addresses are used first. If no loopback interfaces are configured, OSPF will choose from physical interfaces instead.

Hello/Dead interval   The period between Hello packets is the Hello time, which is 10 seconds by default. The dead time is the length of time allotted for a Hello packet to be received before a neighbor is considered down—four times the Hello interval, unless otherwise configured.

Neighbors   The information includes a list of the router IDs for all the originating router's neighbors, neighbors being defined as routers that are attached to a common IP subnet and use identical subnet masks.

Area ID   This represents the area that the originating router interface belongs to.

Router priority   The priority is an 8-bit value used to aid in the election of the DR and BDR. This isn't set on point-to-point links!

DR IP address   This is the router ID of the current DR.

BDR IP address   This is the router ID of the current BDR.

Authentication data   This is the authentication type and corresponding information (if configured).

The mandatory information within the Hello update that must match exactly are the hello and dead timer values intervals, area ID, OSPF area type, subnet, and authentication data if used. If any of those don't match perfectly, no adjacency will occur!

Neighbor States

Before we move on to configuration, verification, and troubleshooting OSPF, it's important for you to grasp how OSPF routers traverse different states when adjacencies are being established.

When OSPF routers are initialized, they first start exchanging information using the Hello protocol via the multicast address 224.0.0.5. After the neighbor relationship is established between routers, the routers synchronize their link-state database (LSDB) by reliably exchanging LSAs. They actually exchange quite a bit of vital information when they start up.

The relationship that one router has with another consists of eight possible states. All OSPF routers begin in the DOWN state, and if all is well, they'll progress to either the 2WAY or FULL state with their neighbors. Figure 5.6 shows this neighbor state progression.

FIGURE 5.6   OSPF neighbor states, part 1

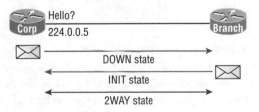

The process starts by sending out Hello packets. Every listening router will then add the originating router to the neighbor database. The responding routers will reply with all of their Hello information so that the originating router can add them to its own neighbor table. At this point, we will have reached the 2WAY state—only certain routers will advance beyond this to establish adjacencies.

Here's a definition of the eight possible relationship states:

DOWN In the *DOWN state*, no Hello packets have been received on the interface. Bear in mind that this does not imply that the interface itself is physically down.

ATTEMPT In the *ATTEMPT state*, neighbors must be configured manually. It applies only to nonbroadcast multi-access (NBMA) network connections.

INIT In the *INIT state*, Hello packets have been received from another router. Still, the absence of the router ID for the receiving router in the Neighbor field indicates that bidirectional communication hasn't been established yet.

2WAY In the *2WAY state*, Hello packets that include their own router ID in the Neighbor field have been received. Bidirectional communication has been established. In broadcast multi-access networks, an election can occur after this point.

After the DR and BDR have been selected, the routers will enter into the EXSTART state and the routers are ready to discover the link-state information about the internetwork and create their LSDB. This process is illustrated in Figure 5.7.

FIGURE 5.7 OSPF router neighbor states, part 2

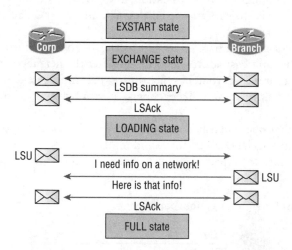

EXSTART In the *EXSTART state*, the DR and BDR establish adjacencies with each router in the network. A master-slave relationship is created between each router and its adjacent DR and DBR. The router with the highest RID becomes the master, and the master-slave election dictates which router will start the exchange. Once routers exchange DBD packets, the routers will move into the EXCHANGE state.

One reason two neighbor routers won't get past the EXSTART state is that they have different MTUs.

EXCHANGE   In the *EXCHANGE state*, routing information is exchanged using Database Description (DBD or DD) packets, and Link-State Request (LSR) and Link-State Update packets may also be sent. When routers start sending LSRs, they're considered to be in the LOADING state.

LOADING   In the *LOADING state*, Link-State Request (LSR) packets are sent to neighbors to request any Link-State Advertisements (LSAs) that may have been missed or corrupted while the routers were in the EXCHANGE state. Neighbors respond with Link-State Update (LSU) packets, which are in turn acknowledged with Link-State Acknowledgement (LSAck) packets. When all LSRs have been satisfied for a given router, the adjacent routers are considered synchronized and enter the FULL state.

FULL   In the *FULL state*, all LSA information is synchronized among neighbors and adjacency has been established. OSPF routing can begin only after the FULL state has been reached!

It's important to understand that routers should be in the 2WAY and FULL states and the others are considered transitory. Routers shouldn't remain in any other state for extended period of times. Let's configure OSPF now to see what we've covered so far in action.

Basic Multi-area Configuration

Basic multi-area configuration isn't all that hard. Understanding your design, layout, and types of LSAs and DRs and configuring the elections, troubleshooting, and fully comprehending what's happening in the background are really the most complicated aspects of OSPF.

As I was saying, configuring OSPF is pretty simple, and you'll see toward the end of this chapter that configuring OSPFv3 is even easier! After I show you the basic OSPF multi-area configuration in this section, we'll work on the verification of OSPF and then go through a detailed troubleshooting scenario just as we did with EIGRP. Let's get the ball rolling with the multi-area configuration shown in Figure 5.8.

We'll use the same routers we've been working with throughout all the chapters, but we're going to create three areas. The routers are still configured with the IPv6 addresses from my last EIGRPv6 section in Chapter 3, and I've also verified that the IPv4 addresses are on the interfaces and working as well since then, so we're all set to rock the configs for this chapter! Here's the Corp configuration:

```
Corp#config t
Corp(config)#router ospf 1
Corp(config-router)#router-id 1.1.1.1
```

Reload or use "clear ip ospf process" command, for this to take effect

```
Corp(config-router)#network 10.10.0.0 0.0.255.255 area 0
Corp(config-router)#network 172.16.10.0 0.0.0.3 area 1
Corp(config-router)#network 172.16.10.4 0.0.0.3 area 2
```

FIGURE 5.8 Our internetwork

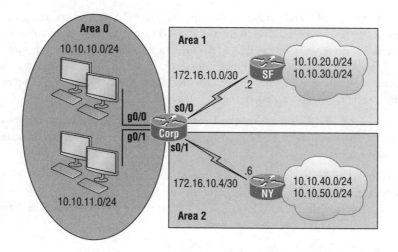

Pretty straightforward, but let's talk about it anyway. First I started the OSPF process with the router ospf *process-id* command, using any number from 1–65,535 because they're only locally significant, so they don't need to match my neighbor routers. I set the RID of the router only to remind you that this can be configured under the router process, but with our small network it wouldn't really be necessary to mess with RIDs if this was an actual production network. The one thing that you need to keep in mind here is that in OSPF, the RID must be different on each router. With EIGRP, they can all be the same because they are not as important in that process. Still, as I showed you in the EIGRPv6 section, we still need them!

Anyway, at this point in the configurations I needed to choose my network statements for the OSPF process to use, which allowed me to place my four interfaces on the Corp router into three different areas. In the first network statement, 10.10.0.0 0.0.255.255, I placed the g0/0 and g0/1 interfaces into area 0. The second and third statements needed to be more exact since there are /30 networks. 172.16.10.0 0.0.0.3 tells OSPF process 1 to go find an active interface that's configured with 172.16.10.1 or .2 and to place that interface into area 1. The last line tells the OSPF process to go find any active interface configured with 172.16.10.5 or .6 and place that interface into area 2. The wildcard of 0.0.0.3 means the first three octets can match any value, but the last octet is a block size of 4.

The only thing different about these configurations from those in the single-area OSPF is the different areas at the end of the command—that's it!

Here is the configuration for the SF and NY routers:

```
SF(config)#router ospf 1
SF(config-router)#network 10.10.0.0 0.0.255.255 area 1
SF(config-router)#network 172.16.0.0 0.0.255.255 area 1

NY(config)#router ospf 1
NY(config-router)#network 0.0.0.0 255.255.255.255 area 2
00:01:07: %OSPF-5-ADJCHG: Process 1, Nbr 1.1.1.1 on Serial0/0/0 from LOADING
to FULL,
Loading Done
```

I configured each one slightly different from the Corp router, but since they didn't have an interface in more than area 1, I had more leeway in configuring them. For the NY router I just configured a network statement (0.0.0.0 255.255.255.255) that says "go find any active interface and place it into area 2!" I'm not recommending that you configure your routers in such a broad manner; I just wanted to show you your options.

Before we move onto verifying our network, let me show you another way that the CCNA objectives configure OSPF. For the Corp router, we had three network statements, which covered the four interfaces used. We could have configured the OSPF process like this on the Corp router (or all routers); it doesn't matter which way you choose:

```
Corp(config)#router ospf 1
Corp(config-router)#router-id 1.1.1.1
Corp(config-router)#int g0/0
Corp(config-if)#ip ospf 1 area 0
Corp(config-if)#int g0/1
Corp(config-if)#ip ospf 1 area 0
Corp(config-if)#int s0/0
Corp(config-if)#ip ospf 1 area 1
Corp(config-if)#int s0/1
Corp(config-if)#ip ospf 1 area 2
```

First I chose my process ID, then set my RID (this absolutely must be different on every router in your internetwork!), then I just went to each interface and told it what area it was in. Easy! No network commands to screw up! Nice. Again, you can configure it with the network statement or the interface statement, it doesn't matter, but you need to really remember this for the CCNA objectives!

Now that our three routers are configured, let's verify our internetwork.

Verifying and Troubleshooting Multi-area OSPF Networks

Cisco's IOS has several show and debug commands that can help you monitor and trouble-shoot OSPF networks. A sampling of these commands, which can be used to gain information about various OSPF characteristics, is included in Table 5.1.

TABLE 5.1   OSPF verification commands

Command	Provides the following
show ip ospf neighbor	Verifies your OSPF-enabled interfaces
show ip ospf interface	Displays OSPF-related information on an OSPF-enabled interface
show ip protocols	Verifies the OSPF process ID and that OSPF is enabled on the router
show ip route	Verifies the routing table, and displays any OSPF injected routes
show ip ospf database	Lists a summary of the LSAs in the database, with one line of output per LSA, organized by type

Let's go through some verification commands—the same commands we used to verify our single-area OSPF network—then we'll move onto the OSPF troubleshooting scenario section.

Okay, once you've checked the link between your neighbors and can use the Ping program, the best command when verifying a routing protocol is to always check the status of your neighbor's connection first. The show ip ospf neighbor command is super useful because it summarizes the pertinent OSPF information regarding neighbors and their adjacency state. If a DR or BDR exists, that information will also be displayed. Here's a sample:

```
Corp#sh ip ospf neighbor
Neighbor ID     Pri   State        Dead Time    Address       Interface
172.16.10.2       0   FULL/  -     00:00:34     172.16.10.2   Serial0/0/0
172.16.10.6       0   FULL/  -     00:00:31     172.16.10.6   Serial0/0/1

SF#sh ip ospf neighbor
Neighbor ID     Pri   State        Dead Time    Address       Interface
1.1.1.1           0   FULL/  -     00:00:39     172.16.10.1   Serial0/0/0
```

```
NY#sh ip ospf neighbor
Neighbor ID    Pri   State        Dead Time   Address       Interface
1.1.1.1          0   FULL/  -     00:00:34    172.16.10.5   Serial0/0/0
```

The reason that the Corp connections to SF and LA don't have a DR or BDR listed in the output is that by default, elections don't happen on point-to-point links and they show FULL/-. But we can see that the Corp router is fully adjacent to all three routers from its output.

The output of this command shows the neighbor ID, which is the RID of the router. Notice in the output of the Corp router that the RIDs for the SF and NY routers were chosen based on highest IP address of any active interface when I started the OSPF process on those routers. Both the SF and NY routers see the Corp router RID as 1.1.1.1 because I set that manually under the router ospf process command.

Next we see the Pri field, which is the priority field that's set to 1 by default. Don't forget that on point-to-point links, elections don't happen, so the interfaces are all set to 0 in this example because none of these routers will have elections on these interfaces with each other over this serial WAN network. The state field shows Full/-, which means all routers are synchronized with their LSDB, and the /- means there is no election on this type of interface. The dead timer is counting down, and if the router does not hear from this neighbor before this expires, the link will be considered down. The Address field is the actual address of the neighbor's interface connecting to the router.

The *show ip ospf* Command

We use the show ip ospf command to display OSPF information for one or all OSPF processes running on the router. Information contained therein includes the router ID, area information, SPF statistics, and LSA timer information. Let's check out the output from the Corp router:

```
Corp#sh ip ospf
 Routing Process "ospf 1" with ID 1.1.1.1
 Supports only single TOS(TOS0) routes
 Supports opaque LSA
 It is an area border router
 SPF schedule delay 5 secs, Hold time between two SPFs 10 secs
 Minimum LSA interval 5 secs. Minimum LSA arrival 1 secs
 Number of external LSA 0. Checksum Sum 0x000000
 Number of opaque AS LSA 0. Checksum Sum 0x000000
 Number of DCbitless external and opaque AS LSA 0
 Number of DoNotAge external and opaque AS LSA 0
 Number of areas in this router is 3. 3 normal 0 stub 0 nssa
 External flood list length 0
```

```
Area BACKBONE(0)
    Number of interfaces in this area is 2
    Area has no authentication
    SPF algorithm executed 19 times
    Area ranges are
    Number of LSA 7. Checksum Sum 0x0384d5
    Number of opaque link LSA 0. Checksum Sum 0x000000
    Number of DCbitless LSA 0
    Number of indication LSA 0
    Number of DoNotAge LSA 0
    Flood list length 0
Area 1
    Number of interfaces in this area is 1
    Area has no authentication
    SPF algorithm executed 43 times
    Area ranges are
    Number of LSA 7. Checksum Sum 0x0435f8
    Number of opaque link LSA 0. Checksum Sum 0x000000
    Number of DCbitless LSA 0
    Number of indication LSA 0
    Number of DoNotAge LSA 0
    Flood list length 0
Area 2
    Number of interfaces in this area is 1
    Area has no authentication
    SPF algorithm executed 38 times
    Area ranges are
    Number of LSA 7. Checksum Sum 0x0319ed
    Number of opaque link LSA 0. Checksum Sum 0x000000
    Number of DCbitless LSA 0
    Number of indication LSA 0
    Number of DoNotAge LSA 0
    Flood list length 0
```

You'll notice that most of the preceding information wasn't displayed with this command output in single-area OSPF. We have more displayed here because it's providing information about each area we've configured on this router.

The *show ip ospf interface* Command

The show ip ospf interface command displays all interface-related OSPF information. Data is displayed for all OSPF-enabled interfaces or for specified interfaces. I'll highlight some important portions I want you to pay special attention to.

```
Corp#sh ip ospf interface gi0/0
GigabitEthernet0/0 is up, line protocol is up
  Internet address is 10.10.10.1/24, Area 0
  Process ID 1, Router ID 1.1.1.1, Network Type BROADCAST, Cost: 1
  Transmit Delay is 1 sec, State DR, Priority 1
  Designated Router (ID) 1.1.1.1, Interface address 10.10.10.1
  No backup designated router on this network
  Timer intervals configured, Hello 10, Dead 40, Wait 40, Retransmit 5
    Hello due in 00:00:05
  Index 1/1, flood queue length 0
  Next 0x0(0)/0x0(0)
  Last flood scan length is 1, maximum is 1
  Last flood scan time is 0 msec, maximum is 0 msec
  Neighbor Count is 0, Adjacent neighbor count is 0
  Suppress hello for 0 neighbor(s)
```

Let's take a look at a serial interface so we can compare it to the Gigabit Ethernet interface just shown. The Ethernet network is a broadcast multi-access network by default, and the serial interface is a point-to-point nonbroadcast multi-access network, so they will act differently with OSPF:

```
Corp#sh ip ospf interface s0/0/0
Serial0/0/0 is up, line protocol is up
  Internet address is 172.16.10.1/30, Area 1
  Process ID 1, Router ID 1.1.1.1, Network Type POINT-TO-POINT, Cost: 64
  Transmit Delay is 1 sec, State POINT-TO-POINT, Priority 0
  No designated router on this network
  No backup designated router on this network
  Timer intervals configured, Hello 10, Dead 40, Wait 40, Retransmit 5
    Hello due in 00:00:02
  Index 3/3, flood queue length 0
  Next 0x0(0)/0x0(0)
  Last flood scan length is 1, maximum is 1
  Last flood scan time is 0 msec, maximum is 0 msec
  Neighbor Count is 1 , Adjacent neighbor count is 1
    Adjacent with neighbor 172.16.10.2
  Suppress hello for 0 neighbor(s)
```

The following information is displayed via this command:

- Interface IP address
- Area assignment
- Process ID
- Router ID

- Network type
- Cost
- Priority
- DR/BDR election information (if applicable)
- Hello and dead timer intervals
- Adjacent neighbor information

I used the show ip ospf interface gi0/0 command first because I knew that there would be a designated router elected on the Ethernet broadcast multi-access network on the Corp router, even though it has no one to run against, which means the Corp router automatically wins. The information that I bolded is all very important! What are the hello and dead timers set to by default? Even though I haven't talked much about the cost output on an interface, it can also be very important. Two OSPF routers still could create an adjacency if the costs don't match, but it could lead to certain links not being utilized. We'll discuss this more at the end of the verification section.

 Real World Scenario

Neighbor Routers Don't Form an Adjacency

I'd like to talk more about the adjacency issue and how the show ip ospf interface command can help you solve problems, especially in multi-vendor networks.

Years ago I was consulting with the folks at a large PC/laptop manufacturer and was helping them build out their large internetwork. They were using OSPF because their company was a worldwide company and used many types of routers from all manufacturers.

I received a call from a remote branch informing me that they installed a new router but it was not seeing the Cisco router off their Ethernet interface. Of course it was an emergency because this new router was holding some important WAN links to a new remote location that needed to be up yesterday!

After calming down the person on the phone, I simply had the admin use the show ip ospf interface fa0/0 command and verify the hello and dead timers and the area configured for that interface and then had him verify that the IP addresses were correct between routers and that there was no passive interface set.

Then I had him verify that same information on the neighbor, and sure enough the neighbor's hello and dead timers didn't match. Quick and easy fix on the interface of the Cisco router with the ip ospf dead 30 command, and they were up!

Always remember that OSPF can work with multi-vendor routers, but no one ever said it works out of the box between various vendors!

The *show ip protocols* Command

The show ip protocols command is also useful, whether you're running OSPF, EIGRP, RIP, BGP, IS-IS, or any other routing protocol that can be configured on your router. It provides an excellent overview of the actual operation of all currently running protocols.

Check the output from the Corp router:

```
Corp#sh ip protocols
Routing Protocol is "ospf 1"
  Outgoing update filter list for all interfaces is not set
  Incoming update filter list for all interfaces is not set
  Router ID 1.1.1.1
  Number of areas in this router is 3. 3 normal 0 stub 0 nssa
  Maximum path: 4
  Routing for Networks:
    10.10.0.0 0.0.255.255 area 0
    172.16.10.0 0.0.0.3 area 1
    172.16.10.4 0.0.0.3 area 2
  Routing Information Sources:
    Gateway         Distance      Last Update
    1.1.1.1             110        00:17:42
    172.16.10.2         110        00:17:42
    172.16.10.6         110        00:17:42
  Distance: (default is 110)
```

Here we can determine the OSPF process ID, OSPF router ID, type of OSPF area, networks, and the three areas configured for OSPF as well as the OSPF router IDs of neighbors—that's a lot. Read efficient!

The *show ip route* Command

Now would be a great time to issue a show ip route command on the Corp router. The Corp router shows only four dynamic routes for our internetwork, with the O representing OSPF internal routes. The Cs clearly represent our directly connected networks, but our four remote networks are also showing up—nice! Notice the 110/65, which is the administrative distance/metric:

```
Corp#sh ip route
[output cut]
     10.0.0.0/8 is variably subnetted, 8 subnets, 2 masks
C       10.10.10.0/24 is directly connected, GigabitEthernet0/0
L       10.10.10.1/32 is directly connected, GigabitEthernet0/0
C       10.10.11.0/24 is directly connected, GigabitEthernet0/1
```

```
L       10.10.11.1/32 is directly connected, GigabitEthernet0/1
O       10.10.20.0/24 [110/65] via 172.16.10.2, 02:18:27, Serial0/0/0
O       10.10.30.0/24 [110/65] via 172.16.10.2, 02:18:27, Serial0/0/0
O       10.10.40.0/24 [110/65] via 172.16.10.6, 03:37:24, Serial0/0/1
O       10.10.50.0/24 [110/65] via 172.16.10.6, 03:37:24, Serial0/0/1
        172.16.0.0/16 is variably subnetted, 4 subnets, 2 masks
C       172.16.10.0/30 is directly connected, Serial0/0/0
L       172.16.10.1/32 is directly connected, Serial0/0/0
C       172.16.10.4/30 is directly connected, Serial0/0/1
L       172.16.10.5/32 is directly connected, Serial0/0/1
```

In addition, you can use the show ip route ospf command to get only OSPF-injected routes in your routing table. I can't stress enough how useful this is when dealing with large networks!

```
Corp#sh ip route ospf
        10.0.0.0/8 is variably subnetted, 8 subnets, 2 masks
O       10.10.20.0 [110/65] via 172.16.10.2, 02:18:33, Serial0/0/0
O       10.10.30.0 [110/65] via 172.16.10.2, 02:18:33, Serial0/0/0
O       10.10.40.0 [110/65] via 172.16.10.6, 03:37:30, Serial0/0/1
O       10.10.50.0 [110/65] via 172.16.10.6, 03:37:30, Serial0/0/1
```

Now that's a really nice-looking OSPF routing table! Troubleshooting and fixing an OSPF network is as vital a skill to have as it is in any other networking environment, which is why I always use the show ip int brief command when configuring my routing protocols. It's very easy to make little mistakes with OSPF, so pay very close attention to the details—especially when troubleshooting!

The *show ip ospf database* Command

Using the show ip ospf database command will give you information about the number of routers in the internetwork (AS), plus the neighboring router's ID. This is the topology database I referred to earlier.

The output is broken down by area. Here's a sample, again from Corp:

```
Corp#sh ip ospf database
          OSPF Router with ID (1.1.1.1) (Process ID 1)

            Router Link States (Area 0)

Link ID         ADV Router      Age       Seq#       Checksum Link count
1.1.1.1         1.1.1.1         196       0x8000001a 0x006d76 2
```

```
            Summary Net Link States (Area 0)
Link ID        ADV Router      Age       Seq#        Checksum
172.16.10.0    1.1.1.1         182       0x80000095 0x00be04
172.16.10.4    1.1.1.1         177       0x80000096 0x009429
10.10.40.0     1.1.1.1         1166      0x80000091 0x00222b
10.10.50.0     1.1.1.1         1166      0x80000092 0x00b190
10.10.20.0     1.1.1.1         1114      0x80000093 0x00fa64
10.10.30.0     1.1.1.1         1114      0x80000094 0x008ac9
```

Router Link States (Area 1)

```
Link ID        ADV Router      Age       Seq#        Checksum Link count
1.1.1.1        1.1.1.1         1118      0x8000002a 0x00a59a 2
172.16.10.2    172.16.10.2     1119      0x80000031 0x00af47 4

            Summary Net Link States (Area 1)
Link ID        ADV Router      Age       Seq#        Checksum
10.10.10.0     1.1.1.1         178       0x80000076 0x0021a5
10.10.11.0     1.1.1.1         178       0x80000077 0x0014b0
172.16.10.4    1.1.1.1         173       0x80000078 0x00d00b
10.10.40.0     1.1.1.1         1164      0x80000074 0x005c0e
10.10.50.0     1.1.1.1         1164      0x80000075 0x00eb73
```

Router Link States (Area 2)

```
Link ID        ADV Router      Age       Seq#        Checksum Link count
1.1.1.1        1.1.1.1         1119      0x8000002b 0x005cd6 2
172.16.10.6    172.16.10.6     1119      0x8000002d 0x0020a3 4

            Summary Net Link States (Area 2)
Link ID        ADV Router      Age       Seq#        Checksum
10.10.10.0     1.1.1.1         179       0x8000007a 0x0019a9
10.10.11.0     1.1.1.1         179       0x8000007b 0x000cb4
172.16.10.0    1.1.1.1         179       0x8000007c 0x00f0ea
10.10.20.0     1.1.1.1         1104      0x80000078 0x003149
10.10.30.0     1.1.1.1         1104      0x80000079 0x00c0ae
Corp#
```

Considering we only have eight networks configured in our internetwork, there's a huge amount of information in this database! You can see all the routers and the RID of each—the highest IP address related to individual routers. And each output under each area represents LSA Type 1, indicating the area they're connected to.

The router output also shows the link ID. Remember that an interface is also a link, as is the RID of the router on that link under the ADV router—the advertising router.

So far, this has been a great chapter, brimming with detailed OSPF information, a whole lot more than what was needed to meet past Cisco objectives, for sure! Next, we'll use the same sample network that I built in Chapter 3 on EIGRP and run through a troubleshooting scenario using multi-area OSPF.

Troubleshooting OSPF Scenario

When you notice problems with your OSPF network, it's wise to first test your layer 3 connectivity with Ping and the traceroute command to see if your issue is a local one. If all looks good locally, then follow these Cisco-provided guidelines:

1. Verify your adjacency with your neighbor routers using the show ip ospf neighbors command. If you are not seeing your neighbor adjacencies, then you need to verify that the interfaces are operational and enabled for OSPF. If all is well with the interfaces, verify the hello and dead timers next, and establish that the interfaces are in the same area and that you don't have a passive interface configured.

2. Once you've determined that your adjacencies to all neighbors are working, use the show ip route to verify your layer 3 routes to all remote networks. If you see no OSPF routes in the routing table, you need to verify that you don't have another routing protocol running with a lower administrative distance. You can use show ip protocols to see all routing protocols running on your router. If no other protocols are running, then verify your network statements under the OSPF process. In a multi-area network, make sure all non–backbone area routers are directly connected to area 0 through an ABR or they won't be able to send and receive updates.

3. If you can see all the remote networks in the routing table, move on to verify the path for each network and that each path for each specific network is correct. If not, you need to verify the cost on your interfaces with the show ip ospf interface command. You may need to adjust the cost on an interface either higher or lower, depending on which path you want OSPF to use for sending packets to a remote network. Remember—the path with the lowest cost is the preferred path!

Okay, with our marching orders for troubleshooting OSPF in hand, let's take a look at Figure 5.9, which we'll use to verify our network now.

FIGURE 5.9 Our internetwork

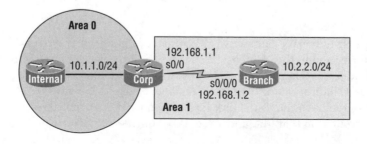

Here's the OSPF configuration on the three routers:

```
Corp(config-if)#router ospf 1
Corp(config-router)#network 10.1.1.0 0.0.0.255 area 0
Corp(config-router)#network 192.168.1.0 0.0.0.3 area 1

Internal(config)#router ospf 3
Internal(config-router)#network 10.1.1.2 0.0.0.0 area 0

Branch(config-if)#router ospf 2
Branch(config-router)#network 192.168.1.2 0.0.0.0 area 1
Branch(config-router)#network 10.2.2.1 0.0.0.0 area 1
```

Let's check out our network now, beginning by checking the layer 1 and layer 2 status between routers:

```
Corp#sh ip int brief
Interface          IP-Address      OK? Method Status          Protocol
FastEthernet0/0    10.1.1.1        YES manual up                up
Serial0/0          192.168.1.1     YES manual up                up
```

The IP addresses look correct and the layer 1 and 2 status is up/up, so next we'll use the Ping program to check connectivity like this:

```
Corp#ping 192.168.1.2
Type escape sequence to abort.
Sending 5, 100-byte ICMP Echos to 192.168.1.2, timeout is 2 seconds:
!!!!!
Success rate is 100 percent (5/5), round-trip min/avg/max = 1/2/4 ms
Corp#ping 10.1.1.2
Type escape sequence to abort.
Sending 5, 100-byte ICMP Echos to 10.1.1.2, timeout is 2 seconds:
!!!!!
Success rate is 100 percent (5/5), round-trip min/avg/max = 1/2/4 ms
```

Nice—I can ping both directly connected neighbors, so this means layers 1, 2, and 3 are working between neighbor routers. This is a great start, but it still doesn't mean OSPF is actually working yet. If any of the preceding commands had failed, I first would've verified layers 1 and 2 to make sure my data link was working between neighbors and then moved on to verify my layer 3 IP configuration.

Since our data link appears to be working between each neighbor, our next move is to check the OSPF configuration and status of the routing protocol. I'll start with the interfaces:

```
Corp#sh ip ospf interface s0/0
Serial0/0 is up, line protocol is up
```

```
Internet Address 192.168.1.1/30, Area 1
Process ID 1, Router ID 192.168.1.1, Network Type POINT_TO_POINT, Cost: 100
Transmit Delay is 1 sec, State POINT_TO_POINT
Timer intervals configured, Hello 10, Dead 40, Wait 40, Retransmit 5
  oob-resync timeout 40
  Hello due in 00:00:03
Supports Link-local Signaling (LLS)
Cisco NSF helper support enabled
IETF NSF helper support enabled
Index 1/2, flood queue length 0
Next 0x0(0)/0x0(0)
Last flood scan length is 1, maximum is 1
Last flood scan time is 0 msec, maximum is 0 msec
Neighbor Count is 1, Adjacent neighbor count is 1
  Adjacent with neighbor 192.168.1.2
Suppress hello for 0 neighbor(s)
```

I've highlighted the important statistics that you should always check first on an OSPF interface. You need to verify that the interface is configured in the same area as the neighbor and that the hello and dead timers match. A cost mismatch won't stop an adjacency from forming, but it could cause ugly routing issues. We'll explore that more in a minute.

For now let's take a look at the LAN interface that's connecting to the Internal router:

```
Corp#sh ip ospf int f0/0
FastEthernet0/0 is up, line protocol is up
  Internet Address 10.1.1.1/24, Area 0
  Process ID 1, Router ID 192.168.1.1, Network Type BROADCAST, Cost: 1
  Transmit Delay is 1 sec, State DR, Priority 1
  Designated Router (ID) 192.168.1.1, Interface address 10.1.1.1
  Backup Designated router (ID) 10.1.1.2, Interface address 10.1.1.2
  Timer intervals configured, Hello 10, Dead 40, Wait 40, Retransmit 5
    oob-resync timeout 40
    Hello due in 00:00:00
  Supports Link-local Signaling (LLS)
  Cisco NSF helper support enabled
  IETF NSF helper support enabled
  Index 1/1, flood queue length 0
  Next 0x0(0)/0x0(0)
  Last flood scan length is 1, maximum is 1
  Last flood scan time is 0 msec, maximum is 0 msec
  Neighbor Count is 1, Adjacent neighbor count is 1
    Adjacent with neighbor 10.1.1.2   (Backup Designated Router)
  Suppress hello for 0 neighbor(s)
```

We'll focus on the same key factors on a LAN interface that we did on our serial interface: the area ID and hello and dead timers. Notice that the cost is 1. According to Cisco's method of calculating cost, anything 100 Mbps or higher will always be a cost of 1 and serial links with the default bandwidth are always 64. This can cause problems in a large network with lots of high-bandwidth links. One thing to take special note of is that there's a designated and backup designated router on a broadcast multi-access network. DRs and BDRs won't cause a routing problem between neighbors, but it's still a consideration when designing and configuring in a really large internetwork environment. But we won't be focusing on that for our purposes here. It's just something to keep in mind.

Staying with the troubleshooting step of checking our interfaces, look at the error I received when I tried to verify OSPF on the fa0/1 interface of the Corp router (which we're not using):

```
Corp#sh ip ospf int fa0/1
%OSPF: OSPF not enabled on FastEthernet0/1
```

I got this error because the network statements under the OSPF process are not enabled for the network on the fa0/1 interface. If you receive this error, immediately check your network statements!

Next, let's check out the networks we're routing for with the show ip protocols command:

```
Corp#sh ip protocols
Routing Protocol is "ospf 1"
  Outgoing update filter list for all interfaces is not set
  Incoming update filter list for all interfaces is not set
  Router ID 192.168.1.1
  It is an area border router
  Number of areas in this router is 2. 2 normal 0 stub 0 nssa
  Maximum path: 4
  Routing for Networks:
    10.1.1.0 0.0.0.255 area 0
    192.168.1.0 0.0.0.3 area 1
  Reference bandwidth unit is 100 mbps
  Routing Information Sources:
    Gateway         Distance      Last Update
    192.168.1.2          110      00:28:40
  Distance: (default is 110)
```

From this output we can check our process ID as well as reveal if we have an ACL set on our routing protocol, just as we found when troubleshooting EIGRP in Chapter 3. But this time, we'll first examine the network statements and the area they're configured for—most important, the specific areas that each interface is configured for. This is key, because if your neighbor's interface isn't in the same area, you won't be able to form an adjacency!

This command's output provides a great view of what exactly we typed in for the network statements under the OSPF process. Also, notice that the default reference bandwidth is set to 100 Mbps. I'll talk about this factor at the end of this section.

I want to point out that the neighbor IP address and administrative distance is listed. OSPF uses 110 by default, so remember that if EIGRP were running here, we wouldn't see OSPF routes in the routing table because EIGRP has an AD of 90!

Next, we'll look at our neighbor table on the Corp router to find out if OSPF has formed an adjacency with the Branch router:

```
Corp#sh ip ospf neighbor
Neighbor ID    Pri   State        Dead Time    Address      Interface
10.1.1.2         1   FULL/BDR     00:00:39     10.1.1.2     FastEthernet0/0
```

Okay, we've finally zeroed in on our problem—the Corp router can see the Internal router in area 0 but not the Branch router in area 1! What now?

First, let's review what we know so far about the Corp and Branch router. The data link is good, and we can use Ping successfully between the routers. This shouts out that we have a routing protocol issue, so we'll look further into the details of the OSPF configuration on each router. Let's run a show ip protocols on the Branch router:

```
Branch#sh ip protocols
Routing Protocol is "eigrp 20"
  Outgoing update filter list for all interfaces is not set
  Incoming update filter list for all interfaces is not set
  Default networks flagged in outgoing updates
  Default networks accepted from incoming updates
  EIGRP metric weight K1=1, K2=0, K3=1, K4=0, K5=0
  EIGRP maximum hopcount 100
  EIGRP maximum metric variance 1
  Redistributing: eigrp 20
  EIGRP NSF-aware route hold timer is 240s
  Automatic network summarization is not in effect
  Maximum path: 4
  Routing for Networks:
    10.0.0.0
    192.168.1.0
  Routing Information Sources:
    Gateway          Distance       Last Update
    (this router)          90       3d22h
    192.168.1.1            90       00:00:07
  Distance: internal 90 external 170
```

```
Routing Protocol is "ospf 2"
  Outgoing update filter list for all interfaces is not set
  Incoming update filter list for all interfaces is not set
  Router ID 192.168.1.2
  Number of areas in this router is 1. 1 normal 0 stub 0 nssa
  Maximum path: 4
  Routing for Networks:
    10.2.2.1 0.0.0.0 area 1
    192.168.1.2 0.0.0.0 area 1
Reference bandwidth unit is 100 mbps
  Passive Interface(s):
    Serial0/0/0
  Routing Information Sources:
    Gateway        Distance      Last Update
    192.168.1.1        110       03:29:07
  Distance: (default is 110)
```

Do you see two routing protocols running on the Branch router? Both EIGRP and OSPF are running, but that's not necessarily our problem. The Corp router would need to be running EIGRP, and if so, we would have only EIGRP routes in our routing table because EIGRPs have the lower AD of 90 versus OSPF's AD of 110.

Let's check the routing table of the Branch router and see if the Corp router is also running EIGRP. This will be easy to determine if we discover EIGRP-injected routes in the table:

```
Branch#sh ip route
[output cut]
     10.0.0.0/24 is subnetted, 2 subnets
C       10.2.2.0 is directly connected, FastEthernet0/0
D       10.1.1.0 [90/2172416] via 192.168.1.1, 00:02:35, Serial0/0/0
     192.168.1.0/30 is subnetted, 1 subnets
C       192.168.1.0 is directly connected, Serial0/0/0
```

Okay—so yes, the Corp router is clearly running EIGRP. This is a leftover configuration from Chapter 3. All I need to do to fix this issue is disable EIGRP on the Branch router. After that, we should see OSPF in the routing table:

```
Branch#config t
Branch(config)#no router eigrp 20
Branch(config)#do sh ip route
[output cut]
     10.0.0.0/24 is subnetted, 1 subnets
```

```
C       10.2.2.0 is directly connected, FastEthernet0/0
    192.168.1.0/30 is subnetted, 1 subnets
C       192.168.1.0 is directly connected, Serial0/0/0
```

That's not so good—I disabled the EIGRP protocol on the Branch router, but we still didn't receive OSPF updates! Let investigate further using the show ip protocols command on the Branch router:

```
Branch#sh ip protocols
Routing Protocol is "ospf 2"
  Outgoing update filter list for all interfaces is not set
  Incoming update filter list for all interfaces is not set
  Router ID 192.168.1.2
  Number of areas in this router is 1. 1 normal 0 stub 0 nssa
  Maximum path: 4
  Routing for Networks:
    10.2.2.1 0.0.0.0 area 1
    192.168.1.2 0.0.0.0 area 1
 Reference bandwidth unit is 100 mbps
  Passive Interface(s):
    Serial0/0/0
  Routing Information Sources:
    Gateway         Distance      Last Update
    192.168.1.1          110      03:34:19
  Distance: (default is 110)
```

Do you see the problem? There's no ACL, the networks are configured correctly, but see the passive interface for Serial0/0/0? That will definitely prevent an adjacency from happening between the Corp and Branch routers! Let's fix that:

```
Branach#show run
[output cut]
!
router ospf 2
 log-adjacency-changes
 passive-interface Serial0/0/0
 network 10.2.2.1 0.0.0.0 area 1
 network 192.168.1.2 0.0.0.0 area 1
!
[output cut]
Branch#config t
Branch(config)#router ospf 2
Branch(config-router)#no passive-interface serial 0/0/0
```

Let's see what our neighbor table and routing table look like now:

```
Branch#sh ip ospf neighbor
Neighbor ID     Pri   State          Dead Time   Address       Interface
192.168.1.1       0   FULL/  -       00:00:32    192.168.1.1   Serial0/0/0

Branch#sh ip route
     10.0.0.0/24 is subnetted, 2 subnets
C       10.2.2.0 is directly connected, FastEthernet0/0
O IA    10.1.1.0 [110/65] via 192.168.1.1, 00:01:21, Serial0/0/0
     192.168.1.0/30 is subnetted, 1 subnets
C       192.168.1.0 is directly connected, Serial0/0/0
```

Awesome—our little internetwork is finally happy! That was actually pretty fun and really not all that hard once you know what to look for.

But there's one more thing we need to cover before moving onto OSPFv3—load balancing with OSPF. To explore that, we'll use Figure 5.10, wherein I added another link between the Corp and Branch routers.

FIGURE 5.10   Our internetwork with dual links

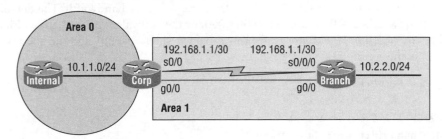

First, it's clear that having a Gigabit Ethernet interface between our two routers is way better than any serial link we could possibly have, which means we want the routers to use the LAN link. We can either disconnect the serial link or use it as a backup link.

Let's start by looking at the routing table and seeing what OSPF found:

```
Corp#sh ip route ospf
     10.0.0.0/8 is variably subnetted, 3 subnets, 2 masks
O       10.2.2.0 [110/2] via 192.168.1.6, 00:00:13, GigabitEthernet0/1
```

Look at that! OSPF wisely went with the Gigabit Ethernet link because it has the lowest cost. Although it's possible you'll have to mess with the links to help OSPF choose the best paths, it's likely best to just leave it alone at this point.

But that wouldn't be very much fun, now would it? Instead, let's configure OSPF to fool it into thinking the links are equal so it will use both of them by setting the cost on the interfaces to the same value:

```
Corp#config t
Corp(config)#int g0/1
```

```
Corp(config-if)#ip ospf cost 10
Corp(config-if)#int s0/0/0
Corp(config-if)#ip ospf cost 10
```

Obviously you need to deploy this configuration on both sides of the link, and I've already configured the Branch router as well. Now that both sides are configured with the same cost, let's check out our routing table now:

```
Corp#sh ip route ospf
     10.0.0.0/8 is variably subnetted, 3 subnets, 2 masks
O       10.2.2.0 [110/11] via 192.168.1.2, 00:01:23, Serial0/0/0
                 [110/11] via 192.168.1.6, 00:01:23, GigabitEthernet0/1
```

I'm not saying you should configure a serial link and Gigabit Ethernet link as equal costs as I just demonstrated, but there are times when you need to adjust the cost for OSPF. If you don't have multiple links to any remote networks, you really don't need to worry about this, but with regard to the objectives, you absolutely must understand the cost, how it works, and how to set it so OSPF can choose a preferred path. And there's still one more thing about cost I want to cover with you.

It's possible to change the reference bandwidth of the router, but you need to make sure all the routers within the OSPF AS have the same reference bandwidth. The default reference bandwidth is 10^8, which is 100,000,000, or the equivalent of the bandwidth of Fast Ethernet, which is 100 Mbps, as demonstrated via show ip ospf and the show ip protocols command:

```
Routing for Networks:
    10.2.2.1 0.0.0.0 area 1
    192.168.1.2 0.0.0.0 area 1
Reference bandwidth unit is 100 mbps
```

This will basically make any interface running 100 Mbps or higher have a cost of 1. The default is 100, and if you change it to 1,000, it will increase the cost by a factor of 10. Again, if you do want to change this, you must make sure to configure the change on all routers in your AS! Here is how you would do that:

```
Corp(route)#router ospf 1
Corp(config-router)#auto-cost reference-bandwidth ?
  <1-4294967>  The reference bandwidth in terms of Mbits per second
```

Simple Troubleshooting OSPF for the CCNA

Let's do a troubleshooting scenario. You have two routers not forming an adjacency. What would you do first? Well, we went through a lot in this chapter, but let me make it super easy for you when troubleshooting on the CCNA exam.

All you need to do is perform a *show running-config* on each router. That's it! You can then fix anything regarding OSPF because all the problems will be shown there if you know what to look for. Unlike with EIGRP, where you don't need to see a neighbor router's configuration to verify the protocol, with OSPF we need to compare directly connected interfaces to make sure they match up.

Let's look at each router's configuration and determine what the problems are.

Here is the first router's configuration:

```
R1#sh run
Building configuration...
!
interface Loopback0
 ip address 10.1.1.1 255.255.255.255
 ip ospf 3 area 0
!
int FastEthernet0/0
 Description **Connected to R2 F0/0**
 ip address 192.168.16.1 255.255.255.0
 ip ospf 3 area 0
 ip ospf hello-interval 25
!
router ospf 3
 router-id 192.168.3.3
```

Here is the neighbor router's configuration:

```
R2#sh run
Building configuration...
!
interface Loopback0
 ip address 10.1.1.2 255.255.255.255
 ip ospf 6 area 0
!
 Description **Connected to R1 F0/0**
 int FastEthernet0/0
 ip address 192.168.17.2 255.255.255.0
 ip ospf 6 area 1
!
router ospf 6
 router-id 192.168.3.3
```

Can you see the problems? Pretty simple. Just use the show running-config on each router and compare directly connected interfaces.

The loopbacks on each router are fine. I don't see a problem with their configuration, and they don't connect to each other, so whatever configuration they would have wouldn't matter.

However on the FastEthernet 0/0 interface of each router, where the description tells us that R1 and R2 are directly connected with interface f0/0, we can see a few problems. First, R1 is not using the default hellointerval of 10 seconds as R2 is, so that will never work. On R1 under the f0/0 interface, configure the no ip ospf hello-interval 25 command.

Let's dig deeper. Both routers have a different process ID, but that's not a problem. However, the areas are configured differently on each interface, and the IP addresses are not in the same subnet.

Last, they are both using the same RID under their process ID—this will never work! Now, finally, let's get to the easy section of the chapter!

OSPFv3

The new version of OSPF continues the trend of routing protocols having a lot in common with their IPv4 versions. The foundation of OSPF remains the same—it's still a link-state routing protocol that divides an entire internetwork or autonomous system into areas, establishing a hierarchy.

In OSPF version 2, the router ID (RID) is determined by the highest IP addresses assigned to the router. And as you now know, the RID can be assigned. In version 3, nothing has really changed because you can still assign the RID, area ID, and link-state ID, which remain 32-bit values.

Adjacencies and next-hop attributes now use link-local addresses, but OSPFv3 still uses multi-cast traffic to send its updates and acknowledgements. It uses the addresses FF02::5 for OSPF routers and FF02::6 for OSPF-designated routers. These new addresses are the replacements for 224.0.0.5 and 224.0.0.6, respectively.

Other, less flexible IPv4 protocols don't give us the ability that OSPFv2 does to assign specific networks and interfaces into the OSPF process, but this is still configured under the router configuration process. And with OSPFv3, just as with the EIGRPv6 routing protocols we've talked about, the interfaces and therefore the networks attached to them are configured directly on the interface in interface configuration mode.

The configuration of OSPFv3 is going to look like this: First, optionally start by assigning the RID, but if you have IPv4 addresses assigned to your interface, you can let OSPF pick the RID just as we did with OSPFv2:

```
Router(config)#ipv6 router ospf 10
Router(config-rtr)#router-id 1.1.1.1
```

You get to perform some other configurations from router configuration mode, like summarization and redistribution, but again, we don't even need to configure OSPFv3 from this prompt if we configure it from the interface!

A simple interface configuration looks like this:

```
Router(config-if)#ipv6 ospf 10 area 0.0.0.0
```

So, if we just go to each interface and assign a process ID and area—poof, we're done! See? Easy! As the configuration shows, I configured the area as 0.0.0.0, which is the same thing as just typing area `0`. We'll use Figure 5.11, which is the same network and IPv6-addressing we used in the EIGRPv6 section in Chapter 3.

FIGURE 5.11   Configuring OSPFv3

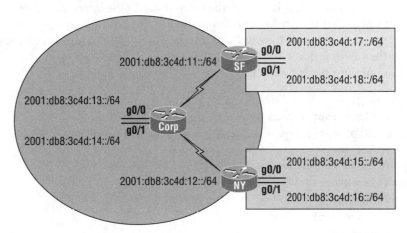

Okay, so all we have to do to enable OSPF on the internetwork is go to each interface that we want to run it on. Here's the Corp configuration:

```
Corp#config t
Corp(config)#int g0/0
Corp(config-if)#ipv6 ospf 1 area 0
Corp(config-if)#int g0/1
Corp(config-if)#ipv6 ospf 1 area 0
Corp(config-if)#int s0/0/0
Corp(config-if)#ipv6 ospf 1 area 0
Corp(config-if)#int s0/0/1
Corp(config-if)#ipv6 ospf 1 area 0
```

That wasn't so bad—much easier than it was with IPv4! To configure OSPFv3, you just need to establish the specific interfaces you'll be using! Let's configure the other two routers now:

```
SF#config t
SF(config)#int g0/0
```

```
SF(config-if)#ipv6 ospf 1 area 1
SF(config-if)#int g0/1
SF(config-if)#ipv6 ospf 1 area 1
SF(config-if)#int s0/0/0
SF(config-if)#ipv6 ospf 1 area 0
01:03:55: %OSPFv3-5-ADJCHG: Process 1, Nbr 192.168.1.5 on Serial0/0/0 from
LOADING to
FULL, Loading Done
```

Sweet—the SF has become adjacent to the Corp router! One interesting output line I want to point out is that the IPv4 RID is being used in the OSPFv3 adjacent change. I didn't set the RIDs manually because I knew I had interfaces with IPv4 addresses already on them, which the OSPF process would use for a RID.

Now let's configure the NY router:

```
NY(config)#int g0/0
NY(config-if)#ipv6 ospf 1 area 2
%OSPFv3-4-NORTRID:OSPFv3 process 1 could not pick a router-id,please configure
manually
NY(config-if)#ipv6 router ospf 1
NY(config-rtr)#router-id 1.1.1.1
NY(config-if)#int g0/0
NY(config-if)#ipv6 ospf 1 area 2
NY(config-if)#int g0/1
NY(config-if)#ipv6 ospf 1 area 2
NY(config-if)#int s0/0/0
NY(config-if)#ipv6 ospf 1 area 0
00:09:00: %OSPFv3-5-ADJCHG: Process 1, Nbr 192.168.1.5 on Serial0/0/0 from
LOADING to
FULL, Loading Done
```

Our adjacency popped up—this is great. But did you notice that I had to set the RID? That's because there wasn't an IPv4 32-bit address already on an interface for the router to use as the RID, so it was mandatory to set the RID manually!

Without even verifying our network, it appears it's up and running. Even so, it's always important to verify!

Verifying OSPFv3

I'll start as usual with the show ipv6 route ospf command:

```
Corp#sh ipv6 route ospf
OI  2001:DB8:3C4D:15::/64 [110/65]
    via FE80::201:C9FF:FED2:5E01, Serial0/0/1
```

```
OI  2001:DB8:3C4D:16::/64 [110/65]
     via FE80::201:C9FF:FED2:5E01, Serial0/0/1
O   2001:DB8:C34D:11::/64 [110/128]
     via FE80::2E0:F7FF:FE13:5E01, Serial0/0/0
OI  2001:DB8:C34D:17::/64 [110/65]
     via FE80::2E0:F7FF:FE13:5E01, Serial0/0/0
OI  2001:DB8:C34D:18::/64 [110/65]
     via FE80::2E0:F7FF:FE13:5E01, Serial0/0/0
```

Perfect. I see all six subnets. Notice the O and OI? The O is intra-area and the OI is inter-area, meaning it's a route from a different area. You can't simply distinguish the area by looking at the routing table though. Plus, don't forget that the routers communicate with their neighbor via link-local addresses: via FE80::2E0:F7FF:FE13:5E01, Serial0/0/0, for example.

Let's take a look at the show ipv6 protocols command:

```
Corp#sh ipv6 protocols
IPv6 Routing Protocol is "connected"
IPv6 Routing Protocol is "static
IPv6 Routing Protocol is "ospf 1"
  Interfaces (Area 0)
    GigabitEthernet0/0
    GigabitEthernet0/1
    Serial0/0/0
    Serial0/0/1
```

This just tells us which interfaces are part of OSPF process 1, area 0. To configure OSPFv3, you absolutely have to know which interfaces are in use. Show ip int brief can really help you if you're having a problem finding your active interfaces.

Let's take a look at the Gigabit Ethernet OSPFv3 active interface on the Corp router:

```
Corp#sh ipv6 ospf int g0/0
GigabitEthernet0/0 is up, line protocol is up
  Link Local Address FE80::2E0:F7FF:FE0A:3301 , Interface ID 1
  Area 0, Process ID 1, Instance ID 0, Router ID 192.168.1.5
  Network Type BROADCAST, Cost: 1
  Transmit Delay is 1 sec, State DR, Priority 1
  Designated Router (ID) 192.168.1.5, local address FE80::2E0:F7FF:FE0A:3301
  No backup designated router on this network
  Timer intervals configured, Hello 10, Dead 40, Wait 40, Retransmit 5
    Hello due in 00:00:09
  Index 1/1, flood queue length 0
```

```
Next 0x0(0)/0x0(0)
Last flood scan length is 1, maximum is 1
Last flood scan time is 0 msec, maximum is 0 msec
Neighbor Count is 0, Adjacent neighbor count is 0
Suppress hello for 0 neighbor(s)
```

This is basically the same information we saw earlier in the verification and trouble-shooting section. Let's take a look at the neighbor table on the Corp router via show ipv6 ospf neighbor:

```
Corp#sh ipv6 ospf neighbor
Neighbor ID     Pri   State         Dead Time   Interface ID   Interface
2.2.2.2          0    FULL/  -      00:00:36    4              Serial0/0/1
192.168.1.6      0    FULL/  -      00:00:39    4              Serial0/0/0
```

Okay, we can see our two neighbors, and there's also a slight difference in this version's command from OSPFv2. We still see the RID on the left and that we're also fully adjacent with both our neighbors—the dash is there because there are no elections on serial point-to-point links. But we don't see the neighbor's IPv6 address listed as we did with OSPFv2's IPv4 addresses, which were listed in the interface ID field.

There's one other command I want to finish with—the show ipv6 ospf command:

```
Corp#sh ipv6 ospf
 Routing Process "ospfv3 1" with ID 192.168.1.5
 SPF schedule delay 5 secs, Hold time between two SPFs 10 secs
 Minimum LSA interval 5 secs. Minimum LSA arrival 1 secs
 LSA group pacing timer 240 secs
 Interface flood pacing timer 33 msecs
 Retransmission pacing timer 66 msecs
 Number of external LSA 0. Checksum Sum 0x000000
 Number of areas in this router is 1. 1 normal 0 stub 0 nssa
 Reference bandwidth unit is 100 mbps
    Area BACKBONE(0)
        Number of interfaces in this area is 4
        SPF algorithm executed 10 times
        Number of LSA 10. Checksum Sum 0x05aebb
        Number of DCbitless LSA 0
        Number of indication LSA 0
        Number of DoNotAge LSA 0
        Flood list length 0
```

This shows the process ID and RID, our reference bandwidth for this interface, and how many interfaces we have in each area, which in our example is only area 0.

Holy output! Now that's what I call a fun chapter. The best thing you can do to get a solid grasp of OSPF and OSPv3 multi-area networks is to gather up some routers and spend some quality time with them, practicing everything we've covered!

Summary

In this chapter, you learned about the scalability constraints of a single-area OSPF network, and you were introduced to the concept of multi-area OSPF as a solution to these scalability limitations.

You're now able to identify the different categories of routers used in multi-area configurations, including the backbone router, internal router, area border router, and autonomous system boundary router.

I detailed the function of different OSPF Link-State Advertisements (LSAs) and you discovered how these LSAs can be minimized through the effective implementation of specific OSPF area types. I discussed the Hello protocols and the different neighbor states experienced when an adjacency is taking place.

Verification and troubleshooting are very large parts of the objectives, and I covered everything you need to know in order to verify and troubleshoot OSPFv2 and meet those requirements.

Finally, we ended the chapter with the easiest part: configuring and verifying OSPFv3.

Exam Essentials

Know the scalability issues multi-area OSPF addresses.   The primary problems in single-area OSPF networks are the large size of the topology and routing tables as well as the excessive computation of the SPF algorithm due to the large number of link-state updates that occur in this single area.

Know the different types of OSPF routers.   Backbone routers have at least one interface in area 0. Area border routers (ABRs) belong to two or more OSPF areas simultaneously. Internal routers have all of their interfaces within the same area. Autonomous system boundary routers (ASBRs) have at least one interface connected to an external network.

Know the different types of LSA packets.   There are seven different types of LSA packets that Cisco uses, but here are the ones you need to remember: Type 1 LSAs (router link advertisements), Type 2 LSAs (network link advertisements), Type 3 and 4 LSAs (summary LSAs), and Type 5 LSAs (AS external link advertisements). Know how each functions.

Be able to monitor multi-area OSPF.   There are a number of commands that provide information useful in a multi-area OSPF environment: show ip route ospf, show ip ospf neighbor, show ip ospf, and show ip ospf database. It's important to understand what each provides.

Be able to troubleshoot OSPF networks.   It's important that you can work your way through the troubleshooting scenario that I presented in this chapter. Be able to look for neighbor adjacencies, and if they are not there, look for ACLs set on the routing protocol, passive interfaces, and wrong network statements.

Understand how to configure OSPFv3.   OSPFv3 uses the same basic mechanisms that OSPFv2 uses, but OSPFv3 is more easily configured by placing the configuring OSPFv3 on a per-interface basis with `ipv6 ospf` `process-ID` area `area`.

Written Lab 5

You can find the answers to this lab in Appendix A, "Answers to Written Labs."

1. What type of LSAs are sent by an ASBR?

2. What state would a router adjacency be in after the INIT state has finished?

3. What LSA types are sent by ABR toward the area external to the one in which they were generated?

4. When would you see an adjacency show this: `FULL/-`?

5. True/False: OSPFv3 is configured per area, per interface.

6. Which OSPF state uses DBD packets and LSRs?

7. Which LSA type is referred to as a router link advertisement (RLA)?

8. What is the command to configure OSPFv3 on an interface with process ID 1 into area 0?

9. What must match exactly between two routers to form an adjacency when using OSPFv3?

10. How can you see all the routing protocols configured and running on your router from user mode?

Hands-on Labs

In this section, you will use the following network and add OSPF and OSPFv3 routing.

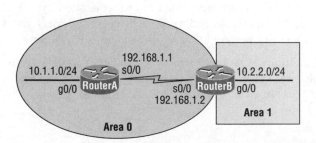

The first lab requires you to configure two routers with OSPF and then verify the configuration. In the second, you will be asked to enable OSPFv3 routing on the same network. Note that the labs in this chapter were written to be used with real equipment—real cheap equipment, that is. As with the chapter on EIGRP, I wrote these labs with the cheapest, oldest routers I had lying around so you can see that you don't need expensive gear to get through some of the hardest labs in this book. However, you can use the free LammleSim IOS version simulator or Cisco's Packet Tracer to run through these labs.

The labs in this chapter are as follows:

Lab 5.1: Configuring and Verifying Multi-Area OSPF

Lab 5.2: Configuring and Verifying OSPFv3

Hands-on Lab 5.1: Configuring and Verifying OSPF Multi-Area

In this lab, you'll configure and verify multi-area OSPF:

1. Implement OSPFv2 on RouterA based on the information in the diagram.

```
RouterA#conf t
RouterA(config)#router ospf 10
RouterA(config-router)#network 10.0.0.0 0.255.255.255 area 0
RouterA(config-router)#network 192.168.1.0 0.0.0.255 area 0
```

2. Implement OSPF on RouterB based on the diagram.

```
RouterB#conf t
RouterB(config)#router ospf 1
RouterB(config-router)#network 192.168.1.2 0.0.0.0 area 0
RouterB(config-router)#network 10.2.2.0 0.0.0.255 area 1
```

3. Display all the LSAs received on RouterA.

```
RouterA#sh ip ospf database

        OSPF Router with ID (192.168.1.1) (Process ID 10)

        Router Link States (Area 0)

Link ID        ADV Router      Age     Seq#        Checksum Link count
10.1.1.2       10.1.1.2        380     0x80000035 0x0012AB 1
192.168.1.1    192.168.1.1     13      0x8000000A 0x00729F 3
192.168.1.2    192.168.1.2     10      0x80000002 0x0090F9 2

        Net Link States (Area 0)

Link ID        ADV Router      Age     Seq#        Checksum
10.1.1.2       10.1.1.2        381     0x80000001 0x003371
```

```
            Summary Net Link States (Area 0)

Link ID          ADV Router       Age        Seq#        Checksum
10.2.2.0         192.168.1.2      8          0x80000001 0x00C3FD
```

4. Display the routing table for RouterA.

```
RouterA#sh ip route
Codes: C - connected, S - static, R - RIP, M - mobile, B - BGP
       D - EIGRP, EX - EIGRP external, O - OSPF, IA - OSPF inter area
       N1 - OSPF NSSA external type 1, N2 - OSPF NSSA external type 2
       E1 - OSPF external type 1, E2 - OSPF external type 2
       i - IS-IS, su - IS-IS summary, L1 - IS-IS level-1, L2 - IS-IS level-2
       ia -IS-IS inter area,* - candidate default,U - per-user static route
       o - ODR, P - periodic downloaded static route

Gateway of last resort is not set

     10.0.0.0/24 is subnetted, 2 subnets
O IA    10.2.2.0 [110/101] via 192.168.1.2, 00:00:29, Serial0/0
C       10.1.1.0 is directly connected, FastEthernet0/0
     192.168.1.0/30 is subnetted, 1 subnets
C       192.168.1.0 is directly connected, Serial0/0
```

5. Display the neighbor table for RouterA.

```
RouterA#sh ip ospf neighbor

Neighbor ID     Pri   State       Dead Time   Address        Interface
192.168.1.2      0    FULL/  -    00:00:35    192.168.1.2    Serial0/0
10.1.1.2         1    FULL/DR     00:00:34    10.1.1.2       FastEthernet0/0
```

6. Use the show ip ospf command on RouterB to see that it is an ABR.

```
RouterB#sh ip ospf
 Routing Process "ospf 1" with ID 192.168.1.2
 Start time: 1w4d, Time elapsed: 00:07:04.100
 Supports only single TOS(TOS0) routes
 Supports opaque LSA
 Supports Link-local Signaling (LLS)
 Supports area transit capability
 It is an area border router
 Router is not originating router-LSAs with maximum metric
```

```
Initial SPF schedule delay 5000 msecs
Minimum hold time between two consecutive SPFs 10000 msecs
Maximum wait time between two consecutive SPFs 10000 msecs
Incremental-SPF disabled
Minimum LSA interval 5 secs
Minimum LSA arrival 1000 msecs
LSA group pacing timer 240 secs
Interface flood pacing timer 33 msecs
Retransmission pacing timer 66 msecs
Number of external LSA 0. Checksum Sum 0x000000
Number of opaque AS LSA 0. Checksum Sum 0x000000
Number of DCbitless external and opaque AS LSA 0
Number of DoNotAge external and opaque AS LSA 0
Number of areas in this router is 2. 2 normal 0 stub 0 nssa
Number of areas transit capable is 0
External flood list length 0
    Area BACKBONE(0)
        Number of interfaces in this area is 1
        Area has no authentication
        SPF algorithm last executed 00:06:44.492 ago
        SPF algorithm executed 3 times
        Area ranges are
        Number of LSA 5. Checksum Sum 0x020DB1
        Number of opaque link LSA 0. Checksum Sum 0x000000
        Number of DCbitless LSA 0
        Number of indication LSA 0
        Number of DoNotAge LSA 0
        Flood list length 0
    Area 1
        Number of interfaces in this area is 1
        Area has no authentication
        SPF algorithm last executed 00:06:45.640 ago
        SPF algorithm executed 2 times
        Area ranges are
        Number of LSA 3. Checksum Sum 0x00F204
        Number of opaque link LSA 0. Checksum Sum 0x000000
        Number of DCbitless LSA 0
        Number of indication LSA 0
        Number of DoNotAge LSA 0
        Flood list length 0
```

Hands-on Lab 5.2: Configuring and Verifying OSPFv3

In this lab, you will configure and verify OSPFv3:

1. Implement OSPFv3 on RouterA. Since the routers have IPv4 addresses, we don't need to set the RID of the router.

    ```
    RouterA#config t
    RouterA(config)#int g0/0
    RouterA(config-if)#ipv6 ospf 1 area 0
    RouterA(config-if)#int s0/0
    RouterA(config-if)#ipv6 ospf 1 area 0
    ```

    That's all there is to it! Nice.

2. Implement OSPFv3 on RouterB.

    ```
    RouterB#config t
    RouterB(config)#int s0/0/0
    RouterB(config-if)#ipv6 ospf 1 area 0
    RouterB(config-if)#int f0/0
    RouterB(config-if)#ipv6 ospf 1 area 1
    ```

    Again, that's all there is to it!

3. Display the routing table for RouterA.

    ```
    RouterA#sh ipv6 route ospf
    IPv6 Routing Table - 11 entries
    Codes: C - Connected, L - Local, S - Static, R - RIP, B - BGP
           U - Per-user Static route
           I1 - ISIS L1, I2 - ISIS L2, IA - ISIS interarea, IS - ISIS summary
           O - OSPF intra, OI - OSPF inter, OE1 - OSPF ext 1, OE2 - OSPF ext 2
           ON1 - OSPF NSSA ext 1, ON2 - OSPF NSSA ext 2
           D - EIGRP, EX - EIGRP external
    OI  2001:DB8:3C4D:15::/64 [110/65]
         via FE80::21A:2FFF:FEE7:4398, Serial0/0
    ```

    Notice that the one route OSPFv3 found is an inter-area route, meaning the network is in another area.

4. Display the neighbor table for RouterA.

    ```
    RouterA#sh ipv6 ospf neighbor

    Neighbor ID    Pri  State       Dead Time   Interface ID   Interface
    192.168.1.2     1   FULL/  -    00:00:32    6              Serial0/0
    ```

5. Display the show `ipv6 ospf` command on RouterB.

```
RouterB#sh ipv6 ospf
 Routing Process "ospfv3 1" with ID 192.168.1.2
 It is an area border router
 SPF schedule delay 5 secs, Hold time between two SPFs 10 secs
 Minimum LSA interval 5 secs. Minimum LSA arrival 1 secs
 LSA group pacing timer 240 secs
 Interface flood pacing timer 33 msecs
 Retransmission pacing timer 66 msecs
 Number of external LSA 0. Checksum Sum 0x000000
 Number of areas in this router is 2. 2 normal 0 stub 0 nssa
 Reference bandwidth unit is 100 mbps
    Area BACKBONE(0)
        Number of interfaces in this area is 1
        SPF algorithm executed 3 times
        Number of LSA 7. Checksum Sum 0x041C1B
        Number of DCbitless LSA 0
        Number of indication LSA 0
        Number of DoNotAge LSA 0
        Flood list length 0
    Area 1
        Number of interfaces in this area is 1
        SPF algorithm executed 2 times
        Number of LSA 5. Checksum Sum 0x02C608
        Number of DCbitless LSA 0
        Number of indication LSA 0
        Number of DoNotAge LSA 0
        Flood list length 0
```

Review Questions

The following questions are designed to test your understanding of this chapter's material. For more information on how to get additional questions, please see www.lammle.com/ccna.

You can find the answers to these questions in Appendix B, "Answers to Review Questions."

1. Which of the following are scalability issues with single-area OSPF networks? (Choose all that apply.)

    A. Size of the routing table

    B. Size of the OSPF database

    C. Maximum hop-count limitation

    D. Recalculation of the OSPF database

2. Which of the following describes a router that connects to an external routing process (e.g., EIGRP)?

    A. ABR

    B. ASBR

    C. Type 2 LSA

    D. Stub router

3. Which of the following must match in order for an adjacency to occur between routers? (Choose three.)

    A. Process ID

    B. Hello and dead timers

    C. Link cost

    D. Area

    E. IP address/subnet mask

4. In which OSPF state do two routers forming an adjacency appear as in the show ip ospf neighbor output after adding neighbors into the table and exchanging hello information?

    A. ATTEMPT

    B. INIT

    C. 2WAY

    D. EXSTART

    E. FULL

5. You need to set up a preferred link that OSPF will use to route information to a remote network. Which command will allow you to set the interface link as preferred over another?

    A. ip ospf preferred 10

    B. ip ospf priority 10

   C. `ospf bandwidth 10`

   D. `ip ospf cost 10`

6. When would a router's neighbor table show the FULL/DR state?

   A. After the first Hello packets are received by a neighbor

   B. When all information is synchronized among adjacent neighbors

   C. When the router's neighbor table is too full of information and is discarding neighbor information

   D. After the EXSTART state

7. Which is/are true regarding OSPFv3? (Choose all that apply.)

   A. You must add network statements under the OSPF process.

   B. There are no network statements in OSPFv3 configurations.

   C. OSPFv3 uses a 128-bit RID.

   D. If you have IPv4 configured on the router, it is not mandatory that you configure the RID.

   E. If you don't have IPv4 configured on the router, it is mandatory that you configure the RID.

   F. OSPFv3 doesn't use LSAs like OSPFv2 does.

8. When a router undergoes the exchange protocol within OSPF, in what order does it pass through each state?

   A. EXSTART state > LOADING state > EXCHANGE state > FULL state

   B. EXSTART state > EXCHANGE state > LOADING state > FULL state

   C. EXSTART state > FULL state > LOADING state > EXCHANGE state

   D. LOADING state > EXCHANGE state > FULL state > EXSTART state

9. Which type of LSA is generated by DRs and referred to as a network link advertisement (NLA)?

   A. Type 1

   B. Type 2

   C. Type 3

   D. Type 4

   E. Type 5

10. Which type of LSA is generated by ABRs and is referred to as a summary link advertisement (SLA)?

   A. Type 1

   B. Type 2

   C. Type 3

   D. Type 4

   E. Type 5

11. Which command will show all the LSAs known by a router?

   A. `show ip ospf`

   B. `show ip ospf neighbor`

    C. `show ip ospf interface`

    D. `show ip ospf database`

12. Using the following illustration, what is the cost from R1's routing table to reach the network with Server 1? Each Gigabit Ethernet link has a cost of 4, and each serial link has a cost of 15.

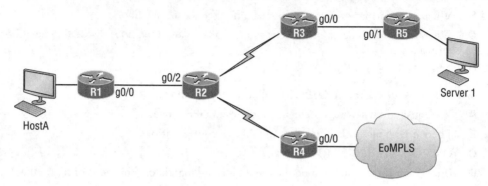

    A. 100

    B. 23

    C. 64

    D. 19

    E. 27

13. Using the following illustration, which of the following are true? (Choose all that apply.)

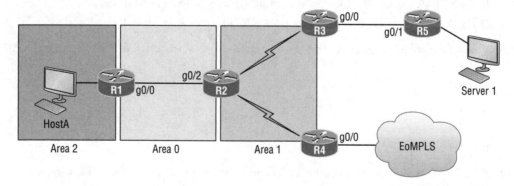

    A. R1 is an internal router.

    B. R3 would see the networks connected to the R1 router as an inter-area route.

    C. R2 is an ASBR.

    D. R3 and R4 would receive information from R2 about the backbone area, and the same LSA information would be in both LSDBs.

    E. R4 is an ABR.

14. Which of the following could cause two routers to not form an adjacency? (Choose all that apply.)

  A. They are configured in different areas.

  B. Each router sees the directly connected link as different costs.

  C. Two different process IDs are configured.

  D. ACL is configured on the routing protocol.

  E. There is an IP address/mask mismtach.

  F. Passive interface is configured.

  G. They both have been configured with the same RID.

15. Which of the following IOS commands shows the state of an adjacency with directly connected routers?

  A. debug ospf events

  B. show ip ospf border-routers

  C. show ip ospf neighbor

  D. show ip ospf database

16. What command will show you the DR and DBR address of the area you are connected to directly with an interface?

  A. show interface s0/0/0

  B. show interface fa0/0

  C. show ip ospf interface s0/0/0

  D. show ip ospf interface fa0/0

17. Which of the following could be causing a problem with the Corp router not forming an adjacency with its neighbor router? (Choose all that apply.)

```
Corp#sh ip protocols
Routing Protocol is "ospf 1"
  Outgoing update filter list for all interfaces is not set
  Incoming update filter list for all interfaces is 10
  Router ID 1.1.1.1
  Number of areas in this router is 3. 3 normal 0 stub 0 nssa
  Maximum path: 4
  Routing for Networks:
    10.10.0.0 0.0.255.255 area 0
    172.16.10.0 0.0.0.3 area 1
    172.16.10.4 0.0.0.3 area 2
Reference bandwidth unit is 100 mbps
  Passive Interface(s):
    Serial0/0/0
Routing Information Sources:
    Gateway         Distance      Last Update
    1.1.1.1             110       00:17:42
    172.16.10.2         110       00:17:42
    172.16.10.6         110       00:17:42
  Distance: (default is 110)
```

    A. The routers are configured with the wrong network statements.

    B. They have different maximum paths configured.

    C. There is a passive interface configured.

    D. There is an ACL set stopping Hellos.

    E. The costs of the links between the routers are configured differently.

    F. They are in different areas.

18. Which of the following is/are true? (Choose all that apply.)

    A. The reference bandwidth for OSPF and OSPFv3 is 1.

    B. The reference bandwidth for OSPF and OSPFv3 is 100.

    C. You change the reference bandwidth from global config with the command `auto-cost reference bandwidth` *number*.

    D. You change the reference bandwidth under the OSPF router process with the command `auto-cost reference bandwidth` *number*.

    E. Only one router needs to set the reference bandwidth if it is changed from its default.

    F. All routers in a single area must set the reference bandwidth if it is changed from its default.

    G. All routers in the AS must set the reference bandwidth if it is changed from its default.

19. Which two statements about the OSPF router ID are true? (Choose two.)

    A. It identifies the source of a Type 1 LSA.

    B. It should be the same on all routers in an OSPF routing instance.

    C. By default, the lowest IP address on the router becomes the OSPF router ID.

    D. The router automatically chooses the IP address of a loopback as the OSPF router ID.

    E. It is created using the MAC address of the loopback interface.

20. What are two benefits of using a single OSPF area network design? (Choose two.)

    A. It is less CPU intensive for routers in the single area.

    B. It reduces the types of LSAs that are generated.

    C. It removes the need for virtual links.

    D. It increases LSA response times.

    E. It reduces the number of required OSPF neighbor adjacencies.

Chapter

6

Troubleshooting IP, IPv6, and VLANs

THE FOLLOWING ICND2 EXAM TOPICS ARE COVERED IN THIS CHAPTER:

✓ **1.7 Describe common access layer threat mitigation techniques**

  ▪ 1.7.c Nondefault native VLAN

✓ **4.0 Infrastructure Services**

✓ **4.4 Configure, verify, and troubleshoot IPv4 and IPv6 access list for traffic filtering**

  ▪ 4.4.a Standard

  ▪ 4.4.b Extended

  ▪ 4.4.c Named

✓ **5.0 Infrastructure Maintenance**

✓ **5.2 Troubleshoot network connectivity issues using ICMP echo-based IP SLA**

✓ **5.3 Use local SPAN to troubleshoot and resolve problems**

In this chapter, especially at first, it's going to seem like we're going over lot of the same ground and concepts already covered in other chapters. The reason for this is that trouble-shooting is such a major focus of the Cisco ICND1 and ICND2 objectives that I've got to make sure I've guided you through this vital topic in depth. If not, then I just haven't done all I can to really set you up for success! So to make that happen, we're going to thoroughly examine troubleshooting with IP, IPv6, and *virtual LANs (VLANs)* now. And I can't stress the point enough that you absolutely must have a solid, fundamental understanding of IP and IPv6 routing as well as a complete understanding of VLANs and trunking nailed down tight if you're going to win at this!

To help you do that, I'll be using different scenarios to walk you through the Cisco troubleshooting steps to correctly solve the problems you're likely to be faced with. Although it's hard to tell exactly what the ICND1 and ICND2 exams will throw at you, you can read and completely understand the objectives so that no matter what, you'll be prepared, equipped, and up to the challenge. The way to do this is by building upon a really strong foundation, including being skilled at troubleshooting. This chapter is precisely designed, and exactly what you need, to seriously help solidify your trouble-shooting foundation.

The previous chapters on EIGRP and OSPF each had their own troubleshooting section. Troubleshooting WAN protocols will be thoroughly covered in Chapter 7. In this chapter we'll concentrate solely on IP, IPv6, and VLAN troubleshooting.

To find up-to-the-minute updates for this chapter, please see www.lammle.com/ccna or the book's web page at www.sybex.com/go/ccna.

Troubleshooting IP Network Connectivity

Let's start out by taking a moment for a short and sweet review of IP routing. Always remember that when a host wants to transmit a packet, IP looks at the destination address and determines if it's a local or remote request. If it's determined to be a local request, IP just broadcasts a frame out on the local network looking for the local host using an ARP request. If it's a remote request, the host sends an ARP request to the default gateway to discover the MAC address of the router.

Once the hosts have the default gateway address, they'll send each packet that needs to be transmitted to the Data Link layer for framing, and newly framed packets are then sent out on the local collision domain. The router will receive the frame and remove the packet from the frame, and IP will then parse the routing table looking for the exit interface on the router. If the destination is found in the routing table, it will packet-switch the packet to the exit interface. At this point, the packet will be framed with new source and destination MAC addresses.

Okay, with that short review in mind, what would you say to someone who called you saying they weren't able to get to a server on a remote network? What's the first thing you would have this user do (besides reboot Windows) or that you would do yourself to test network connectivity? If you came up with using the Ping program, that's a great place to start. The Ping program is a great tool for finding out if a host is alive on the network with a simple ICMP echo request and echo reply. But being able to ping the host as well as the server doesn't guarantee that all is well in the network! Keep in mind that there's more to the Ping program than just being used as a quick and simple testing protocol.

To be prepared for the exam objectives, it's a great idea to get used to connecting to various routers and pinging from them. Of course, pinging from a router is not as good as pinging from the host reporting the problem, but that doesn't mean we can't isolate some problems from the routers themselves.

Let's use Figure 6.1 as a basis to run through some troubleshooting scenarios.

FIGURE 6.1 Troubleshooting scenario

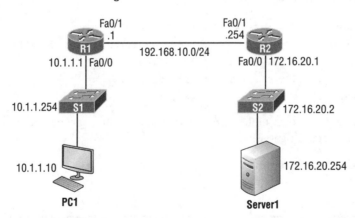

In this first scenario, a manager calls you and says that he cannot log in to Server1 from PC1. Your job is to find out why and fix it. The Cisco objectives are clear on the troubleshooting steps you need to take when a problem has been reported, and here they are:

1. Check the cables to find out if there's a faulty cable or interface in the mix and verify the interface's statistics.

2. Make sure that devices are determining the correct path from the source to the destination. Manipulate the routing information if needed.

3. Verify that the default gateway is correct.

4. Verify that name resolution settings are correct.

5. Verify that there are no *access control lists (ACLs)* blocking traffic.

In order to effectively troubleshoot this problem, we'll narrow down the possibilities by process of elimination. We'll start with PC1 and verify that it's configured correctly and also that IP is working correctly.

There are four steps for checking the PC1 configuration:

1. Test that the local IP stack is working by pinging the loopback address.

2. Test that the local IP stack is talking to the Data Link layer (LAN driver) by pinging the local IP address.

3. Test that the host is working on the LAN by pinging the default gateway.

4. Test that the host can get to remote networks by pinging remote Server1.

Let's check out the PC1 configuration by using the ipconfig command, or ifconfig on a Mac:

```
C:\Users\Todd Lammle>ipconfig

Windows IP Configuration

Ethernet adapter Local Area Connection:

    Connection-specific DNS Suffix  . : localdomain
    Link-local IPv6 Address . . . . . : fe80::64e3:76a2:541f:ebcb%11
    IPv4 Address. . . . . . . . . . . : 10.1.1.10
    Subnet Mask . . . . . . . . . . . : 255.255.255.0
    Default Gateway . . . . . . . . . : 10.1.1.1
```

We can also check the route table on the host with the route print command to see if it truly does know the default gateway:

```
C:\Users\Todd Lammle>route print
[output cut]
IPv4 Route Table
=====================================================================
Active Routes:
Network Destination      Netmask         Gateway        Interface  Metric
        0.0.0.0          0.0.0.0         10.1.1.10      10.1.1.1   10
[output cut]
```

Between the output of the ipconfig command and the route print command, we can be assured that the hosts are aware of the correct default gateway.

For the Cisco objectives, it's extremely important to be able to check and verify the default gateway on a host and also that this address matches the router's interface!

So, let's verify that the local IP stack is initialized by pinging the loopback address now:

```
C:\Users\Todd Lammle>ping 127.0.0.1

Pinging 127.0.0.1 with 32 bytes of data:
Reply from 127.0.0.1: bytes=32 time<1ms TTL=128
Reply from 127.0.0.1: bytes=32 time<1ms TTL=128
Reply from 127.0.0.1: bytes=32 time<1ms TTL=128
Reply from 127.0.0.1: bytes=32 time<1ms TTL=128

Ping statistics for 127.0.0.1:
    Packets: Sent = 4, Received = 4, Lost = 0 (0% loss),
Approximate round trip times in milli-seconds:
    Minimum = 0ms, Maximum = 0ms, Average = 0ms
```

This first output confirms the IP address and configured default gateway of the host, and then I verified the fact that the local IP stack is working. Our next move is to verify that the IP stack is talking to the LAN driver by pinging the local IP address.

```
C:\Users\Todd Lammle>ping 10.1.1.10

Pinging 10.1.1.10 with 32 bytes of data:
Reply from 10.1.1.10: bytes=32 time<1ms TTL=128
Reply from 10.1.1.10: bytes=32 time<1ms TTL=128
Reply from 10.1.1.10: bytes=32 time<1ms TTL=128
Reply from 10.1.1.10: bytes=32 time<1ms TTL=128

Ping statistics for 10.1.1.10:
    Packets: Sent = 4, Received = 4, Lost = 0 (0% loss),
Approximate round trip times in milli-seconds:
    Minimum = 0ms, Maximum = 0ms, Average = 0ms
```

And now that we know the local stack is solid and the IP stack is communicating to the LAN driver, it's time to check our local LAN connectivity by pinging the default gateway:

```
C:\Users\Todd Lammle>ping 10.1.1.1

Pinging 10.1.1.1 with 32 bytes of data:
Reply from 10.1.1.1: bytes=32 time<1ms TTL=128
Reply from 10.1.1.1: bytes=32 time<1ms TTL=128
Reply from 10.1.1.1: bytes=32 time<1ms TTL=128
Reply from 10.1.1.1: bytes=32 time<1ms TTL=128
```

```
Ping statistics for 10.1.1.1:
    Packets: Sent = 4, Received = 4, Lost = 0 (0% loss),
Approximate round trip times in milli-seconds:
    Minimum = 0ms, Maximum = 0ms, Average = 0ms
```

Looking good! I'd say our host is in good shape. Let's try to ping the remote server next to see if our host is actually getting off the local LAN to communicate remotely:

```
C:\Users\Todd Lammle>ping 172.16.20.254

Pinging 172.16.20.254 with 32 bytes of data:
Request timed out.
Request timed out.
Request timed out.
Request timed out.

Ping statistics for 172.16.20.254:
    Packets: Sent = 4, Received = 0, Lost = 4 (100% loss),
```

Well, looks like we've confirmed local connectivity but not remote connectivity, so we're going to have to dig deeper to isolate our problem. But first, and just as important, it's key to make note of what we can rule out at this point:

1. The PC is configured with the correct IP address and the local IP stack is working.
2. The default gateway is configured correctly and the PC's default gateway configuration matches the router interface IP address.
3. The local switch is working because we can ping through the switch to the router.
4. We don't have a local LAN issue, meaning our Physical layer is good because we can ping the router. If we couldn't ping the router, we would need to verify our physical cables and interfaces.

Let's see if we can narrow the problem down further using the traceroute command:

```
C:\Users\Todd Lammle>tracert 172.16.20.254

Tracing route to 172.16.20.254 over a maximum of 30 hops

  1     1 ms     1 ms    <1 ms   10.1.1.1
  2     *        *        *      Request timed out.
  3     *        *        *      Request timed out.
```

Well, we didn't get beyond our default gateway, so let's go over to R2 and see if we can talk locally to the server:

```
R2#ping 172.16.20.254

Pinging 172.16.20.254 with 32 bytes of data:
Reply from 172.16.20.254: bytes=32 time<1ms TTL=128
```

```
Reply from 172.16.20.254: bytes=32 time<1ms TTL=128
Reply from 172.16.20.254: bytes=32 time<1ms TTL=128
Reply from 172.16.20.254: bytes=32 time<1ms TTL=128

Ping statistics for 172.16.20.254:
    Packets: Sent = 4, Received = 0, Lost = 4 (100% loss),
```

Okay, we just eliminated a local LAN problem by connecting to Server1 from the R2 router, so we're good there. Let's summarize what we know so far:

1. PC1 is configured correctly.

2. The switch located on the 10.1.1.0 LAN is working.

3. PC1's default gateway is configured correctly.

4. R2 can communicate to Server1, so we don't have a remote LAN issue.

But something is still clearly wrong, so what should we check now? Now would be a great time to verify the Server1 IP configuration and make sure the default gateway is configured correctly. Let's take a look:

```
C:\Users\Server1>ipconfig

Windows IP Configuration

Ethernet adapter Local Area Connection:

    Connection-specific DNS Suffix  . : localdomain
    Link-local IPv6 Address . . . . . : fe80::7723:76a2:e73c:2acb%11
    IPv4 Address. . . . . . . . . . . : 172.16.20.254
    Subnet Mask . . . . . . . . . . . : 255.255.255.0
    Default Gateway . . . . . . . . . : 172.16.20.1
```

Okay—the Server1 configuration looks good and the R2 router can ping the server, so it seems that the server's local LAN is solid, the local switch is working, and there are no cable or interface issues. But let's zoom in on interface Fa0/0 on R2 and talk about what to expect if there were errors on this interface:

```
R2#sh int fa0/0
FastEthernet0/0 is up, line protocol is up
[output cut]
  Full-duplex, 100Mb/s, 100BaseTX/FX
  ARP type: ARPA, ARP Timeout 04:00:00
  Last input 00:00:05, output 00:00:01, output hang never
  Last clearing of "show interface" counters never
  Input queue: 0/75/0/0 (size/max/drops/flushes); Total output drops: 0
  Queueing strategy: fifo
  Output queue: 0/40 (size/max)
  5 minute input rate 0 bits/sec, 0 packets/sec
```

```
5 minute output rate 0 bits/sec, 0 packets/sec
   1325 packets input, 157823 bytes
   Received 1157 broadcasts (0 IP multicasts)
   0 runts, 0 giants, 0 throttles
   0 input errors, 0 CRC, 0 frame, 0 overrun, 0 ignored
   0 watchdog
   0 input packets with dribble condition detected
   2294 packets output, 244630 bytes, 0 underruns
   0 output errors, 0 collisions, 3 interface resets
   347 unknown protocol drops
   0 babbles, 0 late collision, 0 deferred
   4 lost carrier, 0 no carrier
   0 output buffer failures, 0 output buffers swapped out
```

You've got to be able to analyze interface statistics to find problems there if they exist, so let's pick out the important factors relevant to meeting that challenge effectively now.

Speed and duplex settings   Good to know that the most common cause of interface errors is a mismatched duplex mode between two ends of an Ethernet link. This is why it's so important to make sure that the switch and its hosts (PCs, router interfaces, etc.) have the same speed setting. If not, they just won't connect. And if they have mismatched duplex settings, you'll receive a legion of errors, which cause nasty performance issues, intermittent connectivity—even total loss of communication!

Using autonegotiation for speed and duplex is a very common practice, and it's enabled by default. But if this fails for some reason, you'll have to set the configuration manually like this:

```
Switch(config)#int gi0/1
Switch(config-if)#speed ?
   10    Force 10 Mbps operation
   100   Force 100 Mbps operation
   1000  Force 1000 Mbps operation
   auto  Enable AUTO speed configuration
Switch(config-if)#speed 1000
Switch(config-if)#duplex  ?
   auto  Enable AUTO duplex configuration
   full  Force full duplex operation
   half  Force half-duplex operation
Switch(config-if)#duplex  full
```

If you have a duplex mismatch, a telling sign is that the late collision counter will increment.

Input queue drops   If the input queue drops counter increments, this signifies that more traffic is being delivered to the router that it can process. If this is consistently high, try to determine exactly when these counters are increasing and how the events relate to CPU usage. You'll see the ignored and throttle counters increment as well.

Output queue drops   This counter indicates that packets were dropped due to interface congestion, leading to queuing delays. When this occurs, applications like VoIP will experience performance issues. If you observe this constantly incrementing, consider QoS.

Input errors   Input errors often indicate high errors such as CRCs. This can point to cabling problems, hardware issues, or duplex mismatches.

Output errors   This is the total number of frames that the port tried to transmit when an issue such as a collision occurred.

We're going to move on in our troubleshooting process of elimination by analyzing the routers' actual configurations. Here's R1's routing table:

```
R1>sh ip route
[output cut]
Gateway of last resort is 192.168.10.254 to network 0.0.0.0

S*    0.0.0.0/0 [1/0] via 192.168.10.254
      10.0.0.0/8 is variably subnetted, 2 subnets, 2 masks
C        10.1.1.0/24 is directly connected, FastEthernet0/0
L        10.1.1.1/32 is directly connected, FastEthernet0/0
      192.168.10.0/24 is variably subnetted, 2 subnets, 2 masks
C        192.168.10.0/24 is directly connected, FastEthernet0/1
L        192.168.10.1/32 is directly connected, FastEthernet0/1
```

This actually looks pretty good! Both of our directly connected networks are in the table and we can confirm that we have a default route going to the R2 router. So now let's verify the connectivity to R2 from R1:

```
R1>sh ip int brief
Interface            IP-Address      OK? Method Status                Protocol
FastEthernet0/0      10.1.1.1        YES manual up                    up
FastEthernet0/1      192.168.10.1    YES manual up                    up
Serial0/0/0          unassigned      YES unset  administratively down down
Serial0/1/0          unassigned      YES unset  administratively down down
R1>ping 192.168.10.254
Type escape sequence to abort.
Sending 5, 100-byte ICMP Echos to 192.168.10.254, timeout is 2 seconds:
!!!!!
Success rate is 100 percent (5/5), round-trip min/avg/max = 1/2/4 ms
```

This looks great too! Our interfaces are correctly configured with the right IP address and the Physical and Data Link layers are up. By the way, I also tested layer 3 connectivity by pinging the R2 Fa0/1 interface.

Since everything looks good so far, our next step is to check into the status of R2's interfaces:

```
R2>sh ip int brief
Interface              IP-Address     OK? Method Status          Protocol
FastEthernet0/0        172.16.20.1    YES manual up                up
FastEthernet0/1        192.168.10.254 YES manual up                up
R2>ping 192.168.10.1
Type escape sequence to abort.
Sending 5, 100-byte ICMP Echos to 192.168.10.1, timeout is 2 seconds:
!!!!!
Success rate is 100 percent (5/5), round-trip min/avg/max = 1/2/4 ms
```

Well, everything still checks out at this point. The IP addresses are correct and the Physical and Data Link layers are up. I also tested the layer 3 connectivity with a ping to R1, so we're all good so far. We'll examine the routing table next:

```
R2>sh ip route
[output cut]
Gateway of last resort is not set

     10.0.0.0/24 is subnetted, 1 subnets
S       10.1.1.0 is directly connected, FastEthernet0/0
     172.16.0.0/16 is variably subnetted, 2 subnets, 2 masks
C       172.16.20.0/24 is directly connected, FastEthernet0/0
L       172.16.20.1/32 is directly connected, FastEthernet0/0
     192.168.10.0/24 is variably subnetted, 2 subnets, 2 masks
C       192.168.10.0/24 is directly connected, FastEthernet0/1
L       192.168.10.254/32 is directly connected, FastEthernet0/1
```

Okay—we can see that all our local interfaces are in the table, as well as a static route to the 10.1.1.0 network. But do you see the problem? Look closely at the static route. The route was entered with an exit interface of Fa0/0, and the path to the 10.1.1.0 network is out Fa0/1! Aha! We've found our problem! Let's fix R2:

```
R2#config t
R2(config)#no ip route 10.1.1.0 255.255.255.0 fa0/0
R2(config)#ip route 10.1.1.0 255.255.255.0 192.168.10.1
```

That should do it. Let's verify from PC1:

```
C:\Users\Todd Lammle>ping 172.16.20.254
```

```
Pinging 172.16.20.254 with 32 bytes of data:
Reply from 172.16.20.254: bytes=32 time<1ms TTL=128
Reply from 172.16.20.254: bytes=32 time<1ms TTL=128
Reply from 172.16.20.254: bytes=32 time<1ms TTL=128
Reply from 172.16.20.254: bytes=32 time<1ms TTL=128

Ping statistics for 172.16.20.254
    Packets: Sent = 4, Received = 4, Lost = 0 (0% loss),
Approximate round trip times in milli-seconds:
    Minimum = 0ms, Maximum = 0ms, Average = 0ms
```

Our snag appears to be solved, but just to make sure, we really need to verify with a higher-level protocol like Telnet:

```
C:\Users\Todd Lammle>telnet 172.16.20.254
Connecting To 172.16.20.254...Could not open connection to the host, on
port 23: Connect failed
```

Okay, that's not good! We can ping to Server1, but we can't telnet to it. In the past, I've verified that telnetting to this server worked, but it's still possible that we have a failure on the server side. To find out, let's verify our network first, starting at R1:

```
R1>ping 172.16.20.254
Type escape sequence to abort.
Sending 5, 100-byte ICMP Echos to 172.16.20.254, timeout is 2 seconds:
!!!!!
Success rate is 100 percent (5/5), round-trip min/avg/max = 1/1/4 ms
R1>telnet 172.16.20.254
Trying 172.16.20.254 ...
% Destination unreachable; gateway or host down
```

This is some pretty ominous output! Let's try from R2 and see what happens:

```
R2#telnet 172.16.20.254
Trying 172.16.20.254 ... Open

User Access Verification

Password:
```

Oh my—I can ping the server from a remote network, but I can't telnet to it; however, the local router R2 can! These factors eliminate the server being a problem since I can telnet to the server when I'm on the local LAN.

And we know we don't have a routing problem because we fixed that already. So what's next? Let's check to see if there's an ACL on R2:

```
R2>sh access-lists
```

```
Extended IP access list 110
    10 permit icmp any any (25 matches)
```

Seriously? What a loopy access list to have on a router! This ridiculous list permits ICMP, but that's it. It denies everything except ICMP due to the implicit deny `ip any any` at the end of every ACL. But before we uncork the champagne, we need to see if this foolish list has been applied to our interfaces on R2 to confirm that this is really our problem:

```
R2>sh ip int fa0/0
FastEthernet0/0 is up, line protocol is up
  Internet address is 172.16.20.1/24
  Broadcast address is 255.255.255.255
  Address determined by setup command
  MTU is 1500 bytes
  Helper address is not set
  Directed broadcast forwarding is disabled
  Outgoing access list is 110
  Inbound  access list is not set
```

There it is—that's our problem all right! In case you're wondering why R2 could telnet to Server1, it's because an ACL filters only packets trying to go through the router—not packets generated at the router. Let's get to work and fix this:

```
R2#config t
R2(config)#no access-list 110
```

I just verified that I can telnet from PC1 to Server1, but let's try telnetting from R1 again:

```
R1#telnet 172.16.20.254
Trying 172.16.20.254 ... Open

User Access Verification

Password:
```

Nice—looks like we're set, but what about using the name?

```
R1#telnet Server1
Translating "Server1"...domain server (255.255.255.255)

% Bad IP address or host name
```

Well, we're not all set just yet. Let's fix R1 so that it can provide name resolution:

```
R1(config)#ip host Server1 172.16.20.254
```

```
R1#telnet Server1
Trying Server1 (172.16.20.254)... Open

User Access Verification

Password:
```

Great—things are looking good from the router, but if the customer can't telnet to the remote host using the name, we've got to check the DNS server to confirm connectivity and for the correct entry to the server. Another option would be to configure the local host table manually on PC1.

The last thing to do is to check the server to see if it's responding to HTTP requests via the telnet command, believe it or not! Here's an example:

```
R1#telnet 172.16.20.254 80
Trying 172.16.20.254, 80 ... Open
```

Yes—finally! Server1 is responding to requests on port 80, so we're in the clear.

Using IP SLA for Troubleshooting

I want to mention one more thing that can help you troubleshoot your IP network, and this is using IP service-level agreements (SLAs), which will allow us to use IP SLA ICMP echo to test far-end devices instead of pinging manually.

There are several reasons to use the IP SLA measurements:

- Edge-to-edge network availability monitoring
    - For example, packet loss statistics
- Network performance monitoring and network performance visibility
    - For example, network latency and response time
- Troubleshooting basic network operation
    - For example, end-to-end network connectivity

Step 1: Enable an IP SLA operation that enters the IP SLA configuration mode. Chose any number from 1 to 2.1 billion as an operation number.

```
R1(config)#ip sla 1
```

Step 2: Configure the IP SLA ICMP echo test and destination.

```
R1(config-ip-sla)#icmp?
icmp-echo  icmp-jitter

R1(config-ip-sla)#icmp-echo ?
  Hostname or X:X:X:X::X
  Hostname or A.B.C.D  Destination IPv6/IP address or hostname

R1(config-ip-sla)#icmp-echo 172.16.20.254
```

Step 3: Set the test frequency.

```
R1(config-ip-sla-echo)#frequency ?
 <1-604800>  Frequency in seconds (default 60)

R1(config-ip-sla-echo)#frequency 10
```

Step 4: Schedule your IP SLA test.

```
R1(config-ip-sla-echo)#exit
R1(config)#ip sla schedule ?
 <1-2147483647>  Entry number

R1(config)#ip sla schedule 1 life ?
 <0-2147483647>  Life seconds (default 3600)
 forever         continue running forever

R1(config)#ip sla schedule 1 life forever start-time ?
 after     Start after a certain amount of time from now
 hh:mm     Start time (hh:mm)
 hh:mm:ss  Start time (hh:mm:ss)
 now       Start now
 pending   Start pending

R1(config)#ip sla schedule 1 life forever start-time now
```

Step 5: Verify the IP SLA operation. Use the following commands:

```
Show ip sla configuration
Show ip sla statistics
```

R1 should have an ICMP Echo test configured to the remote server address, and the test should run every 10 seconds and be scheduled to run forever.

```
R1#show ip sla configuration
IP SLAs Infrastructure Engine-II
Entry number: 1
Owner:
Tag:
Type of operation to perform: icmp-echo
Target address/Source address: 172.16.20.254/0.0.0.0
Type Of Service parameter: 0x0
Request size (ARR data portion): 28
Operation timeout (milliseconds): 5000
Verify data: No
```

```
Vrf Name:
Schedule:
   Operation frequency (seconds): 10  (not considered if randomly scheduled)
   Next Scheduled Start Time: Start Time already passed
   Group Scheduled : FALSE
   Randomly Scheduled : FALSE
   Life (seconds): Forever
   Entry Ageout (seconds): never
   Recurring (Starting Everyday): FALSE
   Status of entry (SNMP RowStatus): Active
[output cut]
```

R1#sh ip sla statistics
```
IPSLAs Latest Operation Statistics

IPSLA operation id: 1
Type of operation: icmp-echo
        Latest RTT: 1 milliseconds
Latest operation start time: *15:27:51.365 UTC Mon Jun 6 2016
Latest operation return code: OK
Number of successes: 38
Number of failures: 0
Operation time to live: Forever
```

The IP SLA 1 test on R1 has been successfully performed 38 times and the test never failed.

Using SPAN for Troubleshooting

A traffic sniffer can be a valuable tool for monitoring and troubleshooting your network. However, since the inception of switches into our networks more than 20 years ago, troubleshooting has become more difficult because we can't just plug an analyzer into a switch port and be able to read all the network traffic. Before we had switches, we used hubs, and when a hub received a digital signal on one port, the hub sent that digital signal out on all ports except the port it was received on. This allows a traffic sniffer that is connected to a hub port to receive all traffic in the network.

Modern local networks are essentially switched networks. After a switch boots, it starts to build up a layer 2 forwarding table based on the source MAC addresses of the different packets that the switch receives. After the switch builds this forwarding table, it forwards traffic that is destined for a MAC address directly to the exit port. By default, this prevents a traffic sniffer that is connected to another port from receiving the unicast traffic. The SPAN feature was therefore introduced on switches to help solve this problem (see Figure 6.2).

FIGURE 6.2   Using SPAN for troubleshooting

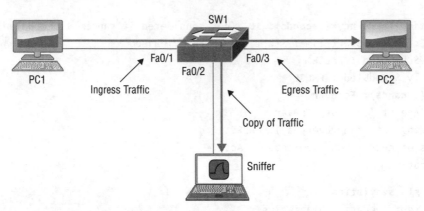

The SPAN feature allows you to analyze network traffic passing through the port and send a copy of the traffic to another port on the switch that has been connected to a network analyzer or other monitoring device. SPAN copies the traffic that the device receives and/or sends on source ports to a destination port for analysis.

For example, if you would like to analyze the traffic flowing from PC1 to PC2, shown in Figure 6.2, you need to specify a source port where you want to capture the data. You can either configure the interface Fa0/1 to capture the ingress traffic or configure the interface Fa0/3 to capture the egress traffic—your choice! Next, specify the destination port interface where the sniffer is connected and will capture the data, in this example Fa0/2. The traffic flowing from PC1 to PC2 will then be copied to that interface, and you will be able to analyze it with a traffic sniffer.

Step 1: Associate a SPAN session number with the source port of what you want to monitor.

```
S1(config)#monitor session 1 source interface f0/1
```

Step 2: Associate a SPAN session number of the sniffer with the destination interface.

```
S1(config)#monitor session 1 dest interface f0/2
```

Step 3: Verify that the SPAN session has been configured correctly.

```
S1(config)#do sh monitor
Session 1
---------
Type                 : Local Session
Source Ports         :
    Both             : Fa0/1
Destination Ports    : Fa0/2
    Encapsulation    : Native
          Ingress    : Disabled
```

Now connect up your network analyzer into port F0/2 and enjoy!

Configuring and Verifying Extended Access Lists

Even though I went through some very basic troubleshooting with ACLs earlier in this chapter, let's dig a little deeper to make sure we really understand extended named ACLs before hitting IPv6.

First off, you should be familiar with ACLs from your ICND1 studies; if not, head back and read that chapter, including the standard and extended ACLs section. I'm going to focus solely on extended named ACLs, since that is what the ICND2 objectives are all about.

As you know, standard access lists focus only on IP or IPv6 source addresses. Extended ACLs, however, filter based on the source *and* destination layer 3 addresses at a minimum, but in addition can filter using the protocol field in the IP header (Next Header field in IPv6), as well as the source and destination port numbers at layer 4, all shown in Figure 6.3

FIGURE 6.3   Extended ACLs

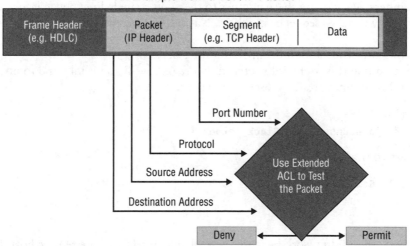

Using the network layout in Figure 6.1, let's create an extended named ACL that blocks Telnet to the 172.16.20.254 server from 10.1.1.10. It's an extended list, so we'll place it closest to the source address as possible.

Step 1: Test that you can telnet to the remote host.

```
R1#telnet 172.16.20.254
Trying 172.16.20.254 ... Open
Server1>
```

Okay, great!

Step 2: Create an ACL on R1 that stops telnetting to the remote host of 172.16.20.254. Using a named ACL, start with the protocol (IP or IPv6), choose either a standard or extended list, and then name it. The name is absolutely case sensitive when applying to an interface.

```
R1(config)#ip access-list extended Block_Telnet
R1(config-ext-nacl)#
```

Step 3: Once you have created the named list, add your test parameters.

```
R1(config-ext-nacl)#deny tcp host 10.1.1.1 host 172.16.20.254 eq 23
R1(config-ext-nacl)#permit ip any any
```

Step 4: Verify your access list.

```
R1(config-ext-nacl)#do sh access-list
Extended IP access list Block_Telnet
    10 deny tcp host 10.1.1.1 host 172.16.20.254 eq telnet
    20 permit ip any any
```

Notice the numbers 10 and 20 on the left side for each test statement. These are called sequence numbers. We can use these number to then edit a single line, delete it, or even add a new line in between two sequence numbers. Named ACLs can be edited; numbered ACLs cannot.

Step 5: Configure your ACL on your router interface.

Since we're adding this to the R1 router in Figure 6.3, we'll add it inbound to interface FastEthernet 0/0, stopping traffic closest to the source.

```
R1(config)#int fa0/0
R1(config-if)#ip access-group Block_Telnet in
```

Step 6: Test your access list.

```
R1#telnet 172.16.20.254
Trying 172.16.20.254 ... Open
Server1>
```

Hmm...okay, that didn't work because I'm still able to telnet to the remote host. Let's take a look at our list, verify our interface, and then fix the problem.

```
R1#sh access-list
Extended IP access list Block_Telnet
    10 deny tcp host 10.1.1.1 host 172.16.20.254 eq telnet
    20 permit ip any any
```

By verifying the IP addresses in the deny statement in line sequence 10, you can see that my source address is 10.1.1.1 and instead should have been 10.1.1.10.

Step 7: Fix and/or edit your access list. Delete the bad line and reconfigure the ACL to the correct IP.

```
R1(config)#ip access-list extended Block_Telnet
R1(config-ext-nacl)#no 10
R1(config-ext-nacl)#10 deny tcp host 10.1.1.10 host 172.16.20.254 eq 80
```

Verify that your list is working.

```
R1#telnet 172.16.20.254
Trying 172.16.20.254 ...
% Destination unreachable; gateway or host down
```

Step 8: Display the ACL again and observe the updated hit counters with each line, and also verify that the interface is set with the ACL.

```
R1#sh access-list
Extended IP access list Block_Telnet
    10 deny tcp host 10.1.1.10 host 172.16.20.254 eq telnet (58 matches)
    20 permit ip any any (86 matches)


R1#sh ip int f0/0
FastEthernet0/0 is up, line protocol is up
  Internet address is 10.10.10.1/24
  Broadcast address is 255.255.255.255
  Address determined by non-volatile memory
  MTU is 1500 bytes
  Helper address is not set
  Directed broadcast forwarding is disabled
  Multicast reserved groups joined: 224.0.0.10
  Outgoing access list is not set
  Inbound  access list is Block_Telnet
  Proxy ARP is enabled
[output cut]
```

The interface was up and working, so verifying at this point was a little overkill, but you must be able to look at an interface and troubleshoot issues, such as ACLs set on an interface. So be sure to remember the show ip interface command.

Now, let's mix things up a little by adding IPv6 to our network and work through the same troubleshooting steps.

Troubleshooting IPv6 Network Connectivity

I'm going to be straight with you: there isn't a lot that's going to be much different between this section and the process you just went through with the IPv4 troubleshooting steps. Except regarding the addressing of course! So other than that key factor, we'll take the same approach, using Figure 6.4, specifically because I really want to highlight the differences associated with IPv6. So the problem scenario I'm going to use will also stay the same: PC1 cannot communicate to Server1.

FIGURE 6.4   IPv6 troubleshooting scenario

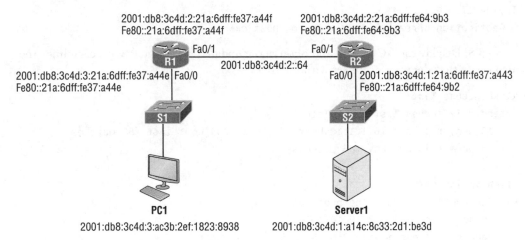

I want to point out that this is not an "introduction to IPv6" chapter, so I'm assuming you've got some IPv6 fundamentals down.

Notice that I documented both the *link-local* and *global addresses* assigned to each router interface in Figure 6.4. We need both in order to troubleshoot, so right away, you can see that things get a bit more complicated because of the longer addresses and the fact that there are multiple addresses per interface involved!

But *before* we start troubleshooting the IPv6 network in Figure 6.4, I want to refresh your memory on the ICMPv6 protocol, which is an important protocol in our troubleshooting arsenal.

ICMPv6

IPv4 used the ICMP workhorse for lots of tasks, including error messages like destination unreachable and troubleshooting functions like Ping and Traceroute. ICMPv6 still does those things for us, but unlike its predecessor, the v6 flavor isn't implemented as a separate layer 3 protocol. Instead, it's an integrated part of IPv6 and is carried after the basic IPv6 header information as an extension header.

ICMPv6 is used for router solicitation and advertisement, for neighbor solicitation and advertisement (i.e., finding the MAC addresses for IPv6 neighbors), and for redirecting the host to the best router (default gateway).

Neighbor Discovery (NDP)

ICMPv6 also takes over the task of finding the address of other devices on the local link. The Address Resolution Protocol is used to perform this function for IPv4, but that's been renamed Neighbor Discovery (ND or NDP) in ICMPv6. This process is now achieved via a multicast address called the solicited node address because all hosts join this multicast group upon connecting to the network.

Neighbor discovery enables these functions:

- Determining the MAC address of neighbors
- Router solicitation (RS) FF02::2
- Router advertisements (RA) FF02::1
- Neighbor solicitation (NS)
- Neighbor advertisement (NA)
- Duplicate address detection (DAD)

The part of the IPv6 address designated by the 24 bits farthest to the right is added to the end of the multicast address FF02:0:0:0:0:1:FF/104. When this address is queried, the corresponding host will send back its layer 2 address. Devices can find and keep track of other neighbor devices on the network in pretty much the same way. When I talked about RA and RS messages earlier in the CCENT chapters, and told you that they use multicast traffic to request and send address information, that too is actually a function of ICMPv6—specifically, neighbor discovery.

In IPv4, the protocol IGMP was used to allow a host device to tell its local router that it was joining a multicast group and would like to receive the traffic for that group. This IGMP function has been replaced by ICMPv6, and the process has been renamed multicast listener discovery.

With IPv4, our hosts could have only one default gateway configured, and if that router went down we had to fix the router, change the default gateway, or run some type of virtual default gateway with other protocols created as a solution for this inadequacy in IPv4. Figure 6.5 shows how IPv6 devices find their default gateways using neighbor discovery.

FIGURE 6.5   Router solicitation (RS) and router advertisement (RA)

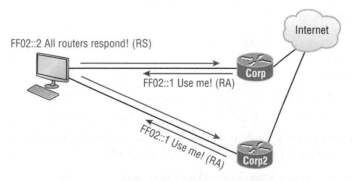

IPv6 hosts send a router solicitation (RS) onto their data link asking for all routers to respond, and they use the multicast address FF02::2 to achieve this. Routers on the same link respond with a unicast to the requesting host, or with a router advertisement (RA) using FF02::1.

But that's not all! Hosts also can send solicitations and advertisements between themselves using a neighbor solicitation (NS) and neighbor advertisement (NA), as shown in Figure 6.6.

FIGURE 6.6   Neighbor solicitation (NS) and neighbor advertisement (NA)

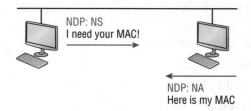

Remember that RA and RS gather or provide information about routers and NS and NA gather information about hosts. Also, remember that a "neighbor" is a host on the same data link or VLAN.

With that foundation review in mind, here are the troubleshooting steps we'll progress through in our investigation:

1. Check the cables because there might be a faulty cable or interface. Verify interface statistics.

2. Make sure that devices are determining the correct path from the source to the destination. Manipulate the routing information if needed.

3. Verify that the default gateway is correct.

4. Verify that name resolution settings are correct, and especially for IPv6, make sure the DNS server is reachable via IPv4 and IPv6.

5. Verify that there are no ACLs that are blocking traffic.

In order to troubleshoot this problem, we'll use the same process of elimination, beginning with PC1. We must verify that it's configured correctly and that IP is working properly. Let's start by pinging the loopback address to verify the IPv6 stack:

```
C:\Users\Todd Lammle>ping ::1

Pinging ::1 with 32 bytes of data:
Reply from ::1: time<1ms
Reply from ::1: time<1ms
Reply from ::1: time<1ms
Reply from ::1: time<1ms
```

Well, the IPv6 stack checks out, so let's ping the Fa0/0 of R1, which PC1 is directly connected to on the same LAN, starting with the link-local address:

```
C:\Users\Todd Lammle>ping fe80::21a:6dff:fe37:a44e
```

```
Pinging fe80:21a:6dff:fe37:a44e with 32 bytes of data:
Reply from fe80::21a:6dff:fe37:a44e: time<1ms
Reply from fe80::21a:6dff:fe37:a44e: time<1ms
Reply from fe80::21a:6dff:fe37:a44e: time<1ms
Reply from fe80::21a:6dff:fe37:a44e: time<1ms
```

Next, we'll ping the global address on Fa0/0:

```
C:\Users\Todd Lammle>ping 2001:db8:3c4d:3:21a:6dff:fe37:a44e

Pinging 2001:db8:3c4d:3:21a:6dff:fe37:a44e with 32 bytes of data:
Reply from 2001:db8:3c4d:3:21a:6dff:fe37:a44e: time<1ms
Reply from 2001:db8:3c4d:3:21a:6dff:fe37:a44e: time<1ms
Reply from 2001:db8:3c4d:3:21a:6dff:fe37:a44e: time<1ms
Reply from 2001:db8:3c4d:3:21a:6dff:fe37:a44e: time<1ms
```

Okay—looks like PC1 is configured and working on the local LAN to the R1 router, so we've confirmed the Physical, Data Link, and Network layers between the PC1 and the R1 router Fa0/0 interface.

Our next move is to check the local connection on Server1 to the R2 router to verify that LAN. First we'll ping the link-local address of the router from Server1:

```
C:\Users\Server1>ping fe80::21a:6dff:fe64:9b2

Pinging fe80::21a:6dff:fe64:9b2  with 32 bytes of data:
Reply from fe80::21a:6dff:fe64:9b2: time<1ms
Reply from fe80::21a:6dff:fe64:9b2: time<1ms
Reply from fe80::21a:6dff:fe64:9b2: time<1ms
Reply from fe80::21a:6dff:fe64:9b2: time<1ms
```

And next, we'll ping the global address of Fa0/0 on R2:

```
C:\Users\Server1>ping 2001:db8:3c4d:1:21a:6dff:fe37:a443

Pinging 2001:db8:3c4d:1:21a:6dff:fe37:a443 with 32 bytes of data:
Reply from 2001:db8:3c4d:1:21a:6dff:fe37:a443: time<1ms
Reply from 2001:db8:3c4d:1:21a:6dff:fe37:a443: time<1ms
Reply from 2001:db8:3c4d:1:21a:6dff:fe37:a443: time<1ms
Reply from 2001:db8:3c4d:1:21a:6dff:fe37:a443: time<1ms
```

Let's quickly summarize what we know at this point:

1. By using the ipconfig /all command on PC1 and Server1, I was able to document their global and link-local IPv6 addresses.
2. We know the IPv6 link-local addresses of each router interface.
3. We know the IPv6 global address of each router interface.

4. We can ping from PC1 to router R1's Fa0/0 interface.

5. We can ping from Server1 to router R2's Fa0/0 interface.

6. We can eliminate a local problem on both LANs.

From here, we'll go to PC1 and see if we can route to Server1:

```
C:\Users\Todd Lammle>tracert 2001:db8:3c4d:1:a14c:8c33:2d1:be3d

Tracing route to 2001:db8:3c4d:1:a14c:8c33:2d1:be3d over a maximum of 30 hops

 1    Destination host unreachable.
```

Okay, now that's not good. Looks like we might have a routing problem. And on this little network, we're doing static IPv6 routing, so getting to the bottom of things will definitely take a little effort! But before we start looking into our potential routing issue, let's check the link between R1 and R2. We'll ping R2 from R1 to test the directly connected link.

The first thing you need to do before attempting to ping between routers is verify your addresses—yes, verify them again! Let's check out both routers, then try pinging from R1 to R2:

```
R1#sh ipv6 int brief
FastEthernet0/0            [up/up]
    FE80::21A:6DFF:FE37:A44E
    2001:DB8:3C4D:3:21A:6DFF:FE37:A44E
FastEthernet0/1            [up/up]
    FE80::21A:6DFF:FE37:A44F
    2001:DB8:3C4D:2:21A:6DFF:FE37:A44F

R2#sh ipv6 int brief
FastEthernet0/0            [up/up]
    FE80::21A:6DFF:FE64:9B2
    2001:DB8:3C4D:1:21A:6DFF:FE37:A443
FastEthernet0/1            [up/up]
    FE80::21A:6DFF:FE64:9B3
    2001:DB8:3C4D:2:21A:6DFF:FE64:9B3

R1#ping 2001:DB8:3C4D:2:21A:6DFF:FE64:9B3
Type escape sequence to abort.
Sending 5, 100-byte ICMP Echos to ping 2001:DB8:3C4D:2:21A:6DFF:FE64:9B3,
timeout
is 2 seconds:
!!!!!
Success rate is 100 percent (5/5), round-trip min/avg/max = 0/2/8 ms
```

In the preceding output, you can see that I now have the IPv6 addresses for both the R1 and R2 directly connected interfaces. The output also shows that I used the Ping program to verify layer 3 connectivity. Just as with IPv4, we need to resolve the logical (IPv6) address to a MAC address in order to communicate on the local LAN. But unlike IPv4, IPv6 doesn't use ARP—it uses ICMPv6 neighbor solicitations instead—so after the successful ping, we can now see the neighbor resolution table on R1:

```
R1#sh ipv6 neighbors
IPv6 Address                     Age Link-layer Addr State Interface
FE80::21A:6DFF:FE64:9B3            0 001a.6c46.9b09  DELAY Fa0/1
2001:DB8:3C4D:2:21A:6DFF:FE64:9B3 0 001a.6c46.9b09  REACH Fa0/1
```

Let's take a minute to talk about the possible states that a resolved address shows us:

INCMP (incomplete)   Address resolution is being performed on the entry. A neighbor solicitation message has been sent, but the neighbor message has not yet been received.

REACH (reachable)   Positive confirmation has been received confirming that the path to the neighbor is functioning correctly. REACH is good!

STALE   The state is STALE when the interface has not communicated within the neighbor reachable time frame. The next time the neighbor communicates, the state will change back to REACH.

DELAY   Occurs after the STALE state, when no reachability confirmation has been received within what's known as the DELAY_FIRST_PROBE_TIME. This means that the path was functioning but it hasn't had communication within the neighbor reachable time frame.

PROBE   When in PROBE state, the configured interface is resending a neighbor solicitation and waiting for a reachability confirmation from a neighbor.

We can verify our default gateway with IPv6 with the ipconfig command like this:

```
C:\Users\Todd Lammle>ipconfig
   Connection-specific DNS Suffix  . : localdomain
   IPv6 Address. . . . . . . . . . . : 2001:db8:3c4d:3:ac3b:2ef:1823:8938
   Temporary IPv6 Address. . . . . . : 2001:db8:3c4d:3:2f33:44dd:211:1c3d
   Link-local IPv6 Address . . . . . : fe80::ac3b:2ef:1823:8938%11
   IPv4 Address. . . . . . . . . . . : 10.1.1.10
   Subnet Mask . . . . . . . . . . . : 255.255.255.0
   Default Gateway . . . . . . . . . : Fe80::21a:6dff:fe37:a44e%11
                                       10.1.1.1
```

It's important to understand that the default gateway will be the link-local address of the router, and in this case, we can see that the address the host learned is truly the link-local address of the Fa0/0 interface of R1. The %11 is just used to identify an interface and isn't used as part of the IPv6 address.

Temporary IPv6 Addresses

The temporary IPv6 address, listed under the unicast IPv6 address as 2001:db8:3c4d:3:2f33: 44dd:211:1c3d, was created by Windows to provide privacy from the EUI-64 format. This creates a global address for your host without using your MAC address by generating a random number for the interface and hashing it; the result is then appended to the /64 prefix from the router. You can disable this feature with the following commands:

```
netsh interface ipv6 set global randomizeidentifiers=disabled
netsh interface ipv6 set privacy state-disabled
```

In addition to the ipconfig command, we can use the command netsh interface ipv6 show neighbor to verify our default gateway address:

```
C:\Users\Todd Lammle>netsh interface ipv6 show neighbor
[output cut]

Interface 11: Local Area Connection

Internet Address                              Physical Address    Type
---------------------------------------------  -----------------   -----------
2001:db8:3c4d:3:21a:6dff:fe37:a44e            00-1a-6d-37-a4-4e   (Router)
Fe80::21a:6dff:fe37:a44e                      00-1a-6d-37-a4-4e   (Router)
ff02::1                                       33-33-00-00-00-01   Permanent
ff02::2                                       33-33-00-00-00-02   Permanent
ff02::c                                       33-33-00-00-00-0c   Permanent
ff02::16                                      33-33-00-00-00-16   Permanent
ff02::fb                                      33-33-00-00-00-fb   Permanent
ff02::1:2                                     33-33-00-01-00-02   Permanent
ff02::1:3                                     33-33-00-01-00-03   Permanent
ff02::1:ff1f:ebcb                             33-33-ff-1f-eb-cb   Permanent
```

 I've checked the default gateway addresses on Server1 and they are correct. They should be, because this is provided directly from the router with an ICMPv6 RA (router advertisement) message. The output for that verification is not shown.

Let's establish the information we have right now:

1. Our PC1 and Server1 configurations are working and have been verified.

2. The LANs are working and verified, so there is no Physical layer issue.

3. The default gateways are correct.

4. The link between the R1 and R2 routers is working and verified.

So all this tells us is that it's now time to check our routing tables! We'll start with the R1 router:

```
R1#sh ipv6 route
C    2001:DB8:3C4D:2::/64 [0/0]
      via FastEthernet0/1, directly connected
L    2001:DB8:3C4D:2:21A:6DFF:FE37:A44F/128 [0/0]
      via FastEthernet0/1, receive
C    2001:DB8:3C4D:3::/64 [0/0]
      via FastEthernet0/0, directly connected
L    2001:DB8:3C4D:3:21A:6DFF:FE37:A44E/128 [0/0]
      via FastEthernet0/0, receive
L    FF00::/8 [0/0]
      via Null0, receive
```

All we can see in the output is the two directly connected interfaces configured on the router, and that won't help us send IPv6 packets to the 2001:db8:3c4d:1::/64 subnet off of Fa0/0 on R2. So let's find out what R2 can tell us:

```
R2#sh ipv6 route
C    2001:DB8:3C4D:1::/64 [0/0]
      via FastEthernet0/0, directly connected
L    2001:DB8:3C4D:1:21A:6DFF:FE37:A443/128 [0/0]
      via FastEthernet0/0, receive
C    2001:DB8:3C4D:2::/64 [0/0]
      via FastEthernet0/1, directly connected
L    2001:DB8:3C4D:2:21A:6DFF:FE64:9B3/128 [0/0]
      via FastEthernet0/1, receive
S    2001:DB8:3C4D:3::/64 [1/0]
      via 2001:DB8:3C4D:2:21B:D4FF:FE0A:539
L    FF00::/8 [0/0]
      via Null0, receive
```

Now we're talking—that tells us a lot more than R1's table did! We have both of our directly connected configured LANs, Fa0/0 and Fa0/1, right there in the routing table, as well as a static route to 2001:DB8:3C4D:3::/64, which is the remote LAN Fa0/0 off of R1, which is good. Now let's fix the route problem on R1 by adding a route that gives us access to the Server1 network.

```
R1(config)#ipv6 route ::/0 fastethernet 0/1 FE80::21A:6DFF:FE64:9B3
```

I want to point out that I didn't need to make the default route as difficult as I did. I entered both the exit interface and next-hop link-local address when just the exit interface or next-hop global addresses would be mandatory, but not the link-local. So it could have simply just been this:

```
R1(config)#ipv6 route ::/0 fa0/1
```

Next, we'll verify that we can now ping from PC1 to Server1:

```
C:\Users\Todd Lammle>ping 2001:db8:3c4d:1:a14c:8c33:2d1:be3d

Pinging 2001:db8:3c4d:1:a14c:8c33:2d1:be3d with 32 bytes of data:
Reply from 2001:db8:3c4d:1:a14c:8c33:2d1:be3d: time<1ms
Reply from 2001:db8:3c4d:1:a14c:8c33:2d1:be3d: time<1ms
Reply from 2001:db8:3c4d:1:a14c:8c33:2d1:be3d: time<1ms
Reply from 2001:db8:3c4d:1:a14c:8c33:2d1:be3d: time<1ms
```

Sweet—we're looking golden with this particular scenario! But know that it is still possible to have name resolution issues. If that were the case, you would just need to check your DNS server or local host table.

Moving on in the same way we did in the IPv4 troubleshooting section, it's a good time to check into your ACLs, especially if you're still having a problem after troubleshooting all your local LANs and all other potential routing issues.

Troubleshooting IPv6 Extended Access Lists

Let's create an extended IPv6 ACL on R2, pretty much just like we did in the IPv4 troubleshooting section.

First, understand that you can only create named extended IPv6 ACLs, so you don't need to specify standard or extended in your named list, and although you won't see any sequence numbers, you can still somewhat edit a named IPv6 ACL, meaning you can delete a single line but there is no way to insert a line other than at the end of the ACL.

In addition, every IPv4 access list has an implicit deny ip any any at the bottom; however, IPv6 access lists actually have *three* implied statements at the bottom:

- permit icmp any any nd-na
- permit icmp any any nd-ns
- deny ipv6 any any

The two permit statements are required for neighbor discovery, which is an important protocol in IPv6, because it's the replacement for ARP.

Using the network layout and IPv6 addresses in Figure 6.4, let's create an IPv6 extended named ACL that blocks Telnet to Server1 (with an IPv6 address of 2001:db8:3c4d:1:a14c:8c33:2d1:be3d) from PC1 (with a destination IPv6 address of 2001:db8:3c4d:3:2ef:1823:8938). Since it's an IPv6 extended named ACL (always), we'll place it closest to the source address if possible.

Step 1: Test that you can telnet to the remote host.

```
R1#telnet 2001:db8:3c4d:1:a14c:8c33:2d1:be3d
Trying 2001:db8:3c4d:1:a14c:8c33:2d1:be3d... Open

Server1>
```

Okay, great—but that was way too much effort! Let's create an entry into the hosts table of R1 so we don't have to type an IPv6 address when trying to access that host.

```
R1(config)#ipv6 host Server1 2001:db8:3c4d:1:a14c:8c33:2d1:be3d
R1(config)#do sh host
[output cut]

Host Port Flags Age Type Address(es)
Server1 None (perm, OK) 0 IPV6 2001:DB8:3C4D:1:A14C:8C33:2D1:BE3D
```

Now we can just type this from now on (the name is case sensitive).

```
R1#telnet Server1
Trying 2001:DB8:3C4D:1:A14C:8C33:2D1:BE3D... Open

Server1>
```

Or better yet, just the name (Telnet is the default).

```
R1#Server1
Trying 2001:DB8:3C4D:1:A14C:8C33:2D1:BE3D... Open

Server1>exit
```

Also, ping using the name.

```
R1#ping Server1
Type escape sequence to abort.
Sending 5, 100-byte ICMP Echos to 2001:DB8:3C4D:1:A14C:8C33:2D1:BE3D, timeout is
2 seconds:
!!!!!
Success rate is 100 percent (5/5), round-trip min/avg/max = 0/0/1 ms
```

Step 2: Create an ACL on R2 that stops Telnet to the remote host Server1 (2001:db8 :3c4d:1:a14c:8c33:2d1:be3d). The name is absolutely case sensitive when applying to an interface.

```
R2(config)#ipv6 access-list Block_Telnet
R2(config-ipv6-acl)#
```

Step 3: Once you have created the named list, add your test parameters.

```
R2(config-ipv6-acl)#deny tcp host 2001:DB8:3C4D:2:21A:6DFF:FE37:A44F host
2001:DB8:3C4D:1:A14C:8C33:2D1:BE3D eq telnet
R2(config-ipv6-acl)#permit ipv6 any any
```

Step 4: Configure your ACL on your router interface.

Since we're adding this to the R2 router in Figure 6.4, we'll add it to interface FastEthernet 0/1, stopping traffic closest to the source, and use the command ipv6 traffic-filter.

```
R2(config)#int fa0/1
R2(config-if)#ipv6 traffic-filter Block_Telnet out
```

Step 5: Test your access list by telnetting from Server1 on the R1 router.

```
R1#Server1
Trying 2001:DB8:3C4D:1:A14C:8C33:2D1:BE3D ...Open


Server1>
```

Hmm... and I tried really hard not to make a typo! Let's take a look.

```
R2#sh access-lists
IPv6 access list Block_Telnet
      deny tcp host 2001:DB8:3C4D:2:21A:6DFF:FE37:A44F host
2001:DB8:3C4D:1:A14C:8C33:2D1:BE3D eq telnet (96 match(es))
      permit ipv6 any any (181 match(es))
```

By verifying the IPv6 addresses with the interfaces of the routers, this list looks correct. It's important to verify your addresses with a show ipv6 interface brief command. Let's take a look.

```
R1#sh ipv6 int brief
FastEthernet0/0 [up/up]
      FE80::2E0:B0FF:FED2:B701
      2001:DB8:3C4D:3:21A:6DFF:FE37:A44E
FastEthernet0/1 [up/up]
      FE80::2E0:B0FF:FED2:B702
      2001:DB8:3C4D:2:21A:6DFF:FE37:A44F
```

Since R1 Fa0/1 is my source address, we can see that this address is correct in my ACL. Let's take a look at the destination device.

```
Server1#sh ipv6 int br
FastEthernet0/0 [up/up]
      FE80::260:70FF:FED8:DD01
      2001:DB8:3C4D:1:A14C:8C33:2D1:BE3D
```

Yup, this one is correct too! My IPv6 ACL is correct, so now we need to check our interface.

Step 6: Fix and/or edit your access list and/or interfaces.

```
R2#show running-config
[output cut]
!
interface FastEthernet0/0
     no ip address
     duplex auto
     speed auto
     ipv6 address 2001:DB8:3C4D:1:21A:6DFF:FE37:A443/64
     ipv6 rip 1 enable
!
interface FastEthernet0/1
     no ip address
     ipv6 traffic-filter Block_Telnet out
     duplex auto
     speed auto
     ipv6 address 2001:DB8:3C4D:2:21A:6DFF:FE64:9B3/64
     ipv6 rip 1 enable
!
```

Unlike IPv4, where we can use the show ip interface command to see if an ACL is set, we can only use the show running-config command to verify if an IPv6 ACL is set on an interface. In the above output, we can see that I certainly did set the ACL to the interface Fa0/1, but I configured it to out instead of in on the interface. Let's fix that.

```
R2#config t
R2(config)#int fa0/1
R2(config-if)#no ipv6 traffic-filter Block_Telnet out
R2(config-if)#ipv6 traffic-filter Block_Telnet in
```

Step 7: Retest your ACL.

```
R1#Server1

Trying 2001:DB8:3C4D:1:A14C:8C33:2D1:BE3D ...% Connection timed out; remote host
not responding
R1#
```

Looks good! Although I don't recommend using this method to block Telnet to a router, it was a great way to test our IPv6 ACLs.

Troubleshooting VLAN Connectivity

You know by now that VLANs are used to break up broadcast domains in a layer 2 switched network. You've also learned that we assign ports on a switch into a VLAN broadcast domain by using the `switchport access vlan` command.

The access port carries traffic for a single VLAN that the port is a member of. If members of one VLAN want to communicate to members in the same VLAN that are located on a different switch, then a port between the two switches needs to be either configured to be a member of this single VLAN or configured as a trunk link, which passes information on all VLANs by default.

We're going to use Figure 6.7 to reference as we go through the procedures for troubleshooting VLAN and trunking.

FIGURE 6.7   VLAN connectivity

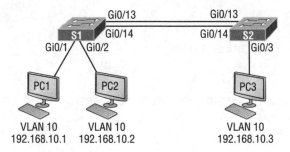

I'm going to begin with VLAN troubleshooting and then move on to trunk troubleshooting.

VLAN Troubleshooting

A couple of key times to troubleshoot VLANs are when and if you lose connectivity between hosts and when you're configuring new hosts into a VLAN but they're not working.

Here are the steps we'll follow to troubleshoot VLANs:

1. Verify the VLAN database on all your switches.

2. Verify your *Content Addressable Memory (CAM)* table.

3. Verify that your port VLAN assignments are configured correctly.

And here's a list of the commands we'll be using in the following sections:

```
Show vlan
Show mac address-table
Show interfaces interface switchport
switchport access vlan vlan
```

VLAN Troubleshooting Scenario

A manager calls and says they can't communicate to the new sales team member that just connected to the network. How would you proceed to solve this issue? Well, because the sales hosts are in VLAN 10, we'll begin with step 1 and verify that our databases on both switches are correct.

First, I'll use the show vlan or show vlan brief command to check if the expected VLAN is actually in the database. Here's a look at the VLAN database on S1:

```
S1#sh vlan

VLAN Name                             Status    Ports
---- -------------------------------- --------- -------------------------------
1    default                          active    Gi0/3, Gi0/4, Gi0/5, Gi0/6
                                                Gi0/7, Gi0/8, Gi0/9, Gi0/10
                                                Gi0/11, Gi0/12, Gi0/13, Gi0/14
                                                Gi0/15, Gi0/16, Gi0/17, Gi0/18
                                                Gi0/19, Gi0/20, Gi0/21, Gi0/22
                                                Gi0/23, Gi0/24, Gi0/25, Gi0/26
                                                Gi0/27, Gi0/28
10   Sales                            active    Gi0/1, Gi0/2
20   Accounting                       active
26   Automation10                     active
27   VLAN0027                         active
30   Engineering                      active
170  VLAN0170                         active
501  Private501                       active
502  Private500                       active
[output cut]
```

This output shows that VLAN 10 is in the local database and that Gi0/1 and Gi0/2 are associated to VLAN 10.

So next, we'll go to step 2 and verify the CAM with the show mac address-table command:

```
S1#sh mac address-table
        Mac Address Table
-------------------------------------------

Vlan    Mac Address       Type        Ports
----    -----------       --------    -----
 All    0100.0ccc.cccc    STATIC      CPU
[output cut]
   1    000d.2830.2f00    DYNAMIC     Gi0/24
   1    0021.1c91.0d8d    DYNAMIC     Gi0/13
   1    0021.1c91.0d8e    DYNAMIC     Gi0/14
   1    b414.89d9.1882    DYNAMIC     Gi0/17
   1    b414.89d9.1883    DYNAMIC     Gi0/18
   1    ecc8.8202.8282    DYNAMIC     Gi0/15
```

```
   1     ecc8.8202.8283     DYNAMIC     Gi0/16
  10     001a.2f55.c9e8     DYNAMIC     Gi0/1
  10     001b.d40a.0538     DYNAMIC     Gi0/2
Total Mac Addresses for this criterion: 29
```

Okay—know that your switch will show quite a few MAC addresses assigned to the CPU at the top of the output; those MAC addresses are used by the switch to manage the ports. The very first MAC address listed is the base MAC address of the switch and used by STP in the bridge ID. In the preceding output, we can see that there are two MAC addresses associated with VLAN 10 and that it was dynamically learned. We can also establish that this MAC address is associated to Gi0/1. S1 looks really good!

Let's take a look at S2 now. First, let's confirm that port PC3 is connected and check its configuration. I'll use the show interfaces *interface* switchport command to do that:

```
S2#sh interfaces gi0/3 switchport
Name: Gi0/3
Switchport: Enabled
Administrative Mode: dynamic desirable
Operational Mode: static access
Administrative Trunking Encapsulation: negotiate
Operational Trunking Encapsulation: native
Negotiation of Trunking: On
Access Mode VLAN: 10 (Inactive)
Trunking Native Mode VLAN: 1 (default)
[output cut]
```

Okay—we can see that the port is enabled and that it's set to dynamic desirable. This means that if it connects to another Cisco switch, it will desire to trunk on that link. But keep in mind that we're using it as an access port, which is confirmed by the operational mode of static access. At the end of the output, the text shows Access Mode VLAN: 10 (Inactive). This is not a good thing! Let's examine S2's CAM and see what we find out:

```
S2#sh mac address-table
        Mac Address Table
-------------------------------------------

Vlan    Mac Address      Type       Ports
----    -----------      --------   -----
All     0100.0ccc.cccc   STATIC     CPU
[output cut]
  1     001b.d40a.0538   DYNAMIC    Gi0/13
  1     0021.1bee.a70d   DYNAMIC    Gi0/13
  1     b414.89d9.1884   DYNAMIC    Gi0/17
```

```
   1    b414.89d9.1885    DYNAMIC    Gi0/18
   1    ecc8.8202.8285    DYNAMIC    Gi0/16
Total Mac Addresses for this criterion: 26
```

Referring back to Figure 6.7, we can see that the host is connected to Gi0/3. The problem here is that we don't see a MAC address dynamically associated to Gi0/3 in the MAC address table. So what do we know so far that can help us? Well first, we can see that Gi0/3 is configured into VLAN 10, but that VLAN is inactive. Second, the host off of Gi0/3 doesn't appear in the CAM table. Now would be a good time to take a look at the VLAN database like this:

S2#**sh vlan brief**

```
VLAN Name                             Status    Ports
---- -------------------------------- --------- -------------------------------
1    default                          active    Gi0/1, Gi0/2, Gi0/4, Gi0/5
                                                Gi0/6, Gi0/7, Gi0/8, Gi0/9
                                                Gi0/10, Gi0/11, Gi0/12, Gi0/13
                                                Gi0/14, Gi0/15, Gi0/16, Gi0/17
                                                Gi0/18, Gi0/19, Gi0/20, Gi0/21
                                                Gi0/22, Gi0/23, Gi0/24, Gi0/25
                                                Gi0/26, Gi0/27, Gi0/28
26   Automation10                     active
27   VLAN0027                         active
30   Engineering                      active
170  VLAN0170                         active
[output cut]
```

Look at that: there is no VLAN 10 in the database! Clearly the problem, but also an easy one to fix by simply creating the VLAN in the database:

S2#**config t**
S2(config)#**vlan 10**
S2(config-vlan)#**name Sales**

That's all there is to it. Now let's check the CAM again:

S2#**sh mac address-table**

```
         Mac Address Table
-------------------------------------------

Vlan    Mac Address       Type        Ports
----    -----------       --------    -----
 All    0100.0ccc.cccc    STATIC      CPU
[output cut]
```

```
 1    0021.1bee.a70d    DYNAMIC    Gi0/13
10    001a.6c46.9b09    DYNAMIC    Gi0/3
Total Mac Addresses for this criterion: 22
```

We're good to go—the MAC address off of Gi0/3 shows in the MAC address table configured into VLAN 10.

That was pretty straightforward, but if the port had been assigned to the wrong VLAN, I would have used the switch access vlan command to correct the VLAN membership. Here's an example of how to do that:

```
S2#config t
S2(config)#int gi0/3
S2(config-if)#switchport access vlan 10
S2(config-if)#do sh vlan

VLAN Name                             Status    Ports
---- -------------------------------- --------- ------------------------------
1    default                          active    Gi0/1, Gi0/2, Gi0/4, Gi0/5
                                                Gi0/6, Gi0/7, Gi0/8, Gi0/9
                                                Gi0/10, Gi0/11, Gi0/12, Gi0/13
                                                Gi0/14, Gi0/15, Gi0/16, Gi0/17
                                                Gi0/18, Gi0/19, Gi0/20, Gi0/21
                                                Gi0/22, Gi0/23, Gi0/24, Gi0/25
                                                Gi0/26, Gi0/27, Gi0/28
10   Sales                            active    Gi0/3
```

Okay, great—we can see that our port Gi0/3 is in the VLAN 10 membership. Now let's try to ping from PC1 to PC3:

```
PC1#ping 192.168.10.3
Type escape sequence to abort.
Sending 5, 100-byte ICMP Echos to 192.168.10.3, timeout is 2 seconds:
.....
Success rate is 0 percent (0/5)
```

No luck, so let's see if PC1 can ping PC2:

```
PC1#ping 192.168.10.2
Type escape sequence to abort.
Sending 5, 100-byte ICMP Echos to 192.168.10.2, timeout is 2 seconds:
!!!!!
Success rate is 100 percent (5/5), round-trip min/avg/max = 1/2/4 ms
PC1#
```

That worked! I can ping a host that's a member of the same VLAN connected to the same switch, but I can't ping to a host on another switch that's a member of the same VLAN, which is VLAN 10. To get to the bottom of this, let's quickly summarize what we've learned so far:

1. We know that the VLAN database is now correct on each switch.

2. The MAC address table shows the ARP entries for each host as well as a connection to each switch.

3. We've verified that our VLAN memberships are now correct on all the ports we're using.

But since we still can't ping to a host on another switch, we need to start checking out the connections between our switches.

Trunk Troubleshooting

You'll need to troubleshoot trunk links when you lose connectivity between hosts that are in the same VLAN but are located on different switches. Cisco refers to this as "VLAN leaking." Seems to me we are leaking VLAN 10 between switches somehow.

These are the steps we'll take to troubleshoot VLANs:

1. Verify that the interface configuration is set to the correct trunk parameters.

2. Verify that the ports are configured correctly.

3. Verify the native VLAN on each switch.

And here are the commands we'll use to perform trunk troubleshooting:

```
Show interfaces trunk
Show vlan
Show interfaces interface trunk
Show interfaces interface switchport
Show dtp interface interface
switchport mode
switchport mode dynamic
switchport trunk native vlan vlan
```

Okay, let's get started by checking ports Gi0/13 and Gi0/14 on each switch because these are what the figure is showing as forming the connection between our switches. We'll start with the show interfaces trunk command:

```
S1>sh interfaces trunk
```

```
S2>sh interfaces trunk
```

Not a scrap of output—that's definitely a bad sign! Let's take another look at the show vlan output on S1 and see what we can find out:

```
S1>sh vlan brief
```

```
VLAN Name                             Status    Ports
---- -------------------------------- --------- --------------------------------
1    default                          active    Gi0/3, Gi0/4, Gi0/5, Gi0/6
                                                Gi0/7, Gi0/8, Gi0/9, Gi0/10
                                                Gi0/11, Gi0/12, Gi0/13, Gi0/14
                                                Gi0/15, Gi0/16, Gi0/17, Gi0/18
                                                Gi0/19, Gi0/20, Gi0/21, Gi0/22
                                                Gi0/23, Gi0/24, Gi0/25, Gi0/26
                                                Gi0/27, Gi0/28
10   Sales                            active    Gi0/1, Gi0/2
20   Accounting                       active
[output cut]
```

Nothing new from when we checked it a few minutes ago, but look there under VLAN 1—we can see interfaces Gi0/13 and Gi0/14. This means that our ports between switches are members of VLAN 1 and will pass only VLAN 1 frames!

Typically I'll tell my students that if you type the show vlan command, you're really typing the nonexistent "show access ports" command since this output shows interfaces in access mode but doesn't show the trunk interfaces. This means that our ports between switches are access ports instead of trunk ports, so they'll pass information about only VLAN 1.

Let's go back over to the S2 switch to verify and see which port interfaces Gi0/13 and Gi0/14 are members of:

S2>**sh vlan brief**

```
VLAN Name                             Status    Ports
---- -------------------------------- --------- -----------------------------
1    default                          active    Gi0/1, Gi0/2, Gi0/4, Gi0/5
                                                Gi0/6, Gi0/7, Gi0/8, Gi0/9
                                                Gi0/10, Gi0/11, Gi0/12, Gi0/13
                                                Gi0/14, Gi0/15, Gi0/16, Gi0/17
                                                Gi0/18, Gi0/19, Gi0/20, Gi0/21
                                                Gi0/22, Gi0/23, Gi0/24, Gi0/25
                                                Gi0/26, Gi0/27, Gi0/28
10   Sales                            active    Gi0/3
```

Again, as with S1, the links between switches are showing in the output of the show vlan command, which means that they are not trunk ports. We can use the show interfaces *interface* switchport command to verify this as well:

S1#**sho interfaces gi0/13 switchport**
Name: Gi0/13

```
Switchport: Enabled
Administrative Mode: dynamic auto
Operational Mode: static access
Administrative Trunking Encapsulation: negotiate
Operational Trunking Encapsulation: native
Negotiation of Trunking: On
Access Mode VLAN: 1 (default)
Trunking Native Mode VLAN: 1 (default)
```

This output tells us that interface Gi0/13 is in dynamic auto mode. But its operational mode is static access, meaning it's not a trunk port. We can look closer at its trunking capabilities with the show interfaces *interface* trunk command:

S1#**sh interfaces gi0/1 trunk**

```
Port        Mode        Encapsulation  Status         Native vlan
Gi0/1       auto        negotiate      not-trunking   1
[output cut]
```

Sure enough—the port is not trunking, but we already knew that. Now we know it again. Notice that we can see that the native VLAN is set to VLAN 1, which is the default native VLAN. This means that VLAN 1 is the default VLAN for untagged traffic.

Now, before we check the native VLAN on S2 to verify that there isn't a mismatch, I want to point out a key fact about trunking and how we would get these ports between switches to do that.

Many Cisco switches support the Cisco proprietary *Dynamic Trunking Protocol (DTP)*, which is used to manage automatic trunk negotiation between switches. Cisco recommends that you don't allow this and to configure your switch ports manually instead. I agree with them!

Okay, with that in mind, let's check out our switch port Gi0/13 on S1 and view its DTP status. I'll use the show dtp interface *interface* command to view the DTP statistics:

S1#**sh dtp interface gi0/13**
```
DTP information for GigabitEthernet0/13:
  TOS/TAS/TNS:                        ACCESS/AUTO/ACCESS
  TOT/TAT/TNT:                        NATIVE/NEGOTIATE/NATIVE
  Neighbor address 1:                 00211C910D8D
  Neighbor address 2:                 000000000000
  Hello timer expiration (sec/state): 12/RUNNING
  Access timer expiration (sec/state): never/STOPPED
```

Did you notice that our port GI0/13 from S1 to S2 is an access port configured to auto-negotiate using DTP? That's interesting, and I want to delve a bit deeper into the different port configurations and how they affect trunking capabilities to clarify why.

Access   Trunking is not allowed on a port set to access mode.

Auto   Will trunk to neighbor switch only if the remote port is set to on or to desirable mode. This creates the trunk based on the DTP request from the neighboring switch.

Desirable   This will trunk with all port modes except access. Ports set to dynamic desirable will communicate via DTP that the interface is attempting to become a trunk if the neighboring switch interface is able to become a trunk.

Nonegotiate   No DTP frames are generated from the interface. Can only be used if the neighbor interface is manually set as trunk or access.

Trunk (on)   Trunks with all switch port modes except access. Automatically enables trunking regardless of the state of the neighboring switch and regardless of any DTP requests.

Let's check out the different options available on the S1 switch with the `switchport mode dynamic` command:

```
S1(config-if)#switchport mode ?
  access       Set trunking mode to ACCESS unconditionally
  dot1q-tunnel set trunking mode to TUNNEL unconditionally
  dynamic      Set trunking mode to dynamically negotiate access or trunk mode
  private-vlan Set private-vlan mode
  trunk        Set trunking mode to TRUNK unconditionally

S1(config-if)#switchport mode dynamic ?
  auto      Set trunking mode dynamic negotiation parameter to AUTO
  desirable Set trunking mode dynamic negotiation parameter to DESIRABLE
```

From interface mode, use the `switch mode trunk` command to turn trunking on. You can also use the `switch mode dynamic` command to set the port to auto or desirable trunking modes. To turn off DTP and any type of negotiation, use the `switchport nonegotiate` command.

Let's take a look at S2 and see if we can figure out why our two switches didn't create a trunk:

```
S2#sh int gi0/13 switchport
Name: Gi0/13
Switchport: Enabled
Administrative Mode: dynamic auto
Operational Mode: static access
Administrative Trunking Encapsulation: negotiate
Operational Trunking Encapsulation: native
Negotiation of Trunking: On
```

Okay—we can see that the port is in dynamic auto and that it's operating as an access port. Let's look into this further:

```
S2#sh dtp interface gi0/13
DTP information for GigabitEthernet0/3:
  DTP information for GigabitEthernet0/13:
  TOS/TAS/TNS:                          ACCESS/AUTO/ACCESS
  TOT/TAT/TNT:                          NATIVE/NEGOTIATE/NATIVE
  Neighbor address 1:                   000000000000
  Neighbor address 2:                   000000000000
  Hello timer expiration (sec/state):   17/RUNNING
  Access timer expiration (sec/state):  never/STOPPED
```

Do you see the problem? Don't be fooled—it's not that they're running in access mode; it's because two ports in dynamic auto will not form a trunk! This is a really common problem to look for since most Cisco switches ship in dynamic auto. The other issue you need to be aware of, as well as check for, is the frame-tagging method. Some switches run 802.1q, some run both 802.1q and *Inter-Switch Link (ISL) routing*, so be sure the tagging method is compatible between all of your switches!

It's time to fix our problem on the trunk ports between S1 and S2. All we need to do is to just fix one side of each link since dynamic auto will trunk with a port set to desirable or on:

```
S2(config)#int gi0/13
S2(config-if)#switchport mode dynamic desirable
23:11:37:%LINEPROTO-5-UPDOWN:Line protocol on Interface GigabitEthernet0/13,
changed state to down
23:11:37:%LINEPROTO-5-UPDOWN:Line protocol on Interface Vlan1, changed state to
down
23:11:40:%LINEPROTO-5-UPDOWN:Line protocol on Interface GigabitEthernet0/13,
changed state to up
23:12:10:%LINEPROTO-5-UPDOWN:Line protocol on Interface Vlan1, changed state to
up
S2(config-if)#do show int trunk

Port       Mode       Encapsulation  Status      Native vlan
Gi0/13     desirable  n-isl          trunking    1
[output cut]
```

Nice—it worked! With one side in Auto and the other now in Desirable, DTPs will be exchanged and they will trunk. Notice in the preceding output that the mode of S2's Gi0/13 link is desirable and that the switches actually negotiated ISL as a trunk encapsulation—go figure! But don't forget to notice the native VLAN. We'll work on the frame-tagging method and native VLAN in a minute, but first, let's configure our other link:

```
S2(config-if)#int gi0/14
S2(config-if)#switchport mode dynamic desirable
23:12:%LINEPROTO-5-UPDOWN:Line protocol on Interface GigabitEthernet0/14,
changed state to down
```

```
23:12:%LINEPROTO-5-UPDOWN:Line protocol on Interface GigabitEthernet0/14,
changed state to up
S2(config-if)#do show int trunk

Port        Mode          Encapsulation  Status       Native vlan
Gi0/13      desirable     n-isl          trunking     1
Gi0/14      desirable     n-isl          trunking     1

Port        Vlans allowed on trunk
Gi0/13      1-4094
Gi0/14      1-4094
[output cut]
```

Great, we now have two trunked links between switches. But I've got to say, I really don't like the ISL method of frame tagging since it can't send untagged frames across the link. So let's change our native VLAN from the default of 1 to 392. The number 392 just randomly sounded good at the moment. Here's what I entered on S1:

```
S1(config-if)#switchport trunk native vlan 392
S1(config-if)#
23:17:40: Port is not 802.1Q trunk, no action
```

See what I mean? I tried to change the native VLAN and ISL basically responded with, "What's a native VLAN?" Very annoying, so I'm going to take care of that now!

```
S1(config-if)#int range gi0/13 - 14
S1(config-if-range)#switchport trunk encapsulation ?
  dot1q      Interface uses only 802.1q trunking encapsulation when trunking
  isl        Interface uses only ISL trunking encapsulation when trunking
  negotiate  Device will negotiate trunking encapsulation with peer on
             interface

S1(config-if-range)#switchport trunk encapsulation dot1q
23:23:%LINEPROTO-5-UPDOWN:Line protocol on Interface GigabitEthernet0/13,
changed state to down
23:23:%LINEPROTO-5-UPDOWN: Line protocol on Interface GigabitEthernet0/14,
changed state to down
23:23:%CDP-4-NATIVE_VLAN_MISMATCH: Native VLAN mismatch discovered on
GigabitEthernet0/13 (392), with S2 GigabitEthernet0/13 (1).
23:23:%LINEPROTO-5-UPDOWN: Line protocol on Interface GigabitEthernet0/14,
changed state to up
23:23:%LINEPROTO-5-UPDOWN: Line protocol on Interface GigabitEthernet0/13,
changed state to up
23:23:%CDP-4-NATIVE_VLAN_MISMATCH: Native VLAN mismatch discovered on
GigabitEthernet0/13 (392), with S2 GigabitEthernet0/13 (1).
```

Okay, that's more like it! As soon as I changed the encapsulation type on S1, DTP frames changed the frame-tagging method between S2 to 802.1q. Since I had already changed the native VLAN on port Gi0/13 on S1, the switch lets us know, via CDP, that we now have a native VLAN mismatch. Let's proceed to deal with this by verifying our interfaces with the show interface trunk command:

```
S1#sh int trunk
Port        Mode        Encapsulation  Status      Native vlan
Gi0/13      auto        802.1q         trunking    392
Gi0/14      auto        802.1q         trunking    1

S2#sh int trunk
Port        Mode        Encapsulation  Status      Native vlan
Gi0/13      desirable   n-802.1q       trunking    1
Gi0/14      desirable   n-802.1q       trunking    1
```

Now notice that both links are running 802.1q and that S1 is in auto mode and S2 is in desirable mode. And we can see a native VLAN mismatch on port Gi0/13. We can also see the mismatched native VLAN with the show interfaces *interface* switchport command by looking at both sides of the link like this:

```
S2#sh interfaces gi0/13 switchport
Name: Gi0/13
Switchport: Enabled
Administrative Mode: dynamic desirable
Operational Mode: trunk
Administrative Trunking Encapsulation: negotiate
Operational Trunking Encapsulation: dot1q
Negotiation of Trunking: On
Access Mode VLAN: 1 (default)
Trunking Native Mode VLAN: 1 (default)

S1#sh int gi0/13 switchport
Name: Gi0/13
Switchport: Enabled
Administrative Mode: dynamic auto
Operational Mode: trunk
Administrative Trunking Encapsulation: dot1q
Operational Trunking Encapsulation: dot1q
Negotiation of Trunking: On
Access Mode VLAN: 1 (default)
Trunking Native Mode VLAN: 392 (Inactive)
```

So this has got to be bad, right? I mean really—are we sending any frames down that link or not? Let's see if we solved our little problem of not being able to ping to hosts from S1 to S2 and find out:

```
PC1#ping 192.168.10.3
Type escape sequence to abort.
Sending 5, 100-byte ICMP Echos to 192.168.10.3, timeout is 2 seconds:
!!!!!
Success rate is 100 percent (5/5), round-trip min/avg/max = 1/1/4 ms
```

Yes, it works! Not so bad after all. We've solved our problem, or at least most of it. Having a native VLAN mismatch only means you can't send untagged frames down the link, which are essentially management frames like CDP, for example. So although it's not the end of the world, it will prevent us from being able to remotely manage the switch, or even sending any other types of traffic down just that one VLAN.

So am I saying you can just leave this issue the way it is? Well, you could, but you won't. No, you'll fix it because if you don't, CDP will send you a message every minute telling you that there's a mismatch, which will drive you mad! So, this is how we'll stop that from happening:

```
S2(config)#int gi0/13
S2(config-if)#switchport trunk native vlan 392
S2(config-if)#^Z
S2#sh int trunk

Port       Mode          Encapsulation  Status     Native vlan
Gi0/13     desirable     n-802.1q       trunking   392
Gi0/14     desirable     n-802.1q       trunking   1
[output cut]
```

All better! Both sides of the same link between switches are now using native VLAN 392 on Gigabit Ethernet 0/13. I want you to know that it's fine to have different native VLANs for each link if that's what works best for you. Each network is different and you have to make choices between options that will end up meeting your particular business requirements the most optimal way.

Summary

This chapter covered troubleshooting techniques from basic to advanced. Although most chapters in this book cover troubleshooting, this chapter focused purely on IPv4, IPv6, and VLAN/trunk troubleshooting.

You learned how to troubleshoot step-by-step from a host to a remote device. Starting with IPv4, you learned the steps to test the host and the local connectivity and then how to troubleshoot remote connectivity.

We then moved on to IPv6 and proceeded to troubleshoot using the same techniques that you learned with IPv4. It's important that you can use the verification commands that I used in each step of this chapter.

Last, I covered VLAN and trunk troubleshooting and how to go step-by-step through a switched network using verification commands and narrowing down the problem.

Exam Essentials

Remember the Cisco steps in troubleshooting an IPv4 and IPv6 network.

1. Check the cables to find out if there's a faulty cable or interface in the mix and verify the interface's statistics.

2. Make sure that devices are determining the correct path from the source to the destination. Manipulate the routing information if needed.

3. Verify that the default gateway is correct.

4. Verify that name resolution settings are correct.

5. Verify that there are no ACLs blocking traffic.

Remember the commands to verify and troubleshoot IPv4 and IPv6.   You need to remember and practice the commands used in this chapter, especially ping and traceroute (tracert on Windows). But we also used the Windows commands ipconfig and route print and Cisco's commands show ip int brief, show interface, and show route.

Remember how to verify an ARP cache with IPv6.   The command show ipv6 neighbors shows the IP-to-MAC-address resolution table on a Cisco router.

Remember to look at the statistics on a router and switch interface to determine problems.   You've got to be able to analyze interface statistics to find problems if they exist, and this includes speed and duplex settings, input queue drops, output queue drops, and input and output errors.

Understand what a native VLAN is and how to change it.   A native VLAN works with only 802.1q trunks and allows untagged traffic to traverse the trunk link. This is VLAN 1 by default on all Cisco switches, but it can be changed for security reasons with the switchport native vlan *vlan* command.

Written Lab 6

You can find the answers to this lab in Appendix A, "Answers to Written Labs."

Write the answers to the following questions:

1. If your IPv6 ARP cache shows an entry of INCMP, what does this mean?

2. You want traffic from VLAN 66 to traverse a trunked link untagged. Which command will you use?

3. What are the five modes you can set a switch port to?

4. You are having a network problem and have checked the cables to find out if there's a faulty cable or interface in the mix and also verified the interface's statistics, made sure that devices are determining the correct path from the source to the destination, and verified that you don't need to manipulate the routing. What are your next troubleshooting steps?

5. You need to find out if the local IPv6 stack is working on a host. What command will you use?

Hands-on Labs for Troubleshooting

Please check www.lammle.com/ccna for the latest information and downloads available for studying when using my books. Preconfigured hands-on troubleshooting labs are available for download, with the answers to the troubleshooting problems found on my forum.

Review Questions

The following questions are designed to test your understanding of this chapter's material. For more information on how to get additional questions, please www.lammle.com/ccna.

You can find the answers to these questions in Appendix B, "Answers to Review Questions."

1. You need to verify the IPv6 ARP cache on a router and see that the state of an entry is REACH. What does REACH mean?

    A.   The router is reaching out to get the address.

    B.   The entry is incomplete.

    C.   The entry has reached the end of life and will be discarded from the table.

    D.   A positive confirmation has been received by the neighbor and the path to it is functioning correctly.

2. What is the most common cause of interface errors?

    A.   Speed mismatch

    B.   Duplex mismatch

    C.   Buffer overflows

    D.   Collisions between a dedicated switch port and an NIC

3. Which command will verify the DTP status on a switch interface?

    A.   `sh dtp status`

    B.   `sh dtp status interface` *interface*

    C.   `sh interface` *interface* `dtp`

    D.   `sh dtp interface` *interface*

4. What mode will not allow DTP frames generated from a switch port?

    A.   Nonegotiate

    B.   Trunk

    C.   Access

    D.   Auto

5. The following output was generated by which command?

```
IPv6 Address                          Age Link-layer Addr State Interface
FE80::21A:6DFF:FE64:9B3                  0 001a.6c46.9b09  DELAY Fa0/1
2001:DB8:3C4D:2:21A:6DFF:FE64:9B3        0 001a.6c46.9b09  REACH Fa0/1
```

    A. show ip arp

    B. show ipv6 arp

    C. show ip neighbors

    D. show ipv6 neighbors

6. Which of the following states tells you that an interface has not communicated within the neighbor-reachable time frame?

    A. REACH

    B. STALE

    C. TIMEOUT

    D. CLEARED

7. You receive a call from a user who says that they cannot log in to a remote server, which only runs IPv6. Based on the output, what could the problem be?

```
C:\Users\Todd Lammle>ipconfig
    Connection-specific DNS Suffix  . : localdomain
    IPv6 Address. . . . . . . . . . . : 2001:db8:3c4d:3:ac3b:2ef:1823:8938
    Temporary IPv6 Address. . . . . . : 2001:db8:3c4d:3:2f33:44dd:211:1c3d
    Link-local IPv6 Address . . . . . : fe80::ac3b:2ef:1823:8938%11
    IPv4 Address. . . . . . . . . . . : 10.1.1.10
    Subnet Mask . . . . . . . . . . . : 255.255.255.0
    Default Gateway . . . . . . . . . : 10.1.1.1
```

    A. The global address is in the wrong subnet.

    B. The IPv6 default gateway has not been configured or received from the router.

    C. The link-local address has not been resolved, so the host cannot communicate to the router.

    D. There are two IPv6 global addresses configured. One must be removed from the configuration.

8. Your host cannot reach remote networks. Based on the output, what is the problem?

```
C:\Users\Server1>ipconfig

Windows IP Configuration

Ethernet adapter Local Area Connection:

    Connection-specific DNS Suffix  . : localdomain
    Link-local IPv6 Address . . . . . : fe80::7723:76a2:e73c:2acb%11
    IPv4 Address. . . . . . . . . . . : 172.16.20.254
    Subnet Mask . . . . . . . . . . . : 255.255.255.0
    Default Gateway . . . . . . . . . : 172.16.2.1
```

    A. The link-local IPv6 address is wrong.

    B. The IPv6 global address is missing.

    C.   There is no DNS server configuration.

    D.   The IPv4 default gateway address is misconfigured.

9. Which two commands will show you if you have a native VLAN mismatch?

    A.   `show interface native vlan`

    B.   `show interface trunk`

    C.   `show interface` *`interface`* `switchport`

    D.   `show switchport interface`

10. You connect two new Cisco 3560 switches together and expect them to use DTP and create a trunk. However, when you check statistics, you find that they are access ports and didn't negotiate. Why didn't DTP work on these Cisco switches?

    A.   The ports on each side of the link are set to auto trunking.

    B.   The ports on each side of the link are set to on.

    C.   The ports on each side of the link are set to dynamic.

    D.   The ports on each side of the link are set to desirable.

Chapter

7

Wide Area Networks

THE FOLLOWING ICND2 EXAM TOPICS ARE COVERED IN THIS CHAPTER:

✓ **3.0 WAN Technologies**

✓ **3.1 Configure and verify PPP and MLPPP on WAN interfaces using local authentication**

✓ **3.2 Configure, verify, and troubleshoot PPPoE client-side interfaces using local authentication**

✓ **3.3 Configure, verify, and troubleshoot GRE tunnel connectivity**

✓ **3.4 Describe WAN topology options**

- 3.4.a Point-to-point

- 3.4.b Hub and spoke

- 3.4.c Full mesh

- 3.4.d Single vs dual-homed

✓ **3.5 Describe WAN access connectivity options**

- 3.5.a MPLS

- 3.5.b MetroEthernet

- 3.5.c Broadband PPPoE

- 3.5.d Internet VPN (DMVPN, site-to-site VPN, client VPN)

✓ **3.6 Configure and verify single-homed branch connectivity using eBGP IPv4 (limited to peering and route advertisement using Network command only)**

The Cisco IOS supports a ton of different wide area network (WAN) protocols that help you extend your local LANs to other LANs at remote sites. And I don't think I have to tell you how essential information exchange between disparate sites is these days—it's absolutely vital! But even so, it wouldn't exactly be cost effective or efficient to install your own cable and connect all of your company's remote locations yourself, would it? A much better way to get this done is to just lease the existing installations that service providers already have in place.

This is exactly why I'm going to devote most of this chapter to covering the various types of connections, technologies, and devices used in today's WANs.

We'll also delve into how to implement and configure High-Level Data-Link Control (HDLC), and Point-to-Point Protocol (PPP). I'll describe Point-to-Point Protocol over Ethernet (PPPoE), cable, digital subscriber line (DSL), MultiProtocol Label Switching (MPLS), and Metro Ethernet plus last mile and long-range WAN technologies. I'll also introduce you to WAN security concepts, tunneling, virtual private networks (VPNs) and how to create a tunnel using GRE (Generic Routing Encapsulation). Finally, I'll close the chapter with a discussion on Border Gateway Protocol (BGP) and how to configure External BGP.

 To find up-to-the-minute updates for this chapter, please see www.lammle .com/ccna or the book's web page at www.sybex.com/go/ccna.

Introduction to Wide Area Networks

Let's begin exploring WAN basics by asking, what's the difference between a *wide area network (WAN)* and a local area network (LAN)? Clearly there's the distance factor, but modern wireless LANs can cover some serious turf, so there's more to it than that. What about bandwidth? Here again, some really big pipes can be had for a price in many places, so that's not it either. What's the answer we're looking for?

A major distinction between a WAN and a LAN is that while you generally own a LAN infrastructure, you usually lease a WAN infrastructure from a service provider. And to be honest, modern technologies even blur this characteristic somewhat, but it still fits neatly into the context of Cisco's exam objectives!

I've already talked about the data link that you usually own back when we covered Ethernet, so now I'm going to focus on the type you usually don't own—the kind you typically lease from a service provider.

There are several reasons why WANs are necessary in corporate environments today.

LAN technologies provide amazing speeds (10/40/100 Gbps is now common) and at a great bang for your buck! But these type of solutions can only work well in relatively small geographic areas. You still need WANs in a communications environment because some business needs require connections to remote sites for many reasons, including the following:

- People in the regional or branch offices of an organization need to be able to communicate and share data.

- Organizations often want to share information with other organizations across large distances.

- Employees who travel on company business frequently need to access information that resides on their corporate networks.

Here are three major characteristics of WANs:

- WANs generally connect devices that are separated by a broader geographic area than a LAN can serve.

- WANs use the services of carriers such as telcos, cable companies, satellite systems, and network providers.

- WANs use serial connections of various types to provide access to bandwidth over large geographic areas.

The first key to understanding WAN technologies is to be familiar with the different WAN topologies, terms, and connection types commonly used by service providers to join your LAN networks together. We'll begin covering these topics now.

WAN Topology Options

A physical topology describes the physical layout of the network, in contrast to logical topologies, which describe the path a signal takes through the physical topology. There are three basic topologies for a WAN design.

Star or hub-and-spoke topology   This topology features a single hub (central router) that provides access from remote networks to a core router. Figure 7.1 illustrates a hub-and-spoke topology:

FIGURE 7.1   Hub-and-spoke

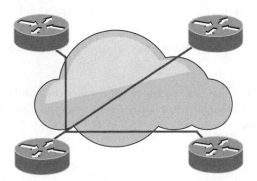

All communication among the networks travels through the core router. The advantages of a star physical topology are less cost and easier administration, but the disadvantages can be significant:

- The central router (hub) represents a single point of failure.

- The central router limits the overall performance for access to centralized resources. It is a single pipe that manages all traffic intended either for the centralized resources or for the other regional routers.

Fully meshed topology   In this topology, each routing node on the edge of a given packet-switching network has a direct path to every other node on the cloud. Figure 7.2 shows a fully meshed topology.

FIGURE 7.2   Fully meshed topology

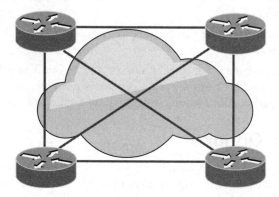

This configuration clearly provides a high level of redundancy, but the costs are the highest. So a fully meshed topology really isn't viable in large packet-switched networks. Here are some issues you'll contend with using a fully meshed topology:

- Many virtual circuits are required—one for every connection between routers, which brings up the cost.

- Configuration is more complex for routers without multicast support in non-broadcast environments.

Partially meshed topology   This type of topology reduces the number of routers within a network that have direct connections to all other routers in the topology. Figure 7.3 depicts a partially meshed topology.

FIGURE 7.3 Partially meshed topology

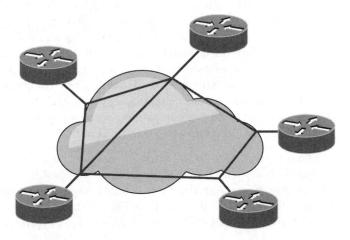

Unlike in the full mesh network, all routers are not connected to all other routers, but it still provides more redundancy than a typical hub-and-spoke design will. This is actually considered the most balanced design because it provides more virtual circuits, plus redundancy and performance.

Defining WAN Terms

Before you run out and order a WAN service type from a provider, you really need to understand the following terms that service providers typically use. Take a look at these in Figure 7.4:

FIGURE 7.4 WAN terms

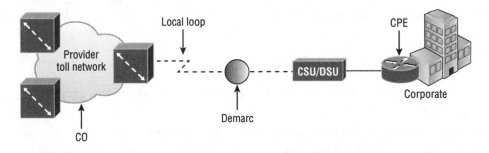

Customer premises equipment (CPE) *Customer premises equipment (CPE)* is equipment that's typically owned by the subscriber and located on the subscriber's premises.

CSU/DSU   A channel service unit/data service unit (CSU/DSU) is a device that is used to connect data terminal equipment (DTE) to a digital circuit, such as a T1/T3 line. A device is considered DTE if it is either a source or destination for digital data—for example, PCs, servers, and routers. In Figure 7.4, the router is considered DTE because it is passing data to the CSU/DSU, which will forward the data to the service provider. Although the CSU/DSU connects to the service provider infrastructure using a telephone or coaxial cable, such as a T1 or E1 line, it connects to the router with a serial cable. The most important aspect to remember for the CCNA objectives is that the CSU/DSU provides clocking of the line to the router. You really need to understand this completely, which is why I'll cover it in depth later in the cabling the serial WAN interface configuration section!

Demarcation point   The *demarcation point* (demarc for short) is the precise spot where the service provider's responsibility ends and the CPE begins. It's generally a device in a telecommunications closet owned and installed by the telecommunications company (telco). It's your responsibility to cable (extended demarc) from this box to the CPE, which is usually a connection to a CSU/DSU, although more recently we see the provider giving us an Ethernet connection. Nice!

Local loop   The *local loop* connects the demarc to the closest switching office, referred to as the central office.

Central office (CO)   This point connects the customer's network to the provider's switching network. Make a mental note that a *central office (CO)* is sometimes also referred to as a *point of presence (POP)*.

Toll network   The *toll network* is a trunk line inside a WAN provider's network. This network is a collection of switches and facilities owned by the Internet service provider (ISP).

Optical fiber converters   Even though I'm not employing this device in Figure 7.4, optical fiber converters are used where a fiber-optic link terminates to convert optical signals into electrical signals and vice versa. You can also implement the converter as a router or switch module.

Definitely familiarize yourself with these terms, what they represent, and where they're located, as shown in Figure 7.4, because they're key to understanding WAN technologies.

WAN Connection Bandwidth

Next, I want you to know these basic but very important bandwidth terms used when referring to WAN connections:

Digital Signal 0 (DS0)   This is the basic digital signaling rate of 64 Kbps, equivalent to one channel. Europe uses the E0 and Japan uses the J0 to reference the same channel speed. Typical to T-carrier transmission, this is the generic term used by several multiplexed digital carrier systems and is also the smallest-capacity digital circuit. One DS0 = One voice/data line.

T1   Also referred to as a DS1, a T1 comprises 24 DS0 circuits bundled together for a total bandwidth of 1.544 Mbps.

E1   This is the European equivalent of a T1 and comprises 30 DS0 circuits bundled together for a bandwidth of 2.048 Mbps.

T3   Referred to as a DS3, a T3 comprises 28 DS1s bundled together, or 672 DS0s, for a bandwidth of 44.736 Mbps.

OC-3   Optical Carrier (OC) 3 uses fiber and is made up of three DS3s bundled together. It's made up of 2,016 DS0s and avails a total bandwidth of 155.52 Mbps.

OC-12   Optical Carrier 12 is made up of four OC-3s bundled together and contains 8,064 DS0s for a total bandwidth of 622.08 Mbps.

OC-48   Optical Carrier 48 is made up of four OC-12s bundled together and contains 32,256 DS0s for a total bandwidth of 2488.32 Mbps.

OC-192   Optical Carrier 192 is four OC-48s and contains 129,024 DS0s for a total bandwidth of 9953.28 Mbps.

WAN Connection Types

You're probably aware that a WAN can use a number of different connection types available on the market today. Figure 7.5 shows the different WAN connection types that can be used to connect your LANs (made up of data terminal equipment, or DTE) together over the data communication equipment (DCE) network.

FIGURE 7.5   WAN connection types

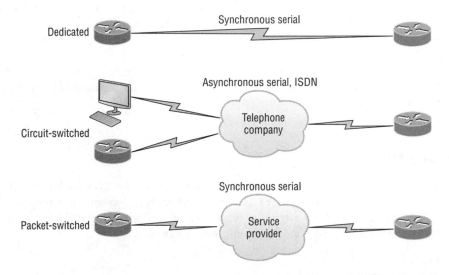

Let me explain the different WAN connection types in detail now:

Dedicated (leased lines)   These are usually referred to as a *point-to-point* or dedicated connections. A *leased line* is a pre-established WAN communications path that goes from the CPE through the DCE switch, then over to the CPE of the remote site. The CPE enables DTE networks to communicate at any time with no cumbersome setup procedures to muddle through before transmitting data. When you've got plenty of cash, this is definitely the way to go because it uses synchronous serial lines up to 45 Mbps. HDLC and PPP encapsulations are frequently used on leased lines, and I'll go over these with you soon.

Circuit switching   When you hear the term *circuit switching*, think phone call. The big advantage is cost; most plain old telephone service (POTS) and ISDN dial-up connections are not flat rate, which is their advantage over dedicated lines because you pay only for what you use, and you pay only when the call is established. No data can transfer before an end-to-end connection is established. Circuit switching uses dial-up modems or ISDN and is used for low-bandwidth data transfers. Okay, I know what you're thinking, "Modems? Did he say modems? Aren't those found only in museums now?" After all, with all the wireless technologies available, who would use a modem these days? Well, some people do have ISDN; it's still viable and there are a few who still use a modem now and then. And circuit switching can be used in some of the newer WAN technologies as well.

Packet switching   This is a WAN switching method that allows you to share bandwidth with other companies to save money, just like a super old party line, where homes shared the same phone number and line to save money. *Packet switching* can be thought of as a network that's designed to look like a leased line yet it charges you less, like circuit switching does. As usual, you get what you pay for, and there's definitely a serious downside to this technology. If you need to transfer data constantly, well, just forget about this option and get a leased line instead! Packet switching will only really work for you if your data transfers are bursty, not continuous; think of a highway, where you can only go as fast as the traffic—packet switching is the same thing. Frame Relay and X.25 are packet-switching technologies with speeds that can range from 56 Kbps up to T3 (45 Mbps).

> MultiProtocol Label Switching (MPLS) uses a combination of both circuit switching and packet switching.

WAN Support

Cisco supports many layer 2 WAN encapsulations on its serial interfaces, including HDLC, PPP, and Frame Relay, which map to the Cisco exam objectives. You can view them via the encapsulation ? command from any serial interface, but understand that the output you'll get can vary based upon the specific IOS version you're running:

```
Corp#config t
Corp(config)#int s0/0/0
Corp(config-if)#encapsulation ?
  atm-dxi     ATM-DXI encapsulation
  frame-relay  Frame Relay networks
```

hdlc	**Serial HDLC synchronous**
lapb	LAPB (X.25 Level 2)
ppp	**Point-to-Point protocol**
smds	Switched Megabit Data Service (SMDS)
x25	X.25

I also want to point out that if I had other types of interfaces on my router, I would have a different set of encapsulation options. And never forget that you can't configure an Ethernet encapsulation on a serial interface or vice versa!

Next, I'm going to define the most prominently known WAN protocols used in the latest Cisco exam objectives: Frame Relay, ISDN, HDLC, PPP, PPPoE, cable, DSL, MPLS, ATM, Cellular 3G/4G, VSAT, and Metro Ethernet. Just so you know, the only WAN protocols you'll usually find configured on a serial interface are HDLC, PPP, and Frame Relay, but who said you're stuck with using only serial interfaces for wide area connections? Actually, we're beginning to see fewer and fewer serial connections because they're not as scalable or cost effective as a Fast Ethernet connection to your ISP.

Frame Relay   A packet-switched technology that made its debut in the early 1990s, *Frame Relay* is a high-performance Data Link and Physical layer specification. It's pretty much a successor to X.25, except that much of the technology in X.25 that was used to compensate for physical errors like noisy lines has been eliminated. An upside to Frame Relay is that it can be more cost effective than point-to-point links, plus it typically runs at speeds of 64 Kbps up to 45 Mbps (T3). Another Frame Relay benefit is that it provides features for dynamic bandwidth allocation and congestion control.

ISDN   *Integrated Services Digital Network (ISDN)* is a set of digital services that transmit voice and data over existing phone lines. ISDN offers a cost-effective solution for remote users who need a higher-speed connection than analog POTS dial-up links can give them, and it's also a good choice to use as a backup link for other types of links, such as Frame Relay or T1 connections.

HDLC   *High-Level Data-Link Control (HDLC)* was derived from Synchronous Data Link Control (SDLC), which was created by IBM as a Data Link connection protocol. HDLC works at the Data Link layer and creates very little overhead compared to Link Access Procedure, Balanced (LAPB).

Generic HDLC wasn't intended to encapsulate multiple Network layer protocols across the same link—the HDLC header doesn't contain any identification about the type of protocol being carried inside the HDLC encapsulation. Because of this, each vendor that uses HDLC has its own way of identifying the Network layer protocol, meaning each vendor's HDLC is proprietary with regard to its specific equipment.

PPP   *Point-to-Point Protocol (PPP)* is a pretty famous, industry-standard protocol. Because all multiprotocol versions of HDLC are proprietary, PPP can be used to create point-to-point links between different vendors' equipment. It uses a Network Control Protocol field in the Data Link header to identify the Network layer protocol being carried and allows authentication and multilink connections to be run over asynchronous and synchronous links.

PPPoE   *Point-to-Point Protocol over Ethernet* encapsulates PPP frames in Ethernet frames and is usually used in conjunction with xDSL services. It gives you a lot of the familiar PPP features like authentication, encryption, and compression, but there's a downside—it has a lower maximum transmission unit (MTU) than standard Ethernet does. If your firewall isn't solidly configured, this little factor can really give you some grief!

Still somewhat popular in the United States, PPPoE's main feature is that it adds a direct connection to Ethernet interfaces while also providing DSL support. It's often used by many hosts on a shared Ethernet interface for opening PPP sessions to various destinations via at least one bridging modem.

Cable   In a modern *hybrid fiber-coaxial (HFC)* network, typically 500 to 2,000 active data subscribers are connected to a certain cable network segment, all sharing the upstream and downstream bandwidth. HFC is a telecommunications industry term for a network that incorporates both optical fiber and coaxial cables to create a broadband network. The actual bandwidth for Internet service over a cable TV (CATV) line can be up to about 27 Mbps on the download path to the subscriber, with about 2.5 Mbps of bandwidth on the upload path. Typically users get an access speed from 256 Kbps to 6 Mbps. This data rate varies greatly throughout the United States and can be much, much higher today.

DSL   Digital subscriber line is a technology used by traditional telephone companies to deliver advanced services such as high-speed data and sometimes video over twisted-pair copper telephone wires. It typically has lower data-carrying capacity than HFC networks, and data speeds can be limited in range by line lengths and quality. Digital subscriber line is not a complete end-to-end solution but rather a Physical layer transmission technology like dial-up, cable, or wireless. DSL connections are deployed in the last mile of a local telephone network—the local loop. The connection is set up between a pair of DSL modems on either end of a copper wire located between the customer premises equipment (CPE) and the Digital Subscriber Line Access Multiplexer (DSLAM). A DSLAM is the device that is located at the provider's central office (CO) and concentrates connections from multiple DSL subscribers.

MPLS   *MultiProtocol Label Switching (MPLS)* is a data-carrying mechanism that emulates some properties of a circuit-switched network over a packet-switched network. MPLS is a switching mechanism that imposes labels (numbers) to packets and then uses them to forward the packets. The labels are assigned on the edge of the MPLS network, and forwarding inside the MPLS network is carried out solely based on the labels. The labels usually correspond to a path to layer 3 destination addresses, which is on par with IP destination-based routing. MPLS was designed to support the forwarding of protocols other than TCP/IP. Because of this, label switching within the network is achieved the same way irrespective of the layer 3 protocol. In larger networks, the result of MPLS labeling is that only the edge routers perform a routing lookup. All the core routers forward packets based on the labels, which makes forwarding the packets through the service provider network faster. This is a big reason most companies have replaced their Frame Relay networks with MPLS service today. Last, you can use Ethernet with MPLS to connect a WAN, and this is called Ethernet over MPLS, or EoMPLS.

ATM   Asynchronous Transfer Mode (ATM) was created for time-sensitive traffic, providing simultaneous transmission of voice, video, and data. ATM uses cells that are a fixed 53 bytes long instead of packets. It also can use isochronous clocking (external clocking) to help the data move faster. Typically, if you're running Frame Relay today, you will be running Frame Relay over ATM.

Cellular 3G/4G   Having a wireless hot spot in your pocket is pretty normal these days. If you have a pretty current cellular phone, then you can probably can gain access through your phone to the Internet. You can even get a 3G/4G card for an ISR router that's useful for a small remote office that's in the coverage area.

VSAT   Very Small Aperture Terminal (VSAT) can be used if you have many locations geographically spread out in a large area. VSAT uses a two-way satellite ground station with dishes available through many companies like Dish Network or Hughes and connects to satellites in geosynchronous orbit. A good example of where VSATs are a useful, cost-effective solution would be companies that use satellite communications to VSATs, like gasoline stations that have hundreds or thousands of locations spread out over the entire country. How could you connect them otherwise? Using leased lines would be cost prohibitive and dial-ups would be way too slow and hard to manage. Instead, the signal from the satellite connects to many remote locations at once, which is much more cost effective and efficient! It's a lot faster than a modem (about 10x faster), but the upload speeds only come in at about 10 percent of their download speeds.

Metro Ethernet   Metropolitan-area Ethernet is a metropolitan area network (MAN) that's based on Ethernet standards and can connect a customer to a larger network and the Internet. If available, businesses can use Metro Ethernet to connect their own offices together, which is another very cost-effective connection option. MPLS-based Metro Ethernet networks use MPLS in the ISP by providing an Ethernet or fiber cable to the customer as a connection. From the customer, it leaves the Ethernet cable, jumps onto MPLS, and then Ethernet again on the remote side. This is a smart and thrifty solution that's very popular if you can get it in your area.

Cisco Intelligent WAN (IWAN)

Bottom line, WANs are expensive, and if they're not deployed correctly, they can be a very costly mistake! Here's a short list of how most companies are currently deployingWANs:

- Using MPLS links for the branch and remote locations to headquarters.
- Leveraging low-cost, high-bandwidth Internet links as backup for the MPLS links.

Still, even these solutions are no longer good enough. The pressure on today's WANs has increased dramatically to make them handle more and more, as shown in Figure 7.6:

- Steadily increasing cloud traffic like Google Docs, Office365, etc.

- Unprecedented proliferation of mobile devices.

- A legion of high-bandwidth applications like Video—lots of video!

FIGURE 7.6   Branch WAN challenges

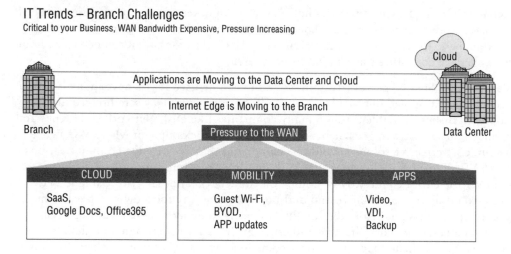

Here are two new winning strategies that many businesses in today's fast paced market utilize:

- Using a low-cost Internet link set in an active/active mode rather than just sitting there idly most of the time in active/standby mode.

- Leveraging the Internet link for remote employees accessing public clouds or the Internet as well as for guest users' access.

These new strategies offer cost reductions for your company plus increased WAN capacity. They result in improved performance and scalability from the end user point of view and pave the way for implementing cloud, mobility, and BYOD effectively.

So what does the Cisco Intelligent WAN (IWAN) have to do with all this? The Cisco IWAN enables application service-level agreements (SLAs), endpoint type, and network conditions so that Cisco IWAN traffic is dynamically routed to deliver the best-quality experience. The savings over traditional WANs not only allows companies to pay for the infrastructure upgrades, they can also free up resources for new business innovation.

IT organizations can now provide more bandwidth to their branch office connections by using less-expensive WAN transport options, all without affecting performance, security, or reliability, as pictured in Figure 7.7:

FIGURE 7.7   Intelligent WAN

Intelligent WAN: Leveraging the Internet

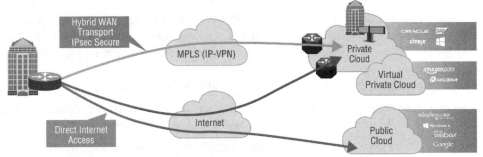

- Saves customers money – 6 month ROI
- Improves application response times
- Enables cloud, mobility, and BYOD in the branch

Cisco's IWAN solution is based upon four technology pillars demonstrated in Figure 7.8:

FIGURE 7.8   IWAN four technology pillars

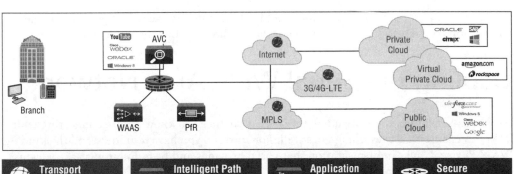

Transport Independent	Intelligent Path Control	Application Optimization	Secure Connectivity
▪ Consistent operational model ▪ Simple Provider migrations ▪ Scalable and Modular design ▪ DMVPN IPsec overlay design	▪ Application best path based on delay, loss, jitter, path preference ▪ Load Balancing for full utilization of all bandwidth ▪ Improved network availability ▪ Performance Routing (PfR)	▪ Application monitoring with Application Visibility and Control (AVC) ▪ Application Acceleration and bandwidth savings with WAAS	▪ Certified strong encryption ▪ Comprehensive threat defense with ASA and IOS Firewall/IPS ▪ Cloud Web Security (CWS) for scalable secure direct Internet access

Transport Independent Connectivity   IWAN should provide consistent connectivity over the entire access network while also providing simplicity, scalability, and modularity. It also allows for a simple, efficient migration strategy. Keep in mind that you don't typically use a design based on DMVPN to achieve this.

Intelligent Path Control   This solution is intended to help utilize full WAN links without oversubscribing lines. Through Intelligent Path Control (Path Selection), routing decisions are made dynamically by looking at application type, policies, and path status. This allows new cloud traffic and guest services as well as video services to easily load-balance across multiple links!

Application Optimization   This solution provides an application-aware network for optimized performance, providing full visibility and control at the Application layer (layer 7). It uses technologies like AVC and NBAR2, NetFlow, QoS, and more to reach optimization goals.

High Secure Connectivity   US government FIPS 140-2 certified IPsec solutions provide security, privacy, and dynamic site-to-site IP Security (IPsec) tunnels with DMVPN. Threat defense with zone-based firewalls permit access to the Internet using the Cloud Web Security (CWS) Connector.

IWAN also gives us more useful technologies, like the following:

Intelligent Virtualization   Cisco's IWAN offers a virtual WAN overlay over any transport type, which doesn't compromise application performance, availability, or security.

Automation   This Cisco IWAN technology provides network services by provisioning security and application policies.

Cloud Integration   An innovation that permits private cloud integration through APIC and public cloud application optimization with security.

Service Virtualization   Cisco's IWAN delivers virtual services on specialized router platforms as well as virtual routers and services on x86 server platforms.

Self-Learning Networks   Using policies, this technology leverages network analytics to proactively optimize the infrastructure.

We're going to pause a second and head back in time to cover some good old serial connections, which still actually happen to be a valid form of connecting via a WAN.

Cabling the Serial Wide Area Network

As you can imagine, there are a few things that you need to know before connecting your WAN to ensure that everything goes well. For starters, you have to understand the kind of WAN Physical layer implementation that Cisco provides and be familiar with the various types of WAN serial connectors involved.

The good news is that Cisco serial connections support almost any type of WAN service. Your typical WAN connection is a dedicated leased line using HDLC or PPP, with speeds that can kick it up to 45 Mbps (T3).

HDLC, PPP, and Frame Relay can use the same Physical layer specifications. I'll go over the various types of connections and then move on to tell you all about the WAN protocols specified in the ICND2 and CCNA R/S objectives.

Serial Transmission

WAN serial connectors use *serial transmission*, something that takes place 1 bit at a time over a single channel.

Older Cisco routers have used a proprietary 60-pin serial connector that you have to get from Cisco or a provider of Cisco equipment. Cisco also has a new, smaller proprietary serial connection that's about one-tenth the size of the 60-pin basic serial cable called the *smart-serial*. You have to verify that you have the right type of interface in your router before using this cable connector.

The type of connector you have on the other end of the cable depends on your service provider and its particular end-device requirements. There are several different types of ends you'll run into:

- EIA/TIA-232—Allowed speed up to 64 Kbps on 24-pin connector

- EIA/TIA-449

- V.35—Standard used to connect to a CSU/DSU, with speeds up to 2.048 Mbps using a 34-pin rectangular connector

- EIA-530

Make sure you're clear on these things: Serial links are described in frequency, or cycles per second (hertz). The amount of data that can be carried within these frequencies is called *bandwidth*. Bandwidth is the amount of data in bits per second that the serial channel can carry.

Data Terminal Equipment and Data Communication Equipment

By default, router interfaces are typically *data terminal equipment (DTE)*, and they connect into *data communication equipment (DCE)* like a *channel service unit/data service unit (CSU/DSU)* using a V.35 connector. CSU/DSU then plugs into a demarcation location (demarc) and is the service provider's last responsibility. Most of the time, the demarc is a jack that has an RJ45 (8-pin modular) female connector located in a telecommunications closet.

Actually, you may already have heard of demarcs. If you've ever had the glorious experience of reporting a problem to your service provider, they'll usually tell you everything tests out fine up to the demarc, so the problem must be the CPE, or customer premises equipment. In other words, it's your problem, not theirs!

Figure 7.9 shows a typical DTE-DCE-DTE connection and the devices used in the network.

FIGURE 7.9   DTE-DCE-DTE WAN connection: Clocking is typically provided by the DCE network to routers. In nonproduction environments, a DCE network is not always present.

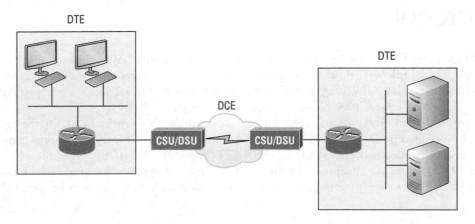

The idea behind a WAN is to be able to connect two DTE networks through a DCE network. The DCE network includes the CSU/DSU, through the provider's wiring and switches, all the way to the CSU/DSU at the other end. The network's DCE device (CSU/DSU) provides clocking to the DTE-connected interface (the router's serial interface).

As mentioned, the DCE network provides clocking to the router; this is the CSU/DSU. If you have a nonproduction network and you're using a WAN crossover type of cable and do not have a CSU/DSU, then you need to provide clocking on the DCE end of the cable by using the clock rate command. To find out which interface needs the clock rate command, use the show controllers *int* command:

```
Corp#sh controllers s0/0/0
Interface Serial0/0/0
Hardware is PowerQUICC MPC860
DCE V.35, clock rate 2000000
```

The preceding output shows a DCE interface that has the clock rate set to 2000000, which is the default for ISR routers. This next output shows a DTE connector, so you don't need enter the clock rate command on this interface:

```
SF#sh controllers s0/0/0
Interface Serial0/0/0
Hardware is PowerQUICC MPC860
DTE V.35 TX and RX clocks detected
```

Terms such as *EIA/TIA-232*, *V.35*, *X.21*, and *HSSI (High-Speed Serial Interface)* describe the Physical layer between the DTE (router) and DCE device (CSU/DSU).

High-Level Data-Link Control (HDLC) Protocol

The High-Level Data-Link Control (HDLC) protocol is a popular ISO-standard, bit-oriented, Data Link layer protocol. It specifies an encapsulation method for data on synchronous serial data links using frame characters and checksums. HDLC is a point-to-point protocol used on leased lines. No authentication is provided by HDLC.

In byte-oriented protocols, control information is encoded using entire bytes. On the other hand, bit-oriented protocols use single bits to represent the control information. Some common bit-oriented protocols are SDLC and HDLC; TCP and IP are byte-oriented protocols.

HDLC is the default encapsulation used by Cisco routers over synchronous serial links. And Cisco's HDLC is proprietary, meaning it won't communicate with any other vendor's

HDLC implementation. But don't give Cisco grief for it—*everyone's* HDLC implementation is proprietary. Figure 7.10 shows the Cisco HDLC format.

FIGURE 7.10 Cisco's HDLC frame format: Each vendor's HDLC has a proprietary data field to support multiprotocol environments.

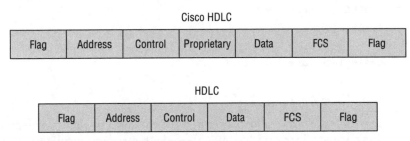

The reason every vendor has a proprietary HDLC encapsulation method is that each vendor has a different way for the HDLC protocol to encapsulate multiple Network layer protocols. If the vendors didn't have a way for HDLC to communicate the different layer 3 protocols, then HDLC would be able to operate in only a single layer 3 protocol environment. This proprietary header is placed in the data field of the HDLC encapsulation.

It's pretty simple to configure a serial interface if you're just going to connect two Cisco routers across a T1, for example. Figure 7.11 shows a point-to-point connection between two cities.

FIGURE 7.11 Configuring Cisco's HDLC proprietary WAN encapsulation

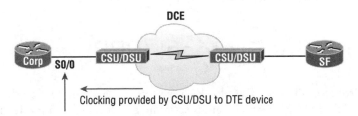

We can easily configure the routers with a basic IP address and then enable the interface. Assuming the link to the ISP is up, the routers will start communicating using the default HDLC encapsulation. Let's take a look at the Corp router configuration so you can see just how easy this can be:

```
Corp(config)#int s0/0
Corp(config-if)#ip address 172.16.10.1 255.255.255.252
Corp(config-if)#no shut

Corp#sh int s0/0
```

```
Serial0/0 is up, line protocol is up
  Hardware is PowerQUICC Serial
  Internet address is 172.16.10.1/30
  MTU 1500 bytes, BW 1544 Kbit, DLY 20000 usec,
    reliability 255/255, txload 1/255, rxload 1/255
  Encapsulation HDLC, loopback not set
  Keepalive set (10 sec)
```

```
Corp#sh run | begin interface Serial0/0
interface Serial0/0
 ip address 172.16.10.1 255.255.255.252
```

Note that all I did was add an IP address before I then enabled the interface—pretty simple! Now, as long as the SF router is running the default serial encapsulation, this link will come up. Notice in the preceding output that the show interface command does show the encapsulation type of HDLC, but the output of show running-config does not. This is important—remember that if you don't see an encapsulation type listed under a serial interface in the active configuration file, you know it's running the default encapsulation of HDLC.

So let's say you have only one Cisco router and you need to connect to a non-Cisco router because your other Cisco router is on order or something. What would you do? You couldn't use the default HDLC serial encapsulation because it wouldn't work. Instead, you would need to go with an option like PPP, an ISO-standard way of identifying the upper-layer protocols. Now is a great time to get into more detail about PPP as well as how to connect to routers using the PPP encapsulation. You can check out RFC 1661 for more information on the origins and standards of PPP.

Point-to-Point Protocol (PPP)

Point-to-Point Protocol (PPP) is a Data Link layer protocol that can be used over either asynchronous serial (dial-up) or synchronous serial media. It relies on Link Control Protocol (LCP) to build and maintain data-link connections. Network Control Protocol (NCP) enables multiple Network layer protocols (routed protocols) to be used on a point-to-point connection.

Because HDLC is the default serial encapsulation on Cisco serial links and it works great, why in the world would you choose to use PPP? Well, the basic purpose of PPP is to transport layer 3 packets across a Data Link layer point-to-point link, and it's nonproprietary. So unless you have all Cisco routers, you need PPP on your serial interfaces because the HDLC encapsulation is Cisco proprietary, remember? Plus, since PPP can encapsulate several layer 3 routed protocols and provide authentication, dynamic addressing, and callback, PPP could actually be the best encapsulation solution for you over HDLC anyway.

Figure 7.12 shows the PPP protocol stack compared to the OSI reference model.

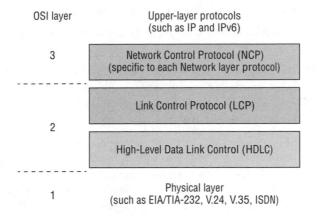

FIGURE 7.12   Point-to-Point Protocol stack

PPP contains four main components:

EIA/TIA-232-C, V.24, V.35, and ISDN   A Physical layer international standard for serial communication.

HDLC   A method for encapsulating datagrams over serial links.

LCP   A method of establishing, configuring, maintaining, and terminating the point-to-point connection. It also provides features such as authentication. I'll give you a complete list of these features in the next section.

NCP   NCP is a method of establishing and configuring different Network layer protocols for transport across the PPP link. NCP is designed to allow the simultaneous use of multiple Network layer protocols. Two examples of protocols here are Internet Protocol Control Protocol (IPCP) and Cisco Discovery Protocol Control Protocol (CDPCP).

Burn it into your mind that the PPP protocol stack is specified at the Physical and Data Link layers only. NCP is used to allow communication of multiple Network layer protocols by identifying and encapsulating the protocols across a PPP data link.

Remember that if you have a Cisco router and a non-Cisco router connected with a serial connection, you must configure PPP or another encapsulation method like Frame Relay because the HDLC default just won't work!

Next, we'll cover the options for LCP and PPP session establishment.

Link Control Protocol (LCP) Configuration Options

Link Control Protocol (LCP) offers different PPP encapsulation options, including the following:

Authentication   This option tells the calling side of the link to send information that can identify the user. The two methods for this task are PAP and CHAP.

Compression   This is used to increase the throughput of PPP connections by compressing the data or payload prior to transmission. PPP decompresses the data frame on the receiving end.

Error detection   PPP uses Quality and Magic Number options to ensure a reliable, loop-free data link.

Multilink PPP (MLP)   Starting with IOS version 11.1, multilink is supported on PPP links with Cisco routers. This option makes several separate physical paths appear to be one logical path at layer 3. For example, two T1s running multilink PPP would show up as a single 3 Mbps path to a layer 3 routing protocol.

PPP callback   On a dial-up connection, PPP can be configured to call back after successful authentication. *PPP callback* can be a very good thing because it allows us to keep track of usage based upon access charges for accounting records and a bunch of other reasons. With callback enabled, a calling router (client) will contact a remote router (server) and authenticate. Predictably, both routers have to be configured for the callback feature for this to work. Once authentication is completed, the remote router will terminate the connection and then reinitiate a connection to the calling router from the remote router.

PPP Session Establishment

When PPP connections are started, the links go through three phases of session establishment, as shown in Figure 7.13:

FIGURE 7.13   PPP session establishment

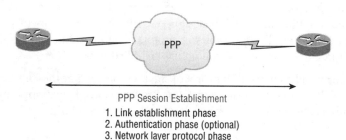

PPP Session Establishment
1. Link establishment phase
2. Authentication phase (optional)
3. Network layer protocol phase

Link-establishment phase   LCP packets are sent by each PPP device to configure and test the link. These packets contain a field called Configuration Option that allows each device to see the size of the data, the compression, and authentication. If no Configuration Option field is present, then the default configurations will be used.

Authentication phase   If required, either CHAP or PAP can be used to authenticate a link. Authentication takes place before Network layer protocol information is read, and it's also possible that link-quality determination will occur simultaneously.

Network layer protocol phase   PPP uses the *Network Control Protocol (NCP)* to allow multiple Network layer protocols to be encapsulated and sent over a PPP data link. Each Network layer protocol (e.g., IP, IPv6, which are routed protocols) establishes a service with NCP.

PPP Authentication Methods

There are two methods of authentication that can be used with PPP links:

Password Authentication Protocol (PAP)   The *Password Authentication Protocol (PAP)* is the less secure of the two methods. Passwords are sent in clear text and PAP is performed only upon the initial link establishment. When the PPP link is first established, the remote node sends the username and password back to the originating target router until authentication is acknowledged. Not exactly Fort Knox!

Challenge Handshake Authentication Protocol (CHAP)   The *Challenge Handshake Authentication Protocol (CHAP)* is used at the initial startup of a link and at periodic checkups on the link to ensure that the router is still communicating with the same host.

After PPP finishes its initial link-establishment phase, the local router sends a challenge request to the remote device. The remote device sends a value calculated using a one-way hash function called MD5. The local router checks this hash value to make sure it matches. If the values don't match, the link is immediately terminated.

CHAP authenticates at the beginning of the session and periodically throughout the session.

Configuring PPP on Cisco Routers

Configuring PPP encapsulation on an interface is really pretty straightforward. To configure it from the CLI, use these simple router commands:

```
Router#config t
Router(config)#int s0
Router(config-if)#encapsulation ppp
Router(config-if)#^Z
```

Of course, PPP encapsulation has to be enabled on both interfaces connected to a serial line in order to work, and there are several additional configuration options available to you via the ppp ? command.

Configuring PPP Authentication

After you configure your serial interface to support PPP encapsulation, you can then configure authentication using PPP between routers. But first, you must set the hostname of the router if it hasn't been set already. After that, you set the username and password for the remote router that will be connecting to your router, like this:

```
Router#config t
Router(config)#hostname RouterA
RouterA(config)#username RouterB password cisco
```

When using the username command, remember that the username is the hostname of the remote router that's connecting to your router. And it's case sensitive too. Also, the password on both routers must be the same. It's a plain-text password that you can see with a show run command, and you can encrypt the password by using the command service password-encryption. You must have a username and password configured for each remote system you plan to connect to. The remote routers must also be similarly configured with usernames and passwords.

Now, after you've set the hostname, usernames, and passwords, choose either CHAP or PAP as the authentication method:

```
RouterA#config t
RouterA(config)#int s0
RouterA(config-if)#ppp authentication chap pap
RouterA(config-if)#^Z
```

If both methods are configured on the same line as I've demonstrated here, then only the first method will be used during link negotiation. The second acts as a backup just in case the first method fails.

There is yet another command you can use if you're using PAP authentication for some reason. The ppp pap sent-username <*username*> password <*password*> command enables outbound PAP authentication. The local router uses the username and password that the ppp pap sent-username command specifies to authenticate itself to a remote device. The other router must have this same username/password configured as well.

Verifying and Troubleshooting Serial Links

Now that PPP encapsulation is enabled, you need to verify that it's up and running. First, let's take a look at a figure of a sample nonproduction network serial link. Figure 7.14 shows two routers connected with a point-to-point serial connection, with the DCE side on the Pod1R1 router.

FIGURE 7.14 PPP authentication example

Pod1R1   Pod1R2

hostname Pod1R1   hostname Pod1R2
username Pod1R2 password cisco   username Pod1R1 password cisco
interface serial 0   interface serial 0
ip address 10.0.1.1 255.255.255.0   ip address 10.0.1.2 255.255.255.0
encapsulation ppp   encapsulation ppp
clock rate 64000   bandwidth 512
bandwidth 512   ppp authentication chap
ppp authentication chap

You can start verifying the configuration with the show interface command like this:

```
Pod1R1#sh int s0/0
Serial0/0 is up, line protocol is up
  Hardware is PowerQUICC Serial
  Internet address is 10.0.1.1/24
  MTU 1500 bytes, BW 1544 Kbit, DLY 20000 usec,
     reliability 239/255, txload 1/255, rxload 1/255
  Encapsulation PPP
  loopback not set
  Keepalive set (10 sec)
  LCP Open
  Open: IPCP, CDPCP
[output cut]
```

The first line of output is important because it tells us that Serial 0/0 is up/up. Notice that the interface encapsulation is PPP and that LCP is open. This means that it has negotiated the session establishment and all is well. The last line tells us that NCP is listening for the protocols IP and CDP, shown with the NCP headers IPCP and CDPCP.

But what would you see if everything isn't so perfect? I'm going to type in the configuration shown in Figure 7.15 to find out.

FIGURE 7.15   Failed PPP authentication

Pod1R1

Pod1R2

```
hostname Pod1R1
username Pod1R2 password Cisco
interface serial 0
ip address 10.0.1.1  255.255.255.0
clock rate 64000
bandwidth 512
encapsulation ppp
ppp authentication chap
```

```
hostname Pod1R2
username Pod1R1 password cisco
interface serial 0
ip address 10.0.1.2  255.255.255.0
bandwidth 512
encapsulation ppp
ppp authentication chap
```

What's wrong here? Take a look at the usernames and passwords. Do you see the problem now? That's right, the C is capitalized on the Pod1R2 username command found in the configuration of router Pod1R1. This is wrong because the usernames and passwords are case sensitive. Now let's take a look at the show interface command and see what happens:

```
Pod1R1#sh int s0/0
Serial0/0 is up, line protocol is down
  Hardware is PowerQUICC Serial
```

```
Internet address is 10.0.1.1/24
MTU 1500 bytes, BW 1544 Kbit, DLY 20000 usec,
    reliability 243/255, txload 1/255, rxload 1/255
Encapsulation PPP, loopback not set
Keepalive set (10 sec)
LCP Closed
Closed: IPCP, CDPCP
```

First, notice that the first line of output shows us that Serial0/0 is up and line protocol is down. This is because there are no keepalives coming from the remote router. The next thing I want you to notice is that the LCP and NCP are closed because the authentication failed.

Debugging PPP Authentication

To display the CHAP authentication process as it occurs between two routers in the network, just use the command debug ppp authentication.

If your PPP encapsulation and authentication are set up correctly on both routers and your usernames and passwords are all good, then the debug ppp authentication command will display an output that looks like the following output, which is called the three-way handshake:

```
d16h: Se0/0 PPP: Using default call direction
1d16h: Se0/0 PPP: Treating connection as a dedicated line
1d16h: Se0/0 CHAP: O CHALLENGE id 219 len 27 from "Pod1R1"
1d16h: Se0/0 CHAP: I CHALLENGE id 208 len 27 from "Pod1R2"
1d16h: Se0/0 CHAP: O RESPONSE id 208 len 27 from "Pod1R1"
1d16h: Se0/0 CHAP: I RESPONSE id 219 len 27 from "Pod1R2"
1d16h: Se0/0 CHAP: O SUCCESS id 219 len 4
1d16h: Se0/0 CHAP: I SUCCESS id 208 len 4
```

But if you have the password wrong as they were previously in the PPP authentication failure example back in Figure 7.15, the output would look something like this:

```
1d16h: Se0/0 PPP: Using default call direction
1d16h: Se0/0 PPP: Treating connection as a dedicated line
1d16h: %SYS-5-CONFIG_I: Configured from console by console
1d16h: Se0/0 CHAP: O CHALLENGE id 220 len 27 from "Pod1R1"
1d16h: Se0/0 CHAP: I CHALLENGE id 209 len 27 from "Pod1R2"
1d16h: Se0/0 CHAP: O RESPONSE id 209 len 27 from "Pod1R1"
1d16h: Se0/0 CHAP: I RESPONSE id 220 len 27 from "Pod1R2"
1d16h: Se0/0 CHAP: O FAILURE id 220 len 25 msg is "MD/DES compare failed"
```

PPP with CHAP authentication is a three-way authentication, and if the username and passwords aren't configured exactly the way they should be, then the authentication will fail and the link will go down.

Mismatched WAN Encapsulations

If you have a point-to-point link but the encapsulations aren't the same, the link will never come up. Figure 7.16 shows one link with PPP and one with HDLC.

FIGURE 7.16   Mismatched WAN encapsulations

Pod1R1   Pod1R2

```
hostname Pod1R1                          hostname Pod1R2
username Pod1R2 password cisco           username Pod1R1 password cisco
interface serial 0                       interface serial 0
ip address 10.0.1.1 255.255.255.0        ip address 10.0.1.2 255.255.255.0
clock rate 64000                         bandwidth 512
bandwidth 512                            encapsulation hdlc
encapsulation ppp
```

Look at router Pod1R1 in this output:

```
Pod1R1#sh int s0/0
Serial0/0 is up, line protocol is down
  Hardware is PowerQUICC Serial
  Internet address is 10.0.1.1/24
  MTU 1500 bytes, BW 1544 Kbit, DLY 20000 usec,
     reliability 254/255, txload 1/255, rxload 1/255
  Encapsulation PPP, loopback not set
  Keepalive set (10 sec)
  LCP REQsent
Closed: IPCP, CDPCP
```

The serial interface is up/down and LCP is sending requests but will never receive any responses because router Pod1R2 is using the HDLC encapsulation. To fix this problem, you would have to go to router Pod1R2 and configure the PPP encapsulation on the serial interface. One more thing: Even though the usernames are configured incorrectly, it doesn't matter because the command ppp authentication chap isn't used under the serial interface configuration. This means that the username command isn't relevant in this example.

You can set a Cisco serial interface back to the default of HDLC with the no encapsulation command like this:

```
Router(config)#int s0/0
Router(config-if)#no encapsulation
*Feb 7 16:00:18.678:%LINEPROTO-5-UPDOWN: Line protocol on Interface Serial0/0,
changed state to up
```

Notice the link came up because it now matches the encapsulation on the other end of the link!

Always remember that you just can't have PPP on one side and HDLC on the other—they don't get along!

Mismatched IP Addresses

A tricky problem to spot is if you have HDLC or PPP configured on your serial interface but your IP addresses are wrong. Things seem to be just fine because the interfaces will show that they are up. Take a look at Figure 7.17 and see if you can see what I mean—the two routers are connected with different subnets—router Pod1R1 with 10.0.1.1/24 and router Pod1R2 with 10.2.1.2/24.

FIGURE 7.17 Mismatched IP addresses

Pod1R1   Pod1R2

hostname Pod1R1   hostname Pod1R2
username Pod1R2 password cisco   username Pod1R1 password cisco
interface serial 0   interface serial 0
ip address 10.0.1.1 255.255.255.0   ip address 10.2.1.2 255.255.255.0
clock rate 64000   bandwidth 512
bandwidth 512   encapsulation ppp
encapsulation ppp   ppp authentication chap
ppp authentication chap

This will never work. Let's take a look at the output:

```
Pod1R1#sh int s0/0
Serial0/0 is up, line protocol is up
  Hardware is PowerQUICC Serial
  Internet address is 10.0.1.1/24
  MTU 1500 bytes, BW 1544 Kbit, DLY 20000 usec,
    reliability 255/255, txload 1/255, rxload 1/255
  Encapsulation PPP, loopback not set
  Keepalive set (10 sec)
  LCP Open
  Open: IPCP, CDPCP
```

See that? The IP addresses between the routers are wrong but the link appears to be working just fine. This is because PPP, like HDLC and Frame Relay, is a layer 2 WAN encapsulation, so it doesn't care about layer three addressing at all. So yes, the link is up, but you can't use IP across this link since it's misconfigured, or can you? Well, yes and no. If you try to ping, you'll see that this actually works! This is a feature of PPP, but not HDLC or Frame Relay. But just because you can ping to an IP address that's not in the same subnet doesn't mean your network traffic and routing protocols will work. So be careful with this issue, especially when troubleshooting PPP links!

Take a look at the routing table of Pod1R1 and see if you can find the mismatched IP address problem:

```
[output cut]
  10.0.0.0/8 is variably subnetted, 2 subnets, 2 masks
C       10.2.1.2/32 is directly connected, Serial0/0
C       10.0.1.0/24 is directly connected, Serial0/0
```

Interesting! We can see our serial interface S0/0 address of 10.0.1.0/24, but what is that other address on interface S0/0—10.2.1.2/32? That's our remote router's interface IP address! PPP determines and places the neighbor's IP address in the routing table as a connected interface, which then allows you to ping it even though it's actually configured on a separate IP subnet.

For the Cisco objectives, you need to be able to troubleshoot PPP from the routing table as I just described.

To find and fix this problem, you can also use the show running-config, show interfaces, or show ip interfaces brief command on each router, or you can use the show cdp neighbors detail command:

```
Pod1R1#sh cdp neighbors detail
-------------------------
Device ID: Pod1R2
Entry address(es):
  IP address: 10.2.1.2
```

Since the layer 1 Physical and layer 2 Data Link is up/up, you can view and verify the directly connected neighbor's IP address and then solve your problem.

Multilink PPP (MLP)

There are many load-balancing mechanisms available, but this one is free for use on serial WAN links! It provides multivendor support and is specified in RFC 1990, which details the fragmentation and packet sequencing specifications.

You can use MLP to connect your home network to an Internet service provider using two traditional modems or to connect a company via two leased lines.

The MLP feature provides a load-balancing functionality over multiple WAN links while allowing for multivendor interoperability. It offers support for packet fragmentation, proper sequencing, and load calculation on both inbound and outbound traffic.

MLP allows packets to be fragmented and then sent simultaneously over multiple point-to-point links to the same remote address. It can work over synchronous and asynchronous serial types.

MLP combines multiple physical links into a logical link called an MLP bundle, which is essentially a single, virtual interface that connects to the remote router. None of the links inside the bundle have any knowledge about the traffic on the other links.

The MLP over serial interfaces feature provides us with the following benefits:

Load balancing MLP provides bandwidth on demand, utilizing load balancing on up to 10 links and can even calculate the load on traffic between specific sites. You don't actually need to make all links the same bandwidth, but doing so is recommended. Another key MLP advantage is that it splits packets and fragments across all links, which reduces latency across the WAN.

Increased redundancy This one is pretty straightforward... If a link fails, the others will still transmit and receive.

Link fragmentation and interleaving The fragmentation mechanism in MLP works by fragmenting large packets, then sending the packet fragments over the multiple point-to-point links. Smaller real-time packets are not fragmented. So interleaving basically means real-time packets can be sent in between sending the fragmented, non-real-time packets, which helps reduce delay on the lines. So let's configure MLP now to get a good feel for how it actually works now.

Configuring MLP

We're going to use Figure 7.18 to demonstrate how to configure MLP between two routers.

FIGURE 7.18   MLP between Corp and SF routers

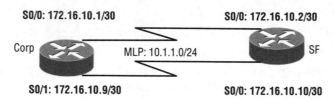

But first, I want you to study the configuration of the two serial interfaces on the Corp router that we're going to use for making our bundle:

```
Corp# show interfaces Serial0/0
Serial0/0 is up, line protocol is up
  Hardware is M4T
  Internet address is 172.16.10.1/30
  MTU 1500 bytes, BW 1544 Kbit/sec, DLY 20000 usec,
     reliability 255/255, txload 1/255, rxload 1/255
  Encapsulation PPP, LCP Open
```

```
  Open: IPCP, CDPCP, crc 16, loopback not set

Corp# show interfaces Serial1/1
Serial1/1 is up, line protocol is up
  Hardware is M4T
  Internet address is 172.16.10.9/30
  MTU 1500 bytes, BW 1544 Kbit/sec, DLY 20000 usec,
      reliability 255/255, txload 1/255, rxload 1/255
  Encapsulation PPP, LCP Open
  Open: IPCP, CDPCP, crc 16, loopback not set
```

Did you notice that each serial connection is on a different subnet (they have to be) and that the encapsulation is PPP?

When you configure MLP, you must first remove your IP addresses off your physical interface. Then, you configure a multilink bundle by creating a multilink interface on both sides of the link. After that, you assign an IP address to this multilink interface, which effectively restricts a physical link so that it can only join the designated multilink group interface.

So first I'm going to remove the IP addresses from the physical interfaces that I'm going to include in my PPP bundle.

```
Corp# config t
Corp(config)# int Serial0/0
Corp(config-if)# no ip address
Corp(config-if)# int Serial1/1
Corp(config-if)# no ip address
Corp(config-if)# end
Corp#


SF# config t
SF(config)# int Serial0/0
SF(config-if)# no ip address
SF(config-if)# int Serial0/1
SF(config-if)# no ip address
SF(config-if)# end
SF#
```

Now we create the multilink interface on each side of the link and the MLP commands to enable the bundle.

```
Corp#config t
Corp(config)# interface Multilink1
Corp(config-if)# ip address 10.1.1.1 255.255.255.0
Corp(config-if)# ppp multilink
```

```
Corp(config-if)# ppp multilink group 1
Corp(config-if)# end

SF#config t
SF(config)# interface Multilink1
SF(config-if)# ip address 10.1.1.2 255.255.255.0
SF(config-if)# ppp multilink
SF(config-if)# ppp multilink group 1
SF(config-if)# exit
```

We can see that a link joins an MLP bundle only if it negotiates to use the bundle when a connection is established and the identification information that has been exchanged matches the info for an existing bundle.

When you configure the ppp multilink group command on a link, that link won't be allowed to join any bundle other than the indicated group interface.

Verifying MLP

To verify that your bundle is up and running, just use the show ppp multilink and show interfaces multilink1 commands:

```
Corp# show ppp multilink

Multilink1
  Bundle name: Corp
  Remote Endpoint Discriminator: [1] SF
  Local Endpoint Discriminator: [1] Corp
  Bundle up for 02:12:05, total bandwidth 4188, load 1/255
  Receive buffer limit 24000 bytes, frag timeout 1000 ms
    0/0 fragments/bytes in reassembly list
    0 lost fragments, 53 reordered
    0/0 discarded fragments/bytes, 0 lost received
    0x56E received sequence, 0x572 sent sequence
  Member links: 2 active, 0 inactive (max 255, min not set)
    Se0/1, since 01:32:05
    Se1/2, since 01:31:31
No inactive multilink interfaces
```

We can see that the physical interfaces, Se0/1 and Se1/1, are members of the logical interface bundle Multilink 1. So now we'll verify the status of the interface Multilink1 on the Corp router:

```
Corp# show int Multilink1
Multilink1 is up, line protocol is up
  Hardware is multilink group interface
```

```
    Internet address is 10.1.1.1/24
   MTU 1500 bytes, BW 1544 Kbit/sec, DLY 20000 usec,
      reliability 255/255, txload 1/255, rxload 1/255
Encapsulation PPP, LCP Open, multilink Open
Open: IPCP, CDPCP, loopback not set
 Keepalive set (10 sec)
[output cut]
```

Let's move on to configure a PPPoE client on a Cisco router.

PPP Client (PPPoE)

Used with ADSL services, PPPoE (Point-to-Point Protocol over Ethernet) encapsulates PPP frames in Ethernet frames and uses common PPP features like authentication, encryption, and compression. But as I said earlier, it can be trouble. This is especially true if you've got a badly configured firewall!

Basically, PPPoE is a tunneling protocol that layers IP and other protocols running over PPP with the attributes of a PPP link. This is done so protocols can then be used to contact other Ethernet devices and initiate a point-to-point connection to transport IP packets.

Figure 7.19 displays typical usage of PPPoE over ADSL. As you can see, a PPP session is connected from the PC of the end user to the router. Subsequently, the subscriber PC IP address is assigned by the router via IPCP.

FIGURE 7.19 PPPoE with ADSL

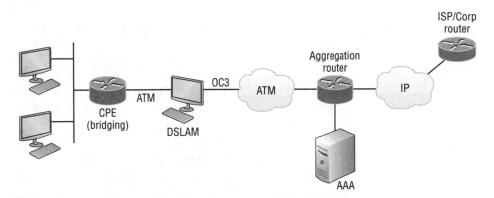

Your ISP will typically provide you with a DSL line and this will act as a bridge if your line doesn't provide enhanced features. This means only one host will connect using PPPoE. By using a Cisco router, you can run the PPPoE client IOS feature which will connect multiple PCs on the Ethernet segment that is connected to the router.

Configuring a PPPoE Client

The PPPoE client configuration is simple and straightforward. First, you need to create a dialer interface and then tie it to a physical interface.

Here are the easy steps:

1. Create a dialer interface using the `interface dialer` *number* command.

2. Instruct the client to use an IP address provided by the PPPoE server with the `ip address negotiated` command.

3. Set the encapsulation type to PPP.

4. Configure the dialer pool and number.

5. Under the physical interface, use the `pppoe-client dial-pool number` *number* command.

On your PPPoE client router, enter the following commands:

```
R1# conf t
R1(config)# int dialer1
R1(config-if)# ip address negotiated
R1(config-if)# encapsulation ppp
R1(config-if)# dialer pool 1
R1(config-if)# interface f0/1
R1(config-if)# no ip address
R1(config-if)# pppoe-client dial-pool-number 1
*May 1 1:09:07.540: %DIALER-6-BIND: Interface Vi2 bound to profile Di1
*May 1 1:09:07.541: %LINK-3-UPDOWN: Interface Virtual-Access2, changed state to
up
```

That's it! Now let's verify the interface with the `show ip interface brief` and the `show pppoe session` commands:

```
R1# show ip int brief
Interface              IP-Address      OK? Method Status         Protocol
FastEthernet0/1        unassigned      YES manual up             up
<output cut>
Dialer1                10.10.10.3      YES IPCP   up             up
Loopback0              192.168.1.1     YES NVRAM  up             up
Loopback1              172.16.1.1      YES NVRAM  up             up
Virtual-Access1        unassigned      YES unset  up             up
Virtual-Access2        unassigned      YES unset  up             up

R1#show pppoe session
    1 client session
```

```
Uniq ID   PPPoE  RemMAC           Port              VT  VA        State
          SID    LocMAC                                 VA-st     Type
   N/A     4     aacb.cc00.1419   FEt0/1            Di1 Vi2       UP
                 aacb.cc00.1f01                         UP
```

Our connection using a PPPoE client is up and running. Now let's take a look at VPNs.

Virtual Private Networks

I'd be pretty willing to bet you've heard the term *VPN* more than once before. Maybe you even know what one is, but just in case, a *virtual private network (VPN)* allows the creation of private networks across the Internet, enabling privacy and tunneling of IP and non-TCP/IP protocols. VPNs are used daily to give remote users and disjointed networks connectivity over a public medium like the Internet instead of using more expensive permanent means.

No worries—VPNs aren't really that hard to understand. A VPN fits somewhere between a LAN and WAN, with the WAN often simulating a LAN link because your computer, on one LAN, connects to a different, remote LAN and uses its resources remotely. The key drawback to using VPNs is a big one—security! So the definition of connecting a LAN (or VLAN) to a WAN may sound the same as using a VPN, but a VPN is actually much more.

Here's the difference: A typical WAN connects two or more remote LANs together using a router and someone else's network, like, say, your Internet service provider's. Your local host and router see these networks as remote networks and not as local networks or local resources. This would be a WAN in its most general definition. A VPN actually makes your local host part of the remote network by using the WAN link that connects you to the remote LAN. The VPN will make your host appear as though it's actually local on the remote network. This means that we now have access to the remote LAN's resources, and that access is also very secure!

This may sound a lot like a VLAN definition, and really, the concept is the same: "Take my host and make it appear local to the remote resources." Just remember this key distinction: For networks that are physically local, using VLANs is a good solution, but for physically remote networks that span a WAN, opt for using VPNs instead.

For a simple VPN example, let's use my home office in Boulder, Colorado. Here, I have my personal host, but I want it to appear as if it's on a LAN in my corporate office in Dallas, Texas, so I can get to my remote servers. VPN is the solution I would opt for to achieve my goal.

Figure 7.20 shows this example of my host using a VPN connection from Boulder to Dallas, which allows me to access the remote network services and servers as if my host were right there on the same VLAN as my servers.

FIGURE 7.20 Example of using a VPN

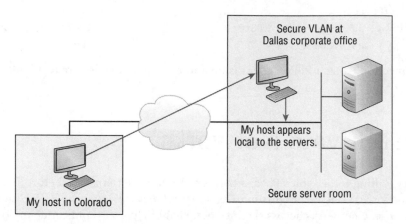

Why is this so important? If you answered, "Because my servers in Dallas are secure, and only the hosts on the same VLAN are allowed to connect to them and use the resources of these servers," you nailed it! A VPN allows me to connect to these resources by locally attaching to the VLAN through a VPN across the WAN. The other option is to open up my network and servers to everyone on the Internet or another WAN service, in which case my security goes "poof." So clearly, it's imperative I have a VPN!

Benefits of VPNs

There are many benefits to using VPNs on your corporate and even home network. The benefits covered in the CCNA R/S objectives are as follows:

Security   VPNs can provide very good security by using advanced encryption and authentication protocols, which will help protect your network from unauthorized access. IPsec and SSL fall into this category. Secure Sockets Layer (SSL) is an encryption technology used with web browsers, which has native SSL encryption, and is known as Web VPN. You can also use the Cisco AnyConnect SSL VPN client installed on your PC to provide an SSL VPN solution, as well as the Clientless Cisco SSL VPN.

Cost savings   By connecting the corporate remote offices to their closest Internet provider, and then creating a VPN tunnel with encryption and authentication, I gain a huge savings over opting for traditional leased point-to-point lines. This also permits higher bandwidth links and security, all for far less money than traditional connections.

Scalability   VPNs scale very well to quickly bring up new offices or have mobile users connect securely while traveling or when connecting from home.

Compatibility with broadband technology   For remote and traveling users and remote offices, any Internet access can provide a connection to the corporate VPN. This allows users to take advantage of the high-speed Internet access of DSL or cable modems.

Enterprise- and Provider-Managed VPNs

VPNs are categorized based upon the role they play in a business—for example, enterprise-managed VPNs and provider-managed VPNs.

You'd use an enterprise-managed VPNs if your company manages its own VPNs, which happens to be a very popular way of providing this service. To get a picture of this, check out Figure 7.21.

FIGURE 7.21   Enterprise-managed VPNs

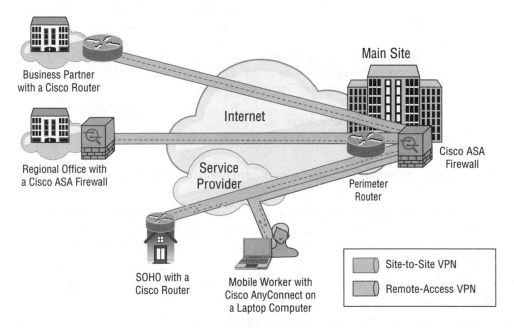

There are three different categories of enterprise-managed VPNs:

Remote-access VPNs allow remote users such as telecommuters to securely access the corporate network wherever and whenever they need to.

Site-to-site VPNs, or intranet VPNs, allow a company to connect its remote sites to the corporate backbone securely over a public medium like the Internet instead of requiring more expensive WAN connections like Frame Relay.

Extranet VPNs allow an organization's suppliers, partners, and customers to be connected to the corporate network in a limited way for business-to-business (B2B) communications.

Provider-managed VPNs are pictured in Figure 7.22.

FIGURE 7.22   Provider-managed VPNs

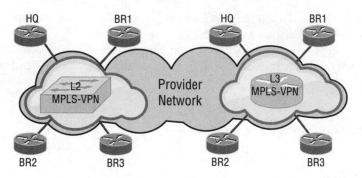

Layer 2 MPLS VPN (VPLS and VPWS):
• Customer routers exchange routes directly.
• Some applications need Layer 2 connectivity to work.

Layer 3 MPLS VPN:
• Customer routers exchange routes with SP routers.
• It provides Layer 3 service across the backbone.

And you need to be familiar with the two different categories of provider-managed VPNs:

Layer 2 MPLS VPN   Layer 2 VPNs are a type of virtual private network (VPN) that use MPLS labels to transport data. The communication occurs between routers known as provider edge routers (PEs) because they sit on the edge of the provider's network, next to the customer's network.

Internet providers who have an existing layer 2 network can opt to use these VPNs instead of the other common layer 3 MPLS VPNs.

There are two typical technologies of layer 2 MPLS VPNs:

Virtual private wire service (VPWS)   VPWS is the simplest form for enabling Ethernet services over MPLS. It is also known as ETHoMPLS (Ethernet over MPLS), or VLL (Virtual Leased Line). VPWS has the characteristics of a fixed relationship between an attachment-virtual circuit and an emulated virtual circuit. VPWS-based services are point-to-point, such as, for example, Frame-Relay/ATM/Ethernet services over IP/MPLS.

Virtual private LAN switching service (VPLS)   This is an end-to-end service and is virtual because multiple instances of this service share the same Ethernet broadcast domain virtually. However, each connection is independent and isolated from the others in the network. A dynamic, "learned" relationship exists between an attachment-virtual circuit and emulated virtual circuits, which is determined by the customer's MAC address.

In this type of network, the customer manages its own routing protocols. One advantage that a layer 2 VPN has over its layer 3 counterpart is that some applications just won't work if nodes are not in the same layer 2 network.

Layer 3 MPLS VPN   Layer 3 MPLS VPN provides a layer 3 service across the backbone. A different IP subnet connects each site. Since you would typically deploy a routing protocol over this VPN, you must communicate with the service provider to participate in the exchange of routes. Neighbor adjacency is established between your router, called CE, and the provider router that's called PE. The service provider network has many core routers called P routers and it's the P routers' job to provide connectivity between the PE routers.

If you really want to totally outsource your layer 3 VPN, then this service is for you. Your service provider will maintain and manage routing for all your sites. From your perspective as a customer who's outsourced your VPNs, this will appear to you that your service provider network is one big virtual switch.

Now you're interested in VPNs, huh? And since VPNs are inexpensive and secure, I'm guessing you just can't wait to find out how to create VPNs now! There's more than one way to bring a VPN into being. The first approach uses IPsec to create authentication and encryption services between endpoints on an IP network. The second way is via tunneling protocols, which allow you to establish a tunnel between endpoints on a network. And understand that the tunnel itself is a means for data or protocols to be encapsulated inside another protocol—pretty clean!

I'm going to go over IPsec in a minute, but first I really want to describe four of the most common tunneling protocols in use today:

Layer 2 Forwarding (L2F) is a Cisco-proprietary tunneling protocol, and it was Cisco's first tunneling protocol created for virtual private dial-up networks (VPDNs). A VPDN allows a device to use a dial-up connection to create a secure connection to a corporate network. L2F was later replaced by L2TP, which is backward compatible with L2F.

Point-to-Point Tunneling Protocol (PPTP) was created by Microsoft and others to allow the secure transfer of data from remote networks to the corporate network.

Layer 2 Tunneling Protocol (L2TP) was created by Cisco and Microsoft to replace L2F and PPTP. L2TP merged the capabilities of both L2F and PPTP into one tunneling protocol.

Generic Routing Encapsulation (GRE) is another Cisco-proprietary tunneling protocol. It forms virtual point-to-point links, allowing for a variety of protocols to be encapsulated in IP tunnels. I'll cover GRE in more detail, including how to configure it, at the end of this chapter.

Now that you're clear on both exactly what a VPN is and the various types of VPNs available, it's time to dive into IPsec.

Introduction to Cisco IOS IPsec

Simply put, IPsec is an industry-wide standard framework of protocols and algorithms that allows for secure data transmission over an IP-based network and functions at the layer 3 Network layer of the OSI model.

Did you notice I said IP-based network? That's really important because by itself, IPsec can't be used to encrypt non-IP traffic. This means that if you run into a situation where you have to encrypt non-IP traffic, you'll need to create a Generic Routing Encapsulation (GRE) tunnel for it (which I explain later) and then use IPsec to encrypt that tunnel!

IPsec Transforms

An *IPsec transform* specifies a single security protocol with its corresponding security algorithm; without these transforms, IPsec wouldn't be able to give us its glory. It's important to be familiar with these technologies, so let me take a second to define the security protocols and briefly introduce the supporting encryption and hashing algorithms that IPsec relies upon.

Security Protocols

The two primary security protocols used by IPsec are *Authentication Header (AH)* and *Encapsulating Security Payload (ESP)*.

Authentication Header (AH)

The AH protocol provides authentication for the data and the IP header of a packet using a one-way hash for packet authentication. It works like this: The sender generates a one-way hash; then the receiver generates the same one-way hash. If the packet has changed in any way, it won't be authenticated and will be dropped since the hash values won't match. So basically, IPsec relies upon AH to guarantee authenticity. AH checks the entire packet, but it doesn't offer any encryption services.

This is unlike ESP, which only provides an integrity check on the data of a packet.

Encapsulating Security Payload (ESP)

It won't tell you when or how the NASDAQ's gonna bounce up and down like a superball, but ESP will provide confidentiality, data origin authentication, connectionless integrity, anti-replay service, and limited traffic-flow confidentiality by defeating traffic flow analysis—which is almost as good! Anyway, there are five components of ESP:

Confidentiality (encryption)   This allows the sending device to encrypt the packets before transmitting in order to prevent eavesdropping. Confidentiality is provided through the use of symmetric encryption algorithms like DES or 3DES. Confidentiality can be selected separately from all other services, but the confidentiality selected must be the same on both endpoints of your VPN.

Data integrity   Data integrity allows the receiver to verify that the data received was not altered in any way along the way. IPsec uses checksums as a simple check of the data.

Authentication   Authentication ensures that the connection is made with the correct partner. The receiver can authenticate the source of the packet by guaranteeing and certifying the source of the information.

Anti-replay service   Anti-replay election is based upon the receiver, meaning the service is effective only if the receiver checks the sequence number. In case you were wondering, a replay attack is when a hacker nicks a copy of an authenticated packet and later transmits it to the intended destination. When the duplicate, authenticated IP packet gets to the destination, it can disrupt services and generally wreak havoc. The *Sequence Number* field is designed to foil this type of attack.

Traffic flow   For traffic flow confidentiality to work, you have to have at least tunnel mode selected. It's most effective if it's implemented at a security gateway where tons of traffic amasses because it's precisely the kind of environment that can mask the true source-destination patterns to bad guys who are trying to breach your network's security.

Encryption

VPNs create a private network over a public network infrastructure, but to maintain confidentiality and security, we really need to use IPsec with our VPNs. IPsec uses various types of protocols to perform encryption. The types of encryption algorithms used today are as follows:

Symmetric encryption   This encryption requires a shared secret to encrypt and decrypt. Each computer encrypts the data before sending info across the network, with this same key being used to both encrypt and decrypt the data. Examples of symmetric key encryption are Data Encryption Standard (DES), Triple DES (3DES), and Advanced Encryption Standard (AES).

Asymmetric encryption   Devices that use asymmetric encryption use different keys for encryption than they do for decryption. These keys are called private and public keys.

Private keys encrypt a hash from the message to create a digital signature, which is then verified via decryption using the public key. Public keys encrypt a symmetric key for secure distribution to the receiving host, which then decrypts that symmetric key using its exclusively held private key. It's not possible to encrypt and decrypt using the same key. This is a variant of public key encryption that uses a combination of both a public and private keys. An example of an asymmetric encryption is Rivest, Shamir, and Adleman (RSA).

As you can see from the amount of information I've thrown at you so far, establishing a VPN connection between two sites takes study, time, and practice. And I am just scratching the surface here! I know it can be difficult at times, and it can take quite a bit of patience. Cisco does have some GUI interfaces to help with this process, and they can be very helpful for configuring VPNs with IPsec. Though highly useful and very interesting, they are just beyond the scope of this book, so I'm not going to delve further into this topic here.

GRE Tunnels

Generic Routing Encapsulation (GRE) is a tunneling protocol that can encapsulate many protocols inside IP tunnels. Some examples would be routing protocols such as EIGRP and OSPF and the routed protocol IPv6. Figure 7.23 shows the different pieces of a GRE header.

FIGURE 7.23   Generic Routing Encapsulation (GRE) tunnel structure

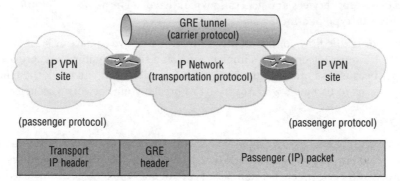

A GRE tunnel interface supports a header for each of the following:

- A passenger protocol or encapsulated protocols like IP or IPv6, which is the protocol being encapsulated by GRE

- GRE encapsulation protocol

- A transport delivery protocol, typically IP

GRE tunnels have the following characteristics:

- GRE uses a protocol-type field in the GRE header so any layer 3 protocol can be used through the tunnel.

- GRE is stateless and has no flow control.

- GRE offers no security.

- GRE creates additional overhead for tunneled packets—at least 24 bytes.

GRE over IPsec

As I just mentioned, GRE by itself provides no security—no form of payload confidentiality or encryption. If the packets are sniffed over the public networks, their contents are in plain-text, and although IPsec provides a secure method for tunneling data across an IP network, it has limitations.

IPsec does not support IP broadcast or IP multicast, preventing the use of protocols that need them, like routing protocols. IPsec also does not support the use of the multiprotocol traffic. GRE is a protocol that can be used to "carry" other passenger protocols like IP broadcast or IP multicast, as well as non-IP protocols. So using GRE tunnels with IPsec allows you to run a routing protocol, IP multicast, as well as multiprotocol traffic across your network.

With a generic hub-and-spoke topology (corp to branch, for example), you can implement static tunnels, typically GRE over IPsec, between the corporate office and branch offices. When you want to add a new spoke to the network, all you need to do is configure it on the hub router. The traffic between spokes has to traverse the hub, where it must exit one tunnel and enter another. Static tunnels can be an appropriate solution for small networks, but this solution actually becomes an unacceptable problem as the number of spokes grows larger and larger!

Cisco DMVPN (Cisco Proprietary)

The Cisco Dynamic Multipoint Virtual Private Network (DMVPN) feature enables you to easily scale large and small IPsec VPNs. The Cisco DMVPN is Cisco's answer to allow a corporate office to connect to branch offices with low cost, easy configuration, and flexibility. DMVPN has one central router, such as a corporate router, which is referred to as the hub, and the branches are called spokes. So the corporate to branch connection is referred to as the hub-and-spoke interconnection. Also supported is the spoke-to-spoke design used for branch-to-branch interconnections. If you're thinking this design sounds eerily similar to your old Frame Relay network, you're right! The DMPVN features enables you to configure a single GRE tunnel interface and a single IPsec profile on the hub router to manage all spoke routers, which keeps the size of the configuration on the hub router basically the same even if you add more spoke routers to the network. DMVPN also allows spoke router to dynamically create VPN tunnels between them as network data travels from one spoke to another.

Cisco IPsec VTI (Cisco Proprietary)

The IPsec Virtual Tunnel Interface (VTI) mode of an IPsec configuration can greatly simplify a VPN configuration when protection is needed for remote access. And it's a simpler option to GRE or L2TP for encapsulation and crypto maps used with IPsec. Like GRE, it sends routing protocol and multicast traffic, but you don't need the GRE protocol and all the overhead that brings. A nice simple configuration and routing adjacency directly over the VTI offers many benefits. Understand that all traffic is encrypted and that it supports only one protocol—either IPv4 or IPv6, just like standard IPsec.

Now let's take a look at how to configure a GRE tunnel. It's actually pretty simple.

Configuring GRE Tunnels

Before you attempt to configure a GRE tunnel, you need to create an implementation plan. Here's a checklist for what you need to configure and implement a GRE:

1. Use IP addressing.
2. Create the logical tunnel interfaces.
3. Specify that you're using GRE tunnel mode under the tunnel interface (this is optional since this is the default tunnel mode).
4. Specify the tunnel source and destination IP addresses.
5. Configure an IP address for the tunnel interface.

Let's take a look at how to bring up a simple GRE tunnel. Figure 7.24 shows the network with two routers.

FIGURE 7.24 Example of GRE configuration

First, we need to make the logical tunnel with the interface tunnel *number* command. We can use any number up to 2.14 billion.

```
Corp(config)#int s0/0/0
Corp(config-if)#ip address 63.1.1.1 255.255.255.252
Corp(config)#int tunnel ?
  <0-2147483647>  Tunnel interface number
Corp(config)#int tunnel 0
*Jan 5 16:58:22.719:%LINEPROTO-5-UPDOWN: Line protocol on Interface Tunnel0,
changed state to down
```

Once we have configured our interface and created the logical tunnel, we need to configure the mode and then the transport protocol.

```
Corp(config-if)#tunnel mode ?
  aurp    AURP TunnelTalk AppleTalk encapsulation
  cayman  Cayman TunnelTalk AppleTalk encapsulation
  dvmrp   DVMRP multicast tunnel
  eon     EON compatible CLNS tunnel
  gre     generic route encapsulation protocol
  ipip    IP over IP encapsulation
  ipsec   IPSec tunnel encapsulation
  iptalk  Apple IPTalk encapsulation
  ipv6    Generic packet tunneling in IPv6
  ipv6ip  IPv6 over IP encapsulation
  nos     IP over IP encapsulation (KA9Q/NOS compatible)
  rbscp   RBSCP in IP tunnel
Corp(config-if)#tunnel mode gre ?
  ip          over IP
  ipv6        over IPv6
  multipoint  over IP (multipoint)

Corp(config-if)#tunnel mode gre ip
```

Now that we've created the tunnel interface, the type, and the transport protocol, we must configure our IP addresses for use inside of the tunnel. Of course, you need to use your actual physical interface IP for the tunnel to send traffic across the Internet, but you also need to configure the tunnel source and tunnel destination addresses.

```
Corp(config-if)#ip address 192.168.10.1 255.255.255.0
Corp(config-if)#tunnel source 63.1.1.1
Corp(config-if)#tunnel destination 63.1.1.2

Corp#sho run interface tunnel 0
Building configuration...

Current configuration : 117 bytes
!
interface Tunnel0
 ip address 192.168.10.1 255.255.255.0
 tunnel source 63.1.1.1
 tunnel destination 63.1.1.2
end
```

Now let's configure the other end of the serial link and watch the tunnel pop up!

```
SF(config)#int s0/0/0
SF(config-if)#ip address 63.1.1.2 255.255.255.252
SF(config-if)#int t0
SF(config-if)#ip address 192.168.10.2 255.255.255.0
SF(config-if)#tunnel source 63.1.1.2
SF(config-if)#tun destination 63.1.1.1
*May 19 22:46:37.099: %LINEPROTO-5-UPDOWN: Line protocol on Interface Tunnel0,
changed state to up
```

Oops—did I forget to set my tunnel mode and transport to GRE and IP on the SF router? No, I didn't need to because it's the default tunnel mode on Cisco IOS. Nice! So, first I set the physical interface IP address (which used a global address even though I didn't have to), then I created the tunnel interface and set the IP address of the tunnel interface. It's really important that you remember to configure the tunnel interface with the actual source and destination IP addresses to use or the tunnel won't come up. In my example, the 63.1.1.2 was the source and 63.1.1.1 was the destination.

Verifying GRP Tunnels

As usual I'll start with my favorite troubleshooting command, show ip interface brief.

```
Corp#sh ip int brief
Interface        IP-Address    OK? Method Status          Protocol
FastEthernet0/0  10.10.10.5    YES manual up              up
```

```
Serial0/0          63.1.1.1        YES manual up                           up
FastEthernet0/1    unassigned      YES unset  administratively down down
Serial0/1          unassigned      YES unset  administratively down down
Tunnel0            192.168.10.1    YES manual up                           up
```

In this output, you can see that the tunnel interface is now showing as an interface on my router. You can see the IP address of the tunnel interface, and the Physical and Data Link status show as up/up. So far so good. Let's take a look at the interface with the show interfaces tunnel 0 command.

```
Corp#sh int tun 0
Tunnel0 is up, line protocol is up
  Hardware is Tunnel
  Internet address is 192.168.10.1/24
  MTU 1514 bytes, BW 9 Kbit, DLY 500000 usec,
     reliability 255/255, txload 1/255, rxload 1/255
  Encapsulation TUNNEL, loopback not set
  Keepalive not set
  Tunnel source 63.1.1.1, destination 63.1.1.2
  Tunnel protocol/transport GRE/IP
    Key disabled, sequencing disabled
    Checksumming of packets disabled
  Tunnel TTL 255
  Fast tunneling enabled
  Tunnel transmit bandwidth 8000 (kbps)
  Tunnel receive bandwidth 8000 (kbps)
```

The show interfaces command shows the configuration settings and the interface status as well as the IP address, tunnel source, and destination address. The output also shows the tunnel protocol, which is GRE/IP. Last, let's take a look at the routing table with the show ip route command.

```
Corp#sh ip route
[output cut]
    192.168.10.0/24 is subnetted, 2 subnets
C    192.168.10.0/24 is directly connected, Tunnel0
L    192.168.10.1/32 is directly connected, Tunnel0
    63.0.0.0/30 is subnetted, 2 subnets
C    63.1.1.0 is directly connected, Serial0/0
L    63.1.1.1/32 is directly connected, Serial0/0
```

The tunnel0 interface shows up as a directly connected interface, and although it's a logical interface, the router treats it as a physical interface, just like serial 0/0 in the routing table.

```
Corp#ping 192.168.10.2

Type escape sequence to abort.
Sending 5, 100-byte ICMP Echos to 192.168.10.2, timeout is 2 seconds:
!!!!!
Success rate is 100 percent (5/5)
```

Did you notice that I just pinged 192.168.10.2 across the Internet? I hope so! Anyway, there's one last thing I want to cover before we move on to EBGP, and that's troubleshooting an output, which is showing a tunnel routing error. If you configure your GRE tunnel and receive this GRE flapping message

```
          Line protocol on Interface Tunnel0, changed state to up
07:11:55: %TUN-5-RECURDOWN:
          Tunnel0 temporarily disabled due to recursive routing
07:11:59: %LINEPROTO-5-UPDOWN:
          Line protocol on Interface Tunnel0, changed state to down
07:12:59: %LINEPROTO-5-UPDOWN:
```

it means that you've misconfigured your tunnel, which will cause your router to try and route to the tunnel destination address using the tunnel interface itself!

Single-Homed EBGP

The *Border Gateway Protocol (BGP)* is perhaps one of the most well-known routing protocols in the world of networking. This is understandable because BGP is the routing protocol that powers the Internet and makes possible what we take for granted: connecting to remote systems on the other side of the country or planet. Because of its pervasive use, it's likely that each of us will have to deal with it at some point in our careers. So it's appropriate that we spend some time learning about BGP.

BGP version 4 has a long and storied history. Although the most recent definition was published in 1995 as RFC 1771 by Rekhter and Li, BGP's roots can be traced back to RFCs 827 and 904, which specified a protocol called the exterior gateway protocol (EGP). These earlier specifications date from 1982 and 1984, respectively—ages ago! Although BGP obsoletes EGP, it uses many of the techniques first defined by EGP and draws upon the many lessons learned from its use.

Way back in 1982, many organizations were connected to the ARPAnet, the noncommercial predecessor of the Internet. When a new network was added to ARPAnet, it would typically be added in a relatively unstructured way and would begin participating in a common routing protocol, the Gateway to Gateway Protocol (GGP). As you might expect, this solution did not scale well. GGP suffered from excessive overhead in managing large routing tables and from the difficulty of troubleshooting in an environment in which there was no central administrative control.

To address these deficiencies, EGP was developed, and with it the concept of *autonomous systems (ASs)*. RFC 827 was very clear in laying out the problems with GGP and in pointing out that a new type of routing protocol was required, an *exterior gateway protocol (EGP)*. The purpose of this new protocol was to facilitate the flow of traffic among a series of autonomous systems by exchanging information about routes contained in each system. The complexities of this network of networks, the Internet, would be hidden from the end user who simply views the Internet as a single address space through which they travel, unaware of the exact path they take.

The BGP that we know today flows directly from this work on EGP and builds upon it. So that you can get a better understanding of BGP, I will provide an overview of its features next.

Protocol Comparison and Overview

Because BGP is the first exterior gateway protocol we've encountered, I'll briefly compare it to a more familiar interior gateway protocol, like OSPF, so that we can put its features into context. After that comes a brief overview of BGP so that you can quickly become aware of its main capabilities.

Just to clarify things, with this comparison, I'm not implying that OSPF could be a substitute for BGP. In fact, there are a number of reasons that BGP is far better suited as an exterior gateway protocol than OSPF. For example, the requirement that all OSPF areas be connected to area 0 simply doesn't allow OSPF to scale to the size required by the Internet. Thousands of areas would have to connect to area 0, overwhelming it with route updates. In addition, OSPF uses a metric based on bandwidth, but in the context of the Internet, routing decisions are also based on political and business issues. OSPF does not have any mechanism to modify path selection based upon factors such as interconnection agreements between Internet service providers.

Although BGP can be thought of as just another routing protocol, the differences between it and protocols like OSPF are significant enough to catapult it into an entirely different category. Table 7.1 contains a comparison of BGP and OSPF.

TABLE 7.1   Comparison of BGP and OSPF

Characteristic	BGP	OSPF
Routing algorithm	Distance vector	Link state
Classless support	Yes	Yes
VLSM support	Yes	Yes
Summarization	Any BGP router	ASBR/ABR

Characteristic	BGP	OSPF
Metric	Various	Bandwidth
Hierarchy	No	Yes
Building blocks	Autonomous systems	Areas
Base protocol	TCP port 179	Protocol value 89
Traffic type	Unicast	Multicast
Neighbors	Specifically configured	Discovered/configured
Route exchange	Only with neighbors	Only with adjacent neighbors
Initial update	Synchronize database	Synchronize database
Update frequency	Incremental	Incremental with 60-minute timer
Hello timer	60 seconds	10 or 30 seconds
Hold timer	180 seconds	40 or 120 seconds
Internal route exchange	Internal BGP sessions	LSA Types 1 and 2
External route exchange	External BGP sessions	LSA Types 3, 4, and 5
Route updates	Contain network, attributes, AS path	Contain network, metric (Types 3 and 4 LSAs)
Network statement	Advertises network	Activates OSPF on interface
Special features	Route reflectors	Stub, totally stubby, NSSA areas

It's easy to get lost in the specific details of BGP, so at the risk of a small amount of repetition later on, the following is a high-level overview of the BGP protocol and its main characteristics as listed in Table 7.1.

BGP is a distance-vector protocol, which means that it advertises all or a portion of its route table to its neighbors. The advertised routes include the network being advertised, a list of attributes that influence the selection of the best path, the next-hop address through which the network can be reached, and a list of autonomous systems (ASs) through which the route update has passed. BGP routers use the list of autonomous systems to ensure a loop-free path by enforcing the rule that no AS path list is allowed to contain the same AS number twice.

BGP supports classless networks, the use of variable length subnet masks (VLSMs), and summarization. These characteristics allow BGP to work with networks that are not organized on purely classful boundaries and to create summaries of networks to reduce the size of the routing tables.

- BGP uses a rich variety of metrics called *attributes* to influence the selection of the best path to remote networks in the event that there are multiple advertised paths. Network administrators far removed from the initial origin of the advertised networks can manipulate these attributes. Paths can be chosen simply because a neighbor AS is preferred for political or economic reasons, thus overriding more traditional measures such as the distance to the advertised route.

- BGP supports a nonhierarchical network structure and allows a complex combination of interconnections among neighbors. There is no counterpart in BGP to the OSPF concept of area 0, which is the single area through which interarea traffic passes. Traffic between different BGP autonomous systems may follow a variety of different paths.

- BGP uses the concept of autonomous systems to define the boundaries of networks and treats communications among neighbors differently depending on whether the neighbors belong to the same autonomous system or not. An autonomous system is a collection of routers that are under a common administrative control and that present a common route policy to the outside world. It is not necessary that all of the routers run the same routing protocol, just that they all be controlled and coordinated by the same administrative authority.

- An AS uses BGP to advertise routes that are in its network and need to be visible outside of the network; it also uses BGP to learn about the reachability of routes by listening to advertisement announcements from other autonomous systems. Each AS can have a specific policy regarding the routes it wishes to advertise externally. These policies can be different for every point in which the AS attaches to the outside world.

- Inside autonomous networks, *interior gateway protocols (IGPs)* are used to discover the connectivity among a set of IP subnets. IGPs are well-known protocols such as the Routing Information Protocol (RIP), Interior Gateway Routing Protocol (IGRP), Open Shortest Path First (OSPF), and Enhanced Interior Gateway Routing Protocol (EIGRP).

BGP relies upon TCP for connection-oriented, acknowledged communications using port 179. BGP routers are specifically configured as neighbors of one another and use unicast packets to exchange route information, keepalives, and a variety of other messages. BGP routers go through a variety of stages as they establish communications with their configured neighbors, verify consistent parameter configuration, and begin the initial synchronization of their route information. After the initial synchronization is complete, BGP neighbors exchange updates on a triggered basis and monitor their connection state via periodic keepalives.

BGP neighbors either live in the same AS, in which case they are referred to as *internal BGP (iBGP) neighbors,* or live in different ASs, in which case they are referred to as *external BGP (eBGP) neighbors.* Internal BGP neighbors do not need to share a common network and can be separated by many other routers that don't need to run BGP. However, every iBGP router must be configured as a neighbor to every other iBGP router in the same area. External BGP neighbors are normally required to share a common network and are directly accessible to each other. There is no requirement that every eBGP router be a neighbor to every other eBGP router.

BGP can advertise networks that are learned dynamically, statically, or through redistribution. The network command, which is used in most other protocols to cause the router's interface(s) to begin listening for and sending route updates, is used in BGP routers to advertise specific networks. There are a number of rules, like the synchronization rule, that govern BGP's interaction with interior gateway protocols and the routes that are advertised as a result of this interaction.

Finally, BGP can implement a variety of mechanisms to improve scalability. Summarization is certainly one of these mechanisms, as is the use of route reflectors. Route reflectors provide a means to eliminate the requirement for a full mesh of neighbor relationships among iBGP neighbors, thus permitting larger BGP environments with less traffic.

Configuring and Verifying EBGP

If you're configuring BGP between a customer network and an ISP, this process is called external BGP (EBGP). If you're configuring BGP peers between two routers in the same AS, it's not considered EBGP.

You must have the basic information to configure EBGP:

- AS numbers (your own, and all remote AS numbers, which must be different)
- All the neighbors (peers) that are involved in BGP, and IP addressing that is used among the BGP neighbors
- Networks that need to be advertised into BGP

For an example of configuring EBGP, here's Figure 7.25.

FIGURE 7.25 Example of EBGP lay layout

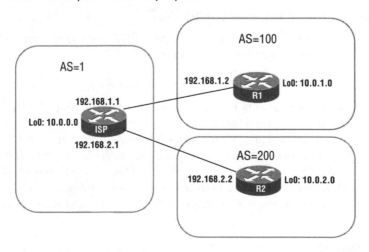

There are three main steps to configure basic BGP:

1. Define the BGP process.
2. Establish one or more neighbor relationships.
3. Advertise the local networks into BGP.

Define the BGP Process

To start the BGP process on a router, use the router bgp *AS* command. Each process must be assigned a local AS number. There can only be one BGP process in a router, which means that each router can only be in one AS at any given time.

Here is an example:

```
ISP#config t
ISP(config)#router bgp ?
<1-65535> Autonomous system number
ISP(config)#router bgp 1
```

Notice the AS number can be from 1 to 65,535.

Establish One or More Neighbor Relationships

Since BGP does not automatically discover neighbors like other routing protocols do, you have to explicitly configure them using the neighbor *peer-ip-address* remote-as *peer-as-number* command. Here is an example of configuring the ISP router in Figure 7.25:

```
ISP(config-router)#neighbor 192.168.1.2 remote-as 100
ISP(config-router)#neighbor 192.168.2.2 remote-as 200
```

Be sure to understand that the above command is the neighbor's IP address and neighbor's AS number.

Advertise the Local Networks Into BGP

To specify your local networks and advertise them into BGP, you use the network command with the mask keyword and then the subnet mask:

```
ISP(config-router)#network 10.0.0.0 mask 255.255.255.0
```

These network numbers must match what is found on the local router's forwarding table exactly, which can be seen with the show ip route or show ip int brief command. For other routing protocols, the network command has a different meaning. For OSPF and EIGRP, for example, the network command indicates the interfaces for which the routing protocol will send and receive route updates. In BGP, the network command indicates which routes should be injected into the BGP table on the local router.

Figure 7.25 displays the BGP routing configuration for the R1 and R2 routers:

```
R1#config t
R1(config)#router bgp 100
```

```
R1(config-router)#neighbor 192.168.1.1 remote-as 1
R1(config-router)#network 10.0.1.0 mask 255.255.255.0

R2#config t
R2(config)#router bgp 200
R2(config-router)#neighbor 192.168.2.1 remote-as 1
R2(config-router)#network 10.0.2.0 mask 255.255.255.0
```

That's it! Pretty simple. Now let's verify our configuration.

Verifying EBGP

We'll use the following commands to verify our little EBGP network.

- show ip bgp summary
- show ip bgp
- show ip bgp neighbors

The *show ip bgp summary* Command

The show ip bgp summary command gives you an overview of the BGP status. Each configured neighbor is listed in the output of the command. The output will display the IP address and AS number of the neighbor, along with the status of the session. You can use this information to verify that BGP sessions are up and established, or to verify the IP address and AS number of the configured BGP neighbor.

```
ISP#sh ip bgp summary
BGP router identifier 10.0.0.1, local AS number 1
BGP table version is 4, main routing table version 6
3 network entries using 396 bytes of memory
3 path entries using 156 bytes of memory
2/2 BGP path/bestpath attribute entries using 368 bytes of memory
3 BGP AS-PATH entries using 72 bytes of memory
0 BGP route-map cache entries using 0 bytes of memory
0 BGP filter-list cache entries using 0 bytes of memory
Bitfield cache entries: current 1 (at peak 1) using 32 bytes of memory
BGP using 1024 total bytes of memory
BGP activity 3/0 prefixes, 3/0 paths, scan interval 60 secs

Neighbor        V    AS MsgRcvd MsgSent   TblVer  InQ OutQ Up/Down State/PfxRcd
192.168.1.2     4   100      56      55        4    0    0 00:53:33           4
192.168.2.2     4   200      47      46        4    0    0 00:44:53           4
```

The first section of the show ip bgp summary command output describes the BGP table and its content:

- The router ID of the router and local AS number.

- The BGP table version is the version number of the local BGP table. This number is increased every time the table is changed.

The second section of the show ip bgp summary command output is a table in which the current neighbor statuses are shown. Here's information about what you see displayed in the output of this command:

- IP address of the neighbor.

- BGP version number that is used by the router when communicating with the neighbor (v4).

- AS number of the remote neighbor.

- Number of messages and updates that have been received from the neighbor since the session was established.

- Number of messages and updates that have been sent to the neighbor since the session was established.

- Version number of the local BGP table that has been included in the most recent update to the neighbor.

- Number of messages that are waiting to be processed in the incoming queue from this neighbor.

- Number of messages that are waiting in the outgoing queue for transmission to the neighbor.

- How long the neighbor has been in the current state and the name of the current state. Interestingly, notice there is no state listed, which is actually what you want because that means the peers are established.

- Number of received prefixes from the neighbor.

- ISP1 has two established sessions with the following neighbors:

  - 192.168.1.2, which is the IP address of R1 router and is in AS 100

  - 192.168.2.2, which is the IP address of R2 router and is in AS 200

- From each of the neighbors, ISP1 has received one prefix (one network).

Now, for the CCNA objectives, remember that if you see this type of output at the end of the show ip bgp summary command, that the BGP session is not established between peers:

```
Neighbor        V    AS MsgRcvd MsgSent   TblVer  InQ OutQ Up/Down State/PfxRcd
192.168.1.2     4    64       0       0        0    0    0 never    Active
```

Notice the state of Active. Remember, seeing no state output is good! Active means we're actively trying to establish with the peer.

The *show ip bgp* Command

With the show ip bgp command, the entire BGP table is displayed. A list of information about each route is displayed, so this is a nice command to get quick information on your BGP routes.

```
ISP#sh ip bgp
BGP table version is 4, local router ID is 10.0.0.1
Status codes: s suppressed, d damped, h history, * valid, > best, i - internal,
r RIB-failure, S Stale
Origin codes: i - IGP, e - EGP, ? - incomplete

Network Next Hop Metric LocPrf Weight Path
*> 10.0.0.0/24 0.0.0.0 0 0 32768 i
*> 10.0.1.0/24 192.168.1.2 0 0 0 100 i
*> 10.0.2.0/24 192.168.2.2 0 0 0 200 i
```

The output is sorted in network number order, and if the BGP table contains more than one route to the same network, the backup routes are displayed on separate lines. We don't have multiple routes, so none are shown.

The BGP path selection process selects one of the available routes to each of the networks as the best. This route is pointed out by the > character in the left column.

ISP1 has the following networks in the BGP table:

- 10.0.0.0/24, which is locally originated via the network command in BGP on the ISP router
- 10.0.1.0/24, which has been advertised from 192.168.1.2 (R1) neighbor
- 10.0.2.0/24, which has been advertised from 192.168.2.2 (R2) neighbor

Since the command displays all routing information, note that network 10.0.0.0/24, with the next-hop attribute set to 0.0.0.0, is also displayed. The next-hop attribute is set to 0.0.0.0 when you view the BGP table on the router that originates the route in BGP. The 10.0.0.0/24 network is the network that I locally configured on ISP1 into BGP.

The *show ip bgp neighbors* Command

The show ip bgp neighbors command provides more information about BGP connections to neighbors than the show ip bgp command does. This command can be used to get information about the TCP sessions and the BGP parameters of the session, as well as the showing the TCP timers and counters, and it's a long output! I'll just give you the top part of the command here:

```
ISP#sh ip bgp neighbors
BGP neighbor is 192.168.1.2, remote AS 100, external link
BGP version 4, remote router ID 10.0.1.1
BGP state = Established, up for 00:10:55
Last read 00:10:55, last write 00:10:55, hold time is 180, keepalive interval is
60 seconds
```

```
Neighbor capabilities:
Route refresh: advertised and received(new)
Address family IPv4 Unicast: advertised and received
Message statistics:
InQ depth is 0
OutQ depth is 0
[output cut]
```

Notice (and remember!) you can use the show ip bgp neighbors command to see the hold time on two BGP peers, and in the above example from the ISP to R1, the holdtime is 180 seconds.

Summary

In this chapter, you learned the difference between the following WAN services: cable, DSL, HDLC, PPP, and PPPoE. You also learned that you can use a VPN once any of those services are up and running as well as create and verify a tunnel interface.

It's so important for you to understand High-Level Data-Link Control (HDLC) and how to verify with the show interface command that HDLC is enabled! You've been provided with some really important HDLC information as well as information on how the Point-to-Point Protocol (PPP) is used if you need more features than HDLC offers or if you're using two different brands of routers. You now know that this is because various versions of HDLC are proprietary and won't work between two different vendors' routers.

When we went through the section on PPP, I discussed the various LCP options as well as the two types of authentication that can be used: PAP and CHAP.

We then discussed virtual private networks, IPsec, and encryption, and I explained GRE and how to configure the tunnel and then verify it.

We finished up the chapter with a discussion on BGP.

Exam Essentials

Remember the default serial encapsulation on Cisco routers.   Cisco routers use a proprietary High-Level Data-Link Control (HDLC) encapsulation on all their serial links by default.

Remember the PPP Data Link layer protocols.   The three Data Link layer protocols are Network Control Protocol (NCP), which defines the Network layer protocols; Link Control Protocol (LCP), a method of establishing, configuring, maintaining, and terminating the point-to-point connection; and High-Level Data-Link Control (HDLC), the MAC layer protocol that encapsulates the packets.

Be able to troubleshoot a PPP link.   Understand that a PPP link between two routers will show up and a ping would even work between the router if the layer 3 addresses are wrong.

Remember the various types of serial WAN connections. The serial WAN connections that are most widely used are HDLC, PPP, and Frame Relay.

Understand the term *virtual private network*. You need to understand why and how to use a VPN between two sites and the purpose that IPsec serves with VPNs.

Understand how to configure and verify a GRE tunnel. To configure GRE, first configure the logical tunnel with the `interface tunnel` *number* command. Configure the mode and transport, if needed, with the `tunnel mode` *mode protocol* command, then configure the IP addresses on the tunnel interfaces, the tunnel source and tunnel destination addresses, and your physical interfaces with global addresses. Verify with the `show interface tunnel` command as well as the Ping protocol.

Written Lab 7

You can find the answers to this lab in Appendix A, "Answers to Written Labs."
  Write the answers to the following WAN questions:

1. True/False: The IWAN allows transport-independent connectivity.

2. True/False: BGP runs between two peers in the same autonomous system (AS). It is referred to as External BGP (EBGP).

3. TCP port 179 is used for which protocol?

4. Which command can you use to know the hold time on the two BGP peers?

5. Which command will not tell you if the GRE tunnel is in up/up state?

6. True/False: A GRE tunnel is considered secure.

7. What protocol would you use if you were running xDSL and needed authentication?

8. What are the three protocols specified in PPP?

9. List two technologies that are examples of layer 2 MPLS VPN technologies.

10. List two VPNs that are examples of VPNs managed by service providers.

Hands-on Labs

In this section, you will configure Cisco routers in three different WAN labs using the figure supplied in each lab. (These labs are included for use with real Cisco routers but work perfectly with the LammleSim IOS version simulator and with Cisco's Packet Tracer program.)

  Lab 7.1: Configuring PPP Encapsulation and Authentication

  Lab 7.2: Configuring and Monitoring HDLC

  Lab 7.3: Configuring a GRE Tunnel

Hands-on Lab 7.1: Configuring PPP Encapsulation and Authentication

By default, Cisco routers use High-Level Data-Link Control (HDLC) as a point-to-point encapsulation method on serial links. If you are connecting to non-Cisco equipment, then you can use the PPP encapsulation method to communicate.

Labs 7.1 and 7.2 will have you configure the network in the following diagram.

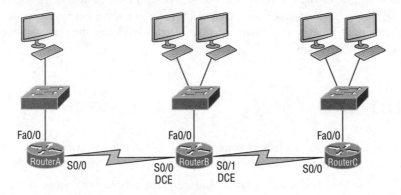

1. Type **sh int s0/0** on RouterA and RouterB to see the encapsulation method.

2. Make sure each router has the hostname assigned.

    ```
    RouterA#config t
    RouterA(config)#hostname RouterA

    RouterB#config t
    RouterB(config)#hostname RouterB
    ```

3. To change the default HDLC encapsulation method to PPP on both routers, use the encapsulation command at interface configuration. Both ends of the link must run the same encapsulation method.

    ```
    RouterA#Config t
    RouterA(config)#int s0
    RouterA(config-if)#encap ppp
    ```

4. Now go to RouterB and set serial 0/0 to PPP encapsulation.

    ```
    RouterB#config t
    RouterB(config)#int s0
    RouterB(config-if)#encap ppp
    ```

5. Verify the configuration by typing **sh int s0/0** on both routers.

6. Notice the IPCP and CDPCP (assuming the interface is up). This is the information used to transmit the upper-layer (Network layer) information across the HDLC at the MAC sublayer.

7. Define a username and password on each router. Notice that the username is the name of the remote router. Also, the password must be the same.

```
RouterA#config t
RouterA(config)#username RouterB password todd

RouterB#config t
RouterB(config)#username RouterA password todd
```

8. Enable CHAP or PAP authentication on each interface.

```
RouterA(config)#int s0
RouterA(config-if)#ppp authentication chap

RouterB(config)#int s0
RouterB(config-if)#ppp authentication chap
```

9. Verify the PPP configuration on each router by using these commands.

```
RouterB(config-if)#shut
RouterB(config-if)#debug ppp authentication
RouterB(config-if)#no shut
```

Hands-on Lab 7.2: Configuring and Monitoring HDLC

There really is no configuration required for HDLC (as it is the default configuration on Cisco serial interfaces), but if you completed Lab 7.1, then the PPP encapsulation would be set on both routers. This is why I put the PPP lab first. This lab allows you to actually configure HDLC encapsulation on a router.

For this second lab, you will use the same configuration you used for Lab 7.1.

1. Set the encapsulation for each serial interface by using the `encapsulation hdlc` command.

```
RouterA#config t
RouterA(config)#int s0
RouterA(config-if)#encapsulation hdlc
```

```
RouterB#config t
RouterB(config)#int s0
RouterB(config-if)#encapsulation hdlc
```

2. Verify the HDLC encapsulation by using the show interface s0 command on each router.

Hands-on Lab 7.3: Configuring a GRE Tunnel

In this lab you will configure two point-to-point routers with a simple IP GRE tunnel. You can use a real router, LammleSim IOS version, or Packet Tracer to do this lab.

1. First, configure the logical tunnel with the interface tunnel number command.

```
Corp(config)#int s0/0/0
Corp(config-if)#ip address 63.1.1.2 255.255.255.252
Corp(config)#int tunnel ?
  <0-2147483647>  Tunnel interface number
Corp(config)#int tunnel 0
*Jan  5 16:58:22.719: %LINEPROTO-5-UPDOWN: Line protocol
on Interface Tunnel0, changed state to down
```

2. Once you have configured your interface and created the logical tunnel, you need to configure the mode and then the transport protocol.

```
Corp(config-if)#tunnel mode ?
  aurp     AURP TunnelTalk AppleTalk encapsulation
  cayman   Cayman TunnelTalk AppleTalk encapsulation
  dvmrp    DVMRP multicast tunnel
  eon      EON compatible CLNS tunnel
  gre      generic route encapsulation protocol
  ipip     IP over IP encapsulation
  ipsec    IPSec tunnel encapsulation
  iptalk   Apple IPTalk encapsulation
  ipv6     Generic packet tunneling in IPv6
  ipv6ip   IPv6 over IP encapsulation
  nos      IP over IP encapsulation (KA9Q/NOS compatible)
  rbscp    RBSCP in IP tunnel
Corp(config-if)#tunnel mode gre ?
  ip         over IP
  ipv6       over IPv6
  multipoint over IP (multipoint)

Corp(config-if)#tunnel mode gre ip
```

3. Now that you have created the tunnel interface, the type, and the transport protocol, you need to configure your IP addresses. Of course, you need to use your actual interface IP for the tunnel, but you also need to configure the tunnel source and tunnel destination addresses.

```
Corp(config-if)#int t0
Corp(config-if)#ip address 192.168.10.1 255.255.255.0
Corp(config-if)#tunnel source 63.1.1.1
Corp(config-if)#tunnel destination 63.1.1.2

Corp#sho run interface tunnel 0
Building configuration...

Current configuration : 117 bytes
!
interface Tunnel0
 ip address 192.168.10.1 255.255.255.0
 tunnel source 63.1.1.1
 tunnel destination 63.1.1.2
end
```

4. Now configure the other end of the serial link and watch the tunnel pop up!

```
SF(config)#int s0/0/0
SF(config-if)#ip address 63.1.1.2 255.255.255.252
SF(config-if)#int t0
SF(config-if)#ip address 192.168.10.2 255.255.255.0
SF(config-if)#tunnel source 63.1.1.2
SF(config-if)#tun destination 63.1.1.1
*May 19 22:46:37.099: %LINEPROTO-5-UPDOWN: Line protocol on Interface
Tunnel0, changed state to up
```

Remember, you don't need to configure your tunnel mode and transport protocol because GRE and IP are the defaults. It's really important that you remember to configure the tunnel interface with the actual source and destination IP addresses to use or the tunnel won't come up. In my example, 63.1.1.2 was the source and 63.1.1.1 was the destination.

5. Verify with the following commands:

```
Corp#sh ip int brief
```

You should see that the tunnel interface is now showing as an interface on your router. The IP address of the tunnel interface and the physical and data link status shows as up/up.

```
Corp#sh int tun 0
```

The show interfaces command shows the configuration settings and the interface status as well as the IP address and tunnel source and destination address.

Corp#**sh ip route**

The tunnel0 interface shows up as a directly connected interface, and although it's a logical interface, the router treats it as a physical interface just like serial0/0 in the routing table.

Review Questions

The following questions are designed to test your understanding of this chapter's material. For more information on how to get additional questions, please see www.lammle.com/ccna.

You can find the answers to these questions in Appendix B, "Answers to Review Questions."

1. Which command will display the CHAP authentication process as it occurs between two routers in the network?

    A. show chap authentication

    B. show interface serial 0

    C. debug ppp authentication

    D. debug chap authentication

2. Which of the following are true regarding the following command? (Choose two.)

    R1(config-router)# **neighbor 10.10.200.1 remote-as 6200**

    A. The local router R1 uses AS 6200.

    B. The remote router uses AS 6200.

    C. The local interface of R1 is 10.10.200.1.

    D. The neighbor IP address is 10.10.200.1.

    E. The neighbor's loopback interface is 10.10.200.1.

3. BGP uses which Transport layer protocol and port number?

    A. UDP/123

    B. TCP/123

    C. UDP/179

    D. TCP/179

    E. UDP/169

    F. TCP/169

4. Which command can you use to know the hold time on the two BGP peers?

    A. show ip bgp

    B. show ip bgp summary

    C. show ip bgp all

    D. show ip bgp neighbor

5. What does a next hop of 0.0.0.0 mean in the show ip bgp command output?

```
    Network            Next Hop          Metric LocPrf Weight Path
 *> 10.1.1.0/24        0.0.0.0                0          32768 ?
 *> 10.13.13.0/24      0.0.0.0                0          32768 ?
```

   A. The router does not know the next hop.

   B. The network is locally originated via the network command in BGP.

   C. It is not a valid network.

   D. The next hop is not reachable.

6. Which two of the following are GRE characteristics? (Choose two.)

   A. GRE encapsulation uses a protocol-type field in the GRE header to support the encapsulation of any OSI layer 3 protocol.

   B. GRE itself is stateful. It includes flow-control mechanisms, by default.

   C. GRE includes strong security mechanisms to protect its payload.

   D. The GRE header, together with the tunneling IP header, creates at least 24 bytes of additional overhead for tunneled packets.

7. A GRE tunnel is flapping with the following error message:

```
07:11:49: %LINEPROTO-5-UPDOWN:
          Line protocol on Interface Tunnel0, changed state to up
07:11:55: %TUN-5-RECURDOWN:
          Tunnel0 temporarily disabled due to recursive routing
07:11:59: %LINEPROTO-5-UPDOWN:
          Line protocol on Interface Tunnel0, changed state to down
07:12:59: %LINEPROTO-5-UPDOWN:
```

What could be the reason for the tunnel flapping?

   A. IP routing has not been enabled on tunnel interface.

   B. There's an MTU issue on the tunnel interface.

   C. The router is trying to route to the tunnel destination address using the tunnel interface itself.

   D. An access list is blocking traffic on the tunnel interface.

8. Which of the following commands will not tell you if the GRE tunnel 0 is in up/up state?

   A. show ip interface brief

   B. show interface tunnel 0

   C. show ip interface tunnel 0

   D. show run interface tunnel 0

9. Which of the following PPP authentication protocols authenticates a device on the other end of a link with an encrypted password?

    A. MD5

    B. PAP

    C. CHAP

    D. DES

10. Which of the following encapsulates PPP frames in Ethernet frames and uses common PPP features like authentication, encryption, and compression?

    A. PPP

    B. PPPoA

    C. PPPoE

    D. Token Ring

11. Shown is the output of a `show interfaces` command on an interface that is configured to use PPP. A ping of the IP address on the other end of the link fails. Which two of the following could be the reason for the problem? (Choose two.)

```
R1# show interfaces serial 0/0/1
Serial0/0/0 is up, line protocol is down
  Hardware is GT96K Serial
Internet address is 10.0.1.1/30
```

    A. The CSU/DSU connected to the other router is not powered on.

    B. The IP address on the router at the other end of the link is not in subnet 192.168.2.0/24.

    C. CHAP authentication failed.

    D. The router on the other end of the link has been configured to use HDLC.

12. You have configured a serial interface with GRE IP commands on a corporate router with a point-to-point link to a remote office. What command will show you the IP addresses and tunnel source and destination addresses of the interfaces?

    A. `show int serial 0/0`

    B. `show ip int brief`

    C. `show interface tunnel 0`

    D. `show tunnel ip status`

    E. `debug ip interface tunnel`

13. Which of the following is true regarding WAN technologies? (Choose three.)

    A. You must use PPP on a link connecting two routers using a point-to-point lease line.

    B. You can use a T1 to connect a customer site to the ISP.

    C. You can use a T1 to connect a Frame Relay connection to the ISP.

   D. You can use Ethernet as a WAN service by using EoMPLS.

   E. When using an Ethernet WAN, you must configure the DLCI.

14. You want to allow remote users to send protected packets to the corporate site, but you don't want to install software on the remote client machines. What is the best solution that you could implement?

   A. GRE tunnel

   B. Web VPN

   C. VPN Anywhere

   D. IPsec

15. Why won't the serial link between the Corp router and the Remote router come up?

```
Corp#sh int s0/0
Serial0/0 is up, line protocol is down
  Hardware is PowerQUICC Serial
  Internet address is 10.0.1.1/24
  MTU 1500 bytes, BW 1544 Kbit, DLY 20000 usec,
     reliability 254/255, txload 1/255, rxload 1/255
  Encapsulation PPP, loopback not set
Remote#sh int s0/0
Serial0/0 is up, line protocol is down
  Hardware is PowerQUICC Serial
  Internet address is 10.0.1.2/24
  MTU 1500 bytes, BW 1544 Kbit, DLY 20000 usec,
     reliability 254/255, txload 1/255, rxload 1/255
  Encapsulation HDLC, loopback not set
```

   A. The serial cable is faulty.

   B. The IP addresses are not in the same subnet.

   C. The subnet masks are not correct.

   D. The keepalive settings are not correct.

   E. The layer 2 frame types are not compatible.

16. Which of the following are benefits of using a VPN in your internetwork? (Choose three.)

   A. Security

   B. Private high-bandwidth links

   C. Cost savings

   D. Incompatibility with broadband technologies

   E. Scalability

17. Which two technologies are examples of layer 2 MPLS VPN technologies? (Choose two.)

  A. VPLS

  B. DMVPM

  C. GETVPN

  D. VPWS

18. Which of the following is an industry-wide standard suite of protocols and algorithms that allows for secure data transmission over an IP-based network that functions at the layer 3 (Network layer) of the OSI model?

  A. HDLC

  B. Cable

  C. VPN

  D. IPsec

  E. xDSL

19. Which of the following describes the creation of private networks across the Internet, enabling privacy and tunneling of non-TCP/IP protocols?

  A. HDLC

  B. Cable

  C. VPN

  D. IPsec

  E. xDSL

20. Which two VPNs are examples of service provider–managed VPNs? (Choose two.)

  A. Remote-access VPN

  B. Layer 2 MPLS VPN

  C. Layer 3 MPLS VPN

  D. DMVPN

Chapter

8

Evolution of Intelligent Networks

THE FOLLOWING ICND2 EXAM TOPICS ARE COVERED IN THIS CHAPTER:

- ✓ **1.6 Describe the benefits of switch stacking and chassis aggregation**

- ✓ **4.2 Describe the effects of cloud resources on enterprise network architecture**
  - 4.2.a Traffic path to internal and external cloud services
  - 4.2.b Virtual services
  - 4.2.c Basic virtual network infrastructure

- ✓ **4.3 Describe basic QoS concepts**
  - 4.3.a Marking
  - 4.3.b Device trust
  - 4.3.c Prioritization
  - 4.3.c.
  - (i) Voice 4.3.c.
  - (ii) Video 4.3.c.
  - (iii) Data
  - 4.3.d Shaping
  - 4.3.e Policing
  - 4.3.f Congestion management

- ✓ **4.5 Verify ACLs using the APIC-EM Path Trace ACL analysis tool**

- ✓ **5.5 Describe network programmability in enterprise network architecture**
  - 5.5.a Function of a controller
  - 5.5.b Separation of control plane and data plane
  - 5.5.c Northbound and southbound APIs

This all-new chapter is totally focused on the CCNA objectives for intelligent networks. I'll start by covering switch stacking using StackWise and then move on to discuss the important realm of cloud computing and its effect on the enterprise network.

I'm going to stick really close to the objectives on the more difficult subjects to help you tune in specifically to the content that's important for the CCNA, including the following: Software Defined Networking (SDN), application programming interfaces (APIs), Cisco's Application Policy Infrastructure Controller Enterprise Module (APIC-EM), Intelligent WAN, and finally, quality of service (QoS). While it's good to understand the cloud and SDN because they're certainly objectives for the CCNA, just know that they aren't as critical for the objectives as the QoS section found in this chapter.

In this chapter, I really only have the space to introduce the concepts of network programmability and SDN because the topic is simply too large in scope. Plus, this chapter is already super challenging because it's a foundational chapter containing no configurations. Just remember that I'm going to spotlight the objectives in this chapter to make this chapter and its vital content as potent but painless as possible! We'll check off every exam objective by the time we're through.

To find up-to-the-minute updates for this chapter, please see www.lammle .com/ccna or the book's web page at www.sybex.com/go/ccna.

Switch Stacking

It's hard to believe that Cisco is using switch stacking to start their "Evolution of Intelligent Networks" objectives because switch stacking has been around since the word *cloud* meant 420 in my home town of Boulder, but I digress.

A typical access closet contains access switches placed next to each other in the same rack and uses high-speed redundant links with copper, or more typically fiber, to the distribution layer switches.

Here are three big drawbacks to a typical switch topology:

- Management overhead is high.

- STP will block half of the uplinks.

- There is no direct communication between switches.

Cisco StackWise technology connects switches that are mounted in the same rack together so they basically become one larger switch. By doing this, you can incrementally add more access ports for each closet while avoiding the cost of upgrading to a bigger switch. So you're adding ports as you grow your company instead of front loading the investment into a pricier, larger switch all at once. And since these stacks are managed as a single unit, it reduces the management in your network.

All switches in a stack share configuration and routing information, so you can easily add or remove switches at any time without disrupting your network or affecting its performance.

Figure 8.1 shows a typical access layer StackWise unit.

FIGURE 8.1   Switch stacking

To create a StackWise unit, you combine individual switches into a single, logical unit using special stack interconnect cables as shown in Figure 8.1. This creates a bidirectional, closed-loop path in the stack.

Here are some other features of StackWise:

- Any changes to the network topology or routing information are updated continuously through the stack interconnect.

- A master switch manages the stack as a single unit. The master switch is elected from one of the stack member switches.

- You can join up to nine separate switches in a stack.

- Each stack of switches has only a single IP address, and the stack is managed as a single object. You'll use this single IP address for managing the stack, including fault detection, VLAN database updates, security, and QoS controls. Each stack has only one configuration file, which is distributed to each switch in the StackWise.

- Using Cisco StackWise will produce some management overhead, but at the same time, multiple switches in a stack can create an EtherChannel connection, eliminating the need for STP.

These are the benefits to using StackWise technology, specifically mapped to the CCNA objectives to memorize:

- StackWise provides a method to join multiple physical switches into a single logical switching unit.

- Switches are united by special interconnect cables.

- The master switch is elected.
- The stack is managed as a single object and has a single management IP address.
- Management overhead is reduced.
- STP is no longer needed if you use EtherChannel.
- Up to nine switches can be in a StackWise unit.

One more very cool thing…When you add a new switch to the stack, the master switch automatically configures the unit with the currently running IOS image as well as the configuration of the stack. So you don't have to do anything to bring up the switch before its ready to operate…nice!

Cloud Computing and Its Effect on the Enterprise Network

Cloud computing is by far one of the hottest topics in today's IT world. Basically, cloud computing can provide virtualized processing, storage, and computing resources to users remotely, making the resources transparently available regardless of the user connection. To put it simply, some people just refer to the cloud as "someone else's hard drive." This is true, of course, but the cloud is much more than just storage.

The history of the consolidation and virtualization of our servers tells us that this has become the de facto way of implementing servers because of basic resource efficiency. Two physical servers will use twice the amount of electricity as one server, but through virtualization, one physical server can host two virtual machines, hence the main thrust toward virtualization. With it, network components can simply be shared more efficiently.

Users connecting to a cloud provider's network, whether it be for storage or applications, really don't care about the underlying infrastructure because as computing becomes a service rather than a product, it's then considered an on-demand resource, described in Figure 8.2.

FIGURE 8.2   Cloud computing is on-demand.

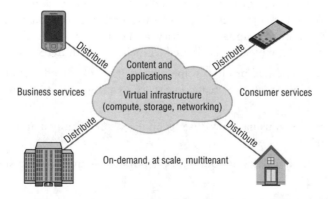

Centralization/consolidation of resources, automation of services, virtualization, and standardization are just a few of the big benefits cloud services offer. Let's take a look in Figure 8.3.

FIGURE 8.3 Advantages of cloud computing

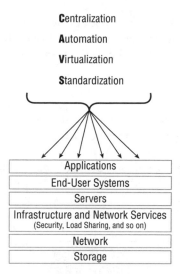

Cloud computing has several advantages over the traditional use of computer resources. Following are advantages to the provider and to the cloud user.

Here are the advantages to a cloud service builder or provider:

- Cost reduction, standardization, and automation
- High utilization through virtualized, shared resources
- Easier administration
- Fall-in-place operations model

Here are the advantages to cloud users:

- On-demand, self-service resource provisioning
- Fast deployment cycles
- Cost effective
- Centralized appearance of resources
- Highly available, horizontally scaled application architectures
- No local backups

Having centralized resources is critical for today's workforce. For example, if you have your documents stored locally on your laptop and your laptop gets stolen, you're pretty much screwed unless you're doing constant local backups. That is so 2005!

After I lost my laptop and all the files for the book I was writing at the time, I swore (yes, I did that too) to never have my files stored locally again. I started using only Google

Drive, OneDrive, and Dropbox for all my files, and they became my best backup friends. If I lose my laptop now, I just need to log in from any computer from anywhere to my service provider's logical drives and presto, I have all my files again. This is clearly a simple example of using cloud computing, specifically SaaS (which is discussed next), and it's wonderful!

So cloud computing provides for the sharing of resources, lower cost operations passed to the cloud consumer, computing scaling, and the ability to dynamically add new servers without going through the procurement and deployment process.

Service Models

Cloud providers can offer you different available resources based on your needs and budget. You can choose just a vitalized network platform or go all in with the network, OS, and application resources.

Figure 8.4 shows the three service models available depending on the type of service you choose to get from a cloud.

FIGURE 8.4 Cloud computing service

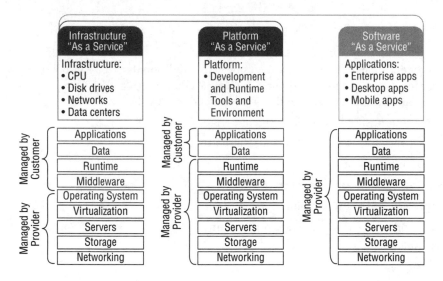

You can see that IaaS allows the customer to manage most of the network, whereas SaaS doesn't allow any management by the customer, and PaaS is somewhere in the middle of the two. Clearly, choices can be cost driven, so the most important thing is that the customer pays only for the services or infrastructure they use.

Let's take a look at each service:

Infrastructure as a Service (IaaS): Provides only the network. Delivers computer infrastructure—a platform virtualization environment—where the customer has the most control and management capability.

Platform as a Service (PaaS): Provides the operating system and the network.   Delivers a computing platform and solution stack, allowing customers to develop, run, and manage applications without the complexity of building and maintaining the infrastructure typically associated with developing and launching an application. An example is Windows Azure.

Software as a Service (SaaS): Provides the required software, operating system, and network.   SaaS is common application software such as databases, web servers, and email software that's hosted by the SaaS vendor. The customer accesses this software over the Internet. Instead of having users install software on their computers or servers, the SaaS vendor owns the software and runs it on computers in its data center. Microsoft Office 365 and many Amazon Web Services (AWS) offerings are perfect examples of SaaS.

So depending on your business requirements and budget, cloud service providers market a very broad offering of cloud computing products from highly specialized offerings to a large selection of services.

What's nice here is that you're is offered a fixed price for each service that you use, which allows you to easily budget wisely for the future. It's true—at first, you'll have to spend a little cash on staff training, but with automation you can do more with less staff because administration will be easier and less complex. All of this works to free up the company resources to work on new business requirements and be more agile and innovative in the long run.

Overview of Network Programmability in Enterprise Network

Right now in our current, traditional networks, our router and switch ports are the only devices that are not virtualized. So this is what we're really trying to do here—virtualize our physical ports.

First, understand that our current routers and switches run an operating system, such as Cisco IOS, that provides network functionality. This has worked well for us for 25 years or so, but it is way too cumbersome now to configure, implement, and troubleshoot these autonomous devices in today's large, complicated networks. Before you even get started, you have to understand the business requirements and then push that out to all the devices. This can take weeks or even months since each device is configured, maintained, and monitored separately.

Before we can talk about the new way to network our ports, you need to understand how our current networks forward data, which happens via these two planes:

Data plane   This plane, also referred to as the forwarding plane, is physically responsible for forwarding frames of packets from its ingress to egress interfaces using protocols managed in the control plane. Here, data is received, the destination interface is looked up, and the forwarding of frames and packets happens, so the data plane relies completely on the control plane to provide solid information.

Control plane   This plane is responsible for managing and controlling any forwarding table that the data plane uses. For example, routing protocols such as OSPF, EIGRP, RIP, and BGP as well as IPv4 ARP, IPv6 NDP, switch MAC address learning, and STP are all managed by the control plane.

Now that you understand that there are two planes used to forward traffic in our current or legacy network, let's take a look at the future of networking.

Application Programming Interfaces (APIs)

If you have worked on any enterprise Wi-Fi installations in the last decade, you would have designed your physical network and then configured a type of network controller that managed all the wireless APs in the network. It's hard to imagine that anyone would install a wireless network today without some type of controller in an enterprise network, where the access points (APs) receive their directions from the controller on how to manage the wireless frames and the APs have no operating system or brains to make many decisions on their own.

The same is now true for our physical router and switch ports, and it's precisely this centralized management of network frames and packets that Software Defined Networking (SDN) provides to us.

SDN removes the control plane intelligence from the network devices by having a central controller manage the network instead of having a full operating system (Cisco IOS, for example) on the devices. In turn, the controller manages the network by separating the control and data (forwarding) planes, which automates configuration and the remediation of all devices.

So instead of the network devices each having individual control planes, we now have a centralized control plane, which consolidates all network operations in the SDN controller. APIs allow for applications to control and configure the network without human intervention. The APIs are another type of configuration interface just like the CLI, SNMP, or GUI interfaces, which facilitate machine-to-machine operations.

The SDN architecture slightly differs from the architecture of traditional networks by adding a third layer, the application plane, as described here and shown in Figure 8.5:

Data (or forwarding) plane   Contains network elements, meaning any physical or virtual device that deals with data traffic.

Control plane   Usually a software solution, the SDN controllers reside here to provide centralized control of the router and switches that populate the data plane, removing the control plane from individual devices.

Application plane   This new layer contains the applications that communicate their network requirements toward the controller using APIs.

FIGURE 8.5 The SDN architecture

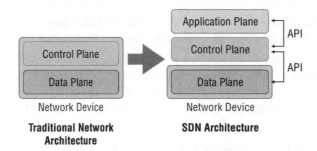

SDN is pretty cool because your applications tell the network what to do based on business needs instead of you having to do it. Then the controller uses the APIs to pass instructions on to your routers, switches, or other network gear. So instead of taking weeks or months to push out a business requirement, the solution now only takes minutes.

There are two sets of APIs that SDN uses and they are very different. As you already know, the SDN controller uses APIs to communicate with both the application and data plane. Communication with the data plane is defined with southbound interfaces, while services are offered to the application plane using the northbound interface. Let's take a deeper look at this oh-so-vital CCNA objective.

Southbound APIs

Logical southbound interface (SBI) APIs (or device-to-control-plane interfaces) are used for communication between the controllers and network devices. They allow the two devices to communicate so that the controller can program the data plane forwarding tables of your routers and switches. SBIs are pictured in Figure 8.6.

FIGURE 8.6 Southbound interfaces

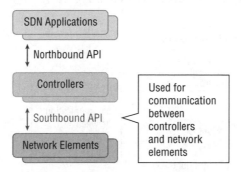

Since all the network drawings had the network gear below the controller, the APIs that talked to the devices became known as southbound, meaning, "out the southbound interface of the controller." And don't forget that with SDN, the term *interface* is no longer referring to a physical interface!

Unlike northbound APIs, southbound APIs have many standards, and you absolutely must know them well for the objectives. Let's talk about them now:

OpenFlow   Describes an industry-standard API, which the ONF (opennetworking.org) defines. It configures white label switches, meaning that they are nonproprietary, and as a result defines the flow path through the network. All the configuration is done through NETCONF.

NETCONF   Although not all devices support NETCONF yet, what this provides is a network management protocol standardized by the IETF. Using RPC, you can install, manipulate, and delete the configuration of network devices using XML.

 NETCONF is a protocol that allows you to modify the configuration of a networking device, but if you want to modify the device's forwarding table, then the OpenFlow protocol is the way to go.

onePK   A Cisco proprietary SBI that allows you to inspect or modify the network element configuration without hardware upgrades. This makes life easier for developers by providing software development kits for Java, C, and Python.

OpFlex   The name of the southbound API in the Cisco ACI world is OpFlex, an open-standard, distributed control system. Understand that OpenFlow first sends detailed and complex instructions to the control plane of the network elements in order to implement a new application policy—something called an imperative SDN model. On the other hand, OpFlex uses a declarative SDN model because the controller, which Cisco calls the APIC, sends a more abstract, "summary policy" to the network elements. The summary policy makes the controller believe that the network elements will implement the required changes using their own control planes, since the devices will use a partially centralized control plane.

Northbound APIs

To communicate from the SDN controller and the applications running over the network, you'll use northbound interfaces (NBIs), pictured in Figure 8.7.

FIGURE 8.7   Northbound interfaces

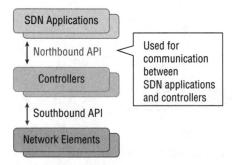

By setting up a framework that allows the application to demand the network setup with the configuration that it needs, the NBIs allow your applications to manage and control the network. This is priceless for saving time because you no longer need to adjust and tweak your network to get a service or application running correctly.

The NBI applications include a wide variety of automated network services, from network virtualization and dynamic virtual network provisioning to more granular firewall monitoring, user identity management, and access policy control. This allows for cloud orchestration applications that tie together, for server provisioning, storage, and networking that enables a complete rollout of new cloud services in minutes instead of weeks!

Sadly, at this writing there is no single northbound interface that you can use for communication between the controller and all applications. So instead, you use various and sundry northbound APIs, with each one working only with a specific set of applications.

Most of the time, applications used by NBIs will be on the same system as the APIC controller, so the APIs don't need to send messages over the network since both programs run on the same system. However, if they don't reside on the same system, REST (Representational State Transfer) comes into play; it uses HTTP messages to transfer data over the API for applications that sit on different hosts.

Cisco APIC-EM

Cisco Application Policy Infrastructure Controller Enterprise Module (APIC-EM) is a Cisco SDN controller, which uses the previously mentioned open APIs for policy-based management and security through a single controller, abstracting the network and making network services simpler. APIC-EM provides centralized automation of policy-based application profiles, and the APIC-EM northbound interface is the only API that you'll need to control your network programmatically. Through this programmability, automated network control helps IT to respond quickly to new business opportunities. The APIC-EM also includes support for greenfield (new installations) and brownfield (current or old installations) deployments, which allows you to implement programmability and automation with the infrastructure that you already have.

APIC-EM is pretty cool, easy to use (that's up for debate), and automates the tasks that network engineers have been doing for well over 20 years. At first glance this seems like it will replace our current jobs, and in some circumstances, people resistant to change will certainly be replaced. But you don't have to be one of them if you start planning now. Figure 8.8 demonstrates exactly where the APCI-EM controller sits in the SDN stack.

FIGURE 8.8   Where APIC-EM fits in the SDN stack

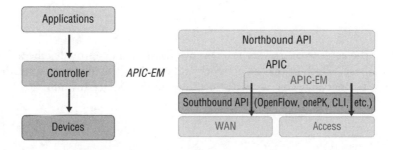

Cisco APIC-EM's northbound interface is only an API, but southbound interfaces are implemented with something called a service abstraction layer (SAL), which talks to the network elements via SNMP and CLI. Using the SNMP and the CLI allows APIC-EM to work with legacy Cisco products, and soon APIC-EM will be able to use NETCONF too.

The network devices can be either physical or virtual, including Nexus data center switches, ASA firewalls, ASR routers, or even third-party load balancers. The managed devices must be specific to ACI; in other words, a special NX-OS or ASR IOS version is required to add the southbound APIs required to communicate with the APIC controller.

The APIC-EM API is REST based, which as you know allows you to discover and control your network using HTTP by using the GET, POST, PUT, and DELETE options along with JSON (JavaScript Object Notation) and XML (eXtensible Markup Language) syntax.

Here are some important features of Cisco APIC-EM that are covered in the CCNA objectives, and shown in Figure 8.9:

FIGURE 8.9   APIC-Enterprise Module

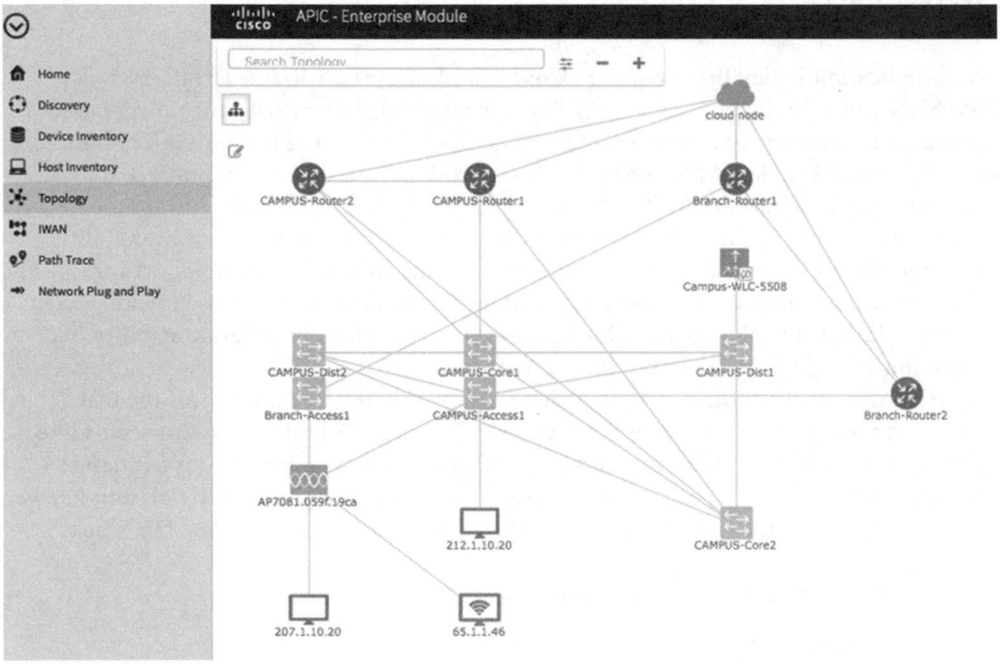

On the left of the screen you can see the Discover button. This provides the network information database, which scans the network and provides the inventory, including all network devices; the network devices are also shown in the Device Inventory.

There's also a network topology visualization, which reveals the physical topology discovered, as shown in the layout on Figure 8.9. This auto-discovers and maps network devices to a physical topology with detailed device-level data, including the discovered hosts. And take note of that IWAN button. It provides the provisioning of IWAN network profiles with simple business policies. Plus there is a Path Trace button, which I will talk about next.

But wait… Before I move on to the Path Trace functionality of APIC-EM, let me go over a few more promising features with you. In the APIC-EM is the Zero-Touch Deployment feature, which finds a new device via the controller scanner and automatically configures it. You can track user identities and endpoints by exchanging the information with the Cisco Identity Service Engine (Cisco ISE) via the Identity Manager. You can also quickly set and enforce QoS priority policies with the QoS deployment and change management feature and accelerate ACL management by querying and analyzing ACLs on each network device. This means you can quickly identify ACL misconfiguration using the ACL analysis! And last but not least, using the Policy Manager, the controller translates a business policy into a network-device-level policy. The Policy Manager can enforce the policy for a specific user at various times of the day, across wired and wireless networks.

Now let's take a look at the very vital path tracing feature of APIC-EM.

Using APIC-EM for Path Tracing

An important objective in this intelligent networks chapter is the path tracing ability in the APIC-EM. Matter of fact, I've mostly been using the APIC-EM for just this feature in order to help me troubleshoot my virtual networks, and it does it very well. And it looks cool too!

Pushing toward staying tight to the CCNA objectives here, you really want to know that you can use the path trace service of APIC-EM for ACL analysis. Doing this allows you to examine the path that a specific type of packet travels as it makes its way across the network from a source to a destination node, and it can use IP and TCP/UDP ports when diagnosing an application issue. If there is an ACL on an interface that blocks a certain application, you'll see this in a GUI output. I cannot tell you how extremely helpful this is in the day-to-day administration of your networks!

The result of a path trace will be a GUI representation of the path that a packet takes across all the devices and links between the source and destination, and you can choose to provide the output of a reverse path as well. Although I could easily do this same work manually, it would certainly be a whole lot more time consuming if I did! APIC-EM's Path Trace app actually does the work for you with just a few clicks at the user interface.

Once you fill in the fields for the source, destination, and optionally, the application, the path trace is initiated. You'll then see the path between hosts, plus the list of each device along the path, illustrated in Figure 8.10.

FIGURE 8.10   APIC-Enterprise Module path trace sample

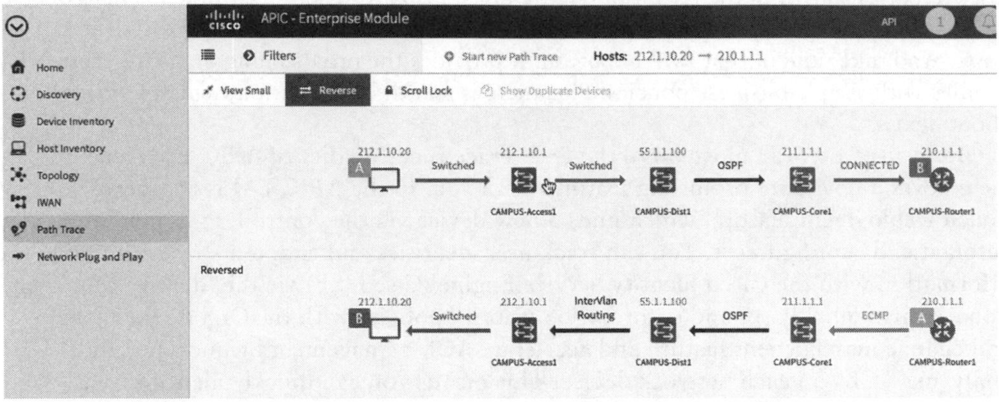

Okay, here you can see the complete path taken from host A to host B. I chose to view the reverse path as well. In this particular case, we weren't being blocked by an ACL, but if a packet actually was being blocked for a certain application, we'd see the exact interface where the application was blocked and why. Here is more detail on how my trace occurred.

First, the APIC-EM Discovery finds the network topology. At this point I can now choose the source and destination address of a packet and, alternately, port numbers and the application that can be used. The MAC address table, IP routing tables, and so on are used by the APIC-EM to find the path of the packet through the network. Finally, the GUI will show you the path, complete with device and interface information.

Last point: The APIC-EM is free, and most of the applications off the NBI are built in and included, but there are some solution applications that need a license. So if you have a VM with at least 64 gigs of RAM, you're set!

Cisco Intelligent WAN

This topic was covered in the chapter "Wide Area Networks," but it's important to at least touch on it here since it's included in the "Evolution of Intelligent Networks" CCNA objectives. We'll also take a peek at the APIC-EM for IWAN in this section. What Cisco's IWAN solution provides is a way to take advantage of cheaper bandwidth at remote locations, without compromising application performance, availability, or even security and in an easy-to-configure manner—nice!

Clearly, this allows us to use low-cost or inexpensive Internet connections, which have become more reliable and cost effective compared to the dedicated WAN links we used to use, and it means that we can now take advantage of this low-cost technology with Cisco's new Cisco Intelligent WAN (Cisco IWAN). Add in the failover and redundancy features that IWAN provides and you'll definitely see the reason large enterprises are deploying

Cisco's IWAN. The downside? Well, nothing to you and me, because we always use Cisco's gear from end to end in all our networks, right?

IWAN can provide great long-distance connections for your organization by dynamically routing based on the application service-level agreement (SLA) while paying attention to network conditions. And it can do this over any type of network!

Figure 8.11 pictures the IWAN Aggregation Site tab on the IWAN screen.

A feature of the APCI-EM is the IWAN discovery and configuration.

FIGURE 8.11   APIC-Enterprise Module IWAN

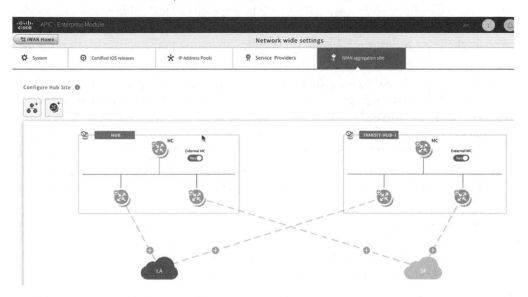

There are four components of Cisco's IWAN:

Transport-independent connectivity   Cisco IWAN provides a type of advanced VPN connection across all available routes to remote locations, providing one network with a single routing domain. This allows you to easily multihome the network across different types of connections, including MPLS, broadband, and cellular.

Intelligent path control   By using Cisco Performance Routing (Cisco PfR), Cisco IWAN improves delivery and WAN efficiency of applications.

Application optimization   Via Cisco's Application Visibility and Control (Cisco AVC), as well as Cisco's Wide Area Application Services (Cisco WAAS), you can now optimize application performance over WAN links.

Highly secure connectivity   Using VPNs, firewalls, network segmentation, and security features, Cisco IWAN helps ensure that these solutions actually provide the security you need over the public Internet.

Quality of Service

Quality of service (QoS) refers to the way the resources are controlled so that the quality of services is maintained. It's basically the ability to provide a different priority to one or more types of traffic over other levels for different applications, data flows, or users so that they can be guaranteed a certain performance level. QoS is used to manage contention for network resources for better end-user experience.

QoS methods focus on problems that can affect data as it traverses network cable:

Delay   Data can run into congested lines or take a less-than-ideal route to the destination, and delays like these can make some applications, such as VoIP, fail. This is the best reason to implement QoS when real-time applications are in use in the network—to prioritize delay-sensitive traffic.

Dropped Packets   Some routers will drop packets if they receive a packet while their buffers are full. If the receiving application is waiting for the packets but doesn't get them, it will usually request that the packets be retransmitted—another common cause of a service(s) delay. With QoS, when there is contention on a link, less important traffic is delayed or dropped in favor of delay-sensitive business-important traffic.

Error   Packets can be corrupted in transit and arrive at the destination in an unacceptable format, again requiring retransmission and resulting in delays such as video and voice.

Jitter   Not every packet takes the same route to the destination, so some will be more delayed than others if they travel through a slower or busier network connection. The variation in packet delay is called *jitter*, and this can have a nastily negative impact on programs that communicate in real time.

Out-of-Order Delivery   Out-of-order delivery is also a result of packets taking different paths through the network to their destinations. The application at the receiving end needs to put them back together in the right order for the message to be completed. So if there are significant delays, or the packets are reassembled out of order, users will probably notice degradation of an application's quality.

QoS can ensure that applications with a required level of predictability will receive the necessary bandwidth to work properly. Clearly, on networks with excess bandwidth, this is not a factor, but the more limited your bandwidth is, the more important a concept like this becomes!

Traffic Characteristics

In today's networks, you will find a mix of data, voice, and video traffic. Each traffic type has different properties.

Figure 8.12 shows the traffic characteristics found in today's network for data, voice, and video.

FIGURE 8.12 Traffic characteristics

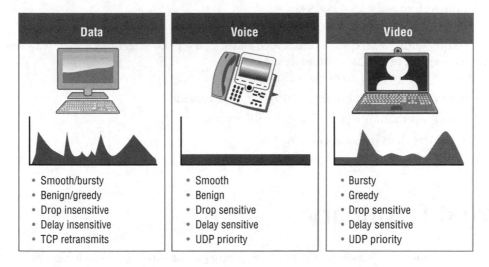

Data traffic is not real-time traffic, and includes data packets comprising of bursty (or unpredictable) traffic and widely varying packet arrival times.

The following are data characteristics on a network, as shown in Figure 8.12:

- Smooth/bursty
- Benign/greedy
- Drop insensitive
- Delay insensitive
- TCP retransmits

Data traffic doesn't really require special handling in today's network, especially if TCP is used. Voice traffic is real-time traffic with constant, predictable bandwidth and known packet arrival times.

The following are voice characteristics on a network:

- Smooth traffic
- Benign
- Drop insensitive
- Delay sensate insensitive
- UDP priority

One-way voice traffic needs the following:

- Latency of less than or equal to 150 milliseconds
- Jitter of less than or equal to 30 milliseconds

- Loss of less than or equal to 1%
- Bandwidth of only 30–128k Kbps

There are several types of video traffic, and a lot of the traffic on the Internet today is video traffic, with Netflix, Hulu, etc. Video traffic can include streaming video, real-time interactive video, and video conferences.

One-way video traffic needs the following:

- Latency of less than or equal to 200–400 milliseconds
- Jitter of less than or equal to 30–50 milliseconds
- Loss of less than or equal to 0.1%–1%
- Bandwidth of 384 Kbps to 20 Mbps or greater

Trust Boundary

The trust boundary is a point in the network where packet markings (which identify traffic such as voice, video, or data) are not necessarily trusted. You can create, remove, or rewrite markings at that point. The borders of a trust domain are the network locations where packet markings are accepted and acted upon. Figure 8.13 shows some typical trust boundaries.

FIGURE 8.13   Trust boundaries

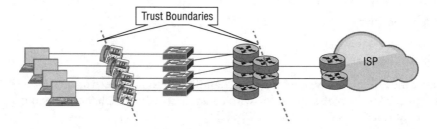

The figure shows that IP phones and router interfaces are typically trusted, but beyond those points are not. Here are some things you need to remember for the exam objectives:

Untrusted domain   This is the part of the network that you are not managing, such as PC, printers, etc.

Trusted domain   This is part of the network with only administrator-managed devices such as switches, routers, etc.

Trust boundary   This is where packets are classified and marked. For example, the trust boundary would be IP phones and the boundary between the ISP and enterprise network. In an enterprise campus network, the trust boundary is almost always at the edge switch.

Traffic at the trust boundary is classified and marked before being forwarded to the trusted domain. Markings on traffic coming from an untrusted domain are usually ignored to prevent end-user-controlled markings from taking unfair advantage of the network QoS configuration.

QoS Mechanisms

In this section we'll be covering these important mechanisms:

- Classification and marking tools
- Policing, shaping, and re-marking tools
- Congestion management (or scheduling) tools
- Link-specific tools

  So let's take a deeper look at each mechanism now.

Classification and Marking

A classifier is an IOS tool that inspects packets within a field to identify the type of traffic that they are carrying. This is so that QoS can determine which traffic class they belong to and determine how they should be treated. It's important that this isn't a constant cycle for traffic because it does take up time and resources. Traffic is then directed to a policy-enforcement mechanism, referred to as policing, for its specific type.

Policy enforcement mechanisms include marking, queuing, policing, and shaping, and there are various layer 2 and layer 3 fields in a frame and packet for marking traffic. You are definitely going to have to understand these marking techniques to meet the objectives, so here we go:

Class of Service (CoS) An Ethernet frame marking at layer 2, which contains 3 bits. This is called the Priority Code Point (PCP) within an Ethernet frame header when VLAN tagged frames as defined by IEEE 802.1Q are used.

Type of Service (ToS) ToS comprises of 8 bits, 3 of which are designated as the IP precedence field in an IPv4 packet header. The IPv6 header field is called Traffic Class.

Differentiated Services Code Point (DSCP or DiffServ) One of the methods we can use for classifying and managing network traffic and providing quality of service (QoS) on modern IP networks is DSCP. This technology uses a 6-bit differentiated services code point in the 8-bit Differentiated Services field (DS field) in the IP header for packet classification. DSCP allows for the creation of traffic classes that can be used to assign priorities. While IP precedence is the old way to mark ToS, DSCP is the new way. DSCP is backward compatible with IP precedence.

Layer 3 packet marking with IP precedence and DSCP is the most widely deployed marking option because layer 3 packet markings have end-to-end significance.

Class Selector   Class Selector uses the same 3 bits of the field as IP precedence and is used to indicate a 3-bit subset of DSCP values.

Traffic Identifier (TID)   TID, used in wireless frames, describe a 3-bit field in the QoS control field in 802.11. It's very similar to CoS, so just remember CoS is wired Ethernet and TID is wireless.

Classification Marking Tools

As discussed in the previous section, classification of traffic determines which type of traffic the packets or frames belong to, which then allows you to apply policies to it by marking, shaping, and policing. Always try to mark traffic as close to the trust boundary as possible.

To classify traffic, we generally use three ways:

Markings   This looks at header informant on existing layer 2 or 3 settings, and classification is based on existing markings.

Addressing   This classification technique looks at header information using source and destinations of interfaces, layer 2 and 3 addresses, and layer 4 port numbers. You can group traffic with devices using IP and traffic by type using port numbers.

Application signatures   This is the way to look at the information in the payload, and this classification technique is called deep packet inspection.

Let's dive deeper into deep packet inspection by discussing something called Network Based Application Recognition (NBAR).

NBAR is a classifier that provides deep-packet inspection on layer 4 to 7 on a packet, however, know that using NBAR is the most CPU intensive technique compared to using addresses (IP or ports) or access control lists (ACLs).

Since it's not always possible to identify applications by looking at just layers 3 and 4, NBAR looks deep into the packet payload and compares the payload content against its signature database called a Packet Description Language Model (PDLM).

There are two different modes of operation used with NBAR:

Passive mode   Using passive mode will give you real-time statistics on applications by protocol or interface as well as the bit rate, packet, and byte counts.

Active mode   Classifies applications for traffic marking so that QoS policies can be applied.

Policing, Shaping, and Re-Marking

Okay—now that we've identified and marked traffic, it's time to put some action on our packet. We do this with bandwidth assignments, policing, shaping, queuing, or dropping. For example, if some traffic exceeds bandwidth, it might be delayed, dropped, or even re-marked in order to avoid congestion.

Policers and shapers are two tools that identify and respond to traffic problems and are both rate limiters. Figure 8.14 shows how they differ.

FIGURE 8.14   Policing and shaping rate limiters

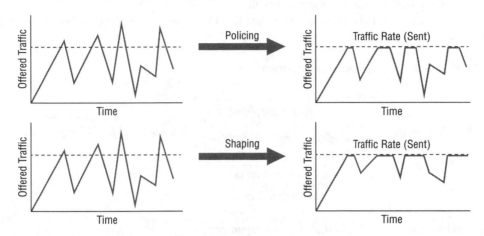

Policers and shapers identify traffic violations in a similar manner, but they differ in their response:

Policers   Since the policers make instant decisions you want to deploy them on the ingress if possible. This is because you want to drop traffic as soon as you receive it if it's going to be dropped anyway. Even so, you can still place them on an egress to control the amount of traffic per class. When traffic is exceeded, policers don't delay it, which means they do not introduce jitter or delay, they just check the traffic and can drop it or re-mark it. Just know that this means there's a higher drop probability, it can cause a significant amount of TCP resends.

Shapers   Shapers are usually deployed between an enterprise network, on the egress side, and the service provider network to make sure you stay within the carrier's contract rate. If the traffic does exceed the rate, it will get policed by the provider and dropped. This allows the traffic to meet the SLA and means there will be fewer TCP resends than with policers. Be aware that shaping does introduce jitter and delay.

Just remember that policers drop traffic and shapers delay it. Policers have significant TCP resends and shapers do not. Shapers introduce delay and jitter, but policers do not.

Tools for Managing Congestion

This section and the next section on congestion avoidance will cover congestion issues. If traffic exceeds network resource (always), the traffic gets queued, which is basically the temporary storage of backed-up packets. You perform queuing in order to avoid dropping packets. This isn't a bad thing. It's actually a good thing or all traffic would immediately be dropped if packets couldn't get processed immediately. However, traffic classes like

VoIP would actually be better off just being immediately dropped unless you can somehow guarantee delay-free bandwidth for that traffic.

When congestion occurs, the congestion management tools are activated. There are two types, as shown in Figure 8.15.

FIGURE 8.15 Congestion management

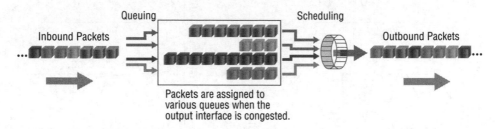

Let's take a closer look at congestion management:

Queuing (or buffering)   Buffering is the logic of ordering packets in output buffers. It is activated only when congestion occurs. When queues fill up, packets can be reordered so that the higher-priority packets can be sent out of the exit interface sooner than the lower-priority ones.

Scheduling   This is the process of deciding which packet should be sent out next and occurs whether or not there is congestion on the link.

Staying with scheduling for another minute, know that there are some schedule mechanisms that exist you really need to be familiar with. We'll go over those, and then I'll head back over to a detailed look at queuing:

Strict priority scheduling   Low-priority queues are only serviced once the high-priority queues are empty. This is great if you are the one sending high-priority traffic, but it's possible that low-priority queues will never be processed. We call this traffic or queue starvation.

Round-robin scheduling   This is a rather fair technique because queues are serviced in a set sequence. You won't have starving queues here, but real-time traffic suffers greatly.

Weighted fair scheduling   By weighing the queues, the scheduling process will service some queues more often than others, which is an upgrade over round-robin. You won't have any starvation here either, but unlike with round-robin, you can give priority to real-time traffic. It does not, however, provide bandwidth guarantees.

Okay, let's run back over and finish queueing. Queuing typically is a layer 3 process, but some queueing can occur at layer 2 or even layer 1. Interestingly, if a layer 2 queue fills up, the data can be pushed into layer 3 queues, and at layer 1 (called the transmit ring or TX-ring queue), when that fills up, the data will be pushed to layer 2 and 3 queues. This is when QoS becomes active on the device.

There are many different queuing mechanisms, with only two typically used today, but let's take a look at the legacy queuing methods first:

First in, first out (FIFO)   A single queue with packets being processed in the exact order in which they arrived.

Priority queuing (PQ)   This is not really a good queuing method because lower-priority queues are served only when the higher-priority queues are empty. There are only four queues, and low-priority traffic many never be sent.

Custom queueing (CQ)   With up to 16 queues and round-robin scheduling, CQ prevents low-level queue starvation and provides traffic guarantees. But it doesn't provide strict priority for real-time traffic, so your VoIP traffic could end up being dropped.

Weighted fair queuing (WFQ)   This was actually a pretty popular way of queuing for a long time because it divided up the bandwidth by the number of flows, which provided bandwidth for all applications. This was great for real-time traffic, but it doesn't offer any guarantees for a particular flow.

Now that you know about all the not so good queuing methods to use, let's take a look at the two newer queuing mechanisms that are recommended for today's rich-media networks, detailed in Figure 8.16).

FIGURE 8.16   Queuing mechanisms

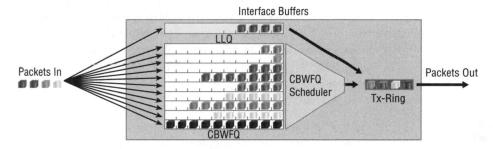

The two new and improved queuing mechanisms you should now use in today's network are class-based weighted fair queuing and low latency queuing:

Class-based weighted fair queuing (CBWFQ)   Provides fairness and bandwidth guarantees for all traffic, but it does not provide latency guarantees and is typically only used for data traffic management.

Low latency queuing (LLQ):   LLQ is really the same thing as CBWFQ but with stricter priorities for real-time traffic. LLQ is great for both data and real-time traffic because it provides both latency and bandwidth guarantees.

In Figure 8.16, you can see the LLQ queuing mechanism, which is suitable for networks with real-time traffic. If you remove the low-latency queue (at the top), you're then left with CBWFQ, which is only used for data-traffic networks.

Tools for Congestion Avoidance

TCP changed our networking world when it introduced sliding windows as a flow-control mechanism in the mid-1990s. Flow control is a way for the receiving device to control the amount of traffic from a transmitting device.

If a problem occurred during a data transmission (always), the previous flow control methods used by TCP and other layer 4 protocols like SPX, that we used before sliding windows, the transmission rate would be in half, and left there at the same rate, or lower, for the duration of the connection. This was certainly a point of contention with users!

TCP actually does cut transmission rates drastically if a flow control issue occurs, but it increases the transmission rate once the missing segments are resolved or the packets are finally processed. Because of this behavior, and although it was awesome at the time, this method can result in what we call tail drop. Tail drop is definitely suboptimal for today's networks because using it, we're not utilizing the bandwidth effectively.

Just to clarify, tail drop refers to the dropping of packets as they arrive when the queues on the receiving interface are full. This is a waste of precious bandwidth since TCP will just keep resending the data until it's happy again (meaning an ACK has been received). So now this brings up another new term, *TCP global synchronization*, where senders will reduce their transmission rate at the same time when packet loss occurs.

Congestion avoidance starts dropping packets before a queue fills, and it drops the packets by using traffic weights instead just randomness. Cisco uses something called weighted random early detection (WRED), which is a queuing method that ensures that high-precedence traffic has lower loss rates than other traffic during congestion. This allows more important traffic, like VoIP, to be prioritized and dropped over what you'd consider less important traffic such as, for example, a connection to Facebook.

Queuing algorithms manage the front of the queue and congestion mechanisms manage the back of the queue.

Figure 8.17 demonstrates how congestion avoidance works.

FIGURE 8.17   Congestion avoidance

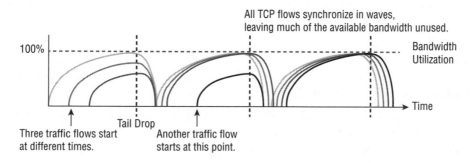

If three traffic flows start at different times, as shown in the example in Figure 8.17, and congestion occurs, using TCP could first cause tail drop, which drops the traffic as soon as it is received if the buffers are full. At that point TCP would start another traffic flow, synchronizing the TCP flows in waves, which would then leave much of the bandwidth unused.

Summary

This all-new chapter was totally focused on the CCNA objectives for intelligent networks. I started the chapter by covering switch stacking using StackWise and then moved on to discuss the important realm of cloud computing and what effect it has on the enterprise network.

Although this chapter had a lot of material, I stuck really close to the objectives on the more difficult subjects to help you tune in specifically to the content that's important for the CCNA, including the following: Software Defined Networking (SDN), application programming interfaces (APIs), Cisco's Application Policy Infrastructure Controller Enterprise Module (APIC-EM), Intelligent WAN, and finally, quality of service (QoS).

Exam Essentials

Understand switch stacking and StackWise.   You can connect up to nine individual switches together to create a StackWise.

Understand basic cloud technology.   Understand cloud services such as SaaS and others and how virtualization works.

Have a deep understanding of QoS.   You must understand QoS, specifically marking; device trust; prioritization for voice, video, and data; shaping; policing; and congestion management in detail.

Understand APIC-EM and the path trace.   Read through the APIC-EM section as well as the APIC-EM path trace section, which cover the CCNA objectives fully.

Understand SDN.   Understand how a controller works, and especially the control and data plane, as well as the northbound and southbound APIs.

Written Lab 8

You can find the answers to this lab in Appendix A, "Answers to Written Labs."
   Write the answers to the following questions:

1. Which QoS mechanism is a 6-bit value that is used to describe the meaning of the layer 3 IPv4 ToS field?

2. Southbound SDN interfaces are used between which two planes?

3. Which QoS mechanism is a term that is used to describe a 3-bit field in the QoS control field of wireless frames?

4. What are the three general ways to classify traffic?

5. CoS is a layer 2 QoS _____?

6. A session is using more bandwidth than allocated. Which QoS mechanism will drop the traffic?

7. What are the three SDN layers?

8. What are two examples of newer queuing mechanisms that are recommended for rich-media networks?

9. What is a layer 4 to 7 deep-packet inspection classifier that is more CPU intensive than marking?

10. _____ APIs are responsible for the communication between the SDN controller and the services running over the network.

Review Questions

 The following questions are designed to test your understanding of this chapter's material. For more information on how to get additional questions, please see www.lammle.com/ccna.

You can find the answers to these questions in Appendix B, "Answers to Review Questions."

1. Which of the following is a congestion-avoidance mechanism?

   A. LMI

   B. WRED

   C. QPM

   D. QoS

2. Which of the following are true regarding StackWise? (Choose two.)

   A. A StackWise interconnect cable is used to connect the switches to create a bidirectional, closed-loop path.

   B. A StackWise interconnect cable is used to connect the switches to create a unidirectional, closed-loop path.

   C. StackWise can connect up to nine individual switches joined in a single logical switching unit.

   D. StackWise can connect up to nine individual switches joined into multiple logical switching units and managed by one IP address.

3. Which of the following is the best definition of cloud computing?

   A. UCS data center

   B. Computing model with all your data at the service provider

   C. On-demand computing model

   D. Computing model with all your data in your local data center

4. Which three features are properties and one-way requirements for voice traffic? (Choose three.)

   A. Bursty voice traffic.

   B. Smooth voice traffic.

   C. Latency should be below 400 ms.

   D. Latency should be below 150 ms.

   E. Bandwidth is roughly between 30 and 128 kbps.

   F. Bandwidth is roughly between 0.5 and 20 Mbps.

5. On which SDN architecture layer does Cisco APIC-EM reside?

    A. Data

    B. Control

    C. Presentation

    D. Application

6. In which cloud service model is the customer responsible for managing the operating system, software, platforms, and applications?

    A. IaaS

    B. SaaS

    C. PaaS

    D. APIC-EM

7. Which statement about QoS trust boundaries or domains is true?

    A. The trust boundary is always a router.

    B. PCs, printers, and tablets are usually part of a trusted domain.

    C. An IP phone is a common trust boundary.

    D. Routing will not work unless the service provider and the enterprise network are one single trust domain.

8. Which statement about IWAN is correct?

    A. The IWAN allows transport-independent connectivity.

    B. The IWAN allows only static routing.

    C. The IWAN does not provide application visibility because only encrypted traffic is transported.

    D. The IWAN needs special encrypting devices to provide an acceptable security level.

9. Which advanced classification tool can be used to classify data applications?

    A. NBAR

    B. MPLS

    C. APIC-EM

    D. ToS

10. The DSCP field constitutes how many bits in the IP header?

    A. 3 bits

    B. 4 bits

    C. 6 bits

    D. 8 bits

11. Between which two planes are SDN southbound interfaces used?

    A. Control

    B. Data

   C. Routing

   D. Application

12. Which option is a layer 2 QoS marking?

   A. EXP

   B. QoS group

   C. DSCP

   D. CoS

13. You are starting to use SDN in your network. What does this mean?

   A. You no longer have to work anymore, but you'll get paid more.

   B. You'll need to upgrade all your applications.

   C. You'll need to get rid of all Cisco switches.

   D. You now have more time to react faster when you receive a new business requirement.

14. Which QoS mechanism will drop traffic if a session uses more than the allotted bandwidth?

   A. Congestion management

   B. Shaping

   C. Policing

   D. Marking

15. Which three layers are part of the SDN architecture? (Choose three.)

   A. Network

   B. Data Link

   C. Control

   D. Data

   E. Transport

   F. Application

16. Which of the following is NOT true about APIC-EM ACL analysis?

   A. Fast comparison of ACLs between devices to visualize difference and identify misconfigurations

   B. Inspection, interrogation, and analysis of network access control policies

   C. Ability to provide layer 4 to layer 7 deep-packet inspection

   D. Ability to trace application-specific paths between end devices to quickly identify ACLs and other problem areas

17. Which two of the following are not part of APIC-EM?

   A. Southbound APIs are used for communication between the controllers and network devices.

   B. Northbound APIs are used for communication between the controllers and network devices.

    C. OnePK is Cisco proprietary.

    D. The control plane is responsible for the forwarding of frames or packets.

18. When stacking switches, which is true? (Choose two.)

    A. The stack is managed as multiple objects and has a single management IP address.

    B. The stack is managed as a single object and has a single management IP address.

    C. The master switch is chosen when you configure the first switch's master algorithm to on.

    D. The master switch is elected from one of the stack member switches.

19. Which of the following services provides the operating system and the network?

    A. IaaS

    B. PaaS

    C. SaaS

    D. None of the above

20. Which of the following services provides the required software, the operating system, and the network?

    A. IaaS

    B. PaaS

    C. SaaS

    D. None of the above

21. Which of the following is NOT a benefit of cloud computing for a cloud user?

    A. On-demand, self-service resource provisioning

    B. Centralized appearance of resources

    C. Local backups

    D. Highly available, horizontally scaled application architectures

Appendix A

Answers to Written Labs

Chapter 1: Enhanced Switched Technologies

Written Lab 1

1. PAgP

2. show spanning-tree summary

3. 802.1w

4. STP

5. BPDU Guard

6. (config-if)#**spanning-tree portfast**

7. Switch#**show etherchannel port-channel**

8. Switch(config)#**spanning-tree vlan 3 root primary**

9. show spanning-tree, then follow the root port that connects to the root bridge using CDP, or show spanning-tree summary.

10. Active and passive

Chapter 2: Network Device Management and Security

Written Lab 2

1. INFORM

2. GET

3. TRAP

4. SET

5. WALK

6. If the active router fails, the standby router takes over with a different virtual IP address, and different to the one configured as the default-gateway address for end devices, so your hosts stop working which defeats the purpose of a FHRP.

7. You'll start receiving duplicate IP address warnings.

8. You'll start receiving duplicate IP address warnings.

9. In version 1, HSRP messages are sent to the multicast IP address 224.0.0.2 and UDP port 1985. HSRP version 2 uses the multicast IP address 224.0.0.102 and UDP port 1985.

10. RADIUS and TACACS+, with TACACS+ being proprietary.

Chapter 3: Enhanced IGRP

Written Lab 3

1. `ipv6 router eigrp` *as*

2. FF02::A

3. False

4. The routers will not form an adjacency.

5. Passive interface

6. A backup route, stored in the topology table

Chapter 4: Open Shortest Path First (OSPF)

Written Lab 4

1. `router ospf 101`

2. `show ip ospf`

3. `show ip ospf interface`

4. `show ip ospf neighbor`

5. `show ip route ospf`

6. Cost (bandwidth)

7. Areas don't match. The routers are not in same subnet. RIDs are the same. Hello and Dead timers don't match.

8. `show ip ospf database`

9. 110

10. 10 and 40

Chapter 5: Multi-Area OSPF

Written Lab 5

1. Type 5 or Type 7

2. 2WAY

3. Type 3, and possibly Type 4 and 5

4. When all LSAs have synchronized with a neighbor on a point-to-point link

5. True

6. EXCHANGE

7. Type 1

8. `ipv6 ospf 1 area 0`

9. OSPFv2 and v3 use the same items when forming an adjacency; Hello and Dead timers, subnet info, and area ID all must match. Authentication must also match if configured.

10. `show ip protocols` and `show ipv6 protocols`

Chapter 6: Troubleshooting IP, IPv6, and VLANs

Written Lab 6

1. The INCMP is an incomplete message, which means a neighbor solicitation message has been sent but the neighbor message has not yet been received.

2. `switchport trunk native vlan 66`

3. Access, auto, desirable, nonegotiate, and trunk (on)

4. Verify that the default gateway is correct. Verify that name resolution settings are correct. Verify that there are no ACLs blocking traffic.

5. `ping ::1`

Chapter 7: Wide Area Networks

Written Lab 7

1. True

2. False

3. BGP

4. `show ip bgp neighbor`

5. `show run interface tunnel tunnel_number`

6. False

7. PPPoE or PPPoA

8. HDLC, LCP, and NCP

9. VPLS, VPWS

10. Layer 2 MPLS VPN, Layer 3 MPLS VPN

Chapter 8: Evolution of Intelligent Networks

Written Lab 8

1. DSCP

2. Control, data

3. TID

4. Markings, addressing, and application signatures

5. Marking

6. Policing

7. Data, control, application

8. CBWFQ, LLW

9. NBAR

10. Northbound

Appendix

B

Answers to Review Questions

Chapter 1: Enhanced Switched Technologies

1. B, D. The switch is not the root bridge for VLAN 1 or the output would tell us exactly that. The root bridge for VLAN 1 is off of interface G1/2 with a cost of 4, meaning it is directly connected. Use the command show cdp nei to find your root bridge at this point. Also, the switch is running RSTP (802.1w), not STP.

2. D. Option A seems like the best answer, and had switches not been configured with the primary and secondary command, then the switch configured with priority 4096 would have been root. However, since the primary and secondary both had a priority of 16384, then the tertiary switch would be a switch with a higher priority in this case.

3. A, D. It is important that you can find your root bridge, and the show spanning-tree command will help you do this. To quickly find out which VLANs your switch is the root bridge for, use the show spanning-tree summary command.

4. A. 802.1w is the also called Rapid Spanning Tree Protocol. It is not enabled by default on Cisco switches, but it is a better STP to run because it has all the fixes that the Cisco extensions provide with 802.1d. Remember, Cisco runs RSTP PVST+, not just RSTP.

5. B. The Spanning Tree Protocol is used to stop switching loops in a layer 2 switched network with redundant paths.

6. C. Convergence occurs when all ports on bridges and switches have transitioned to either the forwarding or blocking states. No data is forwarded until convergence is complete. Before data can be forwarded again, all devices must be updated.

7. C, E. There are two types of EtherChannel: Cisco's PAgP and the IEEE's LACP. They are basically the same, and there is little difference to configuring them. For PAgP, use auto or desirable mode, and with LACP use passive or active. These modes decide which method you are using, and they must be configured the same on both sides of the EtherChannel bundle.

8. A, B, F. RSTP helps with convergence issues that plague traditional STP. Rapid PVST+ is based on the 802.1w standard in the same way that PVST+ is based on 802.1d. The operation of Rapid PVST+ is simply a separate instance of 802.1w for each VLAN.

9. D. BPDU Guard is used when a port is configured for PortFast, or it should be used, because if that port receives a BPDU from another switch, BPDU Guard will shut that port down to stop a loop from occurring.

10. C. To allow for the PVST+ to operate, there's a field inserted into the BPDU to accommodate the extended system ID so that PVST+ can have a root bridge configured on a per-STP

instance. The extended system ID (VLAN ID) is a 12-bit field, and we can even see what this field is carrying via the show spanning-tree command output.

11. C. PortFast and BPDU Guard allow a port to transition to the forwarding state quickly, which is great for a switch port but not for load balancing. You can somewhat load balance with RSTP, but that is out of the scope of our objectives, and although you can use PPP to configure multilink (bundle links), this is performed on asynchronous or synchronous serial links. Cisco's EtherChannel can bundle up to eight ports between switches.

12. D. If the Spanning Tree Protocol is not running on your switches and you connect them together with redundant links, you will have broadcast storms and multiple frame copies being received by the same destination device.

13. B, C, E. All the ports on both sides of every link must be configured exactly the same or it will not work. Speed, duplex, and allowed VLANs must match.

14. D, F. There are two types of EtherChannel: Cisco's PAgP and the IEEE's LACP. They are basically the same, and there is little difference to configure them. For PAgP, use the auto or desirable mode, and with LACP use the passive or active mode. These modes decide which method you are using, and they must be configured the same on both sides of the Ether-Channel bundle.

15. D. You can't answer this question if you don't know who the root bridge is. SC has a bridge priority of 4,096, so that is the root bridge. The cost for SB was 4, with the direct link, but that link went down. If SB goes through SA to SC, the cost would be 4 + 19, or 23. If SB goes to SA to SD to SC, the cost is 4 + 4 + 4 = 12.

16. A, D. To configure EtherChannel, create the port channel from global configuration mode, and then assign the group number on each interface using the active mode to enable LACP. Just configuring the channel-group command under your interfaces will enable the bundle, but options A and D are the best Cisco objective answers.

17. A, D. You can set the priority to any value from 0 through 61,440 in increments of 4,096. Setting it to zero (0) means that the switch will always be a root as long as it has a lower MAC than another switch with its bridge ID also set to 0. You can also force a switch to be a root for a VLAN with the spanning-tree vlan vlan primary command.

18. A. By using per-VLAN spanning tree, the root bridge can be placed in the center of where all the resources are for a particular VLAN, which enables optimal path determination.

19. A, C, D, E. Each 802.1d port transitions through blocking, listening, learning, and finally forwarding after 50 seconds, by default. RSTP uses discarding, learning, and forwarding only.

20. A, C, D, E, F. The roles a switch port can play in STP are root, non-root, designated, non-designated, forwarding, and blocking. Discarding is used in RSTP, and disabled could be a role, but it's not listed as a possible answer.

Chapter 2: Network Device Management and Security

1. B. You can enter the ACL directly in the SNMP configuration to provide security, using either a number or a name.

2. C. 100. By setting a higher number then the default on a router, you are making that router the active router. Setting preempt would assure that if the active router went down, it would become the active router again when it comes back up.

3. D. To enable the AAA commands on a router or switch, use the global configuration command aaa new-model.

4. A, C. To mitigate access layer threats, use port security, DHCP snooping, dynamic ARP inspection, and identity based networking.

5. D. DHCP snooping validates DHCP messages, builds and maintains the DHCP snooping binding database, and rate-limits DHCP traffic for trusted and untrusted source.

6. A, D. TACACS+ uses TCP, is Cisco proprietary, and offers multiprotocol support as well as separated AAA services.

7. B. Unlike with TACACS+, separating AAA services is not an option when configuring RADIUS.

8. A, D. With a read-only community string, no changes can be made to the router. However, SNMPv2c can use GETBULK to create and return multiple requests at once.

9. C. The idea of a first hop redundancy protocol is to provide redundancy for a default gateway.

10. A, B. A router interface can be in many states with HSRP; the states are shown in Table 2.1.

11. A. Only option A has the correct sequence to enable HSRP on an interface.

12. D. This is a question that I used in a lot of job interviews on prospects. The show standby command is your friend when dealing with HSRP.

13. D. There is nothing wrong with leaving the priorities at the defaults of 100. The first router up will be the active router.

14. C. In version 1, HSRP messages are sent to the multicast IP address 224.0.0.2 and UDP port 1985. HSRP version 2 uses the multicast IP address 224.0.0.102 and UDP port 1985.

15. B, C. If HSRP1 is configured to preempt, then it will become active because of the higher priority; if not, HSRP2 will stay the active router.

16. C. In version 1, HSRP messages are sent to the multicast IP address 224.0.0.2 and UDP port 1985. HSRP version 2 uses and the multicast IP address 224.0.0.102 and UDP port 1985.

17. C, D. SNMPv2c introduced the GETBULK and INFORM SNMP messages but didn't have any different security than SNMPv1. SNMPv3 uses TCP and provides encryption and authentication.

18. D. The correct answer is option D. Take your newly created RADIUS group and use it for authentication, and be sure to use the keyword `local` at the end.

19. B. DAI, used with DHCP snooping, tracks IP-to-MAC bindings from DHCP transactions to protect against ARP poisoning. DHCP snooping is required in order to build the MAC-to-IP bindings for DAI validation.

20. A, D, E. There are three roles involved in using client/server access control for identity-based networking on wired and wireless hosts: The client, also referred to as a supplicant, is software that runs on a client and is 802.1x compliant. The authenticator is typically a switch that controls physical access to the network and is a proxy between the client and the authentication server. The authentication server (RADIUS) is a server that authenticates each client before it can access any services.

Chapter 3: Enhanced IGRP

1. B. Only the EIGRP routes will be placed in the routing table because it has the lowest administrative distance (AD), and that is always used before metrics.

2. A, C. EIGRP maintains three tables in RAM: neighbor, topology, and routing. The neighbor and topology tables are built and maintained with the use of Hello and update packets.

3. B. EIGRP does use reported distance, or advertised distance (AD), to tell neighbor routers the cost to get to a remote network. This router will send the FD to the neighbor router and the neighbor router will add the cost to get to this router plus the AD to find the true FD.

4. E. Successor routes are going to be in the routing table since they are the best path to a remote network. However, the topology table has a link to each and every network, so the best answer is topology table and routing table. Any secondary route to a remote network is considered a feasible successor, and those routes are found only in the topology table and used as backup routes in case of primary route failure.

5. C. Any secondary route to a remote network is considered a feasible successor, and those routes are found only in the topology table and used as backup routes in case of primary route failure. You can see the topology table with the `show ip eigrp topology` command.

6. B, C, E. EIGRP and EIGRPv6 routers can use the same RID, unlike OSPF, and this can be set with the `eigrp router-id` command. Also a `variance` can be set to provide unequal-cost load balancing, along with the `maximum-paths` command to set the amount of load-balanced paths.

7. C. There were two successor routes, so by default, EIGRP was load-balancing out s0/0 and s0/1. When s0/0 goes down, EIGRP will just keep forwarding traffic out the second link s0/1. s0/0 will be removed from the routing table.

8. D. To enable EIGRPv6 on a router interface, use the command `ipv6 eigrp` as on individual interfaces that will be part of the EIGRPv6 process.

9. C. The path to network 10.10.50.0 out serial0/0 is more than two times the current FD, so I used a `variance 3` command to load-balance unequal-cost links three times the FD.

10. B, C. First, a maximum hop count of 16 only is associated with RIP, and EIGRP never broadcasts, so we can eliminate A and D as options. Feasible successors are backup routes and stored in the topology table, so that is correct, and if no feasible successor is located, the EIGRP will flood its neighbors asking for a new path to network 10.10.10.0.

11. D. The `show ip eigrp neighbors` command allows you to check the IP addresses as well as the retransmit interval and queue counts for the neighbors that have established an adjacency.

12. C, E. For EIGRP to form an adjacency with a neighbor, the AS numbers must match, and the metric K values must match as well. Also, option F could cause the problem; we can see if it is causing a problem from the output given.

13. A, D. Successor routes are the routes picked from the topology table as the best route to a remote network, so these are the routes that IP uses in the routing table to forward traffic to a remote destination. The topology table contains any route that is not as good as the successor route and is considered a feasible successor, or backup route. Remember that all routes are in the topology table, even successor routes.

14. A, B. Option A will work because the router will change the network statement to 10.0.0.0 since EIGRP uses classful addresses by default. Therefore, it isn't technically a wrong answer, but please understand why it is correct for this question. The 10.255.255.64/27 subnet address can be configured with wildcards just as we use with OSPF and ACLs. The /27 is a block of 32, so the wildcard in the fourth octet will be 31. The wildcard of 0.0.0.0 is wrong because this is a network address, not a host address, and the 0.0.0.15 is wrong because that is only a block of 16 and would only work if the mask was a /28.

15. C. To troubleshoot adjacencies, you need to check the AS numbers, the K values, networks, passive interfaces, and ACLs.

16. C. EIGRP and EIGRPv6 will load-balance across 4 equal-cost paths by default but can be configured to load-balance across equal- and unequal-cost paths, up to 32 with IOS 15.0 code.

17. B, E. EIGRP must be enabled with an AS number from global configuration mode with the `ipv6 router eigrp` as command if you need to set the RID or other global parameters. Instead of configuring EIGRP with the network command as with EIGRP, EIGRPv6 is configured on a per-interface basis with the `ipv6 eigrp` as command.

18. C. There isn't a lot to go on from with the output, but that might make this easier than if there were a whole page of output. Since s0/0/2 has the lowest FD and AD, that would become the successor route. For a route to become a feasible successor, its reported distance must be lower than the feasible distance of the current successor route, so C is our best answer based on what we can see.

19. C. The network in the diagram is considered a discontiguous network because you have one classful address subnetted and separated by another classful address. Only RIPv2, OSPF, and EIGRP can work with discontiguous networks, but RIPv2 and EIGRP won't work by default (except for routers running the new 15.0 code). You must use the no auto-summary command under the routing protocol configuration. There is a passive interface on RouterB, but this is not on an interface between RouterA and RouterB and won't stop an adjacency.

20. A, B, C, D. Here are the documented issues that Cisco says to check when you have an adjacency issue:

- Interfaces between the devices are down.
- The two routers have mismatching EIGRP autonomous system numbers.
- Proper interfaces are not enabled for the EIGRP process.
- An interface is configured as passive.
- K values are mismatched.
- EIGRP authentication is misconfigured.

Chapter 4: Open Shortest Path First (OSPF)

1. B. Only the EIGRP routes will be placed in the routing table because it has the lowest administrative distance (AD), and that is always used before metrics.

2. A, B, C. Any router that is a member of two areas must be an area border router or ABR.

3. A, C. The process ID for OSPF on a router is only locally significant, and you can use the same number on each router, or each router can have a different number—it just doesn't matter. The numbers you can use are from 1 to 65,535. Don't get this confused with area numbers, which can be from 0 to 4.2 billion.

4. B. The router ID (RID) is an IP address used to identify the router. It need not and should not match.

5. C. The router ID (RID) is an IP address used to identify the router. Cisco chooses the router ID by using the highest IP address of all configured loopback interfaces. If no loopback interfaces are configured with addresses, OSPF will choose the highest IP address of all active physical interfaces.

6. A. The administrator typed in the wrong wildcard mask configuration. The wildcard should have been 0.0.0.255 or even 0.255.255.255.

7. A. A dash (-) in the State column indicates no DR election, because they are not required on a point-to-point link such as a serial connection.

8. D. By default, the administrative distance of OSPF is 110.

9.   A. Hello packets are addressed to multicast address 224.0.0.5.

10. A. The `show ip ospf neighbor` command displays all interface-related neighbor information. This output shows the DR and BDR (unless your router is the DR or BDR), the RID of all directly connected neighbors, and the IP address and name of the directly connected interface.

11. A. 224.0.0.6 is used on broadcast networks to reach the DR and BDR.

12. D. The Hello and Dead timers must be set the same on two routers on the same link or they will not form an adjacency (relationship). The default timers for OSPF are 10 seconds for the Hello timer and 40 seconds for the Dead timer.

13.

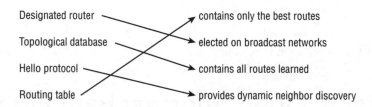

A designated router is elected on broadcast networks. Each OSPF router maintains an identical database describing the AS topology. A Hello protocol provides dynamic neighbor discovery. A routing table contains only the best routes.

14. `passive-interface fastEthernet 0/1`

The command `passive-interface fastEthernet 0/1` will disable OSPF on the specified interface only.

15. B, G. To enable OSPF, you must first start OSPF using a process ID. The number is irrelevant; just choose a number from 1 to 65,535 and you're good to go. After you start the OSPF process, you must configure interfaces on which to activate OSPF using the network command with wildcards and specification of an area. Option F is wrong because there must be a space after the parameter area and before you list the area number.

16. A. The default OSPF interface priority is 1, and the highest interface priority determines the designated router (DR) for a subnet. The output indicates that the router with a router ID of 192.168.45.2 is currently the backup designated router (BDR) for the segment, which indicates that another router became the DR. It can be then be assumed that the DR router has an interface priority higher than 2. (The router serving the DR function is not present in the truncated sample output.)

17. A, B, C. OSPF is created in a hierarchical design, not a flat design like RIP. This decreases routing overhead, speeds up convergence, and confines network instability to a single area of the network.

18. `show ip ospf interface`

The `show ip ospf interface` command displays all interface-related OSPF information. Data is displayed about OSPF information for all OSPF-enabled interfaces or for specified interfaces.

19. A. LSA packets are used to update and maintain the topological database.

20. B. At the moment of OSPF process startup, the highest IP address on any active interface will be the router ID (RID) of the router. If you have a loopback interface configured (logical interface), then that will override the interface IP address and become the RID of the router automatically.

Chapter 5: Multi-Area OSPF

1. A, B, D. As the size of a single-area OSPF network grows, so does the size of the routing table and OSPF database that have to be maintained. Also, if there is a change in network topology, the OSPF algorithm has to be rerun for the entire network.

2. B. An autonomous system boundary router (ASBR) is any OSPF router that is connected to an external routing process (another AS). An ABR, on the other hand, connects one (or more) OSPF areas together to area 0.

3. B, D, E. In order for two OSPF routers to create an adjacency, the Hello and Dead timers must match, and they must both be configured into the same area as well as being in the same subnet. Also, if authentication is configured, that info must match as well.

4. C. The process starts by sending out Hello packets. Every listening router will then add the originating router to the neighbor database. The responding routers will reply with all of their Hello information so that the originating router can add them to its own neighbor table. At this point, we will have reached the 2WAY state—only certain routers will advance beyond this to establish adjacencies.

5. D. If you have multiple links to the same network, you can change the default cost of a link so OSPF will prefer that link over another with the `ip ospf cost cost` command.

6. B. In the FULL state, all LSA information is synchronized among adjacent neighbors. OSPF routing can begin only after the FULL state has been reached. The FULL state occurs after the LOADING state finishes.

7. B, D, E. Configuring OSPFv3 is pretty simple, as long as you know what interfaces you are using on your router. There are no network statements; OSPFv3 is configured on a per-interface basis. OSPFv2 and OSPFv3 both use a 32-bit RID, and if you have an IPv4 address configured on at least one interface, you do not need to manually set a RID when configuring EIGRPv3.

8. B. When OSPF adjacency is formed, a router goes through several state changes before it becomes fully adjacent with its neighbor. The states are (in order) DOWN, ATTEMPT, INIT, 2WAY, EXSTART, EXCHANGE, LOADING, and FULL.

9. B. Referred to as a network link advertisement (NLA), Type 2 LSAs are generated by designated routers (DRs). Remember that a designated router is elected to represent other routers in its network, and it establishes adjacencies with them. The DR uses a Type 2 LSA to send out information about the state of other routers that are part of the same network.

10. C. Referred to as summary link advertisements (SLAs), Type 3 LSAs are generated by area border routers. These ABRs send Type 3 LSAs toward the area external to the one where they were generated. The Type 3 LSA advertises networks, and these LSAs advertise inter-area routes to the backbone area (area 0).

11. D. To see all LSAs a router has learned from its neighbors, you need to see the OSPF LSDB, and you can see this with the show ip ospf database command.

12. B. Based on the information in the question, the cost from R1 to R2 is 4, the cost from R2 to R3 is 15, and the cost from R3 to R5 is 4. 15 + 4 + 4 = 23. Pretty simple.

13. B, D. Since R3 is connected to area 1 and R1 is connected to area 2 and area 0, the routes advertised from R3 would show as OI, or inter-area routes.

14. A, D, E, F, G. For two OSPF routers to form an adjacency, they must be in the same area, must be in the same subnet, and the authentication information must match, if configured. You need to also check if an ACL is set and if a passive interface is configured, and every OSPF router must use a different RID.

15. C. The IOS command show ip ospf neighbor shows neighbor router information, such as neighbor ID and the state of adjacency with the neighboring router.

16. D. The command show ip ospf *interface* on a default broadcast multi-access network will show you DRs and BDRs on that network.

17. A, C, D, F. It's hard to tell from this single output what is causing the problem with the adjacency, but we need to check the ACL 10 to see what that is doing, verify that the routers are in the same area and in the same subnet, and see if passive interface is configured with the interface we're using.

18. B, D, G. The default reference bandwidth is 100 by default, and you can change it under the OSPF process with the auto-cost reference bandwidth *number* command, but if you do, you need to configure this command on all routers in your AS.

19. A, D. An OSPF RID will be used as source of Type 1 LSA, and the router will chose the highest loopback interface as its OSPF router ID (if available).

20. B, C. With single area OSPF you'd use only a couple LSA types, which can save on bandwidth. Also, you wouldn't need virtual links, which is a configuration that allows you to connect an area to another area that is not area 0.

Chapter 6: Troubleshooting IP, IPv6, and VLANs

1. D. Positive confirmation has been received confirming that the path to the neighbor is functioning correctly. REACH is good!

2. B. The most common cause of interface errors is a mismatched duplex mode between two ends of an Ethernet link. If they have mismatched duplex settings, you'll receive a legion of errors, which cause nasty slow performance issues, intermittent connectivity, and massive collisions—even total loss of communication!

3. D. You can verify the DTP status of an interface with the sh dtp interface *interface* command.

4. A. No DTP frames are generated from the interface. Nonegotiate can be used only if the neighbor interface is manually set as trunk or access.

5. D. The command show ipv6 neighbors provides the ARP cache on a router.

6. B. The state is STALE when the interface has not communicated within the neighbor reachable time frame. The next time the neighbor communicates, the state will change back to REACH.

7. B. There is no IPv6 default gateway, which will be the link-local address of the router interface, sent to the host as a router advertisement. Until this host receives the router address, the host will communicate with IPv6 only on the local subnet.

8. D. This host is using IPv4 to communicate on the network, and without an IPv6 global address, the host will be able to communicate to only remote networks with IPv4. The IPv4 address and default gateway are not configured into the same subnet.

9. B, C. The commands show interface trunk and show interface *interface* switchport will show you statistics of ports, which includes native VLAN information.

10. A. Most Cisco switches ship with a default port mode of auto, meaning that they will automatically trunk if they connect to a port that is on or desirable. Remember that not all switches are shipped as mode auto, but many are, and you need to set one side to either on or desirable in order to trunk between switches.

Chapter 7: Wide Area Networks

1. C. The command debug ppp authentication will show you the authentication process that PPP uses across point-to-point connections.

2. B, D. Since BGP does not automatically discover neighbors like other routing protocols do, you have to explicitly configure them using the neighbor peer-ip-address remote-as peer-as-number command.

3. D. BGP uses TCP as the transport mechanism, which provides reliable connection-oriented delivery. BGP uses TCP port 179. Two routers that are using BGP form a TCP connection with one another. These two BGP routers are called "peer routers," or "neighbors."

4. D. The show ip bgp neighbor command is used to see the hold time on two BGP peers.

5. B. The 0.0.0.0 in the next hop field output of the show ip bgp command means that the network was locally entered on the router with the network command into BGP.

6. A, D. GRE tunnels have the following characteristics: GRE uses a protocol-type field in the GRE header so any layer 3 protocol can be used through the tunnel, GRE is stateless and has no flow control, GRE offers no security, and GRE creates additional overhead for tunneled packets—at least 24 bytes.

7. C. If you receive this flapping message when you configure your GRE tunnel, this means that you used your tunnel interface address instead of the tunnel destination address.

8. D. The show running-config interface tunnel 0 command will show you the configuration of the interface, not the status of the tunnel.

9. C. PPP uses PAP and CHAP as authentication protocols. PAP is clear text, CHAP uses an MD5 hash.

10. C. PPPoE encapsulates PPP frames in Ethernet frames and uses common PPP features like authentication, encryption, and compression. PPPoA is used for ATM.

11. C, D. S0/0/0 is up, meaning the s0/0/0 is talking to the CSU/DSU, so that isn't the problem. If the authentication failed or the other end has a different encapsulation than either one of those reasons would be why a data link is not established.

12. C. The show interfaces command shows the configuration settings and the interface status as well as the IP address and tunnel source and destination address.

13. B, C, D. This is just a basic WAN question to test your understanding of connections. PPP does not need to be used, so option A is not valid. You can use any type of connection to connect to a customer site, so option B is a valid answer. You can also use any type of connection to get to the Frame Relay switch, as long as the ISP supports it, and T1 is valid, so option C is okay. Ethernet as a WAN can be used with Ethernet over MPLS (EoMPLS); however, you don't need to configure a DLCI unless you're using Frame Relay, so E is not a valid answer for this question.

14. B. All web browsers support Secure Sockets Layer (SSL), and SSL VPNs are known as Web VPNs. Remote users can use their browser to create an encrypted connection and they don't need to install any software. GRE doesn't encrypt the data.

15. E. This is an easy question because the Remote router is using the default HDLC serial encapsulation and the Corp router is using the PPP serial encapsulation. You should go to the Remote router and set that encapsulation to PPP or change the Corp router back to the default of HDLC by typing no encapsulation under the interface.

16. A, C, E. VPNs can provide very good security by using advanced encryption and authentication protocols, which will help protect your network from unauthorized access. By connecting the corporate remote offices to their closest Internet provider and then creating a VPN tunnel with encryption and authentication, you'll gain a huge savings over opting for traditional leased point-to-point lines. VPNs scale very well to quickly bring up new offices or have mobile users connect securely while traveling or when connecting from home. VPNs are very compatible with broadband technologies.

17. A, D. Internet providers who have an existing Layer 2 network may choose to use layer 2 VPNs instead of the other common layer 3 MPLS VPN. Virtual Pricate Lan Switch (VPLS) and Virtual Private Wire Service (VPWS) are two technologies that provide layer 2 MPLS VPNs.

18. D. IPsec is an industry-wide standard suite of protocols and algorithms that allows for secure data transmission over an IP-based network that functions at the layer 3 Network layer of the OSI model.

19. C. A VPN allows or describes the creation of private networks across the Internet, enabling privacy and tunneling of TCP/IP protocols. A VPN can be set up across any type of link.

20. B, C. Layer 2 MPLS VPNs and the more popular Layer 3 MPLS VPN are service provided to customers and managed by the provider.

Chapter 8: Evolution of Intelligent Networks

1. B. Dropping packets as they arrive is called tail drop. Selective dropping of packets during the time queues are filling up is called congestion avoidance (CA). Cisco uses weighted random early detection (WRED) as a CA scheme to monitor the buffer depth and performs early discards (drops) on random packets when the minimum defined queue threshold is exceeded.

2. A, C. You unite switches into a single logical unit using special stack interconnect cables that create a bidirectional closed-loop path. The network topology and routing information are updated continuously through the stack interconnect.

3. C. A more efficient use of resources has a cost benefit because less physical equipment means less cost. What minimizes the spending is the fact that the customer pays only for the services or infrastructure that the customer uses.

4. B, D, E. Voice traffic is real-time traffic and comprises constant and predictable bandwidth and packet arrival times. One-way requirements incudes latency < 150 ms, jitter <30 ms, and loss < 1%, and bandwidth needs to be 30 to 128 Kbps.

5. B. The control plane represents the core layer of the SDN architecture and is where the Cisco APIC-EM resides.

6. A. Infrastructure as a Service (IaaS) provides only the network and delivers the computer infrastructure (platform virtualization environment).

7. C. A trust boundary is where packets are classified and marked. IP phones and the boundary between the ISP and enterprise network are common examples of trust boundaries.

8. A. The IWAN provides transport-independent connectivity, intelligent path control, application optimization, and highly secure connectivity.

9. A. NBAR is a layer 4 to layer 7 deep-packet inspection classifier. NBAR is more CPU intensive than marking and uses the existing markings, addresses, or ACLs.

10. C. DSCP is a set of 6-bit values that are used to describe the meaning of the layer 3 IPv4 ToS field. While IP precedence is the old way to mark ToS, DSCP is the new way and is backward compatible with IP precedence.

11. A, B. Southbound APIs (or device-to-control-plane interfaces) are used for communication between the controllers and network devices, which puts these interfaces between the control and data planes.

12. D. Class of Service (CoS) is a term to describe designated fields in a frame or packet header. How devices treat packets in your network depends on the field values. CoS is usually used with Ethernet frames and contains 3 bits.

13. D. Although option A is the best answer by far, it is unfortunately false. You will save time working on autonomous devices, which in turn will allow you more time to work on new business requirements.

14. C. When traffic exceeds the allocated rate, the policer can take one of two actions. It can either drop traffic or re-mark it to another class of service. The new class usually has a higher drop probability.

15. C, D, F. The SDN architecture slightly differs from the architecture of traditional networks. It comprises three stacked layers: data, control, and application.

16. C. NBAR is a layer 4 to layer 7 deep-packet inspection classifier.

17. B, D. Southbound APIs (or device-to-control-plane interfaces) are used for communication between the controllers and network devices. Northbound APIs, or northbound interfaces, are responsible for the communication between the SDN controller and the services running over the network. With onePK, Cisco attempting to provide a high-level proprietary API that allows you to inspect or modify the network element configuration without hardware upgrades. The data plane is responsible for the forwarding of frames or packets.

18. B, D. Each stack of switches has a single IP address and is managed as a single object. This single IP management applies to activities such as fault detection, VLAN creation and modification, security, and QoS controls. Each stack has only one configuration file, which is distributed to each member in the stack. When you add a new switch to the stack, the master switch automatically configures the unit with the currently running IOS image and the configuration of the stack. You do not have to do anything to bring up the switch before it is ready to operate.

19. B. Platform as a Service (PaaS) provides the operating system and the network by delivering a computing platform and solution stack.

20. C. Software as a Service (SaaS) provides the required software, operating system, and network by providing ready-to-use applications or software.

21. C. All data that the cloud stores will always be available. This availability means that users do not need to back up their data. Before the cloud, users could lose important documents because of an accidental deletion, misplacement, or computer breakdown.

Index

Q

W-Z

Comprehensive Online Learning Environment

Register on Sybex.com to gain access to the comprehensive online interactive learning environment and test bank to help you study for your Interconnecting Cisco Networking Devices Part 2 (ICND2) exam.

The online test bank includes the following:

- **Assessment Test** to help you focus your study to specific objectives
- **Chapter Tests** to reinforce what you've learned
- **Practice Exams** to test your knowledge of the material
- **Digital Flashcards** to reinforce your learning and provide last-minute test prep before the exam
- **Searchable Glossary** to define the key terms you'll need to know for the exam

Go to http://www.wiley.com/go/sybextestprep **to register and gain access to this comprehensive study tool package.**